FOLLOWING PHI

FOLLOWING PHILO

IN SEARCH OF

The Magdalene

The Virgin

The Men Called Jesus

P.J. Gott and Logan Licht

Leonard Press
Bolivar, Missouri
2015

Leonard Press
P.O. Box 752, Bolivar, MO 65613-0034
www.leonardpress.com

Cover Design: Gott & Licht

Copy of original painting by Giovanni Paolo Panini (National Gallery London) by Bartolomeo Pinelli, with modifications and additions by Cynthia Johnson.

Licensed under Public domain via Wikimedia Commons:
http://commons.wikimedia.org/wiki/File:
Copy_after_Pannini_Roman_Ruins_with_Pyramid.

Philosophers assemble amidst the ruins of a Temple and in the shadow of a pyramid; a crimson-clad couple are the principal figures. The woman may represent women philosophers who disguised themselves as men, several of whom are unveiled in this book. Crimson traditionally represents a royal bloodline; blue, purple and crimson yarns are tied to Moses and the Israelites (Ex 25-39). The statue most likely depicts the man for whom the tomb was built, also identified in this book. The pyramid is one of two constructed between 17 and 12 BCE. The 12th century *Mirabilia Urbis Romae* reports that the marble from the larger was used to construct the floors and stairs of the St. Peter's Basilica that was completed c. 349 CE. Called *The Pyramid of Remus*, it was destroyed c. 1599. The smaller *Pyramid of Cestius*, incorporated into the Aurelian Wall c. 275, still stands in Rome.

ISBN: 0-978-1-934 223-06-2
Library of Congress Control Number: 2015956221

ACKNOWLEDGMENTS

It was around Christmas 2002; I was reading Luke's story of the nativity of Jesus when a number grabbed my attention. After applying my newly-acquired knowledge of mystery school numbers and calculations to Anna's age, I suspected that someone had imbedded Pythagorean sacred numbers in Luke's gospel. When I multiplied the numbers in Chapter One and gazed at the product, 4320, I could almost hear Pythagoras laugh: 4320 halved is the diameter of the moon; 432,000 doubled is the diameter of the sun; 432 squared is the speed of light. Furthermore, John Michell, *The Dimensions of Paradise*, notes (p. 195): "As the man who discovered firm ground for the renewal of traditional culture, Pythagoras had the appropriate number, 864." Michell is referring to ancient Gematria which assigns a number to each letter of the alphabet. When added, the Greek letters that spell *Pythagoras* total 864, 432 doubled.

By the spring of 2011 we had passed through our sacred numbers phase and were wrapped up in equally intriguing historical threads, uncovered as we searched for first century Pythagoreans. And we had a database full of research notes, stacks of resource materials, and a 120,000 word manuscript. We believed what we'd found would be of interest to skeptics, agnostics, and progressive Christians. But we had a loftier goal; we wanted to pique the interest of scholars, especially those tightly bound by rules of scholarship.

And so we sent an introductory e-mail to internationally recognized scholar, Dr. David Trobisch, whose groundbreaking work occasionally intersects with some of our unorthodox hypotheses. After several exchanges we asked for a meeting. We described Philo's version of the Pythagorean method of exegesis and some of what we thought it revealed. Dr. Trobisch's first admonition: "Scholars will demand proof of its efficacy and repeatability." Fortunately, and unexpectedly, he agreed to add us to his busy calendar. We were encouraged that, at the very least, we had managed to pique *his* interest.

For the next thirty months, sometimes by *Skype* from his home in Germany, Dr. Trobisch pointed to gaping holes in some of our conclusions that we couldn't see. He showed us how to construct a clear, continuous path, and how to lead our reader – skeptic or scholar – step-by-step through the process. And he identified confusing weeds to be pulled and a few gems to be set aside for a later volume.

When he warned us of the controversy this book is likely to generate, we assumed his critical review and appraisal would remain unacknowledged. We were overjoyed when he assured us that he feels no need to disassociate himself from a product that may not represent traditional scholarship, but nevertheless deserves investigation and testing. It is the highest compliment we ever hope to receive.

We sincerely thank Dr. Trobisch for sharing his expertise, and we thank his wife Vera for sharing the precious-little time she has with her husband. We are honored to call them friends.

We also want to express our gratitude to Wanda Sue Parrott and Sheila Perryman for saving us from embarrassing typos, spelling, punctuation, and other grammatical errors. Any that remain are in sections added after their painstaking work was finished.

Gott and Licht

We have, in fact, found this man a pestilent fellow,
an agitator among all the Jews throughout the world,
and a ringleader
of the *haireseōs*[1] of the *Nazóraios*.[2]

Acts 24:5

But this I admit to you, that according to *The Way*,
which they call a *hairesin*,[3]
I worship the God of our ancestors,
believing everything laid down according to
the Law or written in the Prophets.

Acts 24:14

---

[1] *Haireseōs; hairesin*: Middle Liddell definition includes: "4. a sect, school, etc.: esp. a religious sect, such as the Sadducees and Pharisees, NTest. 5. a heresy, Eccl."
[2] Translated variously as: Nazarenes, Nasoraeans, or Nasareans.
[3] *Hairesin*: See footnote 1.

DEDICATION

To Joe,
You are the best.

FOREWORD

Have you ever looked up at a towering peak, shaken your head, and said to yourself, "I can't climb that!"? And then you walked away. Feeling guilty, you mutter, "But it would be a waste of time anyway!" Occasionally one finds a scholarly book that prompts the same reaction in the faint-hearted. Gott and Licht's is one of those books. Even a well-read biblical scholar may scan this book and find it too much of a challenge. And it *is* a great challenge, especially to cherished assumptions. One dislikes to have to go back to the drawing board; thus one may uneasily wave away a case, a book, that would require that. But this book, like Robert Eisenman's and Christian Lindtner's, challenges the imagination. It invites the reader to depart from habits of thought, theory, and reading. It may be that a new world awaits, in this case, a completely different way of reading ancient evidence, actually an ancient way which, though strange to us, may turn out to be more realistic, more appropriate, for texts written in an alien world of the past. One thing's for sure: if you're familiar with my work, you're going to think of me as the most retrograde of reactionaries when you're done with *this* one.

Robert M. Price
Author of *The Incredible Shrinking Son of Man*,
The Amazing Colossal Apostle,
and *The Pre-Nicene New Testament*.

PREFACE

By Dané Stoneburner Wallace

Following Philo is a scholarly investigation into ancient texts, but it reads more like a mystery novel than historical-textual analysis.

Judaeus Philo lived in Alexandria, the Roman province of Egypt, from the late first century BCE to about 50 CE. A contemporary of Paul, as well as a possible influence on Pauline thought, Philo was a Hellenistic Jewish philosopher. Through a process of synthesis, he attempted to fuse Greek philosophies

with the messianic and mystical teachings of Judaism. Philo authored some of the earliest known philosophical essays exploring Hebrew traditions through the lens of ancient Greek philosophy. In addition, he established guidelines for approaching scriptural texts, guidelines that at times introduced historical personages who were often concealed, heretofore, in enigmas.

Depiction of Philo Judeaus in the Schedelsche Weltchronik (1493).

Philo's method, "combining great learning of one kind with great learning of another kind," draws associations between the Bible, the philosophies and myths of ancient Greece, and the structural adaptations of ancient literary epics. The revelations of Scripture are juxtaposed to the perceptions of Plato, Homer, Ovid, and others in a systematic method of interpreting the enigmatical modes of expression found in Scripture. The cornerstone of Philo's convergence of Hebrew-Hellenistic thought was found in the concept of Logos. To the earlier He-

10

brews, Logos consisted primarily of God's actions, but for the Greeks, the cosmic Logos was the manifestation of divine actions and contemplations (thoughts). According to Philo, Logos is the mind of God. And in this light, Logos became the mind of God to the multitudes of Christianity.

Philo's method weaves a web of evidence originating from the Bible as well as secular literary sources and local histories. It identifies pre-established word-clues that lead to literal meanings hidden within fictional and non-fictional accounts. The traditional exegetical search for documentation with regard to Jesus and his environment of the first century continues to shun this approach by strictly distinguishing, if not separating, religious from secular literatures and techniques of antiquity.

Philo's twenty-one Rules constitute a form of literary criticism for interpreting the Bible in reference to and in relationship with other sources and genres of ancient literature. These Rules include: the analysis of repetitive phrases; apparent redundancies; alternate formulations; systematically applied synonyms; word plays; symbolic meanings of word particles; comprehensive interpretations of individual words; substituted accents; peculiarities pointing to particular meanings; grammatical idiosyncrasies (such as tense, mood, voice, number, person); manifest presences and patent omissions; artificial interpretations; order of events; positioning of verses; and numerical symbolism.

Did Eve, for instance, "come from Adam's rib" or was she the "giver of life to Adam" according to Philo's resolution (Chapter 11)? Has the Genesis account been informed by earlier Sumerian and Babylonian creation myths containing strikingly parallel references? Can the phonetics for similar-sounding sibilant fricatives (such as the consonants s and z) help to resolve questions about the distinctions of meaning in ancient languages?

For example, three words in Hebrew Scripture are translated "Prince": NZR (NaZiR); NS (NaSi); SR (SaR). Is it possible, therefore, that the name and titles, "Jesus the Nazarene, Prince of Princes," was not derived from a sojourn in Nazareth as Matthew claims (2:23)? Does the preponderance of evidence offered suggest that the name and titles are enigmatic references directing the reader to the Genesis account of Jacob's son Joseph, Israel's first NZR (Gen 49:26)? Was the Sumerians' Lord Ansar (NSR) the inspiration for the Israelites' Nasi Sar (NSSR)?

Another example of Gott and Licht's revealing employ of Philo's method regards the association of Roman Vestal Virgins with the Jewish Temple Virgins (Chapter 12) through the secrecy of their "sacred duties" and the perpetual fire (preserving royal bloodlines) and water (purification). They were forbidden to have sex with mortal men; having sex with men identified as deities, however, was required of them. Was it then, possibly, Mary's duty to preserve the bloodline of the House of David as a Temple Virgin?

How about making sense of the historical sequences of events? Take, for instance, the well-known anachronism of the time of Jesus' birth according to the accounts of Matthew (Herod the Great) and Luke (Quirinius, Governor of Syria). Both figures rank prominently in Roman as well as Jewish histories. The timing of their references, however, reveals a ten-year discrepancy. Herod the Great died before 4 BCE, and the first census under the governorship of Quirinius took place in 6 CE. After consulting historical and non-canonical sources of contemporary familial relations, as well as an important etymology of the name Jesus, Gott and Licht arrive at surprisingly logical conclusions validating both accounts. In addition, as it turns out, the simple answer (Chapter 7) is disclosed in The Four Gospels as well as The Acts of the Apostles.

A second, related example: Suetonius reports that not all Romans believed the eccentric emperor nicknamed "Caligula" was assassinated as alleged. Gott and Licht point to clues that confirm the validity of the doubters' concerns. Where Caligula was and what he was doing after his death will be disturbing for some, but equally enlightening, for others.

Even more notable appears Philo's foresight that historical depictions would be suppressed by the emerging scriptural traditions of competing doctrines. Philo's method, thereby, offers tools for restoring the less adulterated versions – those conforming to the original and ancient points of view, those also informed by the great secular authors of antiquity, both male and female.

Consider, for instance, the millennia old mystery surrounding the Roman poet of the first century, Publius Ovidius Naso, more commonly known as Ovid. Roughly two thousand, seven years ago, a penal sentence of permanent exile was handed down to Ovid, who had been accused of two crimes: carmen et error, in other words, a poem and a mistake. Scholars, poets, and laypeople alike have been trying to solve the mystery behind Ovid's icarion fall from royal grace and the subsequent demise of one of the most laudable poets of his age.

In Ovid's Metamorphoses, creatively imbedded clues may be inferred among the murder, morphings, and mayhem of lovers, sons, fathers, wives, and mothers both mortal and immortal. The author eulogizes Zeus, patriarch of the Greek pantheon, as the benevolent, "first among equals," authoritative father of the Gods, a thinly veiled portrait of Augustus. At the same time, the author vilifies the female goddesses for their selfish, vain, and destructive characteristics, particularly Hera, divine consort of Zeus. Why did Ovid construct such dire qualities in his female characters, while extolling the virtues of compassion and mercy to mainly male characters in his grand metamorphic epic? Is it a bad case of Greco-Roman misogyny? No, actually one could even say that the opposite would be true. Ovid was more of a philogynist in his other works, namely the Heroides [the Heroines] and Ars Amatoria [the Art of Love]. He was one of the earliest writers to empower the female gender, to sing her praises, not only of her physical beauty, but of her mental, and often times, sexual equality as well as her socio-political prowess. Yet Ovid strips the females of any and all virtues in the Metamorphoses, why?

Rumors, both archaic and contemporary, suggest that the key to Ovid's demise was hidden, not in the masculine fist of Emperor Augustus, but rather in the dainty, feminine palm of Livia Drusus, illustrious wife of Augustus and diabolical mother of the potential emperor-in-waiting, Tiberius. What could this poet have possibly done to ignite the wrath of an Empress?

Within the pages of *Following Philo*, a tantalizingly plausible explanation comes to light which might lay this ages old mystery to rest. Ovid's mystery may finally be solved with a little help from contexts, such as incest, infanticide, infidelity, and the future emperor Vespasian.

Speaking of powerful women, this ambitiously insightful text also explores the role of women in antiquity, lending potential voices to the silent names of some of history's powerful females: The Magdalene, Cleopatra, Aspasia, and others. Compelling conjecture suggests that many of the best known and most prolific philosophers and poets were actually women disguised as men: Vergil as the "Virgin of El" also known as Cleopatra; Philo of Alexandria as "Cleopatra Thea-Philo Pater"; Lucius Plutarchus as "Leuce wife of Pluto." How many female minds might have been hidden in masculine guise to assure their works survived the misogyny of patriarchal times?

The possibilities for re-examining, resurrecting and reconstructing historical truths are limitless with the application of Philo's method. The benchmark of the scientific method is simple: can the investigation be accurately applied and will its new conclusions be verifiable and repeatable? In other words, will Philo's method lead to predictions that are substantiated through carefully coordinated research? Gott and Licht establish the logical consequences for developing well-supported general theories. It is now up to readers to test their validity.

An avant-garde work of biblical criticism and a literary romp through the intimate chambers of some of antiquity's most famous writers and thinkers, *Following Philo* offers refreshing impulses to understanding Scripture and the lives, times, and philosophies of ancient minds. Gott and Licht's inquiries also shed new light on the first century circumstances surrounding Jesus, which have remained frustratingly sparse of historical evidence. Writing in painstaking detail, the authors nevertheless keep their narrative approachable and easy to read. I particularly appreciate how they implicitly encourage readers to become inquisitive – how they not only anticipate but also appreciate readers' responses. I look forward to experimenting with Philo's method and debating the results with my colleagues and students.

Dané Stoneburner Wallace
Classical and Global Studies
Missouri State University

TABLE OF CONTENTS

I

II

III

CHAPTER ONE

Enigmas in Scripture: Heresy or History?

Irenaeus, early Church Father and Bishop of Lyons[1] describes a method of biblical exegesis that is, in his opinion, blasphemous – not just another opinion, but a heresy. Irenaeus is critical and dismissive and calls it a *farce* and a *falsehood*.[2] He supports his claims with evidence:

> ... collecting a set of expressions and names scattered here and there, they twist them ... from a natural to a non-natural sense. In so doing, they act like those who bring forward any kind of hypothesis they fancy, and then endeavor to support them out of the poems of Homer, so that the ignorant imagine that Homer actually composed the verses bearing upon that hypothesis, which has, in fact, been but newly constructed...[3]

One of the earliest proponents of this exegetical approach was a man named *Basilides*.[4][5] Irenaeus regarded him as a deceiver – a Gnostic heretic attempting to lure the ignorant away from the authentic church, which was, of course, *his* church. Basilides was the author of two dozen books collectively titled,

---

[1] Irenaeus lived c. 130-202 CE.

[2] Irenaeus, "Against Heresies," Alexander Roberts, ed., *The Gnostic Society Library Online* (1995), 1.9.5, n.p. [cited 2 March 2012].

[3] Irenaeus, 1.9.4.

[4] Suetonius, *The Life of Vespasian*, (Loeb 1914), (Thayer Online 8.7). Suetonius describes Basilides as "Vespasian's freedman."

[5] Tacitus, *Histories*, Alfred John Church and William Jackson Brodribb, trans. *The Complete Works of Tacitus* (1864-1877), (Sacred Texts Online 2.78). Tacitus describes Basilides as a "priest at Mount Carmel." Suetonius and Tacitus agree that Vespasian consulted Basilides before accepting the position as Rome's Emperor in 69 CE and that he was elderly and in poor health at the time. Clement of Alexandria and other Early Church Fathers were apparently unaware of these historians' stories when they moved Basilides from the first to the second century, thereby supporting their contention that the heretical sects were "later than the Catholic Church."

Exegetica and it is this lost, hermeneutical system that Irenaeus wrote against.[6]

First century Jewish philosopher Philo[7] of Alexandria[8] also describes a system of scriptural exegesis that appears to be similar. He sees it as the product of a "Lover of Wisdom," adopts it, and uses it as the foundation for his own system of interpretation. Woven within the extant essays that carry Philo's name is a systematic method for identifying and unraveling clues transmitted in literature. Read these excerpts from Philo's "On Dreams" and carefully consider the exegetical implications:

> I admire the Lover of Wisdom ... collecting and thinking it fit to *weave together* many things, though different, and proceeding *from different sources, into the same web*; for taking the first two elements from the grammatical knowledge ... reading and writing, and taking from ... poets ... and ancient history and ... arithmetic and geometry ... and calculations ... and borrowing from music rhyme, and metre, and harmony, and chromatics, and diatonics, and combined and disjoined melodies; and ... rhetoric and invention ... language, and arrangement, and memory, and action; and from philosophy ... all the other things of which human life consists, he has put together in one most admirably arranged work, combining great learning of one kind with great learning of another kind[9].

Philo compares this method of collecting and weaving to building a web. But the web represents a colorless skeleton of a greater potential; a potential that becomes a work of art in the hands of a craftsman or craftswoman. The skilled weaver pulls disparate threads from multiple sources, and finding their proper place, breathes new life and logic into old stories and superstitions. The finished product is unexpected, sometimes astonishing, and sometimes exhilarating.

---

[6] Irenaeus, *Against Heresies*, Peter Kirby (2001-2015), *Early Christian Writings*, "Basilides."
[7] NAS Exhaustive Concordance of the Bible with Hebrew-Aramaic and Greek Dictionaries Copyright © 1981, 1998 by The Lockman Foundation. All rights reserved. Greek, *Philon* (Strong's Greek 5384, "beloved, dear, friendly"),
[8] Sources report that Philo lived from c. 13 BCE to c. 50 CE.
[9] C.D. Yonge, trans. The Works of Philo: Complete and Unabridged, "On Dreams." (Peabody: Hendrickson Publishers, 2013), (34.205), 383-4. Emphasis added.

Is Philo's Method a "farce," a "fable," and a "falsehood," as Irenaeus judges?[10] Or is it a demonstrably effective tool for scholarly exegesis? What if Philo's directives lead to repeatable, evidence-supported conclusions that unlock mysteries and answer long-standing questions about Jesus, his mission, and his family? What if the clues can be identified, examined, and used to solve biblical puzzles? The core of this endeavor is to demonstrate how Philo's Philology can lead to answers supported by evidence from ancient sources – some textual, some archaeological, and some both.

Although the clues are plainly written, they take time and work to identify and interpret. And sometimes the solutions can be quite disturbing. It is during these moments of discomfort that a message from Jesus – uncovered at Nag Hammadi, Egypt, in 1945 but dated concurrent with the canonical gospels[11] encourages, urges, demands that we continue:

These are the hidden sayings that the living Jesus spoke and Judas Thomas the Twin recorded.

And he said, "Whoever discovers the interpretation of these sayings will not taste death."

Jesus said, "Let one who seeks not stop seeking until one finds. When one finds, one will be troubled. When one is troubled, one will marvel and will reign over all."[12]

---

[10] Irenaeus, "Against Heresies" 1.9.5.

[11] Generally dated c. 70 to c. 120 CE.

[12] Marvin Meyer, ed. *The Nag Hammadi Scriptures: The Revised and Updated Translation of Sacred Gnostic Texts* "The Gospel of Thomas" (New York: HarperOne, 2008), 139.

CHAPTER TWO

Philo's Farce

Irenaeus cites specifically the farce of employing the works of Homer to interpret scripture. Philo adds other works of art, philosophy, history, and science as necessary components of the exegetical process:

Arithmetic and geometry point to Pythagoras' *Canon of Sacred Numbers* (c. 570-500 BCE) and Plato (c. 427–347 BCE).

Philosophy and great learning would include Socrates (c. 469–399 BCE), Archytas (c. 428–347 BCE), and Aristotle (c. 384–322 BCE).

Ancient history encompasses the works of the Father of History, Herodotus of Halicarnassus (c. 480–420 BCE), Ptolemy I Soter (c. 360–283 BCE), Julius Caesar (c. 100–44 BCE), Dionysius of Halicarnassus (c. 60–7 BCE), Livy (c. 59 BCE–17 CE), and Strabo (c. 64 BCE–24 CE).

The dating of the first edition of the Christian Bible in the middle of the second century expands the list to the works of late first and early second century historians: Valerius Maximus, Flavius Josephus, Pliny the Elder, Pliny the Younger, Tacitus, Suetonius, Rufus, Plutarch, Appian, and Arrian.

The science and art of rhyme, harmony, rhetoric, language, arrangement, and philosophy would include virtually all the artists and philosophers known and revered at the time: Vergil, Ovid, Cicero, Seneca, Thrasyllus of Alexandria, and the Jewish scholars and philosophers, Hillel the Elder, Simeon ben Shatah, Gamaliel ben Simeon, and Simeon ben Gamaliel.

We must add these sources to Irenaeus' example of Homer when collecting the threads needed to solve enigmas and interpret sacred scripture.

Of all these, however, no contributor would have been more important to Philo than Aristotle, Plato's most famous and productive student. Aristotle's writings cover the very arts and sciences Philo enumerates as necessary components of the "Lover of Wisdom's" craft. Most important, Aristotle wrote "Peri Hermeneias," an essay on logic and semantics. Philo, whom Clement labeled "The Pythagorean,"[1] would have built his method of exegesis on an Aristotelian foundation, including elements that originated with Pythagoras and were advanced by Plato.

Furthermore, Aristotle had a connection to Philo's home, Alexandria, Egypt. He was head of the Royal Academy of Macedon, and his students included Alexander the Great, for whom Alexandria was named, and Ptolemy I Soter, the man who named the capital of his kingdom "Alexandria." Plutarch and other historians (Arrian, Rufus, Diodorus, and Justin) report that the Oracle of Ammon at Siwa revealed Alexander's father to be Zeus, rather than Philip, King of Macedon, a mere mortal.[2]

Alexander the Great died at the age of thirty-three; Ptolemy became the first Greco-Roman/Macedonian pharaoh of Egypt and the progenitor of the Ptolemaic Dynasty. After Alexander's death, Ptolemy claimed he was Alexander's half-brother and, therefore, his legal successor – and perhaps another son of Zeus.

After explaining the interdisciplinary sources necessary to put his method into practice, Philo goes on to say:

> Now the sacred scripture calls the maker of this compound work "Besaleel," which name being interpreted, signifies "in the shadow of God," for he makes all the copies, and the man by name of Moses makes all the models, as the principal architect; and for this reason it is, that the one only draws outlines as it were, but the other is not content with such sketches, but makes the archetypal

---

[1] Clement of Alexandria, *Stromata*, Peter Kirby, 2001-2015, *Early Christian Writings* (I.15).
[2] P. M. Fraser, *Ptolemaic Alexandria* (Oxford: Oxford University Press, 1972), 215.

natures themselves, and has already adorned the holy places with his variegating art; but the wise man is called the only adorner of the place of wisdom in the oracles delivered in the sacred scriptures.[3]

Besaleel (also *Besalel*; *Bezalel*), is introduced in Philo's *sacred scriptures* in Exodus, where it is written:

> YHWH[4] spoke to Moses: "See, I have called by name Bezalel son of Uri son of Hur, of the tribe of Judah: and I have filled him with the *spirit of Elohim* with ability, intelligence, and knowledge in *every kind of craft*, to devise artistic designs, to work in gold, silver, and bronze, in cutting stones for setting, and in carving wood, in *every kind of craft*" (Ex 31:1-5;).[5]

One of Philo's rules for identifying and solving enigmas is the duplication of a phrase, and "every kind of craft" is a perfect example. These words by definition encompass work beyond the crafts listed and would include the compound work of the "Lover of Wisdom." At the time Philo was writing, and during the time New Testament texts were composed, compiled, and edited, Homer's Pallas-Athena was revered as the goddess of wisdom, weaving, and "every kind of craft."

"Craft" in Hebrew is *melakah*,[6] derived from *malak* which NASB translates as: ambassadors (2), angel (101), angels (9), envoys (1), messenger (24), messengers (76).[7] Also important are the words between the repeated phrase; this placement identifies them as "enigmatic modes of expression" that will reappear in later stories:

> In Hebrew, "devise" is *chashab*,[8] also translated, "to think, account";
>
> "artistic designs" is *machashabah*,[9] also translated "thoughts";

---

[3] Yonge, "On Dreams" (2013); (34.206), 384.
[4] Philo's method requires that YHWH (translated "LORD") and LHM (translated "God") be specified. The reason is fully explained in Chapter Five.
[5] Emphasis added
[6] NAS (Strong's Hebrew 4399).
[7] NASB (Strong's Hebrew 4397).
[8] NAS (Strong's Hebrew 2803).
[9] NAS (Strong's Hebrew 4284).

"to work" is *ashah*,[10] "accomplish"; "bronze" is *nechash*,[11] which can also be rendered *nachash*,[12] translated, "serpent";

"wood is *ets*,[13] translated, "tree, trees, wood."

Enigmatically, Bezalel is identified as "Elohim's angelic messenger," and the words that describe him are identified as clues to enigmas.

The historian Josephus adds context to Philo's Besalel when he provides critical information about Besalel's relationship to Moses: "Moses bade his brother Aaron, and Hur their sister Miriam's husband, to stand on each side of him."[14]

Josephus identifies Hur and Miriam as Besalel's paternal grandparents, which identifies Moses, Miriam's brother, as Besalel's granduncle.

More information about Besalel's craft comes from the Babylonian Talmud, Berakhot 55a; the meaning of the enigmatic phrase duplicated at Ex 31:3 and 31:5, "in every kind of craft," is explained:

> Rab Judah said in the name of Rab [Yehudah Ha Nasi]: "Besalel knew *how to combine the letters* [of Hebrew Scripture] by which the heavens and earth were created. It is written here, 'And He hath filled him with the spirit of God, in wisdom and in understanding, and in knowledge,' and it is written elsewhere, 'The Lord by wisdom founded the earth; by understanding He established the heavens,' and it is also written, 'By His knowledge the depths were broken up.'"
>
> R. Johanan said: "The Holy One, blessed be He, gives wisdom only to one who already has wisdom, as it says, 'He giveth wisdom unto the wise, and knowledge to them that know understanding.'" R. Tahlifa from the West heard and repeated it before R. Abbahu. He said to him: "You learn it from there, but we learn

---

[10] NAS (Strong's Hebrew 6213).

[11] NAS (Strong's Hebrew 5178).

[12] NAS (Strong's Hebrew 5175).

[13] NAS (Strong's Hebrew 6086).

[14] William Whiston, trans. *The New Complete Works of Josephus* (Grand Rapids: Kregel Publications, 1999), *Antiquities* 3.2.4 (54), 116.

it from this text, namely, 'In the hearts of all that are wise-hearted I have put wisdom.'"[15]

The Talmud emphasizes that Besalel's craft requires the knowledge of how to combine letters. Moreover, because Hebrew Scripture is written in consonants without spaces or punctuation, the choice of vowels and spaces can change the meaning, allowing the same consonants to be interpreted in more than one way.

Besalel's name serves as an example of why "wisdom, understanding, and knowledge" are required when interpreting sacred scripture. The consonants BSLL, traditionally rendered *BeSaL eL*, are translated "shadow of El." However, the fragment BSL (BeSaL) means "to strip off" and can be translated as "onion"; therefore, *Besal el* also means "onion of El."

A third equally valid option, however, is most intriguing: aB iSh[16] eL, eL, which word-for-word means, "Father"; "man"; "El"; "El."

Berakhot 55a, quoted above, may hold a clue to the best choice: "Besalel knew how to combine the letters by which the heavens and earth were created." In addition to "Shadow of El" and "Onion of El," Besalel's name can also say that the "Progenitors of Humankind were El and El," an enigma that will be examined in Chapters Four and Five.

Philo alludes to this unique feature of biblical Hebrew when he writes of the Essenes in "Every Good Man is Free":

> Then one takes up the holy volume and reads it, and another of the men of the greatest experience comes forward and *explains what is not very intelligible*, for a great many precepts are delivered in *enigmatical modes of expression*, and allegorically, as the old fashion was.[17]

Two generations after Philo, another prominent first century source for solving enigmas arrived in Greece and opened an academy in the province of Boeotia. His name was Lucius Mes-

---

[15] Emphasis added.

[16] In Biblical Hebrew, *iSh* (Strong's Hebrew 376, "man") can also be rendered *eSh*, "fire" (NAS, Strong's Hebrew 784) and es, "tree" (NAS, Strong's Hebrew 6086).

[17] Yonge (2013): Philo, "Every Good Man is Free (12.82), 690. Emphasis added.

trius Plutarchus (c. 46–120 CE), but he is better known as "Plutarch." In one of his most popular stories, Plutarch writes:

> Pythagoras greatly admired the Egyptian priests, and, copying their *symbolism* and *secret teachings*, incorporated *his doctrines* in enigmas. As a matter of fact, most of the Pythagorean precepts do not at all fall short of the writings that are called hieroglyphs.
>
> ... Whenever you hear the traditional tales which the Egyptians tell about the gods, their wanderings, dismemberments, and many experiences ... *you must not think that any of these tales actually happened in the manner in which they are related.*
>
> If you listen to the *stories about the gods* in this way ... you may avoid superstition which is no less an evil than atheism.[18]

Philo and Plutarch's tacit differentiation between "enigmatical modes of expression" and "allegory" are frequently overlooked even among scholars. Philo's Method of biblical exegesis has traditionally been referred to as the "allegorical interpretation of scripture" when a more accurate definition is: "a systematic method of interpreting enigmatical modes of expression found in scripture."

Like Philo the Jew before him, Plutarch the Greek historian explains that *enigmas* are the preferred means of telling stories about the gods. Enigmas are similar to allegories, but the difference, although subtle, must be fully understood. Merriam-Webster defines "allegory" as:

> 1: the expression by means of symbolic fictional figures and actions of truths or generalizations about human existence; also: an instance (as in a story or painting) of such expression; 2: a symbolic representation.[19]

Synonyms listed include "fable" and "parable." By contrast, Merriam-Webster defines "enigma" as: "1: an obscure speech or writing; 2: something hard to understand or explain; 3: an inscrutable or mysterious person." Synonyms listed include: "mystery"; "puzzle"; "riddle"; "secret.[20]

---

[18] Plutarch. *Isis and Osiris*, "Introduction," (Loeb Classical Library, 1914, Babbit trans.), Bill Thayer's Website. Emphasis added.
[19] Merriam-Webster Dictionary Online
[20] Ibid.

Thus, the solution to an allegory (fable) can be based on an individual's knowledge and personal life experiences. It can, therefore, produce a multitude of *subjective* opinions, but no conclusive solution.

On the other hand, an enigma (mystery; puzzle; riddle; secret) can be solved, but it requires special knowledge or a key. There is but *one* solution, and it cannot be influenced by an individual's subjective interpretation as long as the key is intact and properly utilized. When an enigma is put into writing, its creator also provides the clues which solve the mystery, puzzle, or riddle. Only certain people – the initiated – are given the key. With access to this key, virtually anyone can solve the puzzle and reconstruct the secret hidden within the enigma. Most important, all who do so will reach similar conclusions.

To us, of course, this is a strange method of transmitting information. But it was a common practice two thousand years ago as a way to get the "Losers'" version of events passed through time invisibly attached to the "Victors'" version. The ancient practitioners called it "Philology," and it describes Philo's Method of interpretation: "the study of literary texts and of written records, the establishment of their authenticity and their original form, and the determination of their meaning."[21]

The first evidence of the practice of philology is in Alexandria, Egypt: Philetas of Cos, c. 340–c. 285 BCE[22] and Zenodorus, c. 280 BCE.[23] Plutarch associates the method with Pythagoras, who learned it from the Egyptians. This moves the date further back to the 6th century BCE during Pythagoras' lifetime. When it arrived in Egypt is yet to be determined. What can be said with confidence is that Philo's Method of exegesis is rooted in the ancient "Science of Philology."

---

[21] Dictionary.com.

[22] Livio Sbardella, "Philitas of Cos," Hubert Cancik; Helmut Schneider; Christine F. Salazar (eds). *Brill's New Pauly*–"Antiquity," (Leiden: Brill, 2007).

[23] Jeremy Norman, "Philology Probably Begins at the Royal Library of Alexandria (c. 280 BCE)."

CHAPTER THREE

Philo's Philology
Another Tool for Biblical Exegesis

Although we may be the first in modern times to apply Philo's Philology to ancient texts, we are not the first to recognize it. In a series of eight lectures in 1885, published in 1886 by MacMillan and Company in London as *History of Interpretation*, Frederic W. Farrar read from earlier lectures by the late Rev. John Bampton (1689–1751) as required by Bampton's Last Will and Testament.

Writing of what he called "Philo's Rules," Bampton notes: "All this 'madness' is reduced to 'method' by a set of rules, half Haggadistic, half Stoic, but entirely inapplicable."[1] Like Irenaeus, Bampton – and presumably Farrar – considered Philo's method a heretical farce and argued against it.

Between 1901 and 1906, the editors of The Jewish Encyclopedia published an article, "Philo Judeaus," which is similar in content and sequence to the Philo material that originated in Bampton's and Farrar's lectures. The editors, however, unpacked Bampton's six rules, teased out twenty-one, and incorporated them into their commentary.

It is the Jewish Encyclopedia's simplified enumeration that best serves the purpose of demonstrating the practical implementation of the Method. And it is this enumeration with minor modifications for clarification [in brackets] that will be used in the instructional portions of this text. Following Bampton's lead, we call them "Philo's Rules," and they are:

---

[1] F. W. Farrar, *History of Interpretation: Eight Lectures* (London: MacMillan and Co., 1886), 149.

1. The doubling of a phrase.
2. An apparently superfluous expression in the text.
3. The repetition of statements previously made.
4. A change of phraseology – all these phenomena point to something special that the reader must consider.
5. An entirely different meaning may also be found by disregarding the ordinarily accepted division of the sentence into phrases and clauses and by considering a different combination of the words.
6. Synonyms [and phonetically similar words] must be carefully studied.
7. A play upon words must be utilized for finding a deeper meaning.
8. A definite, allegorical [enigmatical] sense may be gathered from certain particles, adverbs, prepositions, [unclear pronoun antecedents], etc., and in certain cases it can be gathered even from ...
9. the part of a word.
10. Every word must be explained in all its meanings in order that different interpretations may be found.
11. The skillful interpreter may make slight changes in a word, following the rabbinical rule: "Read not so, but so." Philo, therefore, changed accents, breathings, etc., in Greek [and Hebrew] words.[2]
12. Any peculiarity in a phrase justifies the assumption that some special meaning is intended. Details regarding the form of words are very important.
13. Consider the number of the word, if it shows any peculiarity in the singular or the plural: the tense of the verb, etc.
14. The gender of the noun may carry a clue.
15. Note the presence or omission of the article;
16. the artificial interpretation of a single expression;
17. the position of the verses of a passage; [the position of words in a phrase relative to one another];
18. peculiar verse combinations;
19. noteworthy omissions;
20. striking statements [i.e., angel, spirit, Holy Spirit, omen, prophecy, etc.];
21. numeral symbolism [i.e., Platonic; Gematria].[3]

---

[2] The assumption that Philo worked only with the Greek Septuagint is incorrect.
[3] Jewish Encyclopedia Online(1906), "Philo Judaeus," n.p.

Some of these rules act primarily as yellow flags to signal an approaching enigmatic section of text that will require a stop, some thought, and possibly some research. The words most frequently employed are angel, spirit, and prophecy.

Other rules act as red flags, which are the solution or a part of the solution to the puzzle. For example, phrases that are repeated will contain a key word or words that are exactly the same. However, most of Philo's Rules can serve both yellow-flag and red-flag functions.

Our reconstruction of the practical application of these rules is based in part on the work of French literary critic Gérard Genette; he writes: "Hypertextuality refers to any relationship uniting a text B (which I shall call the hypertext) to an earlier text A (I shall, of course, call it the hypotext), upon which it is grafted in a manner that is not that of commentary."[4] Genette calls the process "transformation," meaning Text B (the hypertext) draws from Text A (the hypotext) without specifying it directly.

Dennis R. MacDonald describes this technique as: "a common literary strategy for replacing the values or perspectives of an earlier, targeted text (the 'hypotext') with alternative values or perspectives."[5]

From these sources come four simple steps for solving enigmas:

Identify one or more of Philo's yellow flags in the text being examined (the hypertext), i.e., "Angel of the Lord," that precedes and signals that an enigmatic section of text will follow.

Collect expressions in the text being examined that are identified as "a red-flagged enigmatical mode of expression" on the basis of one or more of the twenty-one Rules, i.e., the duplication of a phrase.

---

[4] Gerard Genette (1997). *Palimpsests: Literature in the Second Degree*; (Lincoln: University of Nebraska Press), 5.

[5] Dennis R. MacDonald, "Luke's Eutychus and Homer's Elpenor: Acts 20:7-12 and Odyssey 10-12," JHC 1 (Fall 1994), 4-24. Institute for Higher Critical Studies; Drew University, Madison, NJ.

Match the expressions with similar elements found in hypotexts (Hebrew and Christian scripture, the works of Homer, Josephus, the Plinys, Tacitus, Suetonius, Plutarch, Ovid, or other sources available in the first and second centuries).

Analyze how the hypotext might add to or alter the meaning when examined alongside the hypertext. The required reference material is a Bible with Apocrypha and annotations. We recommend *The New Oxford Annotated Bible with Apocrypha.*[6]

Philo and Plutarch state unequivocally that scripture – stories about the gods – are written in enigmas – riddles and puzzles – and that interpreting them *accurately* can be done only by those who have the *key* to unlocking the enigmas. Because of Irenaeus and others after him, Christian exegetes have never considered the possibility that Hebrew and Christian scripture were written using "enigmatical modes of expression" or that a key might be available to solve them. Most have erroneously assumed that "enigma" and "allegory" are synonymous and rejected Philo's method as being too subjective for scholarly investigation. *It is this assumption we hope to correct.*

An excellent example of the method comes from The Gospel According to Luke, which opens with these enigmatic words:

Since many have undertaken to set down an orderly account of the events that have been fulfilled among us, just as they were handed on to us by witnesses and servants of the word, I too decided, after investigating everything carefully from the very first, to write an orderly account for you, *kratiste Theophilus*, so that you may know the truth concerning the things about which you have been instructed (Lk 1:1-4).[7]

The Alexandrian Theologian Philo, "The Pythagorean" according to Clement,[8] employs a form of the term "kratistos" more than three hundred times in extant essays; but, the word is found rarely (if at all) in those which scholars classify "definitely spurious." Curiously and notably, the historian Josephus

---

[6] Bruce M. Metzger and Roland E. Murphy, eds. (New York: Oxford University Press, 1994), *The New Oxford Annotated Bible with the Apocrypha: New Revised Standard Version.*
[7] Emphasis added.
[8] Clement, *Stromata* (1.15).

also addresses his benefactor as "kratiste Epaphroditis."[9] How better to associate Josephus with Luke than to dedicate his autobiography to another kratiste, this one "beloved by Aphrodite."

"Kratiste" is the thread that ties Josephus and Luke to one another, and it ties both to Philo. Each of them spins small strands of historical threads that can be tied together and used to weave a new tapestry that reveals the *secret* history.

Furthermore, "Philo" plays a prominent role in Luke's Gospel as a form of the word "Philon" is employed fifteen times plus another three times in The Acts of the Apostles.[10] Notably, no form of the word is found at all in Mark's Gospel, and it appears only once in Matthew's (11:19).

If Philo's Philology can be applied to Christian and Hebrew Scripture – and other "stories about the gods" – and *if* the conclusions reached can be consistently repeated by others applying the same method to the same texts, then it becomes a valid scholarly method. If not, it is – as Plutarch asserts – "nothing more than superstition and no less an evil than atheism."

There is but one way to judge this ancient method of exegesis, and that is by following Philo through the texts.

---

[9] Josephus, 1999, *Life of Flavius Josephus*, 76 (430), 42.
[10] Luke 7:6; 7:34; 11:5 (2); 11:6; 11:8; 12:4; 14:10; 14:12; 15:6; 15:9; 15:29; 16:9; 21:16; 23:12. Acts 10:24; 19:31; 27:3.

CHAPTER FOUR

Following Philo to Bethlehem
House of Bread or Virgin Mother?

No prophecy in Hebrew Scripture appears to foretell that the Jewish Messiah would be called a "Nazarene" (the common New Testament translation), a "Nassarean" (Hebrew nasi and sar, both translated "prince"), or "Nasorean" (perhaps students of the Nasi who studied Pythag-*orean* philosophy). Yet the Gospel of Matthew curiously says, "There he made his home in a town called Nazareth, so that what had been spoken through the prophets might be fulfilled, "He will be called a Nazorean" [Greek, *Nazóraios*] (Mt 2:23).[1]

To which prophets and what prophecy is Matthew referring? The earliest and still most accepted explanation originated with the Church Historian Jerome (c. 347–420). His conclusion includes a harsh, accusatory finger pointed at the translators of the Septuagint as he identifies the mysterious prophet as being,

> ... Isaiah. For in the place where we read and translate, "There shall come forth a rod out of the stem of Jesse, and a *branch* shall grow out of his roots," in the Hebrew idiom it is written thus, "There shall come forth a rod out of the root of Jesse and a *Nazarene* shall grow from his root." How can the Septuagint leave out the word "Nazarene"? Is it not unlawful to substitute one word for another? It is sacrilege to conceal or create a mystery.[2]

---

[1] Some sources translate the Greek terms *Nazóraios, Nazōraion,* and *Nazōraiou* as "Nazarene" while others translate them as "of Nazareth." Philo's Philology will help answer the question: *why the inconsistency?*

[2] Jerome, "Letter to Pammachius." *Nicene and Post Nicene Fathers* (NPNF), Kevin Knight, *New Advent* (2014), Second Series, Vol. 6, Epistle 57.

Curiously, Jerome points in the *direction* of the answer, but he does not *reveal* the answer that solves the mystery he criticizes. And this raises yet another question: Why not?

Jerome quotes Isa 11:1, and the Hebrew word he identifies as "Nazarene" is *NSR*. Because the biblical Hebrew alphabet does not contain vowels, the scribes were left with the task of selecting them. *NSR*, became *neser* then *nêtṣer*, defined as a "sprout, shoot."[3] Therefore, as Jerome explains, Isaiah's Prophecy identifies "Jesus the NSR" as a descendant of Jesse and his son, King David.

Why doesn't Matthew just say that? Why does Matthew claim Jesus resided in Nazareth if the unidentified prophecy explains why he is called "The Nazarene"? Jerome's explanation is at best incomplete and it raises another, weightier question: Why does Matthew seemingly not want to draw attention to Isa 11:1?

Why invoke an unidentified prophecy if your story is designed to give another reason for the terms "Nassarean," "Nasoraean," "Nazarean," and "Nazarene"? Matthew's account of a visit to Nazareth has no apparent relationship to Isaiah's Prophecy, and although NSR and NZR appear dozens of times beginning in Genesis, Nazareth is never mentioned in Hebrew Scripture. This is the underlying mystery that Jerome ignores.

Just as mysterious, Micah's Prophecy that the Messiah would "come from Bethlehem" (Mic 5:2-3) is missing in Mark's Gospel but featured in Matthew's: "'And you, *Bethlehem*, in the land of Judah, are by no means least among the *rulers* of Judah; for *from you shall come* a *ruler* who is to *shepherd* my people Israel'" (Mt 2:6).[4]

Matthew's quote of Micah carries two of Philo's yellow flags:

---

[3] NAS (Strong's Hebrew 5342).
[4] Emphasis added.

1. He repeats a word found but one time in Micah, "ruler." The words between "ruler" are an enigma: "...from *you* shall come..." "You" refers to *BTLHM*.
2. He inserts a word omitted in Micah, "shepherd."

This tells us that the quote holds critical clues to a puzzle and that these two words will be part of the solution. So, let's stop to have a closer look at the hypotexts in Hebrew Scripture.

"Bethlehem" first appears at Gen 35:19-21: "So Rachel died, and she was buried on *the way* to *Ephrath* (that is, *Bethlehem*), and Jacob set up a pillar at her grave; it is the pillar of Rachel's tomb, which is there to this day. Israel journeyed on, and pitched his tent beyond the tower [Hebrew, *MGDL*] of Eder" [English, "flock"]."[5]

Jacob, also called "Israel," repeats the key enigmatic words a few chapters later: "For when I came from Paddan, *Rachel*, alas, died in the land of Canaan on *the way* while there was still some distance to go to *Ephrath*; and I buried her there on *the way* to *Ephrath'* (that is, *Bethlehem*)" (Gen 48:7).[6]

Rachel is the daughter who cared for her father's flock (Gen 29:6, repeated at 29:9 and 10). Therefore, *she* is a shepherd. Rachel's father is Laban; Jacob's mother was Laban's sister Rebekah (Gen 29:10, repeated two more times in the same chapter, at 29:12, and again at 29:13). It must be important for the reader to understand that Rachel is the "watcher of the flock" and that she and Jacob – renamed "Israel" (Gen 35:10) just before Rachel dies (Gen 35:18) – were first cousins as well as husband and wife.

The pillar Jacob erects marking Rachel's tomb becomes the "Tower of the Flock" (Hebrew *MGDL DR*). And that location, which is "on *the way* to *Ephrath*," was named *BTLHM*, the word identified as an enigma.

Tradition says that "Bethlehem" is derived from *Beit* and *lehem*, translated "house of bread." However, adhering to Philo's

---

[5] Emphasis added.
[6] Emphasis added.

instructions and choosing a different break and vowels, the same consonants (BTLHM) can produce "BeTuLaH eM," which is translated "Virgin Mother," and "BaT eL Ha eM," translated, "daughter El the Mother." It should also be noted that "*Jacob* set up a pillar," but "*Israel* journeyed on" after Rachel was buried at BTLHM under the MGDL DR, "Watchtower of the Flock."

The Hebrew word for "ruler" is *mashal*. But the consonants MSL can also be rendered *eM* ("mother") *iSh* ("man" or "humankind") and *eL*. This supports "daughter El the Mother" as the preferred rendering of *BTLHM*.

Seeking the etymology of Rachel's name leads to several intriguing options: *derek* means "way, road, distance, journey, manner"[7]; *racham* means "to love, have compassion"[8]; *rechem* means "womb."[9] Adding *El* to each, *Rach-el* can mean "The Way of El," "the love of El," and/or "the womb of El."

However, another similar Hebrew word is *ruach*, defined as "breath, wind, spirit."[10] And a "breath-thread" generally overlooked in biblical exegesis can be tied to the Sumerian-Babylonian deities EnLil (also known as Ellil, son or grandson of Ansar and Kisar)[11] and his wife NinLiL. *En* means "Lord"; *Nin* means "Lady."

The "breath-thread" is LiL, also defined as "air," "wind," "breath," "spirit." It is important to note that "Lord ElliL" plays a prominent role in the Sumerian-Babylonian creation "myth"[12] just as "Lord El-ohim" and/or "El ha Em" is prominent in the Hebrew creation "history."

---

[7] NAS (Strong's Hebrew 1870), Lockman, *Biblehub.com.*

[8] NAS (Strong's Hebrew 7355), Lockman, *Biblehub.com.*

[9] NAS (Strong's Hebrew 7358), Lockman, *Biblehub.com.*

[10] NAS (Strong's Hebrew 7307), Lockman, *Biblehub.com.*

[11] Nicole Brisch, 'Anšar and Kišar (god and goddess)', *Ancient Mesopotamian Gods and Goddesses*, Oracc and the UK Higher Education Academy, 2012.

[12] Adam Stone, 'Enlil/Ellil (god)', *Ancient Mesopotamian Gods and Goddesses*, Oracc and the UK Higher Education Academy, 2013.

The destination, Ephrath, points to the words *apher* ("dry earth, dust"[13]) and *epher* ("ashes"[14]). It seems Benjamin's birth is tied to the death and burial of "The Spirit of El," *Rachel*, and "The Way of Elohim." The Feminine, "Spirit of El the Mother" was buried under the Watchtower of the Flock. Perhaps the spirit of Rachel is beckoned in ceremonies and occasions when "ashes" and "sackcloth"[15] are invoked.[16]

Moreover, Besalel is tied to Rachel when he is introduced at Ex 31:3: "and I have filled him [Besalel] with the "Spirit of God" [Hebrew, *ruach LHM*], with wisdom, with understanding, with knowledge and with all kinds of skills."[17] An equally valid translation is, "I have filled [Besalel] with the Spirit of El the Mother."

Although Rachel is not identified as a "Betulah," her aunt Rebekah (who is also her mother-in-law) and her daughter-in-law Asenath are: "[Rebekah] was very fair to look upon, a *virgin* [Hebrew *betulah*], whom no *man* had known" (Gen 24:16).[18] The Jewish historian Josephus adds: "[Rachel's son Joseph] married the daughter of Petephres ... she was a *virgin*, and her name was Asenath."[19] These "Virgin Mother" and "Daughter of El the Mother" threads will be picked up several times throughout this work, culminating with the birth of Jesus to the Virgin Mary.

We turn now to Mark's Gospel, the first chronologically;[20] it opens with examples of Philo's Rules: a "prophet," an error,

---

[13] NAS (Strong's Hebrew 6083).

[14] NAS (Strong's Hebrew 665).

[15] "Sackcloth," is used in scripture 47 times, first at Gen 37:34: "Then Jacob tore his garments, and put sackcloth on his loins, and mourned for his son [Joseph] many days." Later "hypertexts" may refer to this "mourning for the return of Rachel's son Joseph" who was identified as "the NZR among his brothers" (Gen 49:26).

[16] "Ashes and Sackcloth": Mt 11:21; Lk 10:13; Esth 4:1; 4:3; Job 16:15; Isa 58:5; Jer 6:26; Dan 9:3; Jonah 3:6.

[17] New International Version (NIV).

[18] Emphasis added.

[19] Josephus, 1999, *Antiquities*, 2.6.1 (91), 86. Emphasis added.

[20] Our research supports the *Farrer-Goulder-Goodacre Hypothesis* but not all the conclusions: Mark Goodacre, *The Case Against Q* Web Site (2002).

and a prophecy borrowed from *two* sources which creates the duplication of a phrase:

"The beginning of the gospel of Jesus Christ, Son of God. As it is written in the prophet Isaiah.[21] 'See, I am sending my messenger [Greek, *angelon*] ahead of you, who will *prepare your way*;[22] [Mal 3:1] the voice of one crying out in the wilderness; '*Prepare the way*[23] of the Lord, make his paths straight'" [Isa 40:3] (Mk 1:1-3).[24]

Matthew's much shorter reiteration is notable for what he omits: "This is the one of whom the prophet Isaiah spoke when he said, 'The voice of one crying out in the wilderness; Prepare the way of the Lord, make his paths straight'" (Mt 3:3).

Matthew omits *angelon*, the striking statement that signals a pending enigma. And he omits the quote from Mal 3:1 that creates the doubling of a phrase, "prepare the way." These noteworthy omissions in Matthew serve to signal a heightened importance of the phrase "Prepare the way." And Rachel links "The Way" to "Bethlehem" at Gen 35:19 and 48:7.

Luke solves more of the puzzle in The Acts of the Apostles:

"But this I admit to you, that according to the Way, which they call a sect [Greek, *hairesin*], I worship the God of our ancestors, believing everything laid down according to the law or written in the prophets" (Acts 24:24).

"We have, in fact, found this man a pestilent fellow, an agitator among all the Jews throughout the world, and a ringleader of the sect [Greek, *hairesin*] of the Nazarenes [Greek, *Nazóraios*]" (Acts 24:5).

According to Luke, the Nazarenes were a heretical sect to be tied to "The Way"; therefore, the question to be answered is, was Jesus affiliated with the Nazóraios sect?

Bethlehem did not exist until the tomb and pillar of Rachel were erected there. The "Bethlehem Prophecy" is one of the

---

[21] Philo's rule no. 20: striking statement: (prophet; prophecy), and an error (quote is from *two* prophets Isaiah *and* Malachi).

[22] Philo's rule no. 1: doubling of a phrase.

[23] Philo's rule no. 1: doubling of a phrase.

[24] Emphasis added.

most frequently cited proofs that Jesus is the Messiah, yet Mark does not mention it – a most noteworthy omission.[25]

Two explanations for Mark's omission of Micah's Prophecy might be considered plausible. The first, that Mark did not believe the prophecy was significant, seems unlikely.

The more plausible explanation comes from biblical scholarship; it suggests that what has come down to us in the New Testament is not a verbatim reproduction of what Mark and the others wrote. For instance, the title of each of the four gospels is exactly the same, "The Gospel According to..." It is unlikely that each writer independently chose exactly the same title, an indication that someone added them at a later date.

Occasionally, someone other than the gospel writer speaks directly to the reader. For example, in the gospel attributed *to* John, the information given at 21:20-24 is *about* John. Therefore, someone *other than* John inserted editorial comments.

Also the arrangement of Matthew, Mark, Luke, and John does not represent the chronological order of their compositions. This serves as additional evidence that they passed through the hands of a compiler and editor which opens the door to the second and more plausible possibility: Mark did not omit the prophecy; a final editor collected the texts and modified all the gospels and epistles, and it was this editor who omitted the prophecy.[26]

One theologian may shine a light on the editor's identity, writing: "I will conclude these considerations with a bold statement: *The New Testament was published by Polycarp of Smyrna between 166 and 168 C.E.*"[27]

This conclusion is intriguing because "Poly-carpus" means "many fruits," the very definition of Philo's words previously quoted: "... collecting and thinking it fit to weave together

---

[25] Philo's rule no. 19: noteworthy omission.
[26] David Trobisch, *The First Edition of the New Testament* (New York: Oxford University Press, 2000), 38.
[27] David Trobisch, "Who Published the New Testament?" Free Inquiry, 28:1 (2007/2008), 30–33.

many things, though different, and proceeding from different sources ["many fruits"], into the same web [the Bible]…"

But this "final editor" option raises still more questions. Was the editor a foe attempting to separate Jesus from the sect of Nazarenes? Or a friendly "Lover of Wisdom" who set about to weave a compound work that carries enigmatical modes of expression and a *Secret History* invisible to Orthodox censors? Were these portions of Matthew's and Mark's gospels modified to draw attention to – and answer – a great debate: Why was Jesus called "The Nazarene" when the early Orthodox Fathers labeled the Nazarenes heretics?

We may now have a way to answer these questions: Foe can be eliminated if Philo's Philology – with the key to solutions – can be identified and objectively applied, and a supported and repeatable conclusion can be reached. This would leave a friend of the Nazarenes as the more reasonable choice.

It is time to look for clues, solutions, and a means to test their validity. And right away we find that Micah's Prophecy would fit quite nicely into an early verse of Mark's gospel. It also comes after one of Philo's yellow flag words that signals enigma. Mark 1:8 concludes with a striking statement ("Holy Spirit") and is immediately followed by 1:9: "In those days Jesus came from Nazareth of Galilee and was baptized by John in the Jordan."

Mark's gospel would include Micah's Prophecy if just one word in the phrase – which "Holy Spirit" flags as an enigma – is changed: "In those days Jesus came from *Bethlehem* to Galilee…"

Furthermore, if *bet-lehem* was intended to be read *betulah-em*,[28] this verse says that Jesus "came from a *virgin mother*." And, if it was intended to be read *bat-El-ha-Em*, then the verse

---

[28] Philo's Rule No. 16: "read not, *Bet Lehem*, but *Betula Em*."

says that Jesus "came from a *daughter of El the Mother*." If either of these equally valid options was the original intent, then Luke's account of a census that required a trip to the ancestral home becomes unnecessary – except for dating the birth of Jesus using Josephus' *Antiquities*.

The evidence suggests that BTLHM (*Bet Lehem, Bet Elohim, Betulah Em* or *Bat El ha Em*) was not just a *place;* it was also the *identity* and *function* of special women who traced their origins to Rachel. Moreover, Rachel was the wife of Jacob, who was renamed *Ish-oR[29]-El* ("man," "light," "El"), or *eSh-uR-eL* ("fire," "flame,"[30] "El").

Notably, "Jacob" constructs Rachel's tomb, but he is called "Israel" as he continues on to Ephrath without her. Therefore, the enigmas infer that the *mother* of the Israelites was the *Betulah Em, daRach-El* ("The Virgin Mother, The Way of El"), and *Bat El Ha Em ruach-El* ("Daughter of El, Spirit of El the Mother"). Just before *Ruachel* died giving birth to Benjamin, LHM gave responsibility for the Israelites to her husband Jacob who was then renamed "Israel."

Mark – or the final editor – could assume readers would know of the sect of Nazarenes if it traced its origins to Isa 11:1 or even earlier to the ancient group in Hebrew Scripture called "Nazirites": "The LORD [Hebrew, YHWH] spoke to Moses, saying: 'Speak to the Israelites and say to them: 'When either men or women make a special vow, the vow of a nazirite, to separate themselves to the LORD'" [Hebrew, *YHWH*]; (Num 6:1-2).

Or perhaps even earlier to the *first* appearance of someone identified as an NZR in Genesis: "Let all these [blessings] rest on the head of Joseph...the NZR among his brothers" (Gen 49:26; NIV).

---

[29] Biblical Hebrew *oR*: NAS (Strong's Hebrew 215): "to be or become light. " NAS (Strong's Hebrew 216): "a light."
[30] Biblical Hebrew *eSh*: NAS (Strong's Hebrew 785): "a fire"; *oR* can also be rendered *uR*, NAS (Strong's Hebrew 217): "a flame."

If it can be demonstrated that Luke – or the final editor – used Philo's Philology to answer the questions and solve the puzzles, foe is eliminated and friend wins the debate.

So what does Luke say, friend or foe? We turn to Luke's Gospel for clues to the answer: "And there appeared to him [Zechariah] an angel of the Lord" (Lk 1:11).

The phrase "angel of the Lord" qualifies as Philo's yellow flag that a clue to an enigma is coming up. The annotations that accompany the verses following "angel of the Lord" indicate they were borrowed from the Book of Judges – the hypotext. And a comparison of the verses turns up one *noteworthy omission*:

Lk 1:11: "Then there appeared to him an angel of the Lord, standing at the right side of the altar of incense."[31]
Judg 13:3: "And the angel of the LORD appeared to the woman..."

Lk 1:13: "'... Your wife Elizabeth will bear you a son...'"
Judg 13:3: "... 'you shall conceive and bear a son.'"

Lk 1:15: "'He must never drink wine or strong drink...'"
Judg 13:4: "'Now be careful not to drink wine or strong drink...'"

Lk 1:16: "'He will turn ... the people of Israel to the Lord their God.'"
Judg 13:5: "'No razor is to come on his head, for the boy shall be a Nazirite[32] to God from birth.'"

The one piece of information provided about Samson that Luke omits when he borrows from Judges is that Samson is a "Nazirite from birth." Therefore, Luke's "enigmatical mode of expression" – the noteworthy omission – ties John the Baptist to "a Nazirite to God from birth."

Next, Luke addresses the baby who will become "Jesus the Nazarene." Luke 1:46-55 is "The Magnificat." It is based largely

---

[31] NRSV excerpted for clarity to compare verses; emphasis added.
[32] Philo's rule no. 19: noteworthy omission.

on the "Song of Hannah" found in 1 Sam 2:1-10. Once again, a comparison reveals a noteworthy omission:

> 1 Sam 2:1: "'My heart rejoices in the LORD...'"[33]
> Lk 1:46: "'My soul glorifies the Lord...'"

> 1 Sam 2:1: "'My heart exults...'"
> Lk 1:47: "'My spirit rejoices...'"

> 1 Sam 2:1: "'...for I delight in your deliverance...'"
> Lk 1:47: "'...my spirit rejoices in God my Savior...'"

> 1 Sam 2:2: "'There is none holy like the LORD...'"
> Lk 1:49: "'...holy is his name...'"

> 1 Sam 2:5; cf. Lk 1:53;
> 1 Sam 2:7-8; cf. Lk 1:52;
> 1 Sam 2:10; cf. Lk 1:51.

Hannah is married to Elkanah, but like John's and Samson's mothers (and Joseph's mother Rachel), she has not been able to conceive:

1 Sam 1:11: She made this vow: "O LORD of hosts, if only you will look on the misery of your servant, and remember me, and not forget your servant, but will give to your servant a male child, then I will set him before you as a nazirite until the day of his death. He shall drink neither wine nor intoxicants, and no razor shall touch his head."

Hannah becomes pregnant and bears a son:

1 Sam 1:22: "But Hannah did not go up, for she said to her husband, 'As soon as the child is weaned, I will bring him, that he may appear in the presence of the LORD, and remain there forever; I will offer him as a nazirite for all time.

Baby Samuel is also a Nazirite. Therefore, Luke's "enigmatical mode of expression" ties Jesus to "a Nazirite for all time."

If the secret message is that Jesus was a Nazarene for all time, a new question is raised: What do we know about the he-

---

[33] NRSV excerpted for clarity to compare verses; emphasis added to each verse.

retical sect identified variously as "Nazarenes," "Nassareans," and/or "Nasoraeans"?

The Gospel of Philip, an ancient Gnostic document found in a desert cave near Nag Hammadi, Egypt, in 1945 and dated between 150 and 300 CE, attempts to explain the etymology of the name "Jesus Christ the Nazarene":

> "Iesous" is a hidden name, "Christ" is a revealed name. For this reason "Iesous" is not particular to any language; rather he is always called by the name "Iesous." While as for "Christ," in Syriac it is "Messiah," in Greek it is "Christ." Certainly all the others have it according to their own language.
>
> "The Nazarene" is "he who reveals what is hidden."[34][35]

"Hidden name" suggests a mystery – an enigma looking for a solution for the name Ie-sous, pronounced "YaH-Zeus." Philip reports that this name did not come from another language; therefore, it is not a derivative of Joshua, Yehosuha, or Yeshua. A reasonable guess might be that "Ie-sous" was created by combining "YHWH" and "Zeus," a thread to be held onto while we search for supporting evidence.

Most of what is known of the Nazarenes depends largely on quotations from the works of those who opposed them, primarily, Hegesippus, Eusebius, Epiphanius, and Jerome. And it is their biased opinions that took root and remain predominant in biblical scholarship.

The most complete and revealing effort to discount the Nazarenes, Naassenes, Nassareans, Nasoraeans, Nazirites, and other NZR and NSR heresies, comes from Epiphanius, Bishop of Salamis (c. 320-403), author of a work titled *Panarion*, written c. 375. In it Epiphanius provides details about the doctrines of 80 heretical sects and philosophies from the time of Adam to the latter part of the fourth century. Some of the unique ele-

---

[34] The Gospel of Philip, c. 150 - ca. 300 CE, n.p. Wesley W. Isenburg, trans.

[35] Meyer, 2008, 164. Marvin Meyer offers a slightly different translation: "Jesus [Gk. Iesous] is a hidden name, Christ is a revealed name. The name Jesus [Iesous] does not exist in any other language, but he is called by the name Jesus [Iesous]. The word for Christ in Syriac is *messias* and in Greek is *christos*, and likewise all other people have a word for it in their own language. Nazarene is the revealed form of the hidden name."

ments Epiphanius addresses suggest he may have had knowledge of the claims quoted above from The Gospel of Philip.

Epiphanius attempts to dispel any suspicion that "Jesus the Nazarene" is to be tied to the Nassaraean or Nazarene sect or the Nazirites of Moses. His very effort suggests that the Orthodox Church had cause to be concerned. People might question Jesus' relationship with Nazirites and Nazarenes – and perhaps questions were being asked at the time Epiphanius wrote *Panarion*. And perhaps the questions were coming from people who were reading Philip's Gospel or the original source from which it may have come.

Epiphanius first addresses the group he identifies as "Nasaraeans," writing:

> The Nasaraeans ... were Jews by nationality ... They acknowledged Moses and believed that he had received laws – *not this law, however, but some other*. And so, they were Jews who kept all the Jewish observances, but they would not offer sacrifice or eat meat. They considered it unlawful to eat meat or make sacrifices with it. They claim that *these Books are fictions*, and that none of these customs were instituted by the fathers. This was the difference between the Nasaraeans and the others.[36]

> Nasaraeans, meaning, "rebels," who forbid all flesh-eating, and do not eat living things at all. They have the holy names of patriarchs which are in the Pentateuch, up through Moses and Joshua the son of Nun, and they believe in them – I mean Abraham, Isaac, Jacob, and the earliest ones, and Moses himself, and Aaron, and Joshua. But they hold that the *scriptures of the Pentateuch* were *not written by Moses*, and maintain that *they have others*.[37]

---

[36] Epiphanius, late third, early fourth century, *Panarion* 1:18. *The Panarion of Epiphanius of Salamis: A Treatise Against Eighty Sects in Three Books.*

[37] Epiphanius, *Panarion* 1:19. Emphasis added.

Let's stop for a moment to consider this statement: "... these Books [the Pentateuch] are fictions ... not written by Moses ... they have others." Most historical-critical scholars agree that Moses did not author the Pentateuch, and some point to evidence of four independent sources.

In *Prolegomena zur Geschichte Israels,*[38] German biblical scholar Julius Wellhausen (1844-1918) supported and expanded the theory first proposed by Karl Heinrich Graf (1815-1869). The "Graf-Wellhausen Hypothesis" became the foundation for similar, competing theories which continue to proliferate and evolve. Wellhausen labeled the sources and dated the evolution of the Pentateuch as: the Jawist (J) c. 900 BCE; the Elohist (E) c. 800 BCE; the Deuteronomist (D) c. 600 BCE; the Priestly (P) c. 500 BCE.

The Babylonian Exile of Judean priests and scribes began c. 609 BCE and lasted until c. 500 BCE, encompassing the time D and P were composed and assimilated with J and E. This synthesis of texts resulted in the first fixed edition of the Tanakh,[39] and it occurred during the time the Judean leaders and their sacred texts were under the control of Babylonian Kings.

When Cyrus the Great released the captives, the scribes and sages emerged as Jewish leaders and the Tanakh became the authoritative text, in effect replacing the need for a central Temple. Judaism could flourish anywhere a scribe or sage had a copy of the Tanakh.

When Ezra returned to Jerusalem from Babylon with the Tanakh c. 458 BCE, modern Judaism arrived with him. A question that should be asked is how much influence did the Babylonians have on the editing of the fixed, approved, and distributed Tanakh? The investigation to answer this question will be carried out in Chapter Five.

---

[38] Julius Wellhausen, *Prolegomena to the History of Israel.* (*Geschichte Israels* appeared in 1878, republished in 1882 as *Prolegomena zur Geschichte Israels.* The official English translation by J. Sutherland Black and Allan Menzies (preface by Prof. W. Robertson Smith) appeared in 1885, and the fifth German edition appeared in 1899.)

[39] The canon of Hebrew Scripture, also known as *Mikra.*

Epiphanius combined with Irenaeus seems to suggest that the "heretical" Nasaraeans – "Gnostics" – had knowledge of the Key that unlocks the history beneath the fiction. Irenaeus' "heretics" employed Homer to interpret scripture; Philo's Philology uses Homer and other hypotexts to interpret scripture as well.

Epiphanius later explains that for a brief period of time the Nazarenes were called "Jessaeans," pointing to Isaiah's Prophecy. He describes the Nazarenes as: "Jewish, attached to the Law, and had circumcision." But he is concerned by how they differed: "... they kindled fire too, in imitation, and set themselves ablaze."[40]

These Nazarenes, Epiphanius writes,

... were impressed by the miracles the apostles performed and came to believe in Jesus, even though they never heard him speak.

But they found that he had been conceived at Nazareth and brought up in Joseph's home, and for this reason is called "Jesus the Nasoraean" in the Gospel as the apostles say, "Jesus the Nasoraean, a man approved by signs and wonders," [Acts 2:22] and so on. Hence, they adopted this name, so as to be called "Nazarenes."[41]

Epiphanius also stresses that Nazarenes, which Luke in *Acts* calls *Nazóraios*, are not to be confused with Nazirites, which he defines as "consecrated persons," explaining that they are an ancient rank belonging to firstborn sons and men dedicated to God. He even gives examples: Samson and John the Baptist.[42] Of course Num 6:1-2 demonstrates that Epiphanius was either poorly informed about Nazirites, or he was intentionally deceptive; Nazirites are specified as being *both* men and women.

Gradually Epiphanius grows more forceful:

Everyone called the Christians "Nasoraeans," as they say in accusing the apostle Paul: "We have found this man a pestilent fellow and a perverter of the people, a ringleader of the sect of the Nasoraeans." And the apostle did not disclaim the name – not to

---

[40] Epiphanius, *Panarion* 29:5.4-5.
[41] Epiphanius, *Panarion*, 29:5.6.
[42] Epiphanius, *Panarion*, 29:5.7.

profess the Nasoraean sect, but he was glad to own the name his adversaries' malice had applied to him for Christ's sake. For he says in court: "They neither found me in the temple disputing with any man, neither raising up the people, nor have I done any of those things whereof they accuse me. But this I confess unto thee, that after The Way, which they call heresy, so worship I, believing all things in the Law and the prophets."[43]

Epiphanius' rhetoric grows even more energetic as he inserts exclamation points to drive home his point:

And no wonder the apostle admitted to being a Nasoraean! In those days everyone called Christians this because of the city of Nazareth – there was no other usage of the name then. People thus gave the name of "Nasoraeans" to believers in Christ, of whom it is written, "He shall be called a Nasoraean."[44]

Christ's disciples called themselves "disciples of Jesus," as indeed they were. But they were not rude when others called them "Nasoraeans," since they saw the intent of those who called them this. They did it because of Christ, since our Lord Jesus was called "Nasoraean" himself – so say the Gospels and the Acts of the Apostles – because of his upbringing in Joseph's home in Nazareth. (Though he was born in the flesh at Bethlehem, of the ever-virgin Mary, Joseph's betrothed. Joseph had settled in Nazareth after leaving Bethlehem and taking up residence in Galilee.)[45]

But these sectarians disregarded the name of Jesus, and did not call themselves "Jessaeans," keep the name "Jews," or term themselves "Christians" – but "Nasoraeans," from the place-name, Nazareth, if you please! However they are simply complete Jews.[46]

Luke's enigmatical modes of expression and resultant revelations beg to differ with Epiphanius dramatically. Luke's enigmatic threads tie the Nazarites in Hebrew Scripture to Luke's Nazarenes (Samson to John and Samuel to Jesus), thereby revealing that Epiphanius' emphatic and repeated claim – that the Nasoraeans took their name from the city of Nazareth – is false. And it is Luke who acknowledges the existence of other

[43] Epiphanius, *Panarion*, 29:6.2-4.
[44] Epiphanius, *Panarion*, 29:6.5-6.
[45] Epiphanius, *Panarion*, 29:6.7-8.
[46] Epiphanius, *Panarion*, 29:7.1.

accounts but promises Theophilus that it is his *orderly account* that carries *the Truth* (Lk 1:1-4). Furthermore, Epiphanius' contemporary Jerome attributes "The Nazarene" to NSR, the Prophecy at Isa 11:1 and a mistake in translation by those who produced the Septuagint.

We see, therefore, that esoteric stories sit alongside the exoteric stories in the verses of the Gospels examined thus far. Philo's Philology identifies them, the four steps for analysis solves them, and a reasonable and repeatable conclusion can be reached about them: The Gospel writers – or the final editor – did *not* agree that Jesus was called "The Nazarene" because he came from Nazareth. The enigmas suggest that Jesus was called "The Nazóraios" for some other reason. And it is the search for the reasons and the people responsible for the deception that will serve as additional tests for Philo's Philology.

This first test demonstrates how yellow and red flags are used. Starting with a popular question for debate among scholars, we set out to find the prophet who predicted that Jesus would be called a "Nazarene" as Matthew claimed. Jerome's answer raised another question: If Nazorean comes from Isa 11:1, *a branch* (wə·nê·ṣer) of Jesse, why does Matthew create a residency in Nazareth to explain the genesis of the term, in effect changing his name to "Jesus of Nazareth"?

Mark opens his gospel with a yellow flag, "angel," signaling a pending enigma. It is immediately followed by the duplicated phrase "prepare The Way" – a red flag. Stopping to give it some thought and checking annotations, we first turned to the quoted Hebrew Scriptures to look for clues. We found "da-Rachel," "The Way of El." And we found that Rachel's Tower was erected on *the way* to Ephrath and its location was called "Bethlehem" – or "Betulah Em."

Luke ties "The Way of El" to the "Nazarene Heresy" at Acts 24:5 and 24:14: "...the heresy of the *Nazarenes*..." and "... *The Way* which they call a heresy." But so little is known of the Nazarenes that we had to ask a follow-up question: Does Luke's gospel offer any clues to this mysterious heresy?

Luke, like Mark, opens with a verse (1:11) that sends up a yellow flag: "Angel of the Lord." The stories of John's and Jesus' births are accompanied by annotations that point to Hebrew Scripture hypotexts. Comparing the similarities line-for-line, we can identify a *noteworthy omission*. One word, "Nazirite," is missing from Luke's version of both stories.

But Epiphanius argues strenuously in support of Matthew's claim that it is neither a sect nor the ancient group that assisted Moses, but the city of Nazareth that gave Jesus his name. For many this has become settled doctrine. Nonetheless, for some it piques curiosity and leads to a continued quest for an alternative answer to the prophecy mystery.

The prophecy thread brought in a companion topic of scholarly debate: Mark's omission of the Bethlehem Prophecy. Again, Philo's rules identify a perfect location for "Bethlehem," and the yellow flag caution is present. But it is not followed by "Bethlehem"; the yellow flag is followed by "Nazareth." This failure forced us to examine the phrase more carefully, concluding that changing just one word in Mk 1:9 would supply the fulfillment of the Bethlehem Prophecy to Mark's gospel.

Proof comes from the hypotext (Gen 35:19) which places "The Way" in close proximity to "Bethlehem." In Mark, however, "The Way" precedes "Nazareth" not "Bethlehem," identifying a possible interpolation. And, restoring "Betulah Em" to Mark also adds the "Virgin Mother" to his story.

We can now reasonably conclude that:

1. Mark's and Luke's gospels were written and/or edited by a friend of Nazarenes – possibly Polycarp – who used the Method to reveal ancient secrets to modern exegetes.

2. The Nazarene sect can be tied to the ancient Nazirites, and their doctrine was called *The Way of Elohim* or *The Way of El the Mother,* Hebrew, *daRach-El ha Em.*

CHAPTER FIVE

Following Philo to
The Son of Man
The Children of Light
The One Who Betrayed Him

Two New Testament questions frequently debated among scholars are: (1) the meaning of "The Son of Man" sayings; (2) the origin of the mysterious "Children of Light":

"No one has ascended into heaven except the one who descended from heaven, the Son of Man. And just as Moses lifted up the serpent in the wilderness, so must the Son of Man be lifted up, that whoever believes in him may have eternal life" (Jn 3:13-15).

"For the *Son of Man* goes as it is written of him, but woe to *that one* by whom the *Son of Man* is betrayed! It would have been better for *that one* not to have been born" (Mk 14:21).[1]

"And his master commended the dishonest manager because he had acted shrewdly; for the children of this age are more shrewd in dealing with their own generation than are the children of light" (Lk 16:8).

"While you have the light, believe in the light, so that you may become children of light" (Jn 12:36).

The questions to be answered in this chapter are:

1. Why does Jesus refer to himself in all four Gospels as "The Son of Man"?
2. Did "The Children of Light" trace their origins to the Hebrew Bible?
3. Who was "that one," the enigmatic person who betrayed "The Son of Man"? Judas is *one* suspect, but Luke points to another.

---

[1] Note the repetition of "The Son of Man" and "That one," signaling *enigmas*. Emphasis added.

The place to start, of course, is Hebrew Scripture which opens with Gen 1:1 and these familiar words:

> "In the beginning God created the heavens and the earth…"

The Hebrew consonants that comprise Genesis 1:1 (in caps), and the vowels and spaces chosen by an interpreter are:

> BeReSiT BaRa eLoHiM[2] eT HaSSaMaYiM We-eT Ha-aReS

As previously shown, Philo and the authors of the Babylonian Talmud suggest that not all first century groups agreed with these choices of vowels and spaces. Both point to "Besalel" as the likely source of "enigmas" in the Torah[3] that only a select few could decipher. Writing of the Essenes, Philo notes:

> Then one takes up the holy volume … and another of the men of the greatest experience … *explains what is not very intelligible*, for a great many precepts are delivered in *enigmatical modes of expression* …[4]

The authors of the Babylonian Talmud add:

> Besalel *knew how to combine the letters* by which the heavens and earth were created.
>
> The Holy One … "giveth wisdom unto the wise, and knowledge to them that know understanding."[5]

Philo and the Babylonian Talmud suggest that the ancient Essenes, "…men of the greatest experience…" and "the wise who have wisdom and knowledge," considered other options for vowels and spaces when interpreting Hebrew Scripture. And the "other options" must be considered in light of *when* the Tanakh first arrived in Jerusalem, from *where* it came, and to *whom* it is attributed: "Some of the people of Israel, and some of the priests and Levites, the singers and gatekeepers, and the temple servants also went up to Jerusalem, in the *seventh year of King Artaxerxes*" (Ezra 7:7). This dates the trip to c. 458 BCE.

---

[2] Also valid is LeHeM, "bread."

[3] The "Five Books of Moses," also known as the "Pentateuch."

[4] Yonge (2013): Philo, "Every Good Man is Free" (XII.82), 690. Emphasis added.

[5] Rabbi Dr. I. Epstein, ed. *Berakoth: Translated into English with Notes, Glossary and Indices,* "Babylonian Talmud, Berakhot 55a." n.p. Maurice Simon, M.A. trans.

Ezra 7:9-12 answers the remaining questions:

On the first day of the first month the journey up *from Babylon* was begun, and on the first day of the fifth month he came to *Jerusalem*, for the gracious hand of his God [Hebrew, *LHM*] was upon him. For Ezra had set his heart to study the law [Hebrew, *tovrat*] of the LORD [Hebrew, *YHWH*], and to do it, and to teach the statutes [Hebrew, *chok*] and ordinances [Hebrew, *mishpat*] in Israel.

This is a copy of the letter that King Artaxerxes gave to the priest *Ezra, the scribe, a scholar of the text of the commandments* [Hebrew, *tovrat*] of the LORD and his statutes [Hebrew, *chukka*] for Israel: "Artaxerxes, king of kings, to the priest Ezra, *the scribe of the law* [Hebrew, *data*] of the God [Hebrew, *LHM*] of heaven: Peace. And now…[6] (Ezra 7:9-12).[7]

Ezra and his group arrived in Jerusalem several decades *after* the Babylonian Exile ended. They arrived *with* "the com-mandments of YHWH" *and* "the *data* of LHM of heaven." Philo's hair-splitting method applied to these carefully composed verses reveals an important distinction: the *tsavah* – the Torah – was written for YHWH's Iudeans, but *chok, mishpat,* and the *"data of LHM shemaiya"* were given to Elohim's Israelites. Therefore two key words, *tsavah* and *mishpat,* require a closer look.

Tsavah, for example "The Ten Commandments," require unquestioning submission to YHWH's written Laws. Conversely, *mishpat*[8] suggests the freedom to judge right from wrong, "good from evil," which *ha nachash* bequeathed to "woman" (*ishshah*), and which she shared with "man" (*ish*) at Gen 3:6.

Ezra 7:9-12 suggests that *two* separate entities, YHWH and LHM, became one during the Babylonian Exile. This "One God" is sometimes written in Hebrew Scripture as "YHWH LHM" ("LORD God"), sometimes as "YHWH" ("LORD") and sometimes as "LHM" (*eLoHiM*, "gods," but translated "God").[9]

---

[6] Note duplication of the phrases, "Torah of YHWH" and "statutes of LHM."
[7] Emphasis added.
[8] NAS (Strong's Hebrew 5921).
[9] *LHM* can also be interpreted *eL Ha eM,* "El the Mother."

This distinction, and the distinction between YHWH's *tsavah* and LHM's *mishpat,* further explains the Nassareans' claim, reported by Epiphanius: "... they hold that the scriptures of the Pentateuch were not written by Moses, and maintain that they have others."

The evidence seems to say that the "other scriptures" of the Pentateuch were compiled by Ezra and his group using Besalel's "enigmatical modes of expression." These "other scriptures" may refer to the *esoteric* Tanakh which can be interpreted only by certain Essenes and "wise men of wisdom." And in his lengthy description of the Essenes, Josephus slips in confirmation that they had "other scriptures":

> "Moreover, he [the Essene] swears to communicate *their doctrines* to no one any otherwise than as he received them himself ... that he will equally *preserve the books belonging to their sect,* and *the names of the Angels* [translator's added note "or messengers"].[10]

Josephus adds that Essenes made judgments based on their own doctrines, not those *commanded* in the Torah:

> "... in *the judgments they exercise* they are most accurate and just..."[11]

Many people are unaware that in the story of the Ten Commandments, Moses brought *two* sets of tablets down from the mountain. The first set "...were the work of LHM, and the writing was the writing of LHM..." (Ex 32:16). However, "As soon as he came near the camp and saw the calf and the dancing, Moses' anger burned hot, and he threw the tablets from his hands and broke them..." (Ex 32:19).

When he returned to the top of the mountain with the bad news about the tablets, "The LORD [*YHWH*] said to Moses, 'Cut two tablets of stone like the former ones, and I will write on the tablets *the words* that were on the former tablets which you broke" (Ex 34:1.)[12]

---

[10] Josephus, 1999, *Wars,* 2.8.7 (142), 737-8.
[11] Josephus, 1999, *Wars,* 2.8.9 (145), 738.
[12] Emphasis added.

"The words" refers to the string of consonants and not the vowels and spaces inserted during interpretation and translation. And as we've previously shown, the same consonants can create quite different words and meanings. Of course, someone would have to reassemble the pieces of the broken tablet, an early version of a jigsaw puzzle that also serves as an enigmatic instruction: "You must put the pieces together!"

Notably, Ezra's name, Hebrew *ZR*, can also be rendered *Ze-Ra*, and *zera* is translated as "a sowing; seed; offspring."[13] It is first used by the scribe who compiled and edited the Tanakh early in Gen:

> "Then God [*LHM*] said, 'Let the earth put forth vegetation: plants yielding seed [*zera*], and their *fruit* [*peri*] trees of every kind on earth that bear *fruit* with the *zera* in it. And it was so" (Gen 1:11), repeated almost verbatim at Gen 1:12.

Note the duplication of the words *zera* and *peri*, identifying them as enigmas. In fact, Ezra, the scribe who worked on the Torah and the mishpat in Babylon and delivered them to Jerusalem, employed the word *ZR*, rendered, *ZeRa*, 230 times, but also rendered *ZaRa*, *ZuR*, *ZiR*, *ZeR*, or *ZeRi* nearly 100 additional times.[14]

With this information in hand, we can now re-examine Gen 1:1 for a second opinion as to vowels and spaces to add to the assigned consonants (in caps):

| BaR iSh eT aB oR eL Ha eM |
| eT Ha iShSha eMYiM We eT Ha oR iSh |

| Son of Man, Father Light, El the Mother, |
| also the women mothers and the light men.[15] |

What emerges is the *heretical* Holy Trinity, "Father, Mother, and Son of Man." Coincidence? Or a clue to the genesis of the claims made by and for The Children of Light? These valid but

---

[13] NAS (Strong's Hebrew 2233).

[14] Lockman, Biblehub.com.

[15] Authors' rendering based on Essene methodology.

alternative words say that a "Son of Man," a "Father of Light,"
and "El the Mother" produced "oR iShShah" and "iSh," "light
women and men," and/or *uR*, "the flame" of ishshah and ish.
And these women and men came *before* Adam and Eve are introduced. In fact, the *Ishshah* and *Ish* are introduced in the
opening words of what must have been the Isshene's Version
of Hebrew Scripture.

In addition to providing an association with Ezra, Gen 1:11
holds critical clues for solving a multitude of biblical puzzles.
The Hebrew words traditionally created for Gen 1:11 are:

> WaYYoMeR eLoHiM **TaDSe** Ha **aReS DeSe** eSeB MaZRia
> **ZeRa** eS **PeRi** oSeH **PeRi** LeMiNoW aSeR **ZaRoW**-BoW aL
> Ha **aReS** WaYHi KeN.[16]

NRSV translates these words:

> Then God said, 'Let the *earth* put forth vegetation: plants
> yielding seed (*zera*), and their *fruit trees* of every kind on
> *earth* that bear *fruit* with the seed (*zera*) in it. And it was so.

Key words and phrases in this verse carry enigmatic threads
that are woven into dozens of stories in Hebrew and Christian
Scripture (the number by each word is assigned by Strong's
Concordance and can be verified online).[17] These words will
become important throughout the rest of this book, so flag this
page for future reference:

1. *TaDSe* [1876], translated "put forth," but equally valid when
   rendered *eT aDa*[18] [1571b] iSh ("adorned man"); and/or, eT *eDa*
   [5713] iSh ("testimony man"); and/or, eT *uD* [5769b] iSh ("bear
   witness man").
2. *DeSe* [1877] *eSeB*, [6212] *MaZRia* [2232] ("vegetation: plants yield-
   ing"); and/or, *aDa iShSha* [802] *'aB* [5645] *eM* [517] *eZeR* [5828]
   ("adorned woman," "cloud," "mother," "helper").
3. *aReS* [776] ("earth"); and/or, *oR* [215] *iSh* (light man"); and/or
   uR [784] *eS* [6086] ("fire tree" or "flaming tree").

---

[16] Lockman, Biblehub.
[17] Ibid.
[18] Hebrew *ada*: "adorned" means the members of this "First Family" are "clothed in
terms" that identify them in later enigmatic stories.

4. *ZeRa* [2233] ("seed," "descendants," "offspring"); and/or, *eZeR* [5828] ("helper"); and/or, *ZuR* (*tSuR*) [6697] ("rock"); and/or *ZaR* [2114] ("stranger").
5. *PeRi* [6529], translated "fruit," but equally valid are *PaRa* [6500] ("fruitful"); and/or, *PeRa* [6544b] ("leader"); and/or, *PeRa* [6545] ("locks (of hair)"); and/or, *PeRe* [6501] ("wild donkey").
6. *eS* [6086] translated "tree" but equally valid are *eSh* [784], "fire" and/or, *"iSh"* [376], "man."

So, beginning with the same consonants, but choosing different vowels and spaces, we find several alternative Hebrew words in Gen 1:11 which produce a totally new meaning:

> WaYY eM oR eL Ha eM et eDa iSh Ha oR iSh eDa iShiSha BaMa eZeR ZuR eSh PeRi eS PeRa aLaM aN[19] We aSheRa ZaR We aB We eLoaH oR eS. WayHi KeN.

> "And Mother Light, *El the Mother,*[20] *adorned* ish-man 'The light man,' *adorned* ish-woman 'high place;[21] helper; rock; fire; wild donkey; tree; fruit; long-haired; hidden;[22] cloud; and Ashera; stranger; and Father; and Eloah;[23] light; fire/flame/tree. And it was so."

Gen 1:11 is one of the most important verses in the Torah because it is "The Key" to interpreting scripture. Gen 1:11 is an itemized listing of enigmatic terms that will "adorn" or "identify" the descendants of the Ishshah and Ishene bloodline whenever they appear in the Bible.

Note that ZR, "eZRa" and/or "ZeRa," is used three times in this verse, suggesting Ezra wanted to be found and recognized for his amazing composition.

---

[19] Hebrew *aN*: NAS (Strong's Hebrew 6051). "aN" also represents "Ansar." *Anna, IoAnna, Ananus,* and *Ananius* identify these people as descendants of *An*-sar and Kisar – the Ish and Ishshah, Ishraelites, Ishenes, and the "princes and princesses," NaZaReans.
[20] Also valid is LHM, "bread."
[21] Hebrew, *BaMa*: NAS (Strong's Hebrew 1116).
[22] Hebrew, *aLaM*: NAS (Strong's Hebrew 5956).
[23] Hebrew, *LH* is Israel's *eLoaH* and refers to the "First Father."

Furthermore, the first use of *ezer* ("helper") subsequent to Gen 1:11 is Gen 2:18: "Then YHWH Elohim said, 'It is not good that adam should be alone; I will make him a *helper* as his partner.'" This identifies the Earth-man's wife, Eve, as an *Ishshah*.

Additionally, when *ish* is part of a name, it also identifies the man as a descendant of "light men" from "Father Light," rather than a descendent of *adam* the "earth men" who came later.

For example, Hagar and Abram's son was Ishmael, *ish eM eL*, identifying him as a descendant of "Light-men," specifically "of *Mother El*." For good measure he is also called a *PeRe*, "wild donkey" (Gen 16:12). Another *Ishene*, Jacob and Leah's son Issachar, is called a "strong donkey" (Gen 49:14).

Ishshah descendants are veiled behind the words *aB* (Hebrew for, "cloud"[24] and/or "father"[25]) and *anan* (another Hebrew word for, "cloud"[26]). In fact, a cloud appears almost two hundred times in the Old and New Testaments combined, and in some of the most important scenes.[27] Let's look at one:

The Greek word for "cloud" is *nephele*,[28] and a most striking "cloud" is one that appears in Mk 9:7, Mt 17:5, and Lk 9:34: "Then *nephele*[29] overshadowed them, and from the *nepheles* there came a voice, 'This is my Son, the Beloved; listen to him!'" (Mk 9:7).[30]

Genesis 1:11 explains that the repeated word "cloud" identifies the speaker ("voice") as a descendant of Ishshah and Ish, an "Essene." This understanding of *who* the word "cloud" identifies turns a supernatural scene into a simple observation. A proud mother, whose ancestors claimed they came from "Father Light," introduces her son to the people he hopes to teach and serve.

---

[24] NAS (Strong's Hebrew 5645).
[25] NAS (Strong's Hebrew 2).
[26] NAS (Strong's Hebrew 6051).
[27] NAS, Lockman.
[28] NAS (Strong's Greek 3507).
[29] The Greek, *nephele* (Strong's No. 3507) is phonetically similar to the Hebrew, *Nephilim* (Strong's No. 5303 from 5307). See Genesis 6:4.
[30] Greek insertions; emphasis added.

Returning now to more of eZRa's esoteric messages: an examination of the Hebrew consonants that are translated, "singers," "gatekeepers," and "temple servants" – and choosing different vowels and spaces – dramatically changes the duties they performed:

Hebrew consonants, WHMSRM:

> Orthodox: We HaM SoRaRiM, "and the singers."
> Essene: We Ha eM iSh oR eM, "and the mother ish ("Essene men") light mother."

Hebrew consonants, WHSSRM:

> Orthodox: We HaS SoaRim, "and the gatekeepers"
> Essene: *We Ha iShSha oR eM*, "and the woman light mother."

Hebrew consonants, WHNNTNM:

> Orthodox: We HaN NeTiNiM, "and the temple servants."
> Essene: We Ha aNNa eT aN eM, "And the Anna, Cloud mother."

The evidence suggests that "iShShah and iSh," introduced at Genesis 1:1 and traveling with Ezra from Babylon to Jerusalem, were "Ishsenes," which evolved into "Essenes." Therefore, those investigating the genesis and etymology of Josephus and Philo's "Essenes," seemingly omitted from Hebrew Scripture, can consider yet another option: read as the Essenes might have read Hebrew Scripture, the "Essene sect of Judaism" is introduced in the opening words.

Josephus associates the Essenes with Pythagoreans: "The Essenes also, as we call a sect of ours ... live the same kind of life as do those whom the Greeks call Pythagoreans..."[31]

These important threads, and the names of prominent men and women derived from *Anan*, will be examined in later chapters.

---

[31] Josephus, 1999, *Antiquities* 15.10.4 (371), 521.

According to Babylonian mythology and the esoteric Torah, the Earth was populated by two genetically different tribes: the Ish-zera of LHM, and the Adam-zera of YHWH. The zera of LHM claimed superiority as "The Children of Light." Furthermore, Cain killed Abel, demonstrating the Adam-man's genetic predisposition for violence and the letting of blood. According to Church Father Epiphanius, the descendants of Ansar – the Nasaraeans – were opposed to the letting of blood:

> The Nasaraeans ... were Jews by nationality ... but *they would not offer sacrifice or eat meat*. They considered it unlawful to eat meat or make sacrifices with it. They claim that ... none of these customs were instituted by the fathers. This was the difference between the Nasaraeans and the others.[32]
>
> Nasaraeans, meaning, "rebels," who forbid all flesh-eating, and do not eat living things at all.[33]

Ezra's NSR, "Nasaraeans," is an enigmatical mode of expression that refers to NSR, "aNSaR eans," "children of the Lord who came from the sky," and "aN iSh oR" ("An's men of light"). They revered Moses, the patriarchs, and the Torah; however, the NSR did not interpret the Torah in the same way as the Judeans, Paul, and the Early Church Fathers. Not only did they reject blood sacrifice, they refused to eat meat!

This presented a problem: How could "Jesus the NaSaRean" *be* a blood sacrifice when the Nasareans *rejected* blood sacrifice? Something had to be done to separate Jesus from the Church's primary adversaries, the heretical Nasaraeans.

The Nasaraeans' earliest adversaries knew, of course, that throughout the Gospels and the Book of Revelation, Jesus claimed the title, "Nazaraean," for himself. "The Son of Man" written in Greek is *huios tou anthropou*; however, in Aramaic – the language of Jesus – "The Son of Man" is written, *Ha BaR eNaS*, which can also be rendered *Ha Bar An iSh*, "The Son of An men."

---

[32] Epiphanius, *Panarion* 1:18. Emphasis added.
[33] Epiphanius, *Panarion* 1:19. Emphasis added.

Furthermore, the same consonants can create *Ha BaR aNa-Sha*, "The Son of serpent." And this brings us back to John 3:14, which solves the mystery of the meaning of "The Son of Man":

> In Hebrew, "lifted up" is *NaSah:*[34] Moses *nasaha anasha* … says that Moses "lifted up the serpent."
>
> In Hebrew, "The Son of Man be lifted up" is *"ha bar anasha nasaha.*

Because the New Testament is written in Greek, the fact that "serpent" and "Son of Man" are identical in the Aramaic language has stood relatively unexamined since the Early Church Fathers dispelled any suspicion that "Jesus" was affiliated with the "heretical" Nazareans, and most scholars accepted their testimony as fact.

However, a book by Charles William King published in 1887, *The Gnostics and Their Remains*, offers some intriguing clues pulled from the works of Hippolytus of Rome (c. 170-235 CE), one of Irenaeus' disciples. Of the Gnostic heresies, King writes:

> The Ophites *should hold by right the first place amongst the schools we are considering*, for that impartial and acute historian of the Gnosis, Hippolytus, styles them, "The Naaseni who specially call themselves 'Gnostics.' But inasmuch as this deception of theirs is multiform and has many heads (a play upon their name of serpent-followers), like the Hydra of fable, if I smite all the heads at once with the wand of Truth, I shall destroy the whole serpent, *for all the other sects differ but little from this one in essentials*." He therefore commences his history of the Gnostic heresies, properly so called, with a minute account of this one, illustrated with copious extracts from their text-books; *on account of their antiquity* and importance bestowing much more of his space upon them than upon any other of their offshoots or competitors.
>
> Their strange-sounding title "Naaseni" – "Followers of the Naas" (the only way in which the Greek, from its want of aspirate letters, could write the Hebrew *Nachash*, "Serpent") was literally rendered by "Ophites," the name which has ever since served to designate

---

[34] NAS (Strong's Hebrew 5375), "lift, carry, take."

them. They first assumed a definite existence about the same time
as the Basilidans, (sic) in the middle of the second century, *although the elements of the doctrine are derived from a source much more
remote. That source was the secret doctrines taught in the various Pagan
Mysteries; and likewise certain philosophic theories of the Greeks, although certainly not to the same extent as the learned Hippolytus labours
so ingeniously to demonstrate.*[35]

Additionally, King seems to suggest that the Early Fathers
were aware that the Nazareans used John 3:14 to explain the
"The Son of Man" sayings and to associate Jesus with "The
Serpent":

> To establish the identity of their *Ophis* with the Saviour, his fol-
> lowers adduced the words of St. John, "For as Moses lifted up the
> serpent in the wilderness, even so must the Son of Man be lifted
> up." All this proves that the section of the Ophites which regarded
> the serpent as *evil* by its nature, had been led astray from *the primi-
> tive doctrine of their sect* by the prevailing Zoroastrian and Jewish
> notions upon that subject. The creed of the *original* Gnostics, the
> *Naaseni*, gave a very different view of the nature of the serpent
> considered merely as a type...[36]

Like most modern translations, NRSV renders the Hebrew
consonants in Gen 3:1, "Now the *Serpent* was more crafty than
any other wild animal that the LORD God had made..."

However, not all translators agree; for example, the International Standard Version reads, "Now *the Shining One* was more
clever than any animal of the field that the [YHWH Elohim]
had made." This unusual option is justified by the elasticity of
the Hebrew word, *nachash* – specifically, whether it is used as a
noun, a verb, or an adjective.

When used as a noun, *nachash* does indeed translate as "serpent." But as a verb, *nachash* means "to practice divination,"
which is associated with the Magoi of the Median tribe whose
high priest was Moses' father-in-law. And Luke identifies Bar-
Jesus as a Magoi (Acts 13:6).

[35] Charles William King, *The Gnostics and Their Remains* (1887), 82. *Sacred Texts Archive.*
[36] King (1887), 102; emphasis added.

When used as an adjective, *nachash* means "shining bronze" or refers to something that has been polished. The addition of *ha* changes the words to "the nachash"; therefore, as an adjective, it is convincingly argued that *ha nachash* means, "the shining one." Moreover, Isaiah supports this option as being the more accurate.[37] "How you have come down from heaven, O Day Star, son of Dawn!" (Isa 14:12; authors' interpretation).

As previously noted, Jesus wasn't the first to be called "a Nazarene." The first NZR appears in Gen 49:26; he is Joseph, Rachel is his mother, and he is Jacob's eleventh son, the only son out of twelve to be identified as NZR: "aN's ZeRa." Indeed, King is right: the doctrine of the Nazaraeans was a "primitive doctrine" from a "remote source" established centuries before Orthodox Christianity abducted "Iesous the NaZaRaean," gave him a new hometown, and renamed him "Iesous of Nazareth."

In his final farewell, Jesus said, "I, Jesus, have sent my angel to testify to you these things for the churches. I am the *root and the descendant of David,* the *bright morning star*" (Rev 22:16).[38]

As with Mark's opening verses, two prophecies are combined to form the key phrases in this verse: "I am the root and the descendant of David" comes from Isa 11:1, the verse Jerome quotes to identify Matthew's unnamed "prophet."

The second phrase, "the bright morning star," comes from Isa 14:12. Both serve as hypotexts as we re-examine Rev 22:16 using Philo's Philology.

The Hebrew Bible version of Isa 11:1 is: "choter miggeza yisay **we neser** missarasaw yif **parah**. NASB translates this verse as, "Then a shoot will spring from the stem of Jesse,[39] And a branch [Hebrew, *neser*] from his roots will *bear fruit.*"

The Hebrew word for "bear fruit," *parah*, is one of the "Ishene adornments" listed in Gen 1:11.[40] So, let's review the

---

[37] Michael S. Heiser, "The Nachash and His Seed: Some Explanatory Notes on Why the 'Serpent' in Genesis 3 Wasn't a Serpent."

[38] NASB; Greek insertion; emphasis added.

[39] Jesse is David's father.

[40] NAS, Lockman.

various possibilities for *PR* and what one or more might reveal about Isa 11:1 and Jesus.

"PR" can be rendered (1) *PeRi* (Strong's 6529, "fruit"); (2) *PeRa* (Strong's 6544b, "leader," "long haired"); (3) *PeRa* (Strong's 6545, "locks (of hair)); and (4) *PeRe* (Strong's 6501, "wild donkey").[41]

"Jesus" of the "Jesus Myth" meets the criteria for all these choices; he was: (1) a "fruit" (Lk 1:41); (2) a "leader" (Heb 12:2); (3) had "long hair" (Num 6:5); arrived in Jerusalem on a donkey that had never been ridden – a "wild donkey" (Mk 11:2).

The key words in the second hypotext, Isa 14:12, are "... heil-il ben shachar." The NASB translation is "...O star of the morning, son of the dawn!" The King James Version, however, is the translation most people know: "... O Lucifer, son of the morning!"

The "star of the morning" is the planet Venus, also known in antiquity as "Ishtar." Ishtar was a popular Babylonian goddess also known as "Astarte."[42] King David's son Solomon "followed Astarte the goddess of the Sidonians..." (1 Kings 11:5) but "... YHWH was angry with Solomon, because his heart had turned away from YHWH, the Elohim of Israel..." (1 Kings 11:9).

Hebrew Scripture refers to this goddess as "Asherah" forty times, and curiously, KJV hides her in the word "groves" in every instance.[43]

The esoteric message hiding in these strange farewell words quoting two of Isaiah's prophecies are revealed in the "heretical" Gospel of Thomas, Saying 18 (2): "Jesus said, 'Have you

---

[41] Ibid.

[42] 1 Kings 11:5; 11:33; 2 Kings 23:13; Sometimes rendered *Asherah* (Strong's Hebrew 842) and *Ashtoreth*, (Strong's Hebrew 6253); *ashtoreth* is also translated "young" (Strong's Hebrew 6251). Similar words: *ashath*, "to think" (NAS, Strong's Hebrew 6245b); *ashar*, "rich" (NAS, Strong's Hebrew 6238); *ashar*, "to go straight, go on, advance" (NAS, Strong's Hebrew 833); *asher*, "who, which, that" (NAS, Strong's Hebrew 834); *esher*, "happiness, blessedness" (NAS, Strong's Hebrew 835); *ashur* or *ashurim*, "perhaps boxwood (a kind of wood) (NAS, Strong's Hebrew 839).

[43] Strong's Hebrew 842 used 40 times from Ex 34:13 to Mic 5:14.

discovered the beginning, then, so that you are seeking the end? *For where the beginning is the end will be.*'"[44]

"The beginning" of Genesis is BRSTBRLHM. In addition to "In the beginning gods…" and the heretical Trinity, "Son of Man, Father Light, El the Mother," BRSTBRLHM can also be rendered *BaR iShTa aB oR eLoHiM*. These Hebrew words are translated, "Son of Morning Star, Father Light, El the Mother."[45]

"The end" of Revelation quotes "the beginning" of Hebrew Scripture. It identifies Jesus as a "descendant of David, *heilil ben sahar*," translated, "the bright morning star," which is Ishtar, also known as, Venus. Her symbol was an eight-pointed star, the same symbol Octavian (Latin for "eight") used on the coins honoring "Augustus Caesar" and the "Divine Julius" (see image, p. 350.

Jesus' adversaries believed they had successfully separated "Jesus of Nazareth" from the "heretical" Nassaraeans. Once that was accomplished they turned Jesus the Nazarene's ancestors – the First Mother and Father, *iShta* and *Ansar* – into *Satan*.[46] The ancestor He claimed in His farewell address, *Heilel ben Shahar* the "Light-Bringer," became *Lucifer*, from the Latin *Luc ferre*.

Today, according to many Orthodox Christians, *Satan* and *Lucifer* – the most terrifying of all boogeymen – are embodied in the dreaded and yet to come "Antichrist." Unfortunately, superstition is easy to sell to men and women who fear anything they can't explain. And it has been used successfully for millennia to manipulate the masses.

Superstition – the irrational fear instilled into believers by the words, "Lucifer," "Satan," and "Antichrist" – explains how, for nearly two thousand years, Jesus' adversaries succeeded in

---

[44] Meyer, 2008, 142. Emphasis added.

[45] And or "bread."

[46] iShTa + aN: *SaTaN*. NASB usage (Strong's Hebrew 7853), Satan: accuse (1), accusers (2), act as my accusers (1), adversaries (1), oppose (1). NASB usage (Strong's Hebrew 7854), Satan: accuser (1), adversary (8), Satan (18).

hiding the esoteric version of Jesus carried through time in the Hebrew and Christian Bibles.

Jesus explains it in his final enigmatic message: *BaR iSh*, "The Son of Man," believed his ancestors were the "First Parents," introduced at Gen 1:1: *Ishtar* and *Ab Or*, known to the Babylonians as *Ansar*. According to their descendants, preserved in Babylonian and Hebrew texts, the "First Parents" came to Earth from the Morning Star, Venus.

One question remains to be answered: Who was Jesus' chief adversary, "The Betrayer" who set the course for the Orthodox Victors and their version of The Nazarean's story?

Luke suggests an "adversary" in a prayer spoken by Zechariah, John the Baptist's father. However, before the prayer commences, Luke inserted two yellow flags: "Zechariah was filled with the *Holy Spirit* and spoke this *prophecy*." And then John's father begins to pray:

> Blessed be the Lord God [Greek, *Kurios Theos*] of Israel ... He has raised up a mighty savior for us in the house of his servant David, as he spoke through the mouth of his *holy prophets* from of old, that we would be *saved from our enemies and from the hand of all who hate us*[47] ... to grant us that we, *being rescued from the hands of our enemies*,[48] might serve him without fear, in holiness and righteousness before him all our days ... By the tender mercy of our God, the dawn from on high will break upon us [hypotext is Mal 4:2], to give light to those who sit in darkness and in the shadow of death [hypotext is Isa 9:2], to guide our feet into *The Way* of Peace" (Lk 1:68-79).[49]

Luke points to the House of David and annotations point to hypotexts in Hebrew Scripture. The repeated statements, "saved from our enemies/rescued from the hand of all who hate us," are quoted from Ps 18:1 and 2 Sam 22:1. But, when Luke incorporates these verses into Zechariah's prayer, he omits the name of the enemy, pointing instead to Hebrew Scripture where the name can be found:

---

[47] Philo's rule no. 3: repetition of statement previously made.
[48] Philo's rule no. 3: repetition of statement previously made.
[49] Pertinent sections excerpted from NRSV; emphasis added.

2 Sam 22:1: "David spoke to YHWH the words of this song on the day when YHWH delivered him from the hand of all his enemies, and from the hand of Saul."

Once Hebrew Scripture relinquishes his name, the next step is to match the name with a character in the Christian Bible. That match may be found in The Acts of the Apostles:

Acts 13:9: "Saul, who is also called Paul."

Why would Luke identify the Apostle Paul as the leading enemy of Jesus? Paul and Jesus never crossed paths. Or did they? Philo's Philology offers a surprising answer as we continue following Philo through ancient texts.

CHAPTER SIX

Following Philo to a Crossing in Paphos
Paul Damns the Son of the Double-crossing Jesus

Did Paul and Jesus cross paths and become enemies? The answer can be found in Luke's story of Saul's encounter with a man called "Bar-Iesous." Luke introduces "John, whose other name was Mark" (Acts 12:25), and then a few verses later at Acts 13:4 he invokes a Holy Spirit,[1] indicating enigmatic language will follow:

> When they arrived at Salamis, they proclaimed the word of *God* in the synagogues of the Jews. And they had John also to assist them. When they had gone through the whole island as far as Paphos, they met a certain *magician*, a Jewish false prophet, named Bar-Jesus. He was with the proconsul, Sergius Paulus, an *intelligent* man, who summoned Barnabas and Saul and wanted to hear the word of *God*. But the *magician Elymas* (for that is the translation of his name) opposed them and tried to turn the proconsul away from the faith. *But Saul, also known as Paul,* filled with the Holy Spirit, looked intently at him and said, "You son of the *devil*, you enemy of all righteousness, full of all deceit and villainy, will you not stop making crooked the straight paths of the Lord? And now listen—the hand of the Lord is against you, and you will be blind for a while, unable to see the sun." Immediately mist and darkness came over *him*, and *he* went about groping for someone to lead him by the hand (Acts 13:5-11).[2]

It seems curious that Saul didn't receive his name change on the road to Damascus when Jesus first came to him in a vision. Luke recites three versions of that one encounter,[3] and in all

---

[1] Philo's rule no. 20: striking statement.
[2] Emphasis added.
[3] Acts 9:3-19; Acts 22:6-16; Acts 26:12-18.

three Saul is temporarily blinded by the light. But it is not at that time – when his sight is restored and he is baptized – that he becomes Paul. "Saulus" is not identified as "Paulus" until this contentious encounter with a "Bar-Jesus" and a proconsul also named "Paulus."

"Bar-Jesus" means "son of Jesus." And one of the earliest translations of the Four Gospels yet to be discovered, the *Syriac Sinaitic*,[4] places a "Jesus Barabbas"[5] in Matthew's version of the Crucifixion:[6] "So after they had gathered, Pilate said to them, 'Whom do you want me to release for you, Jesus Barabbas or Jesus who is called the Messiah?'" (Mt 27:16-17). Mark, Luke, and John agree that "Barabbas" was a key character in the Crucifixion, but notably, the name "Jesus" was either omitted or expunged from all three.

After Paul, Barnabas, and John Mark cross paths and exchange words with Bar-Jesus at Paphos, something notable happens: "Then Paul and his companions set sail from Paphos and came to Perga in Pamphylia. John, however, left them and returned to Jerusalem" (Acts 13:13).

Luke doesn't explain why John Mark returns to Jerusalem nor does he indicate that Paul and Jesus meet at Paphos. But he does state clearly that Paul meets a man called "Bar- Jesus," and his reaction and words are quite revealing – when the words are carefully examined.

The first word to be dissected is "diabolos." In most Bibles this word is translated, "devil." However, "diabolos" comes from the Greek word *diaballo*, defined as "a slanderer; a false accuser,"[7] or these intriguing options: "slanderous, backbiting."[8] Today, we might say, "double crossing."

Paul calls Bar Jesus, "son of my backbiting enemy." The father of a Bar-Jesus would have to be a Jesus, and Paul curses

---

[4] Mk 15:6; Lk 23:18; Jn 18:40.
[5] Bar Abbas means, "Son of Father."
[6] *Syriac Sinaitic*, late 4th century translation.
[7] Perseus: Middle Liddell.
[8] Perseus: LSJ.

him as his betrayer. Philo would advise us to take note of perceived double-crosses in historians' accounts of the time that can be tied to someone named Paulus or Saulus. Josephus tells of one in *Antiquities*, and we will return to investigate him a bit later.

The word translated as "magician" or "sorcerer" (Acts 13:6) is *magos*: "a Magus, Magian, one of a Median tribe ... one of the wise men in Persia who interpreted dreams..."[9] Notably, Moses' father-in-law was Jethro, the High Priest of the Median Tribe.[10]

Sergius Paulus, a *"synetos* man,"* requires careful examination because he is introduced at the very moment "Saulus" becomes "Paulus."

The name "Sergius" comes from the Latin word *servare* meaning "to make safe, save, keep unharmed, preserve, guard, keep, protect, deliver, rescue."[11]

Synetos, translated "intelligent" in most sources, shares its root with "synonymous" and other syn-prefixed words that suggest "sameness."

The enigmas – the proximity of the two names when Paulus is introduced and Sergius is identified as "a synetos man who was saved from harm" – suggest that Saul's name may have been changed to Sergius Paulus and the "Paulus men" in the scene may be but one man. Therefore, we are looking for a historical or mythological "Sergius" and/or "Paulus" who was rescued from some harm, perhaps an alleged assassination.

Following the thread that is "Magoi of the Median tribe" leads to Stephen's bizarre speech that first introduces Saul and ties him to the stoning of Stephen. This lengthy narrative accounts for all of Chapter Seven in *Acts* and contains a number

---

[9] Perseus: Middle Liddell.
[10] Mid-5th century BCE, Herodotus, *Histories* 7.19, 7.37, 1.107, 1.108, 1.120, 1.128 identifies the *magi* as interpreters of omens and dreams.
[11] Crane, Gregory R., ed. (2006); Perseus: Latin word study tool.

of elements that can be matched with the story of Moses' flight to the Medians where he married the High Priest's daughter.[12]

Paul's actions during the encounter at Paphos also provide clues. He calls upon the hand of the Lord to blind Bar-Jesus; mist and darkness come over *him* and *he* needs someone to lead *him* by the hand. Philo's Rule 8: "him" and "he" refer to whom, Bar-Jesus or Paul? We find the answer at Acts 9:8 where, "Saul got up from the ground, and though his eyes were open, he could see nothing; so they *led him by the hand* and brought him into Damascus."

Consequently, according to Luke's first version of Saul's vision of Jesus, it is Paul who was blinded and led by the hand.

This dispute at Paphos that culminates in someone's blindness is between Bar-Jesus – a man of the same Median priesthood as Moses' father-in-law and wife – and Saulus, a man who participated in the stoning of Stephen.

It is also noteworthy that Luke recounts three *contradictory* versions of Saul's vision of Jesus on the road to Damascus. In the first (Acts 9:1-7), Luke uses the same word, *cheiragōgous* – translated, "led him by the hand" – when describing Saul's encounter with Bar-Jesus. Luke's sentence structure and choice of pronouns leaves it unclear which man is blinded after Saul hurled vitriolic and damning words at Bar-Jesus and his father Jesus.

But Luke has already identified the man who is blinded and "led by the hand" at the time of his claimed conversion. It is Saulus, the man who damns Bar-Jesus to blindness, but whom Luke elsewhere identifies as the one who becomes blind.

Curiously, Paul seems unaware of any of Acts' three contradictory versions of his conversion when he describes the experience in his second letter to the Corinthians.[13] The dramatic blindness scene, being led by the hand, and Ananias' miracu-

---

[12] Acts 7:27-29; Ex 2:15-21.
[13] 2 Cor 12:1-10.

lous healing and significant baptism are not mentioned – qualifying as "noteworthy omissions."

More clues emerge in Acts 13:7-9: "[Bar-Jesus] was with the proconsul, Sergius Paulus... But the magician Elymas (for that is the translation of his name) opposed them ... But Saulus, also known as Paulus..."

Another red-flag word in this section of Acts is *Elymas*. The notation in the text, "for that is the translation of his name," has resulted in a longstanding debate over the meaning of *Elymas*. Some sources point to the Arabic word *elymon*, which means "wise."[14] However, this would mean that "Elymas" refers to the word *magos* rather than to "his name."

A more plausible answer is that "Elym-As" is to be tied to the word *elam* (Strong's No. 5867), from *alam* (Strong's No. 5956) defined as, "A primitive root; to veil from sight, i.e. conceal (literally or figuratively)."[15] The author of The Gospel of Philip supports this definition of the name "Iesous": "'Iesous' is a *hidden* name... 'Iesous' is not particular to any language; rather he is always called by the name 'Iesous.'"[16] Furthermore, *alam* is one of the words listed in Gen 1:11 that will "adorn" the descendants of Ansar and Kisar of Ishtar.

But the message carried in Acts 13:8 – the most important information signaled by a second striking statement[17] – is hidden in the phrase that follows Elymas, "... (for that is the *translation* of his name) opposed them and tried to turn the proconsul away from the faith. But Saulus, also known as Paulus..."

The key word in this phrase is "translation," from the Greek, *methermēneuetai*, a combination of *meta* and *herméneuó*. The definition of *meta* includes, "and then, next afterwards, thereafter."[18] Also, "with, among, after."[19]

---

[14] Thayer's Greek Lexicon, 2002; Strong's No. 1681.
[15] NAS (Strong's Hebrew 5956).
[16] Meyer, 2008, 164.
[17] "filled with the Holy Spirit"
[18] Middle Liddell.
[19] NAS (Strong's Greek 3326).

The second half of the word, *herméneuó*, is defined as, "to interpret, put into words, give utterance to; to explain."[20] Therefore Luke's enigma says, "Thus the name (reported) *next afterward*, 'Saulus changed to Paulus,' can be *explained* (by looking at the name in the) *preceding* sentence."

Luke's esoteric message seems to say that Saul was afterward known as the proconsul Sergius Paulus. And this thread is picked up by Pliny the Elder, who recites an anecdote about a man named *Sergius* who strikes down his enemies with an iron hand. An "iron hand" brings to mind Zechariah's concluding words in Lk 1; "the hand of the enemy" that was attached to Saulus.

Pliny writes: "In his second campaign Sergius lost his right hand … He had a right hand made of iron for him and, going into battle with this bound to his arm … saved Placentia and captured twelve enemy camps in Gaul…"[21]

This is an example of a common occurrence when solving puzzles; the sources often hold more clues than is immediately apparent. For instance, Placentia was a city in the country of Aemilia, the location of the Via Aemilia, a road built by, and named for, the Roman consul Marcus Aemilius Lepidus c. 187 BCE. This Marcus Lepidus was the ancestor of Marcus Aemilius Lepidus, the third leg of the Second Triumvirate.[22]

Marcus Aemilius Lepidus the triumvir had a brother, Lucius Aemilius Lepidus *Paulus*, one of several Paulus men who married important Roman women, all of whom gave birth to sons and daughters who would also grow up to be powerful Romans.

First century historian Valerius Maximus writes an amusing and revealing anecdote about Lucius Aemilius Lepidus Paulus:

---

[20] Middle Liddell.

[21] John F. Healy (1991, 2004), *Natural History by Pliny the Elder*, 7.104-5.

[22] *Second Triumvirate* is the name historians give to the official political alliance of Octavian (later known as Augustus Caesar), Marcus Aemilius Lepidus, and Marc Antony. The Second Triumvirate was formed on 26 November 43 BCE with the enactment of the *Les Titia*, which marked the end of the Roman Republic. The Triumvirate existed for two five-year terms, covering the period 43 - 33 BCE.

"When the senate decreed that the temples of Isis and Serapis be demolished and none of the workmen dared touch them, Consul L. Aemilius Paulus took off his official gown, seized an axe, and dashed it against the doors of that temple."[23] Once, again, *iron* in the hand of a *Paulus* is turned against a competing religion.

A similar word, Elymais, is another name for the city of Elam. Josephus tells a story about the temple of Diana in Elymais that was assaulted and besieged by a foreign king. The temple housed many items of value, including armaments left by Alexander the Great. Diana's worshippers fought back, the villainous king fled to Babylon, and the goddess' temple was saved from destruction.[24]

Now look at Luke's similar story in Acts that shares a number of the same elements: Paul arrives in Ephesus on his way to Jerusalem and then Rome. Demetrius, a silversmith, incites a crowd into a frenzy when he warns the people of Ephesus of Paul's mission: "... the temple of the great goddess Diana will be scorned, and she will be deprived of her majesty..." But Paul has been warned it is too dangerous for him to enter the crowded theater, and he stays away. A Jew, "Alexander," attempts to defend Paul's presence in Ephesus, but the crowd drowns him out, chanting "for about two hours,[25] 'Great is Artemis of the Ephesians!'" Paul slips away and quietly leaves for Macedonia. The goddess' temple remains unscathed.[26]

Comparing the two stories, we can pull out matching strands: (1) A foreigner arrives and is perceived to be a threat to the temple of Diana (also known as "Artemis"); (2) the name "Alexander"; (3) the people fight back and prevail; (4) the foreigner slips away and the Temple is saved. A fifth strand might

---

[23] Valerius Maximus, *Famous Words and Deeds,* I, 3.3 (quoting Julius Paris), Loeb Edition Translation.
[24] Josephus, 1999, *Antiquities* 12.9.1 (354-5), 411.
[25] Philo's rule no. 20: striking statement.
[26] Acts 19:21-41.

be an ancient association that identified Rome as the "New Babylon."

Now that the "Saulus known as Paulus" thread has been tentatively tied to Sergius Paulus (whose first name was Lucius), we can begin the search for a historical "Bar-Jesus." And Josephus writes of two men whose sons were called "Jesus." He identifies them in the story of the events that led up to the destruction of the Temple in 70, and he juxtaposes them[27] with a crucial comment about two other men:

> And now *Jesus, the son of Gamaliel, became the successor of Jesus, the son of Damneus*, in the high priesthood... But *Ananias* was too hard for the rest, by his riches, which enabled him to gain those that were most ready to receive. *Costobarus also, and Saulus*, did themselves get together a multitude of wicked wretches ... because they were *of the royal family*; and so they obtained favor among them, because of their *kindred to Agrippa*.[28]

Not only does Josephus identify one Jesus as the "son of Gamaliel" and the other Jesus as the "son of Damneus," he places them adjacent to a man identified as "Saulus," just as Luke does in Acts.[29] Therefore, Luke's thread, "Saulus, the *damned* Bar-Jesus, and his 'double-crossing' father," can be tied to Josephus' thread, "Saulus, Jesus bar Gamaliel, and Jesus bar Damneus."

The relationship between Costobarus and Saulus is reported in Josephus' *Wars*, written about twenty years earlier than *Antiquities*: "Costobarus, therefore, and Saulus, who were brethren."[30]

According to Josephus, Jesus the son of Gamaliel succeeds another Jesus who is the Son of Damneus (Latin from *damno*, "to condemn"). This says – enigmatically – "Jesus, son of one who was damned."

Josephus then tosses the strand to his collaborator Luke who locates the damning at Paphos when "Saulus also known as

---

[27] Philo's rule no. 17: the position of the verses of a passage.
[28] Josephus, 1999, *Antiquities* 20.9.4 (213-214), 657. Emphasis added.
[29] Philo's rule no. 17: position of phrases and verses.
[30] Josephus, 1999, *Wars* 2.20.1 (556), 768.

Paulus" curses the double-crossing Jesus and damns his son Bar-Jesus to blindness.

Luke then hands the strand back to Josephus, who identifies the man who did the damning in the subsequent paragraph, "Costobarus, also, and Saulus..."

It is Luke's turn again, and he ties this thread to the *axe-man* thread at Acts 28:26-27. Luke quotes words from Isa 6:9-12 to conclude *Acts* as Paul calls after the departing "local chief of the Jews." In Hebrew, the word for "chief" is *nasi.* Notably, Luke omits the words that conclude Isaiah Chapter Six.[31] They are, "Even if a tenth part remain in it, it will be burned again, like a terebinth or an oak whose stump remains standing when it is felled [by an axe]. The Holy Seed is its stump" (Isa 6:13).[32]

Bruce M. Metzger and Roland E. Murphy, Editors of the *New Oxford Annotated Bible,* add an intriguing annotation to Isa 6:13: "The last part of the verse is obscure and textually corrupt and perhaps should be restored to read, '...like the terebinth of the goddess and the oak of Asherah, cast out with the pillar of the high places,' that is, like the destroyed furnishings of a pagan high place."[33]

The "axe" and "oak" thread leads to the poet Ovid, another of Luke's favorite sources for solving riddles. Ovid writes an intriguing story of a Pagan goddess, a sacred oak tree, and another axe-wielding man:

> Erysichthon ... violated the grove of [goddess] Ceres with an axe ... Within them stood a great oak ... [Erysichthon] would not hold back the blade ... commanding his servants to fell the sacred oak. When he saw them hesitating at the order, the wretched man snatched the axe from one of them ... And, when his impious hand made a gash in the trunk, blood poured out of its damaged bark, like the crimson tide from its severed neck, when the mighty bull falls, in sacrifice, before the altar.[34]

---

[31] Philo's rule no. 19: noteworthy omissions.

[32] Emphasis added.

[33] *The New Oxford Annotated Bible with Apocrypha* (1991, 1994), 875 OT.

[34] Ovid, *Metamorphoses, Book 6.* Emphasis added.

The words Ovid chose are almost verbatim what his contemporary Valerius Maximus writes of Lucius Aemilius Paulus: "When the senate decreed that the temples of Isis and Serapis be demolished and none of the workmen dared touch them, Consul L. Aemilius Paulus took off his official gown, seized an axe, and dashed it against the doors of that temple."

Axes and violent hands seem to be a recurring theme in stories of the Paulus family. Perhaps "The Acts" [Greek, *agein*] of the Apostles was Luke's enigmatic title for the secret history of "The Axe" [Greek, *axine*] of the Apostle Paulus.[35]

Philo's Philology, applied to the texts, indicates that Paul and Jesus did cross paths. What happened between them that turned Paul against Jesus and generated the immense hatred that spewed forth at Paphos? Perhaps the double-cross is the precipitating event that Josephus associates with the destruction of the Second Temple. It all seems to begin festering when:

> King Agrippa [II] took the high priesthood from [Ananus] after he had ruled only three months, and made *Jesus, the son of Damneus*, high priest. When Albinus arrived at Jerusalem, he destroyed many of the Sicarii. But the high priest Ananias increased in glory daily, and the people favored him and held him in high esteem. He was a great hoarder of money and *cultivated the friendship of Albinus and of the high priest by giving them gifts…*[36]

A thread in *Acts* shares key elements:

> Some days later when Felix came with his wife Drusilla, who was Jewish,[37] he sent for Paul and heard him speak concerning faith in Christ Jesus. And as he discussed justice, self-control, and the coming judgment, Felix became frightened and said, "Go away for the present; when I have an opportunity, I will send for you." At the same time he hoped that money would be given him

---

[35] Gott, *Plutarch's Parable: Lux Gospel and the Axe of the Apostle* (Charleston: Booksurge, 2005), 110.

[36] Josephus, 1999, *Antiquities* 20.9.1-2 (203-205), 656-7. Condensed and paraphrased for clarity; emphasis added.

[37] Philo's No. 2 "superfluous" information.

by Paul, and for that reason he used to send for him very often and converse with him" (Acts 24:24-26).[38]

Two years later Felix, allegedly a freedman, is relieved of his duties and replaced by Festus, "...and since he wanted to grant the Jews a favor, Felix left Paul in prison." The story continues:

> After several days had passed, King Agrippa and Bernice arrived at Caesarea to welcome Festus. Since they were staying there several days, Festus laid Paul's case before the king, saying, "There is a man here who was left in prison by Felix" (Acts 25:14).

Agrippa and his sister Bernice listen to the charges against Paul; Agrippa gives him permission to argue his own case. After Paul's lengthy appeal, which includes the third version of his "Road to Damascus Conversion," King Agrippa concludes, "This man could have been set free if he had not appealed to the emperor" (Acts 26:32).

An important side-note and clue to solving this enigma is that Felix's wife Drusilla is King Agrippa and Bernice's younger sister. The likelihood that a former slave could be married to a Jewish Hasmonean princess is quite remote. (This unlikely "freedman" thread will become important later.)

The evidence may be intriguing, but more is required before a final conclusion can be reached. Additionally, we now have more questions: Who is Ananus? Who are the historical men identified as "Jesus" and "Bar-Jesus," Paul's enemies? Who is "Jesus the son of Gamaliel"? Does "Jesus the son of Damneus" refer to the son of Bar-Jesus whom Paul damns to blindness? What is the betrayal for which Paul blames Bar Jesus' father Jesus? Who is Jesus' father Gamaliel; could he have been another "Jesus"? These are important threads and they must be carefully examined. So, let's have a quick look.

Most of what is known of Gamaliel comes from the Talmud and the Mishnah which report that Gamaliel ben Simeon was the first Nasi of Jerusalem. From c. 50 until c. 70 CE, the Nasi was his son Simeon ben Gamaliel; Simeon's son was Nasi Ga-

---

[38] Emphasis added.

maliel II.[39] "Jesus" is not a part of any of their names – or is it? According to Josephus, Gamaliel *did* have a son whose name was Jesus. Why is this information omitted from the Talmud and other sources?

Philo's Philology can answer these and other questions. However, the evidence cannot be found in one or two places or within the works of one or two historians, philosophers, poets, or gospel writers. As the questions become more complex, a series of small steps revealing tiny strands of larger threads must be taken. Careful analysis of multiple sources, tied together, will eventually lead to the place where the lives of Gamaliel, his father, and his son intersect with the life of Jesus the Nazarean.

---

[39] Michael L. Rodkinson, *The History of the Talmud*, 1.2 (New York: New Talmud Publishing Company, 1903), 8.

CHAPTER SEVEN

Following Philo to Bethlehem's Star
Census of Quirinius *and* when Herod was King

Luke opens Chapters One and Two with statements that have perplexed and confounded biblical scholars for nearly two thousand years: "In the days of King Herod of Judea..." (Lk 1:5). This statement is almost immediately contradicted when Luke writes, "...a decree went out from Emperor Augustus that all the world should be registered. This was the first census and was taken while Quirinius was governor of Syria" (Lk 2:1-2).

The problem with these two statements is that Herod the Great died before 4 BCE and the first census is dated c. 6 CE when Quirinius was governor of Syria, a ten year difference at least. It is a puzzle frequently noted by scholars and added as footnotes to biblical texts.[1]

Josephus dates the census: "Quirinius had disposed of Archelaus' money, and when the census was concluded, which was made in the thirty-seventh year of Caesar's victory over Antony at Actium."[2]

The Battle of Actium was fought c. 31 BCE; therefore, Josephus dates the census and Jesus' birth to c. 6 CE. Herod's reign ended with his death before 4 BCE. The two dates appear to be mutually exclusive, a problem that has defied solution.

Several theories have been presented over the centuries. One that still enjoys some support was offered in 1938 by Herwaert F.M. Heichelheim, who argues that the original meaning of the text was, "This census was the first before that under the

---

[1] *The Complete Gospels, Annotated Scholars Version*, First Harper Collins Paperback Edition, 1994; footnote 2:2, 121; footnote 2:1, 120; footnote 2:3-4, 121.
[2] Josephus, 1999, *Antiquities* 18.2.1 (26), 588.

prefectureship of Quirinius in Syria."[3] In other words, more than one census was conducted while Quirinius was governor of Syria – although no census that required the family to return to their ancestral city can be supported by any historical source or other evidence. And Luke clearly notes this is the *first* census *while* Quirinius was governor of Syria.

Another popular theory is based on the Star of Bethlehem. Colin J. Humphreys concludes that the most likely explanation for the Star of Bethlehem was a comet dated by Chinese sources to 5 BCE between March 9 and April 6 and lasting over 70 days. Humphreys attempts to solve the problem of the Census of Quirinius by *assuming* the census is not for taxation but for pledging allegiance to Caesar, which Josephus (*Antiquities* 17.2.4) dates to a year before the death of King Herod. Humphreys concludes that Jesus was born between March 9 and May 4, 5 BCE.[4] This assumption, of course, ignores the biblical claim that all citizens were required to return to the town of their ancestry.

Jack Kilmon, "History and the New Testament," attributes The Star of Bethlehem to the conjunction of Jupiter and Saturn in Pisces and uses that astrological event to calculate the date of Jesus' birth to be October 3, 7 BCE.[5]

However, most modern scholars take the position that there was but one census and the author of Luke's gospel deviated from history when he connected it with the birth of Jesus.[6]

Philo's method for solving enigmas offers yet another possibility when old assumptions about who Jesus was are set aside and new questions with new implications are asked. However,

---

[3] F.M. Heichelheim, "Roman Syria," in *An Economic Survey of Ancient Rome*, ed. T. Frank (Baltimore: John's Hopkins University Press, 1938), 161.

[4] Colin J. Humphreys, "The Star of Bethlehem…" *Quarterly Journal of the Royal Astronomical Society* 32 (1991), 389-407.

[5] Jack Kilmon (1997), "History and the New Testament," *The Scriptorium*, 1997) n.p.

[6] James Douglas Grant Dunn, *Jesus Remembered* (Grand Rapids: Eerdmans, 2003), 344. Geza Vermes, *The Nativity* (New York: Penguin 2006), 96. John P. Meier, *A Marginal Jew: Rethinking the Historical Jesus* (New York: Doubleday, 1991), Vol. 1, 213.

this requires stepping outside the conventional biblical scholars' box.

Early in his gospel, Luke refers to John the Baptist's mother
Elizabeth as "a relative" (Greek, *suggenes*) of the Virgin Mary.[7]
The first step for the philologist is to seek information about
historical families who had sons born in 6 CE and whose mothers were related to one another.

Four men were born concurrent with the Census of 6 CE,
and it will take most of the rest of this book to unravel the
threads that bind these men together. Moreover, the evidence
suggests that some threads may have been intentionally cut to
protect the guilty.

Julia the Younger and husband Lucius Aemilius Lepidus
Paulus had a son born c. 6 CE. Unfortunately, the genealogy for
this family becomes murky prior to 6, and a number of opinions about Julia's son's name have filtered down through time.

We have gone to the original sources, recognizing that they,
too, may have been transmitted erroneously. Some of the confusion may have come about because Tacitus and Suetonius
often refer to their subjects by one or two of their three or four
names.

For example, when Suetonius writes of *Aemilius Lepidus*,[8] he
could be referring to either *Marcus Aemilius Lepidus* or *Lucius
Aemilius Lepidus Paulus*. It is also possible that subsequent
translators and historians misinterpreted the original texts.
Julia and Lucius Paulus' son is known by more than one name,
including Lucius, Marcus, and Paulus – and perhaps others.

Julia's sister, Agrippina the Elder and husband Germanicus
Julius Caesar, had two sons born c. 6-7 CE: Nero Julius Caesar
Germanicus and Drusus Julius Caesar. They had other names,
as well, which we'll examine later.

The first cousins born in 6 CE, Nero Julius Caesar Germanicus and cousin Lucius Marcus Paulus, were both named after

---

[7] Luke 1:36.
[8] Suetonius, *Life of Caligula* (Loeb, 1914), (Thayer Online 24.3).

their fathers. Germanicus the Elder was born c. 13-15 BCE. He was named after his father, Nero Claudius Drusus Germanicus, born c. 38 BCE, whose elder brother was Emperor Tiberius. Nero Germanicus and Tiberius' mother was the Empress Livia Drusilla, and their step-father was Emperor Augustus Caesar.

It can be said, therefore, that Germanicus and Paulus (the fathers) were born when Herod was King, and Germanicus and Paulus (the sons) were born at the time of the Census of Quirinius.

And so, we have uncovered yet another reasonable option for the apparent contradiction regarding the year of Jesus' birth. Perhaps Jesus the Elder was born when Herod was King, and Bar-Jesus was born in 6 CE, at the time of the Census of Quirinius – and both were known as "Jesus the Nazarene." This solution, of course, requires further investigation.

As demonstrated in Chapter Four, most people have accepted without questioning that Jesus is called "The Nazarene" because he came from Nazareth. However, a closer look at Mark's and Luke's gospels – using Philo's method – found that they disagree with the *common conclusion*, pointing instead to a sect and/or the ancient nazirites as the source for the term Nazarene. And, The Gospel of Philip offers support.

Likewise, people have accepted without questioning that the name "Jesus," Greek *Iesous*, is derived from the Hebrew name, *Yehoshua*, from *YHWH* and *yasha*, defined as "to deliver."[9] The shortened form is *Yeshua* and is found over 700 times in Hebrew Scripture.

However, The Gospel of Philip disputes the claim that Yehoshua/Yeshua is the etymology of the name "Iesous": "Iesous is a hidden name ... Iesous is not particular to any language; rather he is always called by the name Iesous."[10]

What did the author of Philip's gospel know that led him to explain to his readers that the name "Iesous" is not translated

---

[9] NAS (Strong's Hebrew 3091).
[10] Meyer, 2008, 164.

from, and is not to be translated *into*, another language? Why would he term it "hidden" or "mysterious" if it was derived from a *common* Jewish name?

Plutarch offers a possible answer when he sets out to explain how the naming of the god Serapis came about. In the fourth century BCE, Ptolemy I of Egypt, surnamed "The Savior," *created* a new god – Serapis – by merging characteristics and names of competing gods, Osiris and Apis. The name evolved over time: Osir-Apis; Sirapis, Serapis. Serapis was a composite of several deities popular throughout Egypt and the Roman Empire.

Plutarch explains how a statue of Serapis found its way to Alexandria. In a dream state, Ptolemy Soter saw an immense statue of Serapis and was instructed by some "higher power" to find it and move it to Alexandria.[11] However, he had no idea where the statue was located. When he told his friends about the vision and described what he had seen, one of them recalled seeing just such a statue in Sinope. But it was a statue of the god Pluto. Nevertheless, Ptolemy was convinced it was the statue he had seen in his dream and sent two men to steal it away to Alexandria.

Plutarch notes: "It certainly did not bear this name when it came from Sinope, but, after it had been conveyed to Alexandria, *it took to itself the name* which Pluto bears among the Egyptians, that of Serapis."[12]

Shortly thereafter Plutarch adds, "It is better to identify Osiris with Dionysus and Serapis with Osiris, who received this appellation at the time when he changed his nature. For this reason Serapis is a god of all peoples in common, even as Osiris is; and this they who have participated in the Holy Rites well know."[13]

The "Holy Rites" which Plutarch references were the annual pageants held in Egypt which honored Osiris-Serapis and Isis

[11] Philo's rule no. 20: striking statement.
[12] Emphasis added.
[13] Plutarch, *Moralia*: "Isis and Osiris," 1st-2nd Century.

and told their story of love, intrigue, murder, resurrection, and the birth of a son. It consisted of multiple phases over several days, and according to archaeologist Richard H. Wilkinson, "...surviving inscriptional evidence represents ritual and ceremonial activities [were] *performed by the king.*"[14]

According to Julius Firmicus Maternus (fourth century), the play was re-enacted each year by worshippers who "beat their breasts and gashed their shoulders. When they pretend that the mutilated remains of the god have been found and rejoined ... they turn from mourning to rejoicing."[15]

The Serapis pageant was a theatrical performance with a script and probably rehearsals; the supporting roles were played by actors and *the role of Serapis/Osiris was played by the king.* The citizens of the city actively participated in the pageantry. *And the role of Serapis/Osiris was played by the king.*[16]

In some locations the annual celebration also involved the construction of Osiris Beds formed in the shape of Osiris, filled with soil and sown with seed. The germinating seed symbolized Osiris rising from the dead. Archaeologist Howard Carter found an example of this particular prop in the tomb of Tutankhamen.[17]

Some of what is known of the Passion of Osiris was discovered on a stela dated to the Middle Kingdom (c. 2055-1650 BCE). The "Stela of Ikhernofret" confirms the festival's great antiquity.[18] Over time the myth and festival evolved as Osiris became the king of the dead while Horus, his son and heir, became king of the living. In this way the Egyptian Kings reas-

---

[14] Richard H. Wilkinson, *Symbol and Magic in Egyptian Art* (New York: Thames & Hudson, 1994), 149.

[15] Julius Firmicus Maternus, *On The Error of Profane Religions* (*De errore profanarum religionum*, c. 346; Clarence A. Forbes, translation, *The Error of the Pagan Religions* (New York: Paulist Press, 1970), 45.

[16] Repetition is intentional because this is extremely important.

[17] Howard Carter Archives (Burton) "Osiris Bed," Burton photograph, p2024, *The Griffith Institute.*

[18] Mirjam Nebet, *The Egyptian World: The Passion Plays of Osiris.*

sured the masses of the perpetuation of Egypt on two planes –
the dead and the living.

Therefore, many centuries *before* Jesus was crucified, entombed, then resurrected on the third day, the Egyptians were
performing annual pageants to celebrate and honor their own
dying-and-resurrected god Osiris, his son Horus, and his wife
Isis. In Plutarch's version of their tale, Isis and Osiris' mother
took healing herbs and spices to his tomb to anoint and thus
resurrect the god.[19]

Of course Osiris-Serapis never died because he was merely
an invented god – a fictional mythological character. However,
the King who performed the role of Osiris did eventually die,
replaced by his son – the King of the subsequent generation.

Furthermore, Serapis isn't the only such merging of competing gods that preceded Jesus. The gods Hermes and Anubis
were merged to become Hermanubis, an account preserved in
a dedicatory inscription from Delos dated to the second century BCE.[20] And in a story that refers to this deity, Josephus ties a
thread to Plutarch's story of Serapis when he duplicates a sequence of words. Plutarch writes: "...it took to itself the
name...Serapis," and Josephus writes: "...I took to myself the
name of Anubis."[21]

At the time Josephus was writing *Antiquities* c. 80-90 CE,
"Anubis" had been "Hermanubis" for more than two centuries.
This error might be overlooked except for its *peculiar position* in
Antiquities. The story of Anubis – who should have been Her-
manubis – is especially noteworthy because it is found at *An-*

---

[19] Plutarch, *Moralia*: "sis and Osiris," 1st-2nd Century.

[20] Benaissa (2010): "Plutarch cites the name as a designation of Anubis in his under-
worldly aspect (De Is.et Os. 375e), while Porphyry refers to Hermanubis as 'composite,'
and 'half-Greek' (De imaginibus fr. 8, 18.1–2 Bidez). The name has been restored in a
second-century BC dedicatory inscription from Delos (ID 2156.2 ... its earliest attesta-
tion ...it appears in three inscriptions of the Roman period, two from Egypt and one
from Thessalonike. *University of Michigan Library.*

[21] Josephus, 1999, *Antiquities* 18.3.4 (77), 591.

tiquities 18.3.<u>4</u> which immediately follows *Antiquities* 18.3.<u>3</u>,[22] a rather striking introduction to Anubis/Hermanubis:

> Now there was about this time Iesous, a wise man, if it be lawful to call him a man; for he was a doer of wonderful works, a teacher of such men as receive the truth with pleasure. He drew over to him both many of the Jews and many of the Gentiles.[23]

More than three centuries after Ptolemy I Soter combined Osiris and Apis to create Serapis, and two centuries after Hermes and Anubis were combined to create Hermanubis, Jesus the Nazarene arrived in Galilee and Josephus introduces him *immediately before* the Hermanubis error.

In the gospel stories, Jesus fulfills Jewish prophecy that foretells a coming Messiah. But he is also killed, buried, and resurrected, as were Osiris and his replacement, the created and merged god Serapis.

At the time of Jesus, the Most-High of all Pagan deities was Zeus and the Jewish deity was YHWH. And this leads to a possible genesis of the "hidden name," *Iesous*. Like Sar-apis and Herm-anubis, Iesous was created by identifying characteristics of two competing deities and then combining their names: *Ie* (Hebrew *YaH*) combined with *Zeus* becomes *Ie-Zeus* or *Iesous*.

The Gospel of Philip explains: "Iesous is a hidden name ... not particular to any language; rather he is always called by the name Iesous."[24] In other words, *Iesous* is not to be associated with a "common Jewish name" or similar names in any other language. He is Yah Zeus, which can also be translated, "Hail Zeus."[25]

---

[22] Philo's rule no. 17: position of the verses of a passage; Philo's rule no. 18: peculiar verse combinations.

[23] Excerpt. Some scholars argue that portions of the full verse in *Antiquities* are interpolations; however, most agree that Josephus did write a short paragraph about Jesus at this location in *Antiquities*, i.e., G. A. Wells, *The Jesus Legend* (Chicago: Open Court Publishers 1996), 48: "... that Josephus made *some* reference to Jesus, which has been retouched by a Christian hand. This is the view argued by Meier as by most scholars today particularly since S. Pines..."

[24] Meyer, 2008, 164.

[25] Les Aron Gosling, Rebbe, *Biblical Research Institute*. "Yeshu" "Yeshua" or "Jesus" – Which?" "Some authorities, who have spent their entire lives studying the origins of names believe (and they are without doubt quite correct) that 'Jesus' actually means

A defensible solution to the question of when Jesus was born, "Census of Quirinius or when Herod was king," is that *both* statements are true. The man who was called "Iesous" (the Elder) was born when Herod was king. His son, known as "Bar-Iesous," was born at the time of the census in 6 CE. And if the mythological sons born in 6 to Elizabeth and Mary are to be tied to the historical sons born in 6 to Julia and Agrippina, the historical man who was the first to be called "Jesus" can also be identified. So, too, can the man called "John the Baptist."

(according to the rules of the Greek language) – '*Hail Zeus!*' For *Iesous* in Greek IS 'Hail Zeus.' That is, *Ie* translates as 'Hail' and *sous* or *sus* is Zeus. The Jesus of modern Christendom is nothing more than the Egyptian form of Jupiter-Zeus, Serapis.

CHAPTER EIGHT

Following Philo to Contradictions and Coincidences

Part I

The Synoptic Gospels versus Josephus
A New Date for Mark and Luke's Crucifixion

We continue looking for strands of threads from ancient sources that will help answer biblical questions. And some of the clues are found in the contradictions between the Gospel writers and contemporary historians.

Luke dates Jesus' birth by citing the Census of Quirinius;[1] Josephus reports this census was taken c. 6 CE.[2] According to Luke, "Jesus was *about* thirty years old when he began his work" (Lk 3:23).[3]

Therefore, Luke reports that Jesus began his ministry in "about" 36 CE. So, the earliest he could have been crucified is "about" 36 (if the Crucifixion occurred in the year of his arrival); "about" 37 (if he taught just one year); "about" 39 (if his ministry continued for three years).

However, the consensus among scholars is that the Crucifixion occurred between 29 and 34; therefore, either Josephus is wrong about the year of the Census or Luke is wrong about Jesus' age when he began his ministry.

---

[1] Lk 2:2

[2] Josephus, 1999, *Antiquities* 18.2.1 (26), 588. The "… thirty-seventh year of Caesar's victory over Antony at Actium…," which was 31 BCE.

[3] Emphasis added.

Luke adds more confusion when he attempts to date the arrival of John the Baptist:

> In the fifteenth year of the reign of Emperor Tiberius[4] [c. 29], when Pontius Pilate was governor of Judea [c. 26-36], and Herod was ruler of Galilee [c. 6-39], and his brother Philip ruler of the region of Ituraea and Trachonitis [c. 4–BCE-34 (or 36 CE)], and *Lysanias ruler of Abilene* [c. 65-34 *BCE*], during the high priesthood of *Ananas and Caiaphas* [c. 18-36], the word of God came to John son of Zechariah in the wilderness (Lk 3:1-2).[5]

Caiaphas was removed as high priest c. 34 or c. 36 CE.[6] However, reminiscent of Mark's Bethlehem "omission," which was an interpolation, Mark knows *nothing* of Caiaphas.

Matthew, on the other hand, assigns Caiaphas the important role of the High Priest who convicts Jesus of blasphemy and hands him over for execution.[7] This has tied the dating of the Crucifixion to Caiaphas' term as High Priest, even though Mark knows nothing of him.

And as before, Luke steps in to help, returning to the "high priesthood of Ananas *and* Caiaphas" in *Acts*: "The next day their rulers, elders, and scribes assembled in Jerusalem, with *Annas the high priest, Caiaphas, John, and Alexander, and all who were of the high-priestly family*" (Acts 4:5).[8]

This meeting occurs *after* the Crucifixion when Peter and John were taken prisoner and brought before this priestly family to answer for their disobedience.

Following Philo's Rule 5,[9] the sentence can be reconstructed to read, "… their rulers … assembled in Jerusalem, with Annas;

---

[4] Tiberius became Emperor c. 14 CE when Augustus Caesar died.

[5] Emphasis added.

[6] Explanation for these discrepancies will follow.

[7] Mt. 26:3; 26:57-68.

[8] Emphasis added.

[9] "An entirely different meaning may also be found by disregarding the ordinarily accepted division of the sentence into phrases and clauses and by considering a different combination of the words."

the high priest Caiaphas; John; Alexander, and all who were of the high-priestly family."[10]

Luke's philological version renders Matthew's reference to Caiaphas as "High Priest"[11] useless for dating the Crucifixion. Caiaphas is still around *after* the Crucifixion, and Luke suggests he either shares the title of "High Priest" with Annas, or continued as High Priest after the Crucifixion. The "fifteenth year of Tiberius" points to c. 29 CE as John's arrival, assuming this is not an interpolation. But how much time passed before Jesus arrived is not known.

More important, however, is an error in Lk 3:1-2: "Lysanias ruler of Abilene" was the son of Ptolemy of Menneus,[12] an important character who will return in Chapter 11. According to Josephus, Cleopatra ordered Marc Antony to execute Lysanias c. 34 BCE, and of course, he did.[13] Apologists have a vast assortment of explanations for Luke's reference to him as "ruler of Abilene" c. 29 CE, but the fact is, Luke's contribution to dating John's arrival includes a man who had allegedly been dead at least six decades.

So, let's go back to Josephus and see if we can find some threads to pull on.

Emperor Tiberius appointed Pontius Pilate prefect of Judea. Ten years later, according to Josephus, the Samaritan Senate sent an embassy to Vitellius,[14] the president of Syria, and accused Pilate of multiple unwarranted murders:[15]

---

[10] This priestly family of Annas includes five sons and Caiaphas, his son-in-law. They served as High Priests over several decades: Eleazar (16-17 CE); Joseph Caiaphas (18-36 CE); Jonathan (36-37 CE); Theophilus (37-41 CE); Matthias (43 CE); Annas ben Annas (63 CE). Although these are "common" names, the narratives are focused on a small group of people; therefore, we should watch for these names, plus "Alexander," as we continue.

[11] The Nasi of the Great Sanhedrin during this time were descendants of Hillel the Elder: Simeon ben Hillel; Gamaliel ben Simeon; Simeon ben Gamaliel.

[12] Josephus, 1999, *Antiquities* 14.13.4 (330), 479.

[13] Josephus, 1999, *Antiquities* 15.4.1 (92), 498.

[14] Lucius Vitellius the Elder. His son, Aulus Vitellius would serve as Rome's Emperor for eight months in 69 CE, preceding Vespasian.

[15] Josephus, 1999, *Antiquities* 18.4.1 (87), 592.

So Pilate, when he had waited ten years in Judea, *hurried* to Rome, and this in obedience to the orders of Vitellius, which he dared not contradict; *but before he could get to Rome, Tiberius was dead.*[16] But Vitellius came into Judea, and went up to Jerusalem; *it was at the time of that festival which is called the Passover.*[17] Besides, he also deprived Joseph, who was also called Caiaphas, of the high priesthood and appointed Jonathan, the son of Ananus, to succeed him.[18]

Josephus' chronology dates these events to the Passover of 36, the year Pontius Pilate was removed as prefect. Curiously – and notably – Pilate left Jerusalem with orders to return to Rome, and in spite of Josephus reporting that he *"hurried* to Rome," he didn't arrive there until after Tiberius died – March 16, 37.

From Jerusalem to Rome by water during the summer months – depending on the weather – took between fifteen and thirty days – not a year. Therefore, Pilate either didn't "hurry" or he didn't leave for Rome until a year later.

And so we are left with a question: Where was Pilate between Passover of 36 when he was ordered to return to Rome and Passover of 37? We know he wasn't in Rome because he arrived there some unspecified time *after* Caligula became Emperor.

But something else very strange happens at this time; subsequent to reporting these events of 36, Josephus seems to stumble as the chronological order of *Antiquities* breaks down: "About this time Philip, Herod's brother, departed this life in the *twentieth* year of the reign of Tiberius."[19]

Josephus' forward march through time is suddenly reversed. Tiberius became Emperor in 14; add twenty years to 14 and the year is 34. "About this time" in his chronological journey through history was beyond Passover of 36 and before Passover of 37, the year Tiberius died – a three year difference.

---

[16] Josephus, 1999, *Antiquities* 18.4.2 (89), 593. (Tiberius died March 16, 37 CE.)

[17] Josephus, 1999, *Antiquities* 18.4.3 (90), 593.

[18] Josephus, 1999, *Antiquities* 18.4.3 (95), 593. Emphasis added.

[19] Josephus, 1999, *Antiquities* 18.4.6 (106), 594.

This "blip" from the "twenty-third year of Tiberius" back to "the twentieth year of Tiberius" supports those who date the Crucifixion to c. 29-33, and never later than 36 when Pilate was ordered to return to Rome.

The anomaly in Josephus' chronology remains a topic of debate but without any consensus of opinion. One explanation, of course, is that an interpolator changed "the *twenty-third* year of Tiberius" to "the *twentieth* year of Tiberius." We'll look for more threads to support this possibility as we proceed; we will also try to answer why this might have been done.

We turn now to the conflicting stories of John the Baptist. According to Josephus, John was beheaded just before King Aretas of Petra and Damascus defeated Herod's army, and he dates that event to c. 36 CE.[20]

Mark reports that John's beheading came early in Jesus' ministry, *before* the feeding of five thousand, the walk on water, the Transfiguration, and, of course, the Crucifixion.

In addition to contradicting the dating, Josephus attributes John's beheading to something quite different than what is found in Mark's account.[21]

According to Mark, Herod Antipas' wife Herodias held a grudge against John because he criticized the couple for divorcing their spouses in order to marry one another. And Herodias had previously been married to Antipas' brother, Philip, which compounded the sin in John's view.

Herodias' daughter Salome danced for guests at a lavish birthday party given for Antipas. Mark explains that Antipas was so pleased with the girl's performance that he declared, "Ask me for whatever you wish, and I will give it."[22] She turned to her mother for help choosing the gift, and Herodias saw her chance. "The head of John the baptizer,"[23] she said.

---

[20] Josephus, 1999, *Antiquities* 18.5.1 (114) 594.
[21] Josephus, 1999, *Antiquities* 18.5.2 (116-119), 595.
[22] Mark 6:22.
[23] Mark 6:24.

The king immediately sent a soldier to the prison where John was being held with orders to bring them his head. "He went and beheaded him in the prison, brought his head on a platter, and gave it to the girl. Then the girl gave it to her mother" (Mk 6:17-28).

Mark's version contradicts the account in *Antiquities* on a number of key points. Josephus explains that Aretas and Herod Antipas had a quarrel that turned to war because Aretas' daughter was the wife Antipas' divorced to marry Herodias. His version tells of a trip to Rome during which Antipas stayed with his brother Herod Philip. (These were two of Herod the Great's sons with different wives). During this visit, Herod Antipas fell in love with his half-brother's wife and set about to win her heart. She agreed to divorce Herod Philip and marry Herod Antipas *after* he divorced Aretas' daughter. The love-struck Antipas agreed to do so.

However, his wife discovered his plan to divorce her and marry Herodias, and, without telling him why, she demanded that he send her to her father. When she arrived home and told her father what Antipas was planning to do, Aretas declared war and defeated him. Antipas complained to Emperor Tiberius who sent Vitellius with soldiers and orders to take Aretas alive and deliver him in bonds or to kill him and send him his head.[24]

Josephus then interrupts his gripping tale of King Aretas' pending capture or beheading to relate the beheading of John the Baptist:[25]

> Some of the Jews thought that the *destruction of Herod's army*[26] came *from God*,[27] *as punishment* of what he did against John called the Baptist: for Herod killed him, who was a good man ... Herod feared the great influence John had over the people and believed

---

[24] Josephus, 1999, *Antiquities*, 18.5.1 (115), 595.

[25] Philo's rule no. 17: position of verses in passage; Philo's rule no. 18: peculiar verse combinations.

[26] Philo's rule no. 1: doubling of phrase; Philo's rule no. 3: repetition of statement previously made.

[27] Philo's rule no. 20: striking statement, "came from God."

he might raise a rebellion, and therefore thought it best to put him to death ... Herod sent John to King Aretas at Macherus where he was put to death ... The Jews believed that the *destruction of his army* was sent as a *punishment* upon Herod, and a mark of God's displeasure to him.[28]

This seems strange, and the yellow flags that put parentheses around the story say just that. It would be ludicrous to believe that Aretas beheaded John the Baptist *after* his daughter's report of her husband's infidelity, a report which led to war.[29]

Why would Aretas behead John under these circumstances? The answer is, he wouldn't. And Josephus clearly signals this story is not to be taken literally. It carries essential clues and it is up to us to find them and decipher them. So we proceed, paying close attention to what follows and how it might be tied to Gospel stories.

After rudely interrupting his account of King Aretas' predicament, Josephus returns to Vitellius who is still on his way with soldiers to behead Aretas:

> So Vitellius prepared to make war with Aretas ... But as he was leading his army through Judea, the principal men met him, and refused to allow him to march through their land because of the ensigns they carried ... So he ordered the army to march along the great plain, while he himself, with Herod Antipas and his friends, went up to Jerusalem to offer sacrifice to God, an *ancient festival of the Jews* being then just approaching; he was entertained by the multitude of the Jews and stayed in Jerusalem for *three days*, during which he took the High Priesthood from Jonathan and gave it to his brother Theophilus ... But on the fourth day letters came which informed him that *Emperor Tiberius had died*. Therefore, he ordered the multitude to take an oath of fidelity to Gaius [also known as Caligula.][30]

Vitellius, Herod Antipas, and friends are being entertained at an unnamed three-day festival in Jerusalem during which a new High Priest was installed. The death of Emperor Tiberius

---

[28] Josephus, 1999, *Antiquities* 18.5.1-2 (109-119), 594-5. Emphasis added.

[29] Antipas' marriage to Herodias preceded John's beheading, which means Aretas' betrayed daughter had already reported Antipas' offense and John's criticism of it.

[30] Josephus, 1999, *Antiquities* 18.5.3 (120-4), 595. Emphasis added.

confirms 37 as the year of this festival. Luke dates the beginning of Jesus' ministry to *about* 36; a one year ministry[31] dates the Crucifixion to *about* 37; scholarly consensus ranges from 29 to 35. And so, as noted, something seems to be amiss.

We have now gathered enough evidence to begin applying Philo's Philology to these texts. The goal is to solve the puzzles and date Mark's version of the Crucifixion, the *first* version on which Matthew and Luke allegedly relied.

Pilate was removed as prefect of Judea "at the time of that festival which is called the Passover" of 36.[32] Note that Josephus does not identify this festival as "Passover" but a festival that was *concurrent with* Passover.

Mark knows nothing about Caiaphas who was High Priest until "the time of" the Jewish Festival of 36.[33] Mark writes only of Pontius Pilate who, according to Josephus, served from c. 26 to c. 36 CE but did not arrive back in Rome until *after* Tiberius died, March 16, 37.

Mark does know that "the chief priests stirred up the crowd to have Pilate release Barabbas for them" (Mk 15:11), but he offers no names for any of these priests.

Matthew is the first to name Caiaphas and to place him at the Crucifixion. Matthew's "Jesus *OF* Nazareth" and the "Nazareth" in place of "Bethlehem" interpolation in Mark's Gospel have already shown Matthew's Gospel to be unreliable. And it must be considered a possibility that the insertion of Caiaphas into the story might have been for a similar purpose – to hide a secret Jesus' adversaries did not want known.

Josephus' dating of two unnamed annual festivals – 36 and 37 – and Luke's calculation of *about* the year 36 agree. However, Matthew's insertion of Caiaphas as High Priest and the

---

[31] Irenaeus, *Against Heresies*, 2.22.5: "He preached only one year reckoning from His baptism."

[32] Josephus, 1999, *Antiquities* 18.4.2-3 (89-90), 592-3.

[33] The year is 36 CE, according to Josephus' chronological march; 34 if "the twentieth year of Tiberius" is accepted in spite of being out of sequence.

three-year blip in *Antiquities* shifts the Crucifixion back by about three years.

So, what would motivate someone to do this? What difference does it make whether Jesus was crucified in 29, 34, or 37?

Well! A Crucifixion in 37 opens a door to information that would have posed a threat to preserving some of the adversaries' biggest secrets. However, exposing these secrets requires a brief side trip.

Emperor Tiberius' died on March 16, 37 CE; his death coincides with the popular Roman festival that also marks the death of Julius Caesar in 44 BCE: The Ides of March. Cults with characteristics and rituals similar to these annual festivals have been dated to the eighth century BCE in Sumer, the kingdom of Ansar, Kisar, Enlil, Ninlil, their son the Moon-god Sin, and his daughter Inanna.[34]

In Imperial Rome the Ides of March began a holy week of festivals honoring the deities Kybele and Attis.[35] It was a celebration of the myth of Attis' birth, death, and resurrection, and it has striking similarities in Hebrew and Christian traditions.

Like Moses, Attis was found among the reeds on the banks of a river; Attis was rescued by the goddess Kybele, the Great Mother. Sharing elements with "The Jesus Story," on March 22 priests cut down a pine tree, suspended an effigy of Attis from it, claimed he died, and then carried it to the temple of the Magna Mater. After a period of mourning Attis was reborn on the eve of the third day (March 25), the day reckoned as being the vernal equinox.[36] Winter's *death* had come to an end and Spring's *rebirth* of the sources of food had begun.

---

[34] Elizabeth Simpson, "Phrygian Furniture from Gordion," in Georgina Herrmann (ed.), *The Furniture of Ancient Western Asia*, Mainz: Philipp Von Zabern 1996), 198–201. In Phrygian art of the 8th century BCE, the attributes of the Phrygian mother-goddess include attendant lions. The Hurrian goddess *Hannahannah* was also earlier associated with lions, as was Sumerian *Inanna*, daughter of the Moon-god, *Sin*.

[35] Possibly derived from Hebrew words, *Ki aB eL*, "Ki cloud of El" and *eTs*, "Tree," one of the words that "adorns" Ansar and Kisar's descendants.

[36] Sir James George Frazer, *The Golden Bough, Attis Mythology* (New York: MacMillan, 1922), Chapters 34-36, *Sacred Texts Archive Online*. Also, Ovid, *Fasti*, Book III.

Inscriptions in Rome and in Phrygia indicate that Kybele's high-priest – whatever his *real* name might have been – was called "Attis" and *probably played the role of his namesake during the annual festival.*[37] (Read the previous sentence at least two more times!)

On the "Day of Blood," the high priest cut his arms to draw blood, but afterwards an effigy – not the priest – was ritually killed.

Scottish anthropologist Sir James George Frazer notes: "Perhaps we may go a step farther and conjecture that this mimic killing of the priest, accompanied by a real effusion of his blood, was in Phrygia, as it has been elsewhere, a substitute for a human sacrifice which in earlier times was actually offered."[38]

An echo of the "Day of Blood" and the ritual "real effusion of his blood" can be heard in John's Gospel: "One of the soldiers pierced his side with a spear, and at once blood and water came out" (Jn 19:34).

Another popular myth and festival was the story of the founding of Rome by the twins Romulus and Remus, sons of a Vestal Virgin, Rhea Silvia, and the god Mars. Ovid tells the story of the twins' birth:

> Meanwhile Remus and Romulus were growing, and her belly swelled with the divine burden. When only two signs remained for the shining god to travel before the complete year had run its course, Silvia became a mother. They say the images of Vesta covered their eyes with their virgin hands: The altar of the goddess certainly trembled when her priestess gave birth, and the fearful flame sank to its own ashes. When Amulius, knew of this, a man scornful of justice, (since he overcame his own brother and took his power) he ordered the twins drowned in the river. The water shrank from the crime: and the boys were left there on dry land.[39]

Plutarch tells the story of Romulus' death, including an eye-witness to the god's ascension into heaven and an important renaming: "Proculus, a man of note, took oath that he saw

---

[37] Frazer, 1922, Chapter 36, "Human Representatives of Attis."
[38] Frazer, 1922, Chapter 35.
[39] Ovid, *Fasti*, Book III, Introduction.

Romulus caught up into heaven in his arms and vestments, and heard him, as he ascended, cry out that they should hereafter call him by the name of Quirinus."[40]

In Augustan Rome, Quirinus became the double-faced god "Janus Quirinus,"[41] the symbol of change and transitions. He also represented time because he could see into the past with one face and into the future with the other.[42] Janus Quirinus was celebrated with "Quirinal Festivals" at the beginnings of the harvest, planting times, marriages, deaths, and other beginnings and transitions, although February 17 is cited as the date of the annual festival. According to Ovid, Janus was considered the "god of gods":

"Next I said: 'Why, while I placate other gods, Janus, do I bring the wine and incense first to you?' He replied: 'So that *through me*, who guard the threshold, you can have access to whichever god you please.'"[43]

An echo of Janus' words can be heard in John's Gospel: "...No one comes to the Father if not *through me*"[44] (Jn 14:6).

"Janus Quirinus" is the final stage of an evolutionary process that began in ancient Sumer. There, two solar pillars located on the eastern side of temples marked the direction of the rising sun on the two solstices. They were the origin of the theology of the Divine Twins, one of whom is mortal – represented by the Northeast pillar where the sun *never* shines – while the other is immortal – represented by the Southeast pillar where the sun *always* shines. The two pillars evolved into the Egyptian obelisk which represents two torsos, and finally into a

---

[40] Plutarch, *Parallel Lives*: "Life of Numa Pompilius." (Loeb, 1914), (Thayer Online 2.3).
[41] In the prayer of the priests of Jupiter, quoted by Livy (I.32.10); Macrobius (*Saturnalia* I.9.15).
[42] Macrobius *Saturnalia* I. 7, 20 and I. 9, 4: "Antevorta and Postvorta are his associate deities." Ovid *Fasti* I 133-40 states his double head means he is the gatekeeper of the heavenly mansion and can watch both the eastern and western gates of heaven.
[43] Ovid, *Fasti* Book I.
[44] Word-for-word literal translation.

single body with two heads looking in opposite directions, represented by Janus Quirinus.[45]

The evidence suggests that Tiberius' death – coinciding with the Ides of March in 37, eighty-one years after Julius Caesar's assassination – was the event that triggered the *first* Crucifixion Festival recorded in Mark's Gospel. It signaled the shift from the *past* to the *future* – a new Emperor, a new deity, a new annual festival to replace Passover, The Ides of March, and the Isis and Serapis Festival in Egypt.

In 6 CE, the year Jesus, John the Baptist, and the Nasoraean sect of Judaism were born, Emperor Tiberius became the grandfather of twin boys,[46] recorded by the historian and philologist Tacitus: "This, as a rare event, causing joy even in humble homes, so delighted the emperor that he did not refrain from boasting before the senators that no Roman of the same rank had twin offspring ever before been born."[47]

This is one of the most carefully guarded of the secrets that motivated Jesus' adversaries to write Matthew's Gospel and to change "Bethlehem" to "Nazareth" in Mark's.

After thirty years of anxious anticipation – and perhaps an exemption from Roman and Temple taxation for those who converted to "The Way of the Nasoraeans" – the time had come. And John chose to have Jesus himself explain it: "Now is the judgment of this world; now the prince [Hebrew, Nasi] of this world will be driven out. And I, when I am lifted up [Hebrew, *Nasa*] from the earth, will draw all things to myself" (Jn 12:31-2).

Shortly after the Crucifixion, Luke introduces someone who was also known to Josephus: "A Pharisee in the council named Gamaliel, a teacher of the Law, respected by all the people,

---

[45] A. Audin, "Dianus bifrons ou les deux stations solaires, piliers jumeaux et portiques solsticiaux" in *Revue de géographie de Lyon* 1956, 191-198. (N.V.)
[46] The dating of this event is disputed, but circumstantial evidence in later chapters supports 6 CE as the year Tiberius' twin grandsons were born.
[47] Tacitus, *Annals: The Works*(1864-1877); *Sacred Texts Online 2.84).*

stood up..." (Acts 5:34). (The crucial message Gamaliel delivers in his speech will be examined in Part 2 of this chapter.)

According to Josephus, Nasi Gamaliel had a son named "Iesous."[48] According to the Babylonian Talmud, Gamaliel's son was "Nasi Simeon ben Gamaliel."[49] Equally important, Gamaliel has a counterpart in Hebrew Scripture that will become an important hypotext in later chapters:

> "... The leader [Hebrew, *nasi*] of the people of Manasseh[50] shall be Gamaliel..." (Num 2:20).

> "On the eighth day Gamaliel ... the leader [*nasi*] of the Manassites..." (Num 7:54).

Nasi Gamaliel and his son Nasi Simeon ben Gamaliel, also known as "Iesous" and "bar Iesous" is another secret the adversaries wanted to keep. Remember the sentence we asked you to re-read: "Inscriptions in Rome and in Phrygia indicate that *Kybele's* **high-priest** – whatever his **real** name might have been – was called **Attis** and *probably played the role of his namesake during the annual festival.*"

Historians tell us that Greeks and Egyptians were peacefully united when Osiris was merged with Apis to become "Serapis." The annual festival to celebrate Serapis, Isis, and their son Horus was the highlight of the year for the Egyptian people.

A century later, merging Hermes and Anubis to create "Hermanubis" united more warring factions. All that remained was to *peacefully* unite the Orthodox Jews with the Hellenized Jews and the Romans. And so the same proven plan was implemented.

"YH-Zeus the Nazarean" was introduced during a new annual festival celebrating the arrival of the Jewish Messiah and the death and resurrection of the Savior. The Messiah-Savior brought along his benevolent Father of Light, Love, and Compassion, accessible to those who follow Him in "The Way."

---

[48] Josephus, 1999, *Antiquities* 20.9.4 (213), 657.

[49] Rab. Dr. Epstein, ed. *Soncino Babylonian Talmud*: Tractate Gittin; folio 58a. (Longon: The Soncino Press, 1935-1948).

[50] Manasseh was the name of Joseph's first-born son; Manasseh's grandmother was Rachel.

One festival that could be celebrated by all Romans – Pagans, Jews, and Gentiles alike – would bring peace and prosperity. The Golden Age of Rome – The New Jerusalem – was the goal.

Let's take a moment to review: According to Josephus, it was around the year 36 that Herod Antipas agreed to divorce his wife and marry Herodias. His wife discovered his plan and returned to her home to report this betrayal to her father, King Aretas[51] of Petra.

Shortly thereafter Herod Antipas sent John the Baptist to the same King Aretas. Antipas ordered the king to behead John, his daughter's defender – which Aretas allegedly did. Aretas then declared war against the man whose request he fulfilled, a rather unlikely story. Also c. 36 Tiberius ordered Vitellius to capture or behead Aretas, just as John had been beheaded, suggesting enigmatically that "John" may have also been known as "Aretas," and that "beheading" might have referred to removal from high office.

Back in Rome a year later – March 16, 37 – Gaius Julius Caesar, also known as "Caligula," became Emperor, replacing Tiberius. A month or so after that, while on his way to behead Aretas of Petra, Vitellius, Antipas, and friends "…went up to Jerusalem to offer sacrifice to God…," part of *an ancient three-day festival.* Josephus does not say what – *or who* – was sacrificed.

During the festival, Vitellius took the High Priesthood from Jonathan and gave it to his brother Theophilus. News of Tiberius' death was received, dating this festival to the year 37.

According to Josephus, Vitellius deposed Pontius Pilate "at the time of" the Passover of 36; however, Pilate's arrival in Rome *after* Caligula became Emperor indicates he remained in Judea in some capacity until 37. But in what capacity did he

---

[51] It was a tradition that the Kings of Arabia at Petra and Damascus change their names to *Aretas, The New Complete Works of Josephus,* p. 545, Note 2.

serve? Perhaps Pilate was relieved of his *official* duties in 36 so he could play one of the roles in the festival performance of 37.

The collected pieces of evidence say that Mark's Gospel is the written record of this "First Annual Passover-Passion Festival." It was composed and in use *before* Paul began his letter-writing ministry, and it is "the other gospel" he references in Gal 1:8. Before the interpolations were inserted, it may have been the "lost," "Gospel of the Nassaraeans."

The evidence also suggests that Luke's Gospel was written *after* Matthew's falsifications in order to repair the damage done to Mark's Gospel. This suggests that scholars' proposed, "Q Source" never existed; Mark's and Matthew's Gospels were used to compose Luke's Gospel.

The Passover-Passion Festival was repeated annually. The minor modifications with each retelling have been viewed as "discrepancies" when, in fact, they recorded *subsequent* Crucifixions. Perhaps the changes in minor details were inserted in order to reveal this fact.

However, Matthew's changes to Mark's version had a different purpose. Caiaphas was added to the Crucifixion to coordinate with Caiaphas in *Antiquities*; someone then changed Josephus' "twenty-third year of Tiberius" to the "twentieth year of Tiberius" thereby shifting the First Crucifixion away from the year Tiberius died. Fortunately, whoever did it failed to consider that Josephus' dependable chronological method – with help from Luke – would eventually expose this careless interpolation.

Philo's Philology leads to a date for the Crucifixion that falls outside the traditionally accepted range of 30 to 34 CE. April 19, 37,[52] was the date of the first Jewish Passover after the death of Tiberius. The long-anticipated Messiah arrived as a Savior to participate in the "First Annual Passover-Passion Festival." And, "The Watchtower of the Flock" arrived with him.

---

[52] Jesus the Elder, born c. 13-15 BCE, would have been about 50 years of age in 37. Jn 8:57: "Then the Jews said to him, 'You are *not yet fifty years old*, and have you seen Abraham?'"

CHAPTER EIGHT

Following Philo to Contradictions and Coincidences

Part II

Luke versus Josephus
Theudas and Judas – Who came First?

In Part One we identified a contradiction between the Synoptic Gospels and Josephus, and we found a good reason for it: a new and later date for the Crucifixion – April 19, 37 CE. This date coincides with the death of Tiberius and the beginning of Caligula's reign of terror that lasted from March 37 until January 41. The significance of the correlation between the death of Tiberius, the Crucifixion, and the reign of Caligula must not be underestimated.

Curiously, when he became Emperor, rather than following through with Tiberius' orders to capture or behead Aretas, Caligula expanded Aretas' kingdom and awarded him Damascus.[1] Damascus, of course, is Paul's destination when he sees the light, then a vision, and is converted from a ruthless killer of Nasoraean men and women to Jesus' chief apostle.

Luke composed a story in which the Nasi Gamaliel contradicts Josephus. It also carries clues for reweaving "The Secret History of Jesus." It leads to key participants in events from the

---

[1] Archaeologists recovered a Damascus coin with the image of King Aretas and the date 101 (Pompeian era), which converts to 37 CE, the year Caligula became Emperor (T. E. Mionnet, Description des medailles antiques greques et romaines, V [1811], 284f.)

Crucifixion until the destruction of the Jerusalem Temple in 70. Luke writes:

> But a Pharisee in the council named Gamaliel, a teacher of the law, respected by all the people, stood up and ordered the men to be put outside for a short time. Then he said to them, "Fellow *Israelites*, consider carefully what you propose to do to these men. For some time ago Theudas rose up, claiming to be somebody, and a number of men, about four hundred, joined him; but he was killed, and all who followed him were dispersed and disappeared. *After him* Judas the Galilean rose up *at the time of the census* and got people to follow him; he also perished, and all who followed him were scattered (Acts 5:34-37).[2]

Josephus also points to the Census of Quirinius but contradicts Luke's chronology:

> Now it came to pass, while Fadus was procurator of Judea [44-46 CE], that a certain magician [*magos*], whose name was Theudas [perhaps *Theo+Iudas*], persuaded a great part of the people to take their effects with them, and follow him to the river Jordan; for he told them he was a prophet, and that he would, by his own command, divide the river, and afford them an easy passage over it; and many were deluded by his words. However, Fadus sent a troop of horsemen who slew many and took many of them alive. They also took Theudas alive, and cut off his head, and carried it to Jerusalem. This was what befell the Jews in the time of Cuspius Fadus' government.[3]

Josephus agrees that Judas the Galilean rose up at the time of the census in 6 CE and notes that Judas and Sadduc (Zadok) "excited a fourth philosophic sect" in that very year.[4] However, according to Josephus, Theudas rose up nearly forty years *after* Judas, not before.

Josephus continues his story and identifies more important people by name in the subsequent paragraph:

> Then came Tiberius Alexander ... the son of Alexander the Alabarch of Alexandria ... a great famine happened in Judea, in which Queen Helena bought grain in Egypt and contributed it to

---

[2] Emphasis added.

[3] Josephus, 1999, *Antiquities* 20.5.1 (97-99), 648.

[4] Josephus, 1999, *Antiquities* 18.1.1 (4), 585.

those in need. And the sons of Judas of Galilee were now killed; I mean of that Judas who caused the people to revolt, when Quirinius came to take an account of the estates of the Jews, as we have shown in a foregoing book. The names of those sons were James and Simon, whom Alexander commanded to be crucified.[5]

Alexander the Alabarch of Alexandria had two sons. His younger son Marcus married King Herod the Great's great-granddaughter, Princess Bernice.[6] And Bernice, according to Josephus, was "a virgin" who took the Nazirite vow.[7] This is the same Bernice whose brother was King Agrippa and whose sister Drusilla married the freedman Antonius Felix. Coincidentally, Alabarch Alexander was Philo's brother; Marcus Tiberius Alexander and Julius Tiberius Alexander were Philo's nephews.[8]

The second person Josephus identifies is Queen Helena who also took the vow of a nazirite for fourteen (or twenty-one) years.[9] In this one section of *Antiquities*, Josephus identifies two people – Tiberius Alexander and Queen Helena – who can be tied to nazirites: Queen Helena herself, Tiberius Alexander by way of his sister-in-law Bernice.

The crucifixion of James and Simon c. 46 CE, and the historical significance of Tiberius Alexander, his brother Marcus, their father Alabarch Alexander, and Queen Helena, are threads that will be picked up again in Chapter Fifteen.

When Josephus introduces Judas the Galilean in *War of the Jews*, dated c. 75, he devotes one paragraph to Judas and his fourth sect:

Under his administration a certain Galilean, whose name was Judas, prevailed with his countrymen to revolt, and said they were cowards if they would endure to pay a tax to the Romans and would after God submit to mortal men as their lords. This

---

[5] Josephus, 1999, *Antiquities* 20.5.2 (100-102), 648.
[6] Josephus, 1999, *Antiquities* 19.5.1 (276), 633.
[7] Josephus, 1999, *Wars*, 2.15.1 (313), 751.
[8] Josephus, 1999, *Antiquities* 18.8.1 (259), 605.
[9] Talmud: *Nazir* 3.6; see Jewish Encyclopedia 6.334, s.v. Helena.

man was a teacher of *a peculiar sect of his own*, and was not at all like the rest of those their leaders.[10]

Josephus devotes most of the rest of Chapter Two to the Essenes.[11] His only other reference to Judas the Galilean in *Wars* comes five Books later (critical portions excerpted from a lengthy narrative):

> It was ... Eleazar, the commander of these Sicarii ... He was a descendant from that Judas who had persuaded the Jews ... not to submit to the taxation when Quirinius was sent into Judea ...[12] this was ... a pretense and a cloak for the barbarity ...[13] and they ... abused those that reproached them for their wickedness.[14]

According to Josephus, Eleazar's revolt had nothing to do with taxation; he merely used it as an excuse for declaring war against the Romans and enticing others to follow him. Two of his followers are featured:

> They were the Sicarii ... and first became barbarous towards those allied to them ... Yet did John of Gischala demonstrate by his actions that these Sicarii were more moderate than he was himself, for he not only killed all who gave him good counsel to do what was right, but treated them as the most bitter enemies that he had among all the citizens.[15]

Joining Eleazar the Sicarii commander and John of Gischala is a third man:

> There was no crime which Simon the son of Gioras[16] would not commit, and he abused those very freemen who had set him up for a tyrant. Friendship or family did not matter to them, for they looked upon attacking strangers only as a work beneath their courage, but thought their barbarity towards their nearest relations would be a glorious demonstration thereof.[17]

---

[10] Josephus, 1999, *Wars* 2.8.1 (118), 736. Emphasis added.

[11] Philo's rule no. 17: the position of the verses of a passage. The "fourth sect of Judaism" is tied philologically to the Essenes.

[12] Josephus, 1999, *Wars* 7.8.1 (253), 925. (Condensed and paraphrased for clarity.)

[13] Josephus, 1999, *Wars* 7.8.1 (254-7), 925-6.

[14] Josephus, 1999, *Wars* 7.8.1 (258), 926.

[15] Josephus, 1999, *Wars*, 7.8.1 (261-4), 926.

[16] *Gioras*, from *guwr* (Strong's Hebrew 1481), translated at Gen 12:10 as "sojourn."

[17] Josephus, 1999, *Wars*, 7.8.1 (265-7), 926 (condensed and paraphrased).

The worst of the violence, Josephus says, was directed at those *within* the family of Eleazar (a descendant of Judas the Galilean), John of Gischala, and Simon the son of Gioras. Also "abused" were certain "freemen" – those who had the power to set Simon up for "a tyrant." Questions to be answered include, to which family or families did these men belong and who are the influential freedmen who gave power to Simon ben Gioras?

A search of Hebrew Scripture for references to Damascus leads to another interesting coincidence:

> But Abram said, "O Lord GOD [Hebrew, *Adonay YHWH*] what will you give me, for I continue childless, and the heir of my house is *Eliezer of Damascus*?" And Abram said, "You have given me no offspring, and so a slave born in my house is to be my heir" (Gen 15:2-3).[18]

This tells us that the first *Eliezer of Damascus* was a potential heir to Abram's House, but he was not Abram's biological son. Of course, Abram's curse was Eliezer's blessing – until Sarai, Abram's wife, stepped in: "You see that YHWH has prevented me from bearing children; go in to my slave girl; it may be that I shall obtain children by her." And, indeed, Hagar conceived and gave Abram a son, Ishmael, "a wild donkey of a man" (Gen 16:12).

Josephus reports that Herod the Great left his brother's seven-year-old son, Phasaulus[19] ben Phasaulus, with King Malchus of Arabia as collateral for money he borrowed.[20] The money was never repaid and it must be assumed the boy was never returned.

And notably, Josephus makes a slight error in his account of King Malchus. It was a longstanding tradition that the Arabian Kings adopt the name Aretas.[21] Therefore "Malchus," from *malek* which means "king," became King Aretas, and from the

---

[18] Emphasis added.

[19] Also written, "Phasaelus" and "Phasalus." Note that "Salus" is the Roman name for *Hygeia,* the Greek goddess of health and well-being.

[20] Josephus, 1999, *Antiquities,* 14.14.1 (371), 482.

[21] It was a tradition that the Kings of Arabia at Petra and Damascus change their names to *Aretas, The New Complete Works of Josephus,* 545, Note 2.

time Phasaulus ben Phasaulus was seven, he was raised in Aretas' palace in Petra. And he may have been in line to become a
subsequent "Aretas of Arabia," which included Petra and Damascus.

Moreover, Damascus is significant in Saul's biography both
before and after he became Paul. It is his destination when he
sees a life-changing vision, and he concludes his second letter
to the Corinthians with a ranting reference to Aretas and Damascus and Abraham:

> I repeat, let no one think that I am a fool; but if you do, then ac-
> cept me as a fool, so that I too may boast a little. What I am saying
> in regard to this boastful confidence, I am saying not with the
> Lord's authority, but as a fool; since many boast according to hu-
> man standards, I will also boast. For you gladly put up with fools,
> being wise yourselves! For you put up with it when someone
> makes slaves of you, or preys upon you, or takes advantage of
> you, or puts on airs, or gives you a slap in the face. To my shame, I
> must say, we were too weak for that!
>
> But whatever anyone dares to boast of – I am speaking as a fool
> – I also dare to boast of that. Are they Hebrews? So am I. Are they
> Israelites? So am I.[22] *Are they descendants of Abraham? So am I.* Are
> they ministers of Christ? I am talking like a madman – I am a bet-
> ter one: with far greater labors, far more imprisonments, with
> countless floggings, and often near death. Five times I have re-
> ceived from the Jews the forty lashes minus one. Three times I was
> beaten with rods. Once I received a stoning. Three times I was
> shipwrecked; for a night and a day I was adrift at sea; on frequent
> journeys, in danger from rivers, danger from bandits, danger from
> my own people, danger from Gentiles, danger in the city, danger
> in the wilderness, danger at sea, danger from false brothers and
> sisters; in toil and hardship, through many a sleepless night, hun-
> gry and thirsty, often without food, cold and naked. And, besides
> other things, I am under daily pressure because of my anxiety for
> all the churches. Who is weak, and I am not weak? Who is made to
> stumble, and I am not indignant?

---

[22] Note that Paul claims to be "Hebrew" and "Israelite," but he does not claim to be a
Judean; in fact, he identifies "Jews" (Judeans) as those who inflicted punishment on
him.

If I must boast, I will boast of the things that show my weakness. The God and Father of the Lord Jesus (blessed be he forever!) knows that I do not lie. *In Damascus, the governor under King Aretas guarded the city of Damascus in order to seize me*, but I was let down in a basket through a window in the wall, and escaped from his hands (2 Cor 11:16-33).[23]

Luke reports that Paul was from Tarsus, not Damascus,[24] and most scholars have accepted this claim without question. However, supporting evidence is lacking, and one scholar offers compelling evidence that disputes Luke's enigmatic claim:

Maybe Acts' reference to Tarsus is a play on "Tarshish," the mythical city to which the prophet Jonah tried to escape from the presence of God. But instead, Jonah ends up shipwrecked in a sea storm, just as Paul ends up shipwrecked before Malta in Acts ... I decided to take Paul's comment "and then I returned to Damascus" (Gal 1:17) at face value. And once I accepted in my heart the possibility that Paul was a Syrian Jew who grew up in Damascus, everything else fell into place: his animosity to the Judean leadership in Jerusalem, which was shared by many Hellenistic Jews, his identity as an Israelite from the Tribe of Benjamin, which points out that he is not a son of Judah and a Judean, his familiarity with the Scriptures in Greek and with Greek culture, his move to Arabia and many other details referenced to in his letters.[25]

The story of Jonah, in fact, opens with the thrice-repeated word "Tarshish":

Now the word of YHWH came to Jonah son of Amittai, saying "Go at once to Nineveh, that great city, and cry out against it; for their wickedness has come up before me." Jonah set out to flee to *Tarshish* ... he ... found a ship going to *Tarshish* ... paid his fare and went on board, to go with them to *Tarshish*, away from the presence of YHWH" (Jon 1:1-3).[26]

Josephus supports Trobisch's proposition that "Tarshish" was also known as "Tarsus": "Tharsus to the Tharsians, for so was Cilicia of old called; the sign of which is this, that the no-

---

[23] Emphasis added.

[24] Acts 22:3.

[25] David Trobisch, *Talitha and the Eyes of Saint Paul* (Bolivar: Leonard Press; 2013), 177-8.

[26] Key excerpts; emphasis added.

blest city they have, and a metropolis also, is Tarsus, the tau being by change put for the theta."[27]

Other Hebrew Bible references to Tarshish pertinent to our investigation include a reference to another Eliezer:

Then Eliezer son of *Dod*-avahu [*Dod* is Hebrew for "Uncle"; *ava-hu* is "YaH"] of Marashah prophesied ... "YHWH will destroy what you have made." And the ships were wrecked and were not able to go to Tarshish (2 Chr 20:37).

... Jehoshaphat made ships of the Tarshish type to go to Ophir for gold, but they did not go, for the ships were wrecked at Ezion-geber (1 Kings 22:40).

Hebrew Bible "shipwrecks" go hand-in-hand with "Tarshish," also known as "Tarsus." And the name "Eliezer" – Josephus' spelling, "Eleazar" – is tied to a shipwreck and both Damascus and Tarsus. And of course, "Saul known as Paul" is also tied to shipwrecks and both Damascus and Tarsus.[28]

Hebrew Scripture associates Eleazar with Damascus and Tarsus. Likewise, Phasaulus ben Phasaulus and John the Baptist were both sent to the King of Petra and Damascus. Phasaulus was raised there; John was beheaded there according to Josephus.

Finally, "Saulus of Tarsus" was on his way *to* Damascus when struck by a blinding light (Acts 9:11 and 9:30). He was forced to escape *from* Damascus in a basket (Acts 9:25). Damascus and Tarshish/Tarsus tie the characters together, allowing a preliminary identification of the Sicarii commander and his two fellow Zealots. The evidence – with more to follow – seems to suggest that:

1. Eleazar the Zealot and leader of the Sicarii may have also been known as Phasaulus ben Phasaulus of Damascus. He was possibly King Aretas of Damascus' heir even though he was not his biological son. The name Pha-Saulus is very close to Saulus, who was also known as Paulus, whose life was forever changed on the road to Damascus. A new thread to hold onto while

[27] Josephus, 1999, *Antiquities* 1.6.1 (127), 57.
[28] Acts 9:11; 9:30; 11:25; 21:39; 22:3.

looking for additional clues is a Saulus (or Paulus) who (1) is raised by someone other than his biological father, and (2) becomes a ruler by passing over the biological sons of the man who raised him.

2. *Giora* is derived from the Hebrew word, *giyur*, defined as "… temporary dweller, new-comer (no inherited rights)."[29] This may suggest that Simeon Giora's father was a "newcomer" and a "temporary dweller" among the Sicarii.

3. John of Gischala may have also been known as "John, whose other name was Mark." But other than his name, no evidence suggests he was also known as *John the Baptist*.

Damascus, Tarsus, and shipwrecks combined become a short, slender thread that can be tied to others, previously collected and yet to come, that identify Josephus' "Eleazar" – a descendant of Judas the Galilean – as Saulus, also known as the Apostle Paul.

Let's take a moment to review some of the key points as they relate to Gospel stories:

1. Luke identifies John the Baptist as a relative of Jesus the Nazarean, and both were born c. 6 CE.

2. A "Paulus" and his cousin "Germanicus" were born that same year.

3. Another boy reportedly born c. 6 is John the Apostle.[30]

4. And a fourth is Matthias, whose younger son is our philologist-historian, Josephus.

Philo would say, *look at the Greek word from which Matthias is derived*. It is *mathétes* and defined as "disciple." The name suggests that the men called "Matthias" may have carried other names but were addressed using the generic term, "disciple." And a comparison of Mark's, Luke's, and Matthew's gospels reveals that the apostle Matthew is also called Levi.

---

[29] Brown-Driver Briggs.
[30] Wikipedia's "year born" feature offers this name, and several websites have adopted it; however, we continue looking for a confirming source.

Perhaps Matthias and Io-*Cephas* received dual names for a reason, just as Simon Peter received his: "So he appointed the twelve: Simon (to whom he gave the name Petron)" (Mk 3:16). And perhaps the reason was to demonstrate that the principle characters, historical and mythical, carried different names at different times and in different situations.

John adds yet another name to Simon Petron: "He brought Simon to Jesus, who looked at him and said, 'You are Simon son of John. You are to be called *Cephas* (which is translated *Petros*)" (Jn 1:42).

Perhaps the name "John" is a marker pointing to John of Gischala, or perhaps, one of the others born in 6 CE: John the Apostle, Matthias, or John the Baptist. It's another loose thread to be held onto as we proceed.

Another long and unquestioned tradition says *Peter* is Greek for "rock" and *Cephas* is Aramaic for "rock." Recall that "rock" (Hebrew, *ZuR; tSuR*) is one of the words that "adorn" the Ish and Ishshah of Ansar and Kisar (Gen 1:11).

However, it's also possible that Simon was called *Petra* because he was *from* Petra. Also intriguing is the Hebrew word, *peter*,[31] defined as "that which separates, first opens;—construct, i.e. *firstborn, of man* and beast." The Egyptians' "Creator God" was *Ptah* (pronounced *pitah*); the Egyptian words, *Hwt-ka-Ptah*, mean "House of the Ka of Ptah";[32] the title, "Ptolemy," unites *Ptah* with *eL* and *eM*.

The Hebrew Bible naming methodology might explain the etymology of *Peter* thusly: "Jesus called him *Peter* because he was a 'Pitah'" ("first born son"). Or, "Jesus called him *Peter* because he was a 'Ptolemy.'" The names may say the man called "Simon Peter" was *Ha Simonean*, a "Hasmonean"; he was the eldest son of a Ptolemy, and he was a King of Petra and Damascus.

---

[31] Brown-Driver-Briggs (Strong's Hebrew 6363).
[32] Nermin Sami and Jimmy Dunn, *The Origin of the Word, "Egypt."*

Tying this thread to Hebrew Scripture, Jacob's son Simeon had a son named Saul who was "...the son of a Canaanite woman" (Gen 46:10). Canaan is the land where Rachel died and was buried; it is also home of the goddess Shemesh, another name for Ishtar/Asharah/Venus.

"Canaan" appears as *ki-na-ah-na* in the 14th Century BCE Armana letters.[33] And, borrowing Hebrew Bible methodology again to seek its etymology, "This land was home to the descendants of Ki and An; therefore, they called it *Ki an ha an*." *Kianna* evolved into "Canaan," suggesting that Ki and An's descendants were Canaanites before they became *ISh oR El*, Israelites. Archaeologists have found evidence that supports this hypothetical etymology.[34]

A little more digging for similar threads and we may be able to support or discard these preliminary conclusions. We may also be able to find the elusive baptizer John. And as might be expected, Josephus offers more evidence as his story of Judas the Galilean's descendants continues:

> The Idumeans also strove with these men who should be guilty of the greatest madness for they ... cut the throats of the high priests ... they proceeded to destroy the least remains of a political government, and introduced the most complete scene of iniquity under which that sort of people that were called *Zealots* grew up and who indeed corresponded to the name, for they imitated every wicked work, nor, if their memory suggested any evil thing that had formerly been done, they *zealously* sought to do the same; and although they gave themselves that name from their *zeal* for what was good, yet did it agree to them only by way of irony...[35]

If the Zealots had been the "Fourth sect of Judaism," surely Josephus would have described them as a "sect" rather than

---

[33] William L. Moran, *The Armarna Letters* (Baltimore: Johns Hopkins University Press, 1992), 14-5. *Armana Letters*: Diplomatic correspondence between ancient Egypt and Canaan discovered at Armana in Upper Egypt, first c. 1887 with more in 1891 and 1892 during excavations led by William Flinders Petrie.

[34] Ann E. Killebrew, *Biblical Peoples and Ethnicity* (Society of Biblical Literature, 2005), 96.

[35] Josephus, 1999, *Wars*, 7.8.1. (267-271), 926. Condensed and paraphrased; emphasis added.

"that sort of people that were called Zealots who gave themselves that name." There was, of course, a man who claimed to be a Jew and whom, according to *Acts*, admitted to being – like Eleazar, John, and Simon – a Zealot:

> I am a Jew, born in Tarsus in Cilicia, but brought up in this city at the feet of Gamaliel, educated strictly according to our ancestral law, being zealous [Greek, zélótés] for God, just as all of you are today. I persecuted this Way[36] up to the point of death by binding both men and women and putting them in prison, as the high priest and the whole council of elders can testify about me. From them I also received letters to the brothers in Damascus, and I went there in order to bind those who were there and to bring them back to Jerusalem for punishment (Acts 22:3-5).

The phrase "both men and women" hearkens to Num 6:2 where women are specifically approved to take the vow of a nazirite. That it follows "this The Way" is surely not unintentional. And Paul is not the only Zealot to be identified in Acts:

> When they heard it, they *praised God* [Greek, *Theos*]. Then they said to him, "You see, brother, how many thousands of believers there are among the Jews, and they are all *zealous* for the law. They have been told about you that you teach all the Jews living among the Gentiles to forsake Moses, and that you tell them not to circumcise their children or observe the customs. What then is to be done? They will certainly hear that you have come. So do what we tell you. We have four men who are under a vow. Join these men, go through the rite of purification with them, and pay for the shaving of their heads. Thus all will know that there is nothing in what they have been told about you, but that you yourself observe and guard the law (Acts 21:20-4).[37]

In other words, take the Nazirite vow and no one will suspect who you really are or what horrible things you have been doing to the Nasoraeans.

Josephus also writes of four men, including a Jew accused of transgressing their laws. And this unnamed contemporary of Saul-Paul had been driven out of his own country for trans-

---

[36] Greek words translated "this Way" are *tauten ten Hodon,* "this *The* Way."
[37] Emphasis added.

gressing Jewish law – a "wicked man." He lived in Rome and claimed to be a teacher of the Laws of Moses. He partnered with three other men of equally questionable character. They persuaded a Jewess named Fulvia to send purple and gold to the Temple at Jerusalem but used the purple for their own benefit and spent the money on themselves. Fulvia's husband Saturnius complained to Tiberius; Tiberius ordered that all the Jews – four thousand in number – be banished from Rome. "Thus were these Jews banished out of the city by the wickedness of four men."[38]

"Wicked" is a term Josephus also applies to Eleazar, the descendant of Judas the Galilean, when he reveals the taxation issue was: "a pretense for barbarity… and when they were convicted of dishonesty … they abused those that reproached them for their wickedness."[39] Paul – or the final editor on his behalf – confesses to his own wickedness in his letter to the Romans:

> I do not understand my own actions. For I do not do what I want, but I do the very thing I hate. Now if I do what I do not want, I agree that the law is good. But in fact it is no longer I that do it, but sin that dwells within me. For I know that nothing good dwells within me, that is, in my flesh. I can will what is right, but I cannot do it. For I do not do the good I want, but the evil I do not want is what I do. Now if I do what I do not want, it is no longer I that do it, but sin that dwells within me.
>
> So I find it to be a law that when I want to do what is good, evil lies close at hand. For I delight in the law of God in my inmost self, but I see in my members another law at war with the law of my mind, making me captive to the law of sin that dwells in my members. Wretched man that I am! Who will rescue me from this body of death? Thanks be to God through Jesus Christ our Lord!
>
> So then, with my mind I am a slave to the law of God, but with my flesh I am a slave to the law of sin (Rom 7:15-25).

It might be argued that Paul's greatest success was convincing James the brother of Jesus that circumcision should be eliminated as a requirement for men who wanted to join his church.

---

[38] Josephus, 1999, *Antiquities* 18.3.5 (81), 591-2.
[39] Josephus, 1999, *Wars* 7.8.1 (258), 926.

And as soon as the decision is announced to the Council and the Elders, they chose men from among their members – perhaps even those who were not circumcised but now qualified – to take the news to the residents of Antioch, Syria, and Cilicia.[40] They sent four men: Paul also known as Saulus, Barnabas, Silas, and Judas called Barsabbas.

Four men: Saulus, Silas; Barnabas, Barsabbas. Enigmatically, the two "bars" plus "abbas" are sons of two eminent fathers. And the names Saulus and Silas may suggest a relationship – perhaps brothers. Josephus writes of two brothers, explaining that:

> ... many of the most eminent of the Jews swam away from the city, as from a ship when it was going to sink: Costobarus, therefore, and Saulus, who were brothers.[41]
>
> Costobarus also, and Saulus, got together a multitude of *wicked wretches* ... because *they were of the royal family*; and so they obtained favor among them, because of their *relationship*[42] to Agrippa; but still they used violence ... and were ready to plunder those that were weaker ... And from that time it ... came to pass that our city was greatly disordered ... and all things grew worse and worse among us.[43]

Josephus now ties Eleazar's *Sicarii* to the brothers, "Costobarus and Saulus," and he ties *them* to "the royal family" and to "Agrippa." Granted, "Costobarus and Saulus" is not "Silas and Saulus," but examining each part of the name *Costobarus*[44] reveals an important clue: *Costo* is Latin for "rib," and *bar* is Hebrew for "son of."

Therefore, *Costo-barus* can be interpreted as "son of the rib." And the best known *rib* in history was the genesis of women – Adam's rib, the mother of all mothers, Eve. The name indicates, philologically, that Costobarus and Saulus are half-brothers – same mother different fathers. But who is this "Brother-of-the Rib" in history? What was his name?

---

[40] Acts 15:1-22.

[41] Josephus, 1999, *Wars* 2.20.1 (556), 768.

[42] Older versions of Whiston's translation, "...kindred to Agrippa."

[43] Josephus, 1999, *Antiquities* 20.9.4 (214), 657. Emphasis added.

[44] Philo's Rules 9-10: the part of a word; explained in all its meanings.

CHAPTER NINE

Following Philo to Saul's Brother Costobarus

Luke's "Saulus known as Paulus" may be the same man as Josephus' Saulus whose brother was Costobarus. And if "Saulus known as Paulus" is to be positively identified as a member of the family of Lucius and Julia Paulus, this family – first introduced in Chapter Seven – must be re-examined for additional evidence.

As previously noted, Axe-man Paulus' great-grandson was Lucius Aemilius Lepidus Paulus; he married Julia Vipsania, Augustus Caesar's granddaughter. Paulus and Julia had a son, Lucius (and/or Marcus) Paulus, born in 6 CE.

Two years after giving birth to baby Paulus in 6, and while still married to his father, Julia became pregnant by another man. Augustus exiled her and her lover to separate locations. "He would not allow the child born to his granddaughter Julia after her sentence to be recognized or reared."[1] Nothing more was written about the birth or death of that child – or so it seemed.

However, about nine months after Julia Vipsania Paulus became pregnant by a man who was not her husband, a son was born to a woman who was the same age and carried a similar name: "Vespasia Pollia." Her son was Titus Flavius Vespasianus, a future Roman Emperor. Tucked within his biography are these tidbits of useful information: "There is moreover on the top of a mountain, near the sixth milestone on the road from Nursia to Spoletium, a place called 'Vespasiae,' where

---

[1] Suetonius, *The Life of Augustus* (Loeb, 1914), (Thayer Online 65.4).

many monuments of the Vespasii are to be seen, affording strong proof of the renown and antiquity of the house."[2]

A philologist searching for clues to a puzzle is now supposed to ask: Was one of the monuments on that mountainside a headstone for a newborn baby boy marking a tiny but empty grave?

According to Tacitus and Suetonius, Vespasian's father was Titus Flavius Sabinus, a name that can be tied to the Roman Poet Ovid. Coincidentally, Ovid was exiled at the very same time the pregnant Julia Vipsania Paulus was exiled for her dalliance with a Roman Senator, identified as Decimus Junius Silanus.

At *Amores* 2.18.27-34, Ovid writes that Sabinus responded to six of Ovid's *Heroides*, the collection of letters each written by a legendary woman to her absent male lover. These are the kinds of coincidences that demand investigation because they are exactly the kinds of clues "enigmatical modes of expression" employ.

Vespasia Pollia gave birth to Titus Flavius Vespasianus in 9 CE in the *Sabine* country. His biographers describe his family as relatively undistinguished and lacking in pedigree, yet he is the founder of the Flavian Dynasty which ruled the Roman Empire for a quarter century.[3] Anyone attempting to solve puzzles must ask: *How much sense does that make?*

Vespasian's father and his brother share the name "Sabinus" with Ovid's pen-pal who exchanged letters written in the person of a woman to her absent lover.

Furthermore, in one of Ovid's letters, dated c. 15, he writes, "… the one who told Ulysses to write back to Penelope while he was wandering over a hostile sea for two lustra, and who has abandoned his own Troezen and unfinished Dierum Opus with his sudden death. Sabinus."[4]

---

[2] Suetonius, *Life of Vespasian* (Loeb,1914), (Thayer Online 1.2-3).

[3] Suetonius, *Life of Vespasian* (Loeb, 1914).

[4] Ovid, *Ex Ponto*, 4.16.13–16.

Historians have used this sentence to conclude that Sabinus died c. 14. Coincidentally, Augustus Caesar died that same year, rendering the commonly accepted interpretation suspect. Clearly, the letters exchanged between Sabinus and Ovid were written in some sort of code. "The one who told Ulysses to write back to Penelope ... hostile sea ... two lustra" meant something to the author and recipient that others could not easily understand. They were apparently using Homer to relay enigmatic messages.

It is equally plausible that the author of the "unfinished Dierum Opus" who died in 14 was Augustus Caesar, not Sabinus, and that the letter was written *by* Sabinus, rather than *about* him. It must be considered a possibility that this letter reported enigmatically that Caesar was dead, and the letter was signed "Sabinus."

Suetonius supplies most of the biographical data about Vespasian that may answer the question: *Who was Saul's "brother of the rib?* In "Life of Vespasian" Suetonius writes:

> Vespasian was brought up under the care of his paternal grandmother Tertulla on her estates at Cosa.[5] Therefore, even after he became emperor he used constantly to visit the home of his infancy, where the manor house was kept in its original condition, since he did not wish to miss anything which he was wont to see there; and he was so devoted to his grandmother's memory that on religious and festival days he always drank from a little silver cup[6] that had belonged to her.[7]

Vespasian was raised by his father's mother, Tertulla, a nickname for the female cognomen "Tertia," which signifies *third daughter*. Two Tertias appear in the biography of Julius Caesar; one is Mucia Tertia, wife of Pompey the Great and one of Julius' many mistresses.

---

[5] Excavations (intermittent, 1948 to present) indicate an earthquake at Cosa c. 51 CE; by 80 Cosa was virtually deserted. Frank Brown; Lisa Fentress, Archaeologists.

[6] Two "little silver cups" dated to c. 40 BCE were excavated in 2000 near Pompeii. Buried by the eruption of Vesuvius in 79 just weeks after Vespasian's death, they depict Marc Antony, Augustus Caesar, and a young "Virgin of Isis" (see photographs, p. 351).

[7] Suetonius, *Life of Vespasian* (Loeb, 1914), (Thayer Online 2.2).

However, the most intriguing is Junia Tertia, the third daughter born to Servilia Caepionis, Julius' favorite mistress for more than twenty years.[8] Junia Tertia was born during that twenty-year intimate relationship. Furthermore, at the time of Junia's birth, Servilia was married to a man named Decimus Junius Silanus[9] – coincidentally the same name as Julia Paulus' lover and father of her illegitimate child.

Coincidences raise questions and questions help provide a working outline. And the concurrent exile of Julia and Ovid certainly raises questions. In Hebrew, *OVD* means "restorer," appropriate for a historian and a philologist. But was Ovid also known as "Silanus," the father of Julia's illegitimate child, hence their exile at the same time?

Julia Vipsania Paulus had one *legitimate* son, Lucius (and/or Marcus) Aemilius Paulus, born in 6 CE. Julia and Lucius' only other child was a daughter, Aemilia Lepida Paulus. She was betrothed to future Emperor Claudius but married Marcus *Junius Silanus* Torquatus – who was related to her mother's lover, Decimus *Junius Silanus* – coincidentally.

And unfortunately for historians, Aemilia's brother Lucius (or Marcus) was lost amidst the tangled web of "Marcus son of Marcus," "Lucius son of Lucius," and "Marcus son of Lucius." The result is that no one has gone in search of Aemilia Paulus' younger brother, Lucius Aemilius *Paulus* – or her assumed-dead, unnamed half-*brother-of-the-rib* – until now.

Josephus writes that "Costobarus also, and Saulus ... were of the royal family ... kindred to Agrippa."[10] The consensus conclusion among historians has been that "kindred to Agrippa" refers to Judean kings named "Agrippa."[11] King Agrippa I (c. 10 BCE-44 CE was a grandson of Herod the Great); King Agrippa II (c. 27-100 CE was the son of Agrippa I).

[8] Suetonius, *Life of Julius Caesar* (Loeb, 1914), (Thayer Online 50.2).
[9] Suetonius, *Life of Julius Caesar* (Loeb, 1914), (Thayer Online 50.2).
[10] Josephus, 1999, *Antiquities*, 20.9.4 (214), 657.
[11] For example, Robert Eisenman, *The New Testament Code*, 595.

However, although Josephus mentions King Agrippa previously in the paragraph, he does not state specifically that Costobarus and Saulus are kindred to *King* Agrippa. And a family far more royal than the Herodians is the family of the Caesars – biological family and family through marriage.

For instance, Augustus Caesar's son-in-law was Marcus Vipsanius Agrippa (c. 63-12 BCE). Agrippa was a virtual nobody who replaced Marc Antony[12] as Caesar's closest confidant after the Battle of Actium. His ancestry is curiously murky, but his wives and their issue are among the most royal of Rome's royal families.

Prior to marrying Augustus' daughter Julia the Elder, Agrippa was married to Caecilia Pomponia Attica with whom he had a daughter, Vipsania Agrippina, who became Emperor Tiberius' first wife. With Julia the Elder, Marcus Agrippa had five children: Gaius Caesar Agrippa; Julia the Younger; Lucius Caesar Agrippa; Agrippina the Elder (wife of Germanicus the Elder); Agrippa Postumus (a posthumous son).

His granddaughter Agrippina the Younger (Germanicus and Agrippina's daughter) married Emperor Claudius and was the mother of Emperor Nero. It gets no more "royal" than this royal family of Agrippa.

Therefore, it is plausible that by writing, "of the family" and "kindred to Agrippa," Josephus is referring to *Marcus Agrippa*, rather than one of the Herodian King Agrippas. And this leads to a striking revelation: Marcus Agrippa's two daughters were Agrippina the Elder and Julia Vipsania Paulus, mothers of sons born in 6 CE, Paulus the Younger and Germanicus the Younger. And Julia's illegitimate son born in 9 was Paulus the Younger's "brother of the rib." Marcus *Agrippa* is the grandfather of all three.

---

[12] Marc Antony's reported date of birth, January 14, 83 BCE, more likely refers to his father, another "Marcus Antonius." Evidence suggests that Antony was a contemporary of Marcus Agrippa, Marcus Lepidus, and Octavian, and therefore probably born c. 63 BCE.

Recall that Luke introduces Silas and Judas Barsabbas immediately after Paul and Barnabas convince James that uncircumcised men should be accepted as members.[13] It was "then [that] the apostles chose men from among their members to send to Antioch with Paul and Barnabas. They sent Judas called Barsabbas, and Silas, leaders among the brothers..." (Acts 15:22).

This scene in *Acts* can be dated to c. 51. Luke notes that Silas and Barsabbas are "leaders and brothers." New members identified as "leaders" raises questions because it seems unlikely. However, new members could have been "leaders," just not "leaders of the *Assembly*." Other "leaders" would be politicians or military commanders, and one in particular stands out: Vespasian.

When Claudius became Emperor in 41, his powerful freedman Narcissus[14] arranged for Vespasian to be appointed Legate of Legio II Augusta, in Germania.[15] And at about the same time, an inscription identifies Lucius Sergius Paulus and others as being in charge of maintaining the banks and channels of the Tiber River. It reads in part: "... L. Sergius Paullus ... curators of the river Tiberis ... Claudius Caesar.[16] (Claudius was Emperor of Rome from 41 until 54.)

Another inscription found in 1877 a short distance north of Paphos near the town of Soli also names the proconsul, Paulus:

> Apollonius to his father ... consecrated this enclosure and monument according to his family's wishes ... having filled the offices of clerk of the market, prefect, town-clerk, high priest, and having been in charge as manager of the records office. Erected on the 25th of the month Demarchexusius in the 13th year [of the reign of

---

[13] Acts 15:19-21.

[14] Paul–or the New Testament's final editor–addresses *Narcissus*: "Greet those in the Lord who belong to the family of Narcissus" (Rom 16:11).

[15] Suetonius, *Life of Vespasian* (Loeb, 1914), (Thayer Online 4.1

[16] Ben Witherington III, *The Acts of the Apostles: A Socio-Rhetorical Commentary*, 399-400. Witherington, 1998. Rome Inscription: GIL VI.3 1545.

Claudius – 54 CE]. He also altered the senate by means of assessors during the time of the proconsul Paulus.[17]

Under Claudius – from c. 43 until c. 51 – Vespasian, according to Suetonius, was

> sent in command of a legion to Germany, *through the influence of Narcissus*; from there he was transferred to Britain, where he fought thirty battles with the enemy. He reduced to subjection two powerful nations, more than twenty towns, and the island of Vectis, near Britain ... For this he received the triumphal regalia, and shortly after two priesthoods, besides the consulship, which he held for the last two months of the year. *The rest of the time up to his proconsulate he spent in rest and retirement, through fear of Agrippina*, who still had a strong influence over her son and hated any friend of Narcissus, even after the latter's death."[18]

It seems that the freedman Narcissus wielded enough power that he was able to get Vespasian promoted to the position of commander of a legion, two priesthoods, and the consulship. And this is a thread that can be tied to Josephus' Simon ben Gioras: "There was no crime which Simon the son of Gioras would not commit, and *he abused those very freemen who had set him up for a tyrant*." It is a strand to hold onto as we continue following Philo.

Then, c. 51 something happened between Vespasian and Agrippina the Younger, the powerful wife of Emperor Claudius and daughter of Germanicus the Elder. Suddenly, Vespasian's rapidly advancing career up the Roman political ladder came to a screeching halt. And curiously, he disappears from historians' accounts until c. 63. Where, oh where, might Vespasian have been *sojourning* from 51 until 63?

Let's stop for a moment to look at the evidence, circumstantial but compelling, and see what it might reveal:

"Kindred to Agrippa" and "royal family" could refer to Marcus Vipsanius Agrippa whose grandsons – Germanicus the Younger and Paulus the Younger – were born in 6 CE and

---

[17] Ben Witherington III, *The Acts of the Apostles: A Socio-Rhetorical Commentary*, 399-400. Witherington, 1998. *Inscriptiones Graecae ad res Romanas pertinentes* III.930.

[18] Suetonius, *Life of Vespasian*; (Loeb,914), (Thayer Online 4.1-5).

whose sons, grandsons, and great-grandsons became Emperors.

Paulus the Younger. had a half-brother, born in 9 to Julia Vipsania Paulus, a "brother-of-the-rib," Latin *Costo* + *bar*, Aramaic for "son of." Vespasian was also born in 9 to Vespasia Pollia and Sabinus. This couple, like Julia and Lucius Paulus, had a daughter and two younger sons[19] the same order and ages as the Paulus children.

The accumulated enigmas seem to be saying that Julia and Lucius Paulus' son was "Paulus also known as Saulus." They also say that Julia's *illegitimate* son with Silanus, born c. 9, was Josephus' "Costobarus," also known as Vespasian son of Sabinus. The freedman Narcissus "set him up for a tyrant"; however, Vespasian, "son of a *stranger*" (Hebrew, *giyur*, hence, *ben Gioras*) turned on the very people who helped establish his legitimacy.

The evidence suggests that Josephus', "Simon son of Gioras," Luke's, "Silas," Paul's, "Silvanus," and Suetonius', "Silanus" was the same man and also known as Emperor Vespasian. The Royal Family of Marcus Agrippa can claim yet another Emperor among their ranks, in spite of the fact that he was apparently illegitimate.

But more evidence is needed to solidify the case. And so, the search continues.

---

[19] Suetonius, *Life of Vespasian* (Loeb, 1914), (Thayer Online 5.2.

CHAPTER TEN

Following Philo to Paul's Brother of the Rib

Luke's "Silas" is a contraction of Paul's "Silvanus," and most scholars agree that the two names refer to the same man. Curiously, Luke in *Acts* refers to Silas thirty-six times, whereas Paul's Epistles refer to Silvanus just three times; in each case he is paired with Titus.[1]

When Silvanus disappears from Paul's account, a mysterious unnamed "brother" is introduced and also paired with Titus:

> With [Titus] we are sending *the brother* who is famous among all the churches for his proclaiming the good news... he has also been appointed by the churches (2 Cor 8:18-9).
>
> I urged Titus to go and sent *the brother* with him (2 Cor 12:18).[2]

Paul's omission of the name of the brother has drawn the attention of New Testament theologians:

> That the missing name is not just to be seen as a singular accident of text tradition but as a deliberate deletion is confirmed by the second mention of the ominous brother accompanying Titus. There, too, the name is missing.
>
> Consequently this would mean that the brother mentioned here with praise is no longer a friend of Paul's at the time he edited 2 Cor.[3]

The ancient historians' complete blackout regarding Vespasian's whereabouts between 51 and 63 match Luke's chronology of (1) accepting uncircumcised men into the Assembly c. 51 CE; (2) the concurrent introduction of Silas/Silvanus and Judas

---

[1] 2 Cor 1:19; 1 Thess 1:1; 2 Thess 1:1.

[2] Emphasis added.

[3] David Trobisch, *Paul's Letter Collection* (Bolivar: Quiet Waters Publications, 2001), 60.

Barsabbas; (3) the absence of Silvanus, replaced by an unnamed brother after 63.

Apparently, Silvanus was a "sojourner" who joined Paul but then left. Notably, "Silanus" is just one letter shy of "Silvanus," a common tactic for matching threads.

Once again circumstantial evidence supports our hypothesis: Lucius (or Marcus) Aemilius Paulus was the mysteriously disappearing son of Julia the Younger and Lucius Aemilius Paulus the Elder; Lucius Paulus' half-brother was "Costobarus," Saul's "Brother-of-the-Rib," also known as Emperor Vespasian.

The boys' elder sister was Aemilia Lepida [Paulus]; however, historians write of several Aemilias which creates a tangle in these threads that may have been intentional.

Three "Aemilias" are part of the puzzle we're attempting to solve: the first is Aemilia Lepida [Paulus]. Like her younger brother, the genealogy of "Aemilia Lepida," daughter of Lucius Paulus and Julia the Younger, becomes murky around the time of the Census of Quirinius. And her name, which should include "Paulus," does not. In other words, "Paulus" is omitted from the names of these siblings, Lucius and Julia, Emperor Augustus' great-grandchildren.

A second "Aemilia Lepida" was about the same age, but her father was *Marcus* Aemilius Lepidus, who served as consul in 6 CE, the year of the Census. It is almost certain that these two "Aemilia Lepidas" were the same woman and her "fathers" were the same man. This also explains the confusion surrounding her younger brother, Lucius and/or Marcus.

The third "Aemilia Lepida" was a generation older. Her father was also a "Marcus Aemilius Lepidus," differentiated from others by adding "Minor" to his name. Her mother's name is not known – a sign that she is hidden in enigmas.

Tacitus tells an intriguing story about this woman who was the wife of Quirinius, the man whose census dates the birth of Jesus:

In Rome, Aemilia Lepida, who beside the glory of being one of the Amilii was the great grand-daughter of Lucius [*Cornelius*] Sulla and Cneius Pompeius, was accused of pretending to be a mother by Publius Quirinius, a rich and childless man. Then, too, there were charges of adulteries, of poisonings, and of inquiries made through astrologers concerning the imperial house.[4]

On the days of the games which interrupted the trial, Aemilia went into the theatre with some ladies of rank, and as she appealed with piteous wailings to her ancestors and to that very Pompey, the public buildings and statues of whom stood there before their eyes, she roused such sympathy that people burst into tears and shouted without ceasing, savage curses on Quirinius, "to whose childless old-age and miserably obscure family, one once destined to be the wife of Lucius Caesar and the daughter-in-law of the Divine Augustus was being sacrificed."[5]

Tacitus chose this point in *Annals* to insert what *seems* to be unrelated information:[6] "It was some compensation for the misfortunes of great houses ... that Decimus Silanus was now restored to the Junian family."[7]

It is noteworthy, to say the least, that at the very time this "Aemilia Lepida" is condemned and exiled c. 20 CE, Tacitus reports that Julia the Younger's lover, Decimus Junius Silanus, is "restored to the Junian family." Equally noteworthy, Aemilia Lepida, daughter of Paulus, married Marcus Junius Silanus,[8] whose name identifies him as a son or nephew of her mother's lover.

Tacitus' "Aemilia daughter of Paulus" can be tied to Josephus' story of a woman he calls, "Paulina," whom he introduces with an enigma:

    ... another sad calamity put the Jews into disorder, and certain shameful practices happened about the *Temple of Isis* that was at Rome. I will now first take notice of the wicked attempt about the

---

[4] Tacitus, *Annals; The Works* (1864-1877), (Sacred Texts Online 3.22).
[5] Tacitus, *Annals; The Works* (1864-1877), (Sacred Texts Online 3.23).
[6] Philo's rules 17 and 18.
[7] Tacitus, Annals; The Works (1864-1877), (Sacred Texts Online 3.24).
[8] Simon Hornblower and Antony Spawforth, Oxford Classical Library (Second Edition, 1970), 21.

Temple of Isis, and will then give an account of the Jewish affairs...[9]

Josephus ties the twice-referenced "Jews" to the twice-referenced "Temple of Isis," suggesting this story is about both. The villain is a man previously introduced: Decius Mundus, who "took to himself the name of the god Anubis."

A quick synopsis: Decius Mundus lusted for Paulina; however, she was married and not in the least interested. Mundus offered her 250,000 drachmae for the pleasure of sharing her bed, but she rejected his offer. However, the deceiver's loyal freedwoman, Ide, found a way around Paulina's rejection; she gave the most trusted of the temple priests 50,000 drachmae to get Paulina to the temple before leaving for the night.

The priest went to Paulina's home and asked her husband Saturnius for permission to speak with her alone. He told Paulina he was sent by the god Anubis, who requested that she come to him. Paulina was flattered and informed Saturnius that the god Anubis had sent a messenger asking that she dine and then lie with him. Saturnius agreed that she should accept the offer and was "fully satisfied with the chastity of his wife."[10] Under cover of darkness, Mundus, whom Paulina believed to be Anubis, had sex with Saturnius' wife.

But, alas, Mundus could not keep the secret. On the third day after their night of lovemaking, Mundus met Paulina and boasted of what he had done, saying, "Nay, Paulina, you saved me two hundred thousand drachmae ... yet you did not fail to be at my service and do what I invited you to do. As for your reproaches, I do not value the business of names; but I rejoice in the pleasure I reaped by what I did, while I took to myself the name of Anubis."[11]

Paulina was mortified that she has been deceived into having sex in the Temple with a mere mortal. Saturnius complained to Tiberius who ordered the defiled Temple of Isis de-

---

[9] Josephus, 1999, *Antiquities*, 18.3.4 (65), 591.
[10] Josephus, 1999, *Antiquities*, 18.3.4 (73), 591.
[11] Josephus, 1999, *Antiquities* 18.3.4 (77), 591.

stroyed and the priest executed. Tacitus picks up, and adds to, this "executed priest" thread:

> Tiberius spoke on the subject of electing a *priest of Jupiter* in the room of Servius Malugenesis, *deceased*, and of the enactment of a new law. "It was," he said, "the old custom to nominate together *three patricians*, sons of parents wedded according to the primitive ceremony, and of these *one was to be chosen*. Now however there was not the same choice as formerly, the primitive form of marriage[12] having been given up or being observed only by a few persons." For this he assigned several reasons, the chief being men's and women's indifference; then, again, the ceremony itself had its difficulties, which were purposely avoided; and there was the objection that *the man who obtained this priesthood* was emancipated from *the father's* authority, as also was his wife, as passing into the husband's control.[13]

Josephus' account of Paulina's defilement has Emperor Tiberius ordering the execution of a priest; Tacitus' account of Tiberius' enactment of a new law has the position of a priest of Jupiter open, also due to the death of a priest.

The enigmatic phrase "emancipated from the Father's authority" that applies to both husband and wife might refer to the exemption from marital laws permitted of Vestal Virgins and their legitimate deity paramours. The Virgins have children with more than one consort, but they are not Temple Prostitutes having sex with mere mortals; they are Vestal Virgins bearing the children of gods. Unless, of course, the Virgin is deceived into believing she is serving a god, as Josephus reports of Paulina.

Reading between the lines in Tacitus story, it appears this may be what happened to Aemilia Lepida, and Tiberius set about to rectify it:

> So the Senate, Tiberius argued, ought to apply some *remedy by a decree of a law*, as Augustus had accommodated certain relics of a rude antiquity to the modern spirit. It was then decided, after a discussion of religious questions, that the institution of the priests

---

[12] Philo's rule no. 1: doubling of a phrase.

[13] Tacitus, *Annals*; *The Works* (1864-1877) (Sacred Texts Online 4.16). Emphasis added.

of Jupiter should remain unchanged. A law however was passed that the priestess, *in regard to her sacred functions*, was to be under the husband's control, but in other respects to retain the ordinary legal position of women. *Malugenesis, the son, was chosen successor to his father.* To raise the dignity of the priesthood and *to inspire the priests with more zeal in attending to the ceremonial, a gift of two million sesterces was decreed to the Vestal Cornelia*, chosen in the room of Scantia; and, whenever Augusta [Empress Livia Drusilla] entered the theatre, *she was to have a place in the seats of the Vestals.*[14]

Tacitus does not specify exactly what the "primitive form of marriage" required. But he leaves clues: it was ancient ("relic of rude antiquity"), the ceremony "presented difficulties," it "emancipated" both husband and wife from "the Father's authority," and it had something to do with the sacred functions the Priestess was required to perform. And clearly, Vestal Virgins could have husbands.

The Vestal Cornelia, recipient of two million sesterces, can be tied to the condemned Aemilia Lepida, descended from Lucius *Cornelius* Sulla. This generous gift suggests the "Virgin Cornelia" had been falsely accused and wrongly convicted, and was, therefore, awarded compensation.

Furthermore, one notable change was made to the ancient law: the priestess in regard to her sacred functions was to be under the *husband's* control. Never again would a temple priest be permitted to meet with the priestess alone to arrange the sacred function. Henceforth, the husband would handle the arrangements himself. It is probably safe to assume that no Vestal Virgin would ever again be at the mercy of a corrupt or bribable priest.

Josephus does not indicate that Paulina became pregnant as the result of her one-night stand with the mortal who "took to himself" the name of a god. But we've already met three women with similar names: Julia Vipsania Paulus, the mother of Lucius and his "Brother of the Rib"; her daughter, Aemilia Lepida [Paulus]; Vespasia Pollia, the mother of Emperor Vespasian.

---

[14] Tacitus, *Annals; The Works* (1864-1877), (Sacred Texts Online 4.16). Emphasis added.

Seating Empress Livia with the Vestal Virgins amidst these proceedings suggests that she, too, was somehow involved in the relationship that produced an illegitimate son. And to be honored as a "Vestal Virgin" may indicate that one of her sons was the baby's father.

If a Vestal Virgin could prove that the pregnancy and birth of a son – for which she had been condemned and exiled – was because the temple priest failed to protect her from a man claiming to be a deity, perhaps the law would be changed and that power given to the Virgin's husband.

The birth of Emperor Vespasian is dated to 9 CE while Julia was married to Lucius Aemilius Paulus. In that enigmatic story, of course, the exiled mother of Aemilia, Paulus, and their half-brother was Julia the Younger, and the *server* of the seed that resulted in her "malu-genesis" child (*Servius* Malu-genesis) was the senator Decimus Junius Silanus. His return *from* exile just as "Aemilia Lepida" is sent *into* exile ties the two stories together.

Also important to note is that "*Malugenesis*, the son, was chosen successor to his father" as Priest of Jupiter. And according to Suetonius, Vespasian was given "…two priesthoods, besides the consulship…"[15]

The multiple characters named Marcus, Lucius, and Aemilia over multiple generations makes it difficult to sort out the players. The fact that historians have been confused about the relationships between these people of the same name may explain the reason for them. It takes time to examine the stories about each person for clues to threads that can be tied together. This confusion protected the enigmatic stories from being destroyed by the adversaries.

With practice, the threads, although numerous, become easier to identify and re-assemble. One thing should be coming into focus: the Paulus Family holds the key to solving multiple mysteries. And the curtain that hides "Paulus also known as Saulus" is slowly coming apart.

---

[15] Suetonius, *Life of Vespasian;* (Loeb,1914), (Thayer Online 4.1-5).

CHAPTER ELEVEN

Following Philo to Paul's Teacher Gamaliel

Paul's encounter with Bar-Jesus – examined in Chapter Six – is concurrent with the term of Nasi Simeon ben Gamaliel, the great-grandson of Hillel the Elder.[1] Hillel was a first century BCE Jewish scholar and sage who – c. 40 BCE – became the highest authority among the Pharisees and scribes of Jerusalem. He was the founder of the "House of Hillel," a school for sages, and the progenitor of a dynasty of rabbinic sages that continued into the fifth century.[2]

Hillel is credited with laying the foundation for the development of the second-century Mishnah[3] and the Talmud.[4] Hillel's great-great-great grandson, Rabbi Judah the Nasi, generally referred to simply as, "Rabbi," is the Nasi who compiled the Mishnah.[5]

And so Josephus, by writing "Jesus the son of Gamaliel" and "Jesus the son of Damneus," ties the name "Jesus" to the family of Hillel, specifically his grandson Gamaliel. And Luke's "Magos Bar-Jesus," the man Paul *damned* to blindness (Acts 13:10), ties Bar-Jesus to Josephus' "Jesus the son of Damneus."

Luke writes that Paul was brought up in Jerusalem at the feet of Gamaliel and educated strictly according to "ancestral law being *zélótés* for Theos" (Acts 22:3). Note the terms, "ancestral law," not "Torah," which suggests that "God" refers to Elohim, not YHWH. This also indicates that Gamaliel may have been more than a teacher and that Paul lived with Gama-

---

[1] Josephus, 1999, *Vita*, 38 (190), 28.
[2] Jewish Encyclopedia: "Hillel," 1906.
[3] For definition of "Mishnah" see: Jewish Encyclopedia Online.
[4] For definition of "Talmud" see: Jewish Encyclopedia Online.
[5] Rambam Hilkhot Talmud Torah 4:8.

liel's family when he was a child. Therefore, it seems reasonable to question whether Gamaliel was Paul's foster father as well as his teacher.

Luke's "Gamaliel" is Hillel's grandson; he is also Josephus' "Gamaliel," whose son was Jesus the High Priest. Josephus reports that "Jesus son of Gamaliel became the successor of Jesus, the son of Damneus, in the high priesthood..."[6] And in the *next sentence*, he adds that "...Saulus ... gathered a multitude of wicked wretches ... from that time ... our city was greatly disordered, and ... all things grew worse and worse..."[7] This rebellion, of course, resulted in the destruction of the Temple in 70 CE.

The proximity of these two revelations suggests that "Saulus" became enraged when Gamaliel's son "Jesus" was named High Priest. Perhaps Saulus perceived that he had been double-crossed. This might explain why "Saulus also known as Paulus" damned Bar-Jesus to blindness at Paphos. But we need more evidence before he can be positively identified and convicted.

Paul's childhood – when he would have been sitting at Gamaliel's feet – coincides with the first Gamaliel – Hillel's grandson. And Hillel is associated with another Pharisee, a contemporary whose name was "Simeon ben Shatah."[8] Shatah's sister was the Hasmonean, Salome Alexandra, wife of Judean High Priest and King Aristobulus I.

After her husband's death, Salome married Aristobulus' brother, Alexander Jannaeus.[9] The brothers' great-grandfather was Matthias ben Johanan, the progenitor of the Hasmonean Dynasty.

A clever and revealing anecdote is told of Simeon ben Shatah (c. 110-40 BCE) that sheds light on one of his secrets:

---

[6] Josephus, 1999, 20.9.4 (213), 657.
[7] Josephus, 1999, 20.9.4 (214), 657.
[8] First name also *Shimon*, last name also ben *Shatach; Shetach; Shehar; Shechar.*
[9] Babylonian Talmud, *Gemara Brachot* 48a.

Simeon supported himself and his family by dealing in linen goods. One day some of his students gave him a gift of a donkey which they had purchased from a gentile merchant. Using the legal formula prescribed by the Talmud, they told the gentile merchant, "When we pay you, this donkey and everything on it is ours." When Simeon removed the saddle from the donkey he discovered a jewel worth a great deal of money. The students were overjoyed because the legal formula of the sale meant that the jewel was now their beloved teacher's. Simeon, however, replied that even though the letter of the law said they were right, it was clear that the seller had not intended to sell the jewel with the animal. Simeon returned the gem to the merchant, who exclaimed, "Praise be the God of Simeon ben Shatah!"[10]

In the Hebrew language, "Praise be the God" is written, *hallel*, *helel*, or *hillel*; the word "Halleluiah" is derived from *hallel*. Therefore, the Hebrew merchant's exclamation is, "Hillel Simeon ben Shatah!"

Philo's Philology suggests that the Pharisee Simeon ben Shatah – Salome Alexandra's brother – may have been identified enigmatically as another Pharisee of the same era: Hillel, grandfather of the Pharisee Gamaliel in *Acts*.

Hillel and Gamaliel were powerful and influential Jews before, during, and after the time of Jesus. Their story – and their relationship to the Hasmonean Dynasty that preceded them – comes primarily from the Talmud and Josephus.

From the Talmud we learn that Salome Alexandra's brother was Simeon ben Shatah.[11] From Josephus we learn that under Salome Alexandra's leadership, the Pharisees became a powerful force and helped establish many of the policies attributed to her.[12] Her brother, Simeon ben Shatah, was influential in re-establishing the Pharisaic interpretation of the Torah – more liberal and focused on the *Spirit* of the Law rather than the *Letter* of the Law promoted by the Sadducees.

---

[10] *Yerushalmi Bava Metzia* , ii. 8c; *Deuteronomy*, R. iii. 5.

[11] Epstein, *Berakhot*, 48a.

[12] Josephus, 1999, *Antiquities,* 13.16.1-2 (405-15), 451.

Hillel's son is Simeon ben Hillel, father of Gamaliel ben Simeon. Josephus reports that Gamaliel had a son named Jesus, and Damneus had a son named Jesus. And Luke identifies a Bar-Jesus at Paphos who is damned to blindness by an angry Saul who had just been identified as Paul. The questions to be answered are:

1. Is Josephus' "Jesus son of Damneus" the son of Luke's "damned Bar-Jesus" in *Acts?*
2. Is Josephus' "Jesus son of Gamaliel" Luke's "damned Bar-Jesus"?

If the answer to both is yes, then Bar-Jesus at Paphos was also known as "Simeon ben Gamaliel" and his father was Gamaliel the Elder, son of Simeon who was the son of Hillel.

Furthermore, Bar-Jesus' father is identified as Nasi Gamaliel, Paul's teacher and the "double-crosser." The fact that Hillel's son and great-grandson are named "Simeon" lends support to the donkey anecdote that enigmatically identifies Hillel as *"Simeon* ben Shatah."

According to Philip, "Ie-sous" is a unique name, and it hides a secret. Perhaps the name "Ie-sous" is reserved for the members of just one family – the family of Hillel. If so, and the evidence suggests it is, we need to know more about this family.

Hillel was a mysterious Jew from Babylon who changed the course of Jewish History and may have created the foundation for Philo's Philology. And since key clues for solving puzzles have been discovered in Hebrew Scripture, we turn there once again:

> After him Abdon son of *Hillel the Pirathonite* judged Israel. He had forty sons and thirty grandsons, who rode on seventy *donkeys;* he judged Israel eight years. Then Abdon son of *Hillel the Pirathonite*[13] died, and was buried at *Pirathon* in the land of *Ephraim,* in the hill country of the *Amalekites*[14] (Judg 12:13-15)[15].

---

[13] Philo's rule no. 1: doubling of a phrase.
[14] Amalekites: *eM eL Ki,* "Mother El Ki."
[15] Emphasis added.

The name of the thrice-referenced city of Pirathon is said to be derived from the Hebrew word, *PR, pera,* translated by the NASB as "leader and *long-haired.*" But another more fitting option is *pere,* translated, "wild donkey."

The donkey anecdote tied to Simeon ben Shatah and seventy donkeys tied to this earlier Hillel signal that we're on the right track. And remember, Gen 1:11 "adorned" the Ishenes of Ansar and Kisar in the cloak of "wild donkeys."

The stories – or legends – that surround Hillel the Elder report unique threads that tie him to Moses:

> ...the periods of Hillel's life are made parallel to those in the life of Moses. Both were 120 years old; at the age of forty Hillel went to Palestine; forty years he spent in study; and the last third of his life he passed as the spiritual head of Israel. Of this artificially constructed biographical sketch this much may be true, that Hillel went to Jerusalem in the prime of his manhood and attained a great age [*Sifre,* Deut. 357].[16]

In other words, the "constructed" biography of a Babylonian Jew, whose name means "Praise be to El," mirrors the life of Moses. Moreover, this mysterious Babylonian becomes the spiritual leader of Israel and passes this elite position on to his son, his grandson, his great grandson, and onward possibly into the fifth century.

What's more, if Hillel is also Simeon ben Shatah, as enigmas suggest, his sister married into the Hasmonean Dynasty. And since the mother of his son is unknown, Hillel may have also married a Hasmonean, an intriguing possibility that will be pursued momentarily.

Now turning to the name "Gamaliel," the first use in Hebrew Scripture is: "A man from each tribe shall be with you, each man the head of his ancestral house. These are the names of the men who shall assist you..." (Num 1:4-5). "... from Manasseh, Gamaliel son of Pedahzur..." (Num 1:10).

Following this thread to its origin, Manasseh is introduced in Genesis and his story goes something like this:

---

[16] Jewish Encyclopedia: "Hillel."

Manasseh's father was Rachel's son Joseph; his envious brothers sold Joseph to Midianite traders who delivered him to Pharaoh in Egypt where he was sold as a slave.

A series of events in Egypt put Joseph in prison, but his freedom and success came when he and he alone was able to accurately interpret Pharaoh's dreams.[17] Pharaoh rewarded Joseph by giving him a wife, the daughter of one of the Priests of the Temple of the Sun. And Pharaoh renamed Joseph, calling him "Zaphenath-Paneah."[18]

When Josephus repeats this account of Joseph's rise to power in Egypt, he changes his new name from "Zaphenath-Paneah" to "Psothom Phanech" and defines it as "the revealer of secrets." He goes on to say that Joseph's wife Asenath was "a virgin" and her father was "one of the priests of Heliopolis."[19] Josephus literally writes that a careful examination of the name "Psothom Phanech" will reveal secrets.

So, let's have a look. "Phanech" and "Paneah" are similar to the Greek verb *phainei*, defined as, "bring to light, cause to appear, in physical sense; make known, reveal, disclose; show."[20] Modern words "window *pane*" and "cello*phane*" share the same root; both can be *seen through*.

And so it seems that part of Joseph's Egyptian name was derived from the Greek, *phainei*, which evolved into *Pan-eah or Pan-YaH*. And the *secret* in his new name may be that he was also made a priest of "Beit Pan-Yah," the Temple of Pan and Yah, also known as the "Temple of the Sun."

Furthermore, this solution has supporting evidence. The word for "light" in Hebrew is *"Owr,"*[21] and Or-pheus was a mythological musician and poet. The suffix *pheus* can be associated with the Greek *phaios*, also defined as "light." And *phaios*

---

[17] Gen 41:37.
[18] Gen 41:45.
[19] Josephus, 1999, *Antiquities*, 2.6.1 (91), 86.
[20] Liddell Scott. *Phanes* is sometimes called light itself. A related word is *phanos*, defined as "light, bright, brightness").
[21] NAS (Strong's Hebrew 216).

is sometimes used as a metaphor for "deliverance, happiness, victory."[22]

The "Orphic Mysteries" became a popular philosophy among scholars during the Hellenistic era (323–31 BCE). But texts of poems and rituals can be dated as early as Herodotus, Euripides, and Plato in the fifth century BCE. An Orphic text, the Derveni papyrus, is Europe's oldest surviving manuscript, dated c. 340 BCE. This places it during the reign of Philip of Macedon, Alexander the Great's father.

The Derveni papyrus is a commentary on Orphic theogony. It tells of the arrival of the "First-born," *Protogonos*, who was also called "Phanes," "Zeus," and "Pan."[23] The name "Phanes" is translated as "the one who makes (or is) Manifest"[24] and pertains to his solar nature, as explained in this second century BCE Orphic poem: "You scattered the dark mist that lay before your eyes, and flapping your wings you whirled about, and throughout this world you brought pure light. For this I call you Phanes."[25]

According to Plato and the Orphic philosophers, "Pan" is translated as "The All." But the name remains associated with "Light" and represents a Hellenistic harmonizing of Orphic themes with Stoicism.[26]

While in Egypt, "Joseph had two sons bore to him by Asenath, daughter of Poti-*pera* the priest of On. Joseph named the firstborn Manasseh, 'For,' he said, 'Elohim has made me forget all my hardship and all my father's house'" (Gen 41:50-1).

Joseph's first-born son's name "Ma-nasseh" is defined as: "*Menashsheh* from *nashah*: causing to forget":[27] The Hebrew Bi-

---

[22] Middle Liddell.

[23] M.L. West, *The Orphic Poems*, Oxford University Press, 1983, 200. (N.V.) Kirk, Raven, & Schofield, *The Presocratic Philosophers* (Cambridge, 1983, 2nd edition), 30-31. (N.V.)

[24] Ibid.

[25] *Orphic Hymn 6*; translated Athanassakis (1977). (N.V.)

[26] West (1983), 205"). (N.V.)

[27] NAS (Strong's Hebrew 4519).

ble technique – matching the name with the reasoning for it – is demonstrated here, *M-nasseh* and *nashah*."

However, a similar Hebrew word is *nasa/nasah*, defined as "to lift."[28] This choice would render Gen 41:51, "Elohim has *lifted me above* all my hardships and all my father's house." *Em* is Hebrew for "mother," and joined to *nasah*, which means "lift up," *eMaNaSSeH* suggests Manasseh's mother was "from above." Therefore, they named him "Em-nassah." In the New Testament hypertexts, Joseph's son Jesus is called *Ha Nassah-rean*.

Moreover, something important to our search for Paul's teacher is written of Manasseh's descendants: "Next to him shall be the tribe of Manasseh. The *nasi* of the people of Manasseh shall be Gamaliel..." (Num 2:20-21).

Numbers 7:54 repeats the name and title, noting, "On the eighth day Gamaliel ... the *nasi* of the Manassites..."

Remarkably, the introduction of *Nazirites* at Num 6:1-2 is strategically placed *between nasi of Ma-nasseh* at Num 2:20-21 and *nasi of the Ma-nassites* at Num 7:54.

According to Philo, the juxtaposition of the verses implies a relationship.[29] And the phonetic similarity of "Nassarite" and "Ma-nassites" to "Nasi" – as in "Nasi Gamaliel" – cannot be dismissed as merely coincidental. Certainly not when a "Gamaliel" was "Nasi of the Ma-nassites," and a "Gamaliel" was "Nasi of Jerusalem" at the time of "Jesus the Nazarean."

"Nasi" at Num 7:54 is usually translated as "leader" but is also defined as "Prince." However, another ancient Hebrew word for "prince" is *sar*, and combining *Nasi* (leader) with *sar* (prince) results in *nasi-sar* or *nas-sar*, the possible etymology of "Nassarean." It would also be the Hebrew words for "Prince of Princes."

Moving our search to the Talmud leads to more critical information about Hillel and Gamaliel: "R'Levi says, a scroll of

---

[28] NAS (Strong's Hebrew 5375).

[29] Philo's rule no. 17: the position of the verses of a passage.

lineage was found in Jerusalem and Hillel was recorded as being descended from King David."[30] Accumulated enigmas suggest that Hillel was also known as "Simeon ben Shatah," which
identifies one of his parents as "Shatah."

The "morning star" is Venus, also known as "Ishtar" and
"Astar." According to the poet Vergil, the gens Julii, Julius
Caesar's clan, claimed to be descended from Ascanius/Iulus,
his father Aeneas, and ultimately Venus. Vergil replaces the
name "Ascanius" with that of "Julius," thereby linking the Julii
gens to earlier mythology and to the deities, Jupiter (Zeus), Ju-
no, Venus, and Mars.

In *Aeneid*, written between 29 and 19 BCE, Vergil honors the
deified Julius with this catchy little phrase: "Go forth with new
value, boy: thus is the path to the stars; A son of gods that will
have gods as sons."[31]

Vergil is referring to the offspring of Julius Caesar, who was,
indeed, deified: "After his death a statue of Julius Caesar was
placed in the temple of Quirinus with the inscription 'To the
Invincible God.' Quirinus, to the Roman people, was the deified likeness of the city's founder and first King, Romulus."[32]

What's more, Luke ties Jesus to Aeneas, and therefore to Julius Caesar: "...Aeneas Jesus Christ heals you;[33] get up and
make your bed! And immediately he got up" (Acts 9:34).[34]

The strands of evidence continue to imply that Hillel was also known as "Simeon ben Shatah," a descendant of long-haired
leaders and wild donkeys of the family of King David, Moses,
Ma-nassah, and Rachel. Joseph's father-in-law's name, Poti-

---

[30] Jerusalem Talmud, Ta'anit 4:2.
[31] Virgil, *Aeneid* (New York: Penguin Books, 2006), 287. Book IX, line 641, spoken by Apollo to Aeneas' young son Iulus.
[32] Cassius Dio, *Roman History* (Loeb, 1916), (Thayer Online 43.45.3).
[33] Philo's rules, no. 16: the artificial interpretation of a single expression; no 5: an entire-ly different meaning may be found by... disregarding the ordinarily accepted division of the sentence in question into phrases and clauses.
[34] Emphasis added.

pera, carries a word that can be tied to Hillel the Pirathonite: *pera* – "leader," "long-haired,"[35] and "wild donkey."[36]

The city of On in Genesis is located in the area of Cairo. "On" is a Coptic word that in Greek is "Heliopolis" and in Hebrew is "Shemesh." And another city called *Beit Shemesh* was located about 19 miles west of Jerusalem. *Beit Shemesh* is Hebrew for "house" or "temple of the sun." Therefore Manasseh's maternal grandfather is the priest of the Temple of Shemesh. And, the Canaanite sun goddess was known as *Shemesh*.

The *Beit Shemesh* located west of Jerusalem is allotted to the priests of the tribe of Levi (Josh 21:16). And notably, *Beit Shemesh* is featured at 1 Sam 6. Recall that Samuel was one of two nazirites Luke references that associates Jesus and John with "nazirites," which also associates them with Nassaraeans, Naas, Ophites, and the Serpent.

In fact, and notably, a *nachash* is employed by Moses: "So Moses made a *nachashnehoset* ["serpent of bronze"], and put it upon *hannês* ["a pole"]; and whenever a serpent bit someone, that person would look at the *nachashhannəḥōšeṯ* ["serpent of bronze"] and live" (Num 21:9).

It seems that something about this "serpent of bronze" attached to "a pole" turned it into a healing device. And it appears that Moses used it to "practice divination," suggesting that Moses revered the Serpent and the power it represented. However, *Judah's* King Hezekiah did not approve of this miraculous power to heal:

> [Hezekiah] did what was right in the sight of *YHWH,* just as his ancestor David had done. He removed *the high places* [*ha abbā mōwṯ*], broke down *the pillars* [*matstsebah*], and cut down the *sacred pole* [*ha aserah*].[37] He broke in pieces *the bronze serpent* [*nachash hannəḥōšeṯ*] that Moses had *made* [*aserah*], for until those days the peo-

---

[35] NAS (Strong's Hebrew 6546).

[36] NAS (Strong's Hebrew 6501).

[37] The "sacred pole" refers to poles that honored the Goddess Asherah.

ple of Israel had made offerings to it; it was called Nehushtan[38] (2 Kings 18:3-4).

In other words, the tools Moses used to heal the *Israelites* were rejected and destroyed by *Judah's* King Hezekiah – on behalf of YHWH. This supports our hypothesis that Moses was working on behalf of a different deity; not YHWH, but LHM. And this supposition requires a brief side trip into the Old Testament and one of its hypotexts.

But before we embark on a journey into ancient Sumerian and Babylonian myths, it's important to do so with the understanding that the authors probably believed the legends of their people were historical and factual. We are not suggesting that these ancient texts are completely factual, only that they were believed to be so by those who wrote them, those who heard of them, and those who preserved them; therefore, they must be examined with an open mind because myths always contain a kernel of truth at their core.

Another caveat: words evolve over time, erecting a barrier between what the author attempted to convey and what we interpret the words to mean. Therefore, we take seriously Philo's admonition to look at all possible interpretations, including interpretations of phonetically similar words.

And most important for grasping the authors' intended meaning is to look at *YHWH-LHM* as the Babylonians looked and *Enki-Ea* and *EnLiL/NinLiL*. These "Lords and Ladies from the sky" were described as physical beings whose parents were highly-evolved visitors from "a star," specifically, the planet Venus.

The original Sumerian texts, generally dated between 3000 and 2000 BCE,[39] were later adopted by the Babylonians. In the Sumerian-Babylonian creation story which predates Genesis,

---

[38] Nehushtan: *aN Ha iSh Ti aN*: "An the Ish Ti of An." *Ti* is the Sumerian word for "rib" and "to make live."

[39] Based on data prepared by the HEA-funded AMGG project; Nicole Brisch, "Mesopotamian history: the basics," Ancient Mesopotamian Gods and Goddesses, Oracc and the UK Higher Education Academy, 2013.

Ki-sar, which means "Earth-princess" and *An-sar,* "heaven-prince," were parents of *Enlil,* one of three supreme Mesopotamian "Lords" or "Princes." *En Lil* (also called *Ellil*) "had the power to appoint Kings, and his command could not be altered."[40]

Another important character in the Babylonian pantheon is *Nin-ti.* The Sumerian word for "rib" is *ti,* and *Nin-ti* is known as the "Lady of the Rib." But *ti* also means "to make live"; therefore, a play on the Sumerian words identifies *Nin-ti* as "Lady of the Rib who is the life giver."[41]

This explains the Hebrew name translated into English as "Eve"; it is *Chavvah* and defined as "life."[42] The Hebrew word translated as "rib" is *SSL,* traditionally rendered *tsela,* but more reasonably rendered *iShSha eL,* "women of El." Therefore, "Eve" was the "life-giving woman of El," the Hebrew version of the Sumerians' *Ninti.* Eve did not "come from Adam's rib"; Eve was the "giver of life to Adam."

When Assyria conquered Babylon (8th–7th centuries BCE), they adopted the Babylonian creation myths and deities. However, "Enlil" was given a new name to reflect the Assyrian nationality; he became "Ashur," written with the cuneiform signs AN.SHAR. As noted, *An-sar* means "heaven prince"; furthermore, AN.SHAR in the Akkadian language means "whole heaven."

"Ashur," as "Anshar," from "Ansar," became the chief Babylonian deity, replacing the god Marduk in the Assyrian version of the Babylonian creation myth. When Enlil was syncretized with Assur, his wife Ninlil became Assur's wife, identi-

---

[40] Based on data prepared by the HEA-funded AMGG project; Adam Stone, "Enlil/Ellil (god)," Ancient Mesopotamian Gods and Goddesses, Oracc and the UK Higher Education Academy, 2013.

[41] Samuel Noah Kramer, "Mythology of Sumer and Akkad," in *Mythologies of the Ancient World.* Ed. Samuel Noah Kramer. Garden City: Doubleday / Anchor, 1961. 103.

[42] NAS (Strong's Hebrew 2332).

fied with "Šeru'a Mullissu."[43] Ninlil is also identified with "Istar of Kis," "Istar of Arbela," and "Ishtar of Nineveh."[44]

Genesis 1:27 further explains the *Ish* and *Ishshah* were not the same genetically as the Adam males and females: "So eL Ha eM created aDaM, aB iSh eL eM, aB iSh eL eM, eL ha eM created them; zakar and neqebah..." (Gen 1:27). The author seems to say that Adam males (Hebrew, *zakar*) and females (Hebrew, *neqebah*) were hybrids but more closely related to "animals of earth" (*zakar* and *neqebah*) than to "Beings from a star" (*ish* and *ishshah*).

In the Babylonian version – the hypotext – Lord and Lady El, both from *Shatah* ("Venus" and/or "Star"), breathed "consciousness of self" into their son whose name was *SN*, traditionally rendered "Suen" or "Sin," but equally valid when rendered *iSh* (of) *An* and/or *Ishene*. They breathed "consciousness of self" into their daughter Isherah, also known as "Asherah," who was probably none other than Abraham's wife SaRaH, *iShaRaH*. Moreover, *aBRaHaM* was also known as "Father El," which in Hebrew is *aB eL*, and/or *BeL*, and/or *BaaL*.

The *Ishshah* and *Ishenes* of Kisar and Ansar remained in the Garden of DN, not "eDeN," but the Garden of *uD aN*, translated, "witness to An."[45] Perhaps they remained inside the perimeter to assure that their offspring remained pure-blooded Princes and Princesses of *Ish-zera-el*.

The Adam tribe, however, was sent outside An's Garden, and in the Babylonian version they were created to work in Enki-Ea's fields and mines. *Yah Ud*, translated, "witness to Yah," possibly evolved to become *Yah udah* and Yah's people "Iudeans."

It was important that the two tribes not interbreed except as determined by Ansar and Kisar, and these rules were passed

---

[43] *Šeru'a Mullissu* can also be rendered, *Sara eM eLeL iShShah*, "Princess mother of Elohim and Ishshah-women."
[44] Nicole Brisch, "Ninlil (Mulliltu, Mullissu, Mylitta) (goddess)"; *Ancient Mesopotamian Gods and Goddesses*, Oracc and the UK Higher Education Academy, 2013.
[45] NAS (Strong's Hebrew 5749b), "to bear witness."

on to YHWH and LHM. They can be identified in the infamous
Lev 18:22, used for two millennia to inflame hostility against
homosexuality; it is repeated at Lev 20:13. Therefore, according
to Philo's Rules, the words must be examined for an enigmatic
interpretation. Both verses contain YHWH's instructions to
Moses regarding the Israelites, *Elohim's* people. In fact, Leviticus from beginning to end is the story of YHWH attempting to
claim dominion over Elohim's Israelites.[46]

When the Hebrew letters are re-examined and valid alternative vowels and spaces chosen, a vastly different interpretation
comes into light. Leviticus 20:13 repeats 18:22 and adds the
penalty for violations. The Hebrew consonants that comprise
Lev 20:13 are:

WSSRYSKBTZKRMSKBSSHTWBHSSNHMMWTYMTDMHMBM

Adding alternative but valid vowels and breaks, these consonants create a stunning new directive to Moses *from YHWH*:

Hebrew: We aSheRa YiSKaB eT ZaKaR...
And Asherah [Ishsha of Or; Israelite tribe] (who) lies with a zakar
[Adam-male; Judean tribe...]

Hebrew: ...eM iSh KeBeS...
... (and becomes the) Mother (of) an ish [Israelite] lamb (kebes,
Strong's No. 3532) ...

Hebrew: ...SeH ToWB...
... lamb (seh, Strong's No. 2089) (is an) abomination...

Hebrew: ...Ha iShSha aN Ha eM MoWT...
...the woman (of) An [defiled virgin] the mother shall be put to
death...

Hebrew: ...YuMaTu aDaM...
...upon her death (her) adam-child ...

> Hebrew: ...Ha eM aB eM...
> ...(is to be cared for) by the mother and father (of the) mother (Virgin).

YHWH issued a warning to Moses: if sexual intercourse between one of the Israelites' "Asherah Virgins" and a male "Adam-Judean" (Hebrew *zakar*) produces a "lamb," the Virgin is to be "put to death" and her parents will be responsible for the "Adam-child." Evidence to come in later chapters suggests that "put to death" in these cases of "defiled Virgins" meant a "metamorphoses"; the Virgin was exiled from the Temple to give birth to her child and to become nothing more than a "mortal woman."

This harsh declaration and its implementation will be revisited in Chapter Twelve where Dionysius of Halicarnassus describes a similar penalty for Roman "Vestal Virgins." Dionysius provides the second source support that Lev 20:13 has nothing to do with homosexuality – then or now.

The authors of Babylonian and Hebrew Scripture seem to say that "Ea" – YHWH – was originally *given* dominion over the gardeners and miners of Earth, the Adam family that became Judeans. Lord and Lady El were parents of *Ishshah* and *Ish*, the "seed of An," and were given dominion over the Ish zera El's. A time came, however, when YHWH claimed dominion over both groups; Leviticus tells *that* story.

"The Way of El," represented by the name "Rachel," uses enigmas to tell how the "Great Mother" was buried under the "Watchtower of the Flock." BTLHM (*Bat El ha Em, Betulah Em,* and *Bethlehem*) was created to preserve the genesis of the Israelites. The *Ish zera el ites* were "from the seed" of Ishtar and Ab Or, also known as "Ansar," progenitors of the "Tribe of Manasseh," who were the *Em-An Ishshah*. History and scripture are filled with stories of the perpetual battles between these two factions.

The similarities between the Babylonian and Hebrew stories of the first tribes on Earth, YHWH's *zakar* and *neqebah* and Elohim's *ish* and *ishshah,* suggest a single source – an original "hypotext." And this brings us back to the Babylonian Exile and the final editing of Hebrew Scripture before Ezra and other Jewish scribes and sages took it back to the Judeans and the Israelites.

An unexamined coincidence that deserves investigation is that Pythagoras was also a Babylonian Captive alongside Israelites and Judeans. His biographer Iamblichus writes:

> In Egypt he frequented all the temples with the greatest diligence, and most studious research, during which time he won the esteem and admiration of all the priests and prophets with whom he associated. Having most solicitously familiarized himself with every detail, he did not, nevertheless, neglect any contemporary celebrity, whether sage renowned for *wisdom,* or peculiarly performed *mystery;* he did not fail to visit any place where he thought he might discover something worthwhile. That is how he visited all of the Egyptian priests, acquiring all the *wisdom* each possessed. He thus passed twenty-two years in the sanctuaries of temples, studying *astronomy* and *geometry,* and being initiated in no casual or superficial manner in all the mysteries of the Gods. At length, however, *he was taken captive by the soldiers of Cambyses, and carried off to Babylon.* Here he was overjoyed to associate with the Magi, who instructed him in their venerable *knowledge,* and in the most perfect worship of the Gods. Through their assistance, likewise, he studied and completed *arithmetic, music,* and all the other *sciences.* After twelve years, about the fifty-sixth year of his age, he returned to Samos.[47]

The "noteworthy omission" in this narration is that Pythagoras was a captive in Babylon from c. 525 to 520 BCE, *along with* the last remaining captive Jewish priests, scribes, and sages. Ezra did not return to Jerusalem from the Babylonian Exile with the Tanakh until "…the seventh year of King Artaxerxes" (Ezra 7:7). Artaxerxes I was king from 465 to 424 BCE, dating the return of the edited Tanakh to Jerusalem c. 458.

---

[47] Iamblichus, *Life of Pythagoras,* Kenneth Sylvan Guthrie, trans. (Chapter IV: "Studies in Egypt and Babylonia"), 9. Emphasis added.

If Pythagoras studied "all the mysteries of the Gods" looking for "the most perfect worship of the Gods," why would he not also interrogate the Jewish sages and examine their sacred texts?

Josephus answers what Iamblichus omitted, noting that Pythagoras "...took a great many of the laws of the Jews into his own philosophy."[48] Josephus confirms that Pythagoras was familiar with the Torah. However, the evidence points to a different conclusion. Rather than *borrowing from* the Torah, Pythagoras unified it with much of his own philosophy and inserted popular Babylonian myths *into* it.

Plutarch's introduction to "Isis and Osiris" can now be fully comprehended: "Pythagoras greatly admired the Egyptian priests, and, copying their symbolism and secret teachings, incorporated *his doctrines* in enigmas." "*His* doctrines," it appears, are the revised Hebrew Scriptures which Ezra carried from Babylon to Jerusalem.

And Pythagoras may have identified himself as well: the name "Pythagoras" is a compound of "Pythia" and "agora." Pythia was the priestess of Delphi and refers to the Greek myth of a Serpent, i.e., a python. A "Pythia in the agora" may be the inspiration for the "Serpent in the Garden," the serpent who encouraged Eve to eat from the "Tree of Gnosis," the same Serpent representing a *secret Gnosis* that Moses carried on a pole to heal the Israelites.

And so surely it is no coincidence that Hillel, the man whose name means "Praise El and El," is also a descendant of David, he precedes Jesus, and the rest of his name, Simeon ben Shatah, identifies him as an *Ish of Em of Light,* "son of the morning star." The relationship between Hillel-Shatah and Jesus cannot be discounted: Both claimed descent from David and Venus, an obvious attempt to tie Judaism and Greek philosophy together.

Additional evidence that Jesus was a descendant of Hillel-Shatah comes from the Babylonian Talmud. Shabbat 104b de-

[48] Josephus, 1999, *Against Apion*, 1.22 (165), 947.

scribes a well-documented and much discussed second century Jewish controversy that many scholars believe is a reference to Jesus the Nazarene. It would also pertain to Bar-Jesus:

> It was taught (that) R. Eliezer said to the Sages: "But did not ben Stada bring forth witchcraft from Egypt by means of scratches upon his flesh?" "He was a fool," answered they, "and proof cannot be adduced from fools."

"Scratches upon his flesh" is reminiscent of the festival for Kybele which began with a day of mourning for Attis that included the Galli flogging themselves until they bled. The climax of the ceremony was cutting the flesh and drawing blood from the High Priest who was called "Attis."

This ancient ritual that replaced human sacrifice would probably have been incorporated into the annual festivals for Osir-Apis and Herm-Anubis. It was definitely incorporated into the Passover-Passion Festival of 37 CE: Jesus is flogged in the opening scene, and the climactic ending comes when a spear brings "blood and water" from the flesh of Jesus.

In some uncensored editions and manuscripts of Shabbat 104b and Sanhedrin 67a, the debate continues over the identity of Stada, Pandira, and their son or sons:

> And this they did to Ben Stada in Lydda, and they hung him on the eve of Passover. Ben Stada was Ben Pandira. R. Hisda said: "The husband was Stada, the paramour Pandira. But was not the husband Pappos b. Judah? His mother's name was Stada. But his mother was Miriam, a dresser of woman's hair?[49][50].

Twelfth century Spanish Talmudist R. Meir Halevi Abulafia[51] explains that the Hebrew words, *nashaia megadla*, are translated, "women's hairdresser." Therefore, he concludes that *megadla* became "Magdalene" and she was a hairdresser.

[49] Rabbi Epstein, ed. *Soncino Babylonian Talmud: Tractate Sanhedrin*, "Folio 67a, footnote 12." J. Shachter, trans. 2012), n.p.

[50] Peter Schafer, *Jesus in the Talmud* (Princeton: Princeton University Press 2007), 18-19; 143.

[51] Rabbi Meir HaLevi Abulafia, "Tractates on Sanhedrin," (c. 1170; 1244), *Jewish Virtual Library, American-Israeli Cooperative Enterprise 2015.*

This interpretation of her name was accepted, repeated, and is still professed by some.

But a more logical solution to the Shabbat 104b/Sanhedrin 67a puzzle comes from Hebrew scripture. The Hebrew word *MGDL* is found at Mic 4:8: "And you, O MGDL DR, hill of daughter Zion, to you it shall come, the former dominion shall come, the sovereignty of daughter Jerusalem."

Coincidentally, this Hebrew Scripture prophecy comes immediately before the Bethlehem Prophecy (Mic 5:2-3). *MGDL DR* is usually translated as "watchtower of the flock." But Micah also identifies her as "Daughter Jerusalem."

Returning to Shabbat 104b, more questions are asked: "Was he then the son of Stada: surely he was the son of Pandira?"[52]

"Pandira" is a compound of PN and DR. Pan is the ancient deity popular throughout the Roman Empire. He was the god of shepherds and flocks, mountain wilderness, hunting and rustic music produced by the flute.[53] Therefore, *PaN eDeR* seems to identify Pandira as the deity, "Pan of the Flock," a fitting companion for MGDL DR, "Watchtower of the flock."

Plutarch tells a story of the death of Pan and notes that it was the only recorded *permanent* death of any god. In the process, he slips in critical clues to the identity of the Talmud's *Pandira*:

> So when he came opposite Palodes ... Thamus[54] from the stern ... said the words as he had heard them: "Great Pan is dead." Even before he had finished there was a great cry of lamentation ... the story was soon spread abroad in Rome, and Thamus was sent for by Tiberius Caesar. Tiberius became so convinced of the truth of the story that he caused an inquiry and investigation to be made about Pan; and the scholars, who were numerous at his court, conjectured that he was the son born of Hermes and Penelopê.[55]

---

[52] Epstein R. D., 2012, *Soncino Babylonian Talmud*: Sanhedrin 104b, footnote 19.
[53] Aaron Atsma, "Pan," *Theoi Greek Mythology*, 2000.
[54] A similar name *Thomas* is Hebrew for *twin*.
[55] Plutarch, *The Obsolescence of Oracles*, as published in Vol. V of the Loeb Classical Library edition, 1936, (Thayer Online 5.17.1.

Pan was one of the most popular deities in the Roman Empire. Plato portrays Pan as the personification of the entire cosmos, embodying the lower animal nature as well as the higher spiritual nature of humanity.[56] Therefore, the educated Emperor Tiberius would know all about the goat-footed Pan without ordering a scholarly investigation into his parentage.

And immediately after this striking yellow-flag statement, Plutarch writes "his court," clearly referring to the court of Tiberius. And by adding the phrase "conjectured that *he* was the son of Hermes and Penelope," who are Pan's parents, Plutarch – using Philo's Rules 8 and 12 – covertly identifies Tiberius as the personification of Pan.[57]

Finally, in the Hebrew language the name *Stada* can also be written *iShtah-da*, which can be tied to Simeon ben Shatah. Accumulated evidence continues to support our hypothesis that "Shatah" is another name assumed by the Babylonian Jew, Hillel.

The double question, "Was he then the son of Stada: surely he was the son of Pandira," can now be answered: Stada was Hillel-Shatah of Babylon; Pandira was his son. And according to Plutarch's anecdotal enigma, Pandira was also known as "Tiberius Julius Caesar."

It can be seen, therefore, that the information passed on in the *censored* portions of the Talmud is enigmatic and correct. Bar-Jesus was the son of Jesus; Jesus was the son of Pandira; Pandira was the son of Shetah, and Shetah was Hillel the Elder. And Bar-Jesus' mother is Mary Magdalene, not a "woman's hairdresser" but "Purifying Water," "Watchtower of the Flock," "Daughter Jerusalem," "Mother Light." She is a *Nasia*, the companion of the *Nasi* of Jerusalem and the fulfillment of Micah's Prophecy.

---

[56] Plato, *Cratylus.*
[57] Philo rule no. 8: a definite sense may be gathered from certain particles, adverbs, prepositions, etc...; Philo's rule no. 12: any peculiarity in a phrase justifies the assumption that some special meaning is intended...

Furthermore, the same can be said for The Virgin Mary before her – the mother of Jesus the Elder – whose father was Emperor Tiberius, also known as "Pandira." Both of the prophesied "Mayim MGDL" will return in subsequent chapters.

Collecting the threads pulled from Luke, Josephus, Hebrew Scripture, and the Talmud, we can see that:

1. The donkey anecdote associates Hillel with Simeon son of Shatah and suggests enigmatically that they are the same man.
2. Gen 1:11 reveals that the descendants of Ishtar, Father Light, Ansar and El the Mother are "adorned" as "donkeys."
3. Hillel's contemporary Julius Caesar claimed descent from the goddess Venus, also known as ISH-tar (*She-tah*).

And the curious statement that comes from Jesus – when translated into biblical Hebrew – ties it all together: "I am [Hebrew, *aNoKi*[58]] the NZR and ZR of David, *Helel Shahar*" (Rev 22:16). This means, of course, that in biblical Hebrew the "I am sayings," according to Essene interpretation, refer to our "First Parents," Ansar and Kisar. The Essene, says Josephus, "... swears ... that he will ... *preserve the names of the Angels.*"[59] And indeed, they have.

However, Hillel remains a mysterious Jew from Babylon with no genealogy other than a claim of descent from the House of David. So the search continues. And a closer look at Simeon ben Shatah's sister and her descendants leads to another possible identity for Hillel-Simeon ben Shatah.

We'll take these steps slowly because they can be mind-numbingly tedious. Be assured, however, they are of the utmost importance and must be followed carefully. Keep in mind it is the mystery of Hillel and Gamaliel that these puzzle pieces were created to solve:

---

[58] NAS (Strong's Hebrew 595), "I"; "my"; "myself."
[59] Josephus, 1999, *Wars*, 2.8.7 (142), 737-8.

1. Hillel-Shatah's sister Salome Alexandra was married to the Hasmonean High Priest Alexander Jannaeus;[60] their sons, Hyrcanus II and Aristobulus II, were Simeon ben Shatah's *nephews*.[61]

2. Hyrcanus II's son, Antigonus II Matthias, was Hillel-Shatah's *grandnephew*; Hyrcanus II's daughter Alexandra was Shatah's *grandniece*. Alexandra's daughter was Mariamme, Herod the Great's favorite wife; Alexandra was Herod's mother-in-law.[62] Mariamme, therefore, was Hillel-Shatah's *great-grandniece*.

3. Alexandra's grandson, Alexander III (Mariamme's eldest son) was the first of the *Virgin Glapyra's* three husbands.[63] And it is the widow Glapyra's marriage to King Juba of Libya that ties this Bloodline of Royal Jews to Egypt's Ptolemaic Dynasty: Juba's first wife and mother of his children was Cleopatra Selene, Cleopatra's daughter born while she was married to Antony.

But the knot that ties these bloodlines together gets pulled even tighter. Alexandra's husband Alexander Maccabeus, the eldest son of King of Judea Aristobulus II, is thought to be the father of Mariamme and her brother Aristobulus III. However, Josephus composed a puzzle that reveals a secret about Alexandra. And just prior to presenting the puzzle he inserted an enigmatic phrase that helps solve it: "'In Egypt, therefore, this nation is powerful, because the *Jews were originally Egyptians'* …And this is what Strabo says."[64]

Josephus, quoting Strabo, reveals that "the Jews were originally Egyptians." And it is the Jews' *language* that helps solve the puzzle that followed:

Ptolemy, the son of Menneus, [Hebrew, *MNS* same as *Manasseh*] who was the ruler [Hebrew, *nasi*] of Chalcis … [Ptolemy]… took his brothers with him, and sent his son Philippion to … Aristobulus' *wife*, and requested that she send back with him *her* son Antigonus and *her* daughters. Philippion fell in love with the one whose name was Alexandra *and married her*. Afterwards his father

[60] Epstein R. D., Berakhot, 48a.
[61] Josephus, 1999, *Antiquities*, 13.16.1 (407), 451.
[62] Josephus, 1999, *Antiquities* 15.2.5 (23), 493.
[63] Josephus, 1999, Antiquities 16.1.2 (11), 526.
[64] Josephus, 1999, *Antiquities* 14.7.2 (118), 463. Emphasis added.

Ptolemy [son of Menneus] killed him, and *married Alexandra,* and continued to take care of her brothers.[65]

Josephus implies that Antigonus and Alexandra's father was *not* Aristobulus; they were his wife's children. Therefore, Alexandra had *two* secrets: (1) her father is unknown, and (2) she was married two times before she married her cousin Alexander Maccabeus.

Alexandra's first husband was Philippion, her second was the Nasi Ptolemy son of Menneus. And his son was Lysanias, allegedly executed c. 34 BCE but curiously included in Luke's list of "rulers" at the time of John the Baptist.

Ptolemy's father's name suggests he was a descendant of Manasseh the Nasi, Abraham's great-great-grandson. Joseph married the Egyptian daughter of the priest of the Temple of Shemesh; Joseph's son Manasseh established the House of Manassites; the first Gamaliel was the Nasi of the Manassites – *Em An Ishites.* And Gamaliel brings us full circle back to the family of Hillel.

Like Nasi Ptolemy son of Menneus, Cleopatra's father was also a Ptolemy, descended from a Ptolemy who claimed Alexander the Great was his half-brother. Cleopatra's father's nickname was "Auletes," which means "pipes player." Apparently, like the god Pan, Ptolemy enjoyed playing the flute.

Recall that Plutarch's account of the death of Pan identifies Tiberius as the personification of Pan. Therefore, this nickname is a clue to the identity of Cleopatra's father and his relationship to Emperor Tiberius.

Ptolemy the Flute-player's full name, "Ptolemy Neos Dionysos Theos Philopator Theos Philadelphos," means "New Dionysus, God Beloved of his Father, God Beloved of his Brother." According to Plutarch, Marc Antony was a subsequent "New Dionysus."

Genealogists are uncertain about Ptolemy Auletes' genealogy. He may have been an illegitimate son of Ptolemy IX Soter

---

[65] Josephus, 1999, *Antiquities* 14.7.4 (126), 464. Emphasis added.

by an Egyptian woman. Or he may have been the son of Ptolemy IX by Cleopatra IV.[66] Perhaps this uncertainty has something to do with another nickname, "bastard." Conspicuously, Cleopatra's *mother* is unnamed and is unknown,[67] whereas, Mariamme's *father* is a mystery.[68]

However – thanks to Josephus – the Hasmonean Queen Alexandra (Mariamme's mother) is identified as a woman who was married for a time to a "Ptolemy," a contemporary of Cleopatra's father and Pompey. And if this "Nasi Ptolemy son of Menneus" was given the nicknames, "Auletes" and "Bastard," then Josephus' enigmatic story of Queen Alexandra serves as the double knot that ties Hasmoneans (the Simeonite-Israelites) to the Ptolemies (Egyptians). And the mystery of the identity of Cleopatra's mother is solved. She was the Hasmonean Alexandra, Mariamme's mother.

But something more significant is also uncovered. Mariamme's great-grandmother's brother is Simeon ben Shatah – also known as "Hillel," which means he is Mariamme's great-granduncle. And pulling at this thread unravels more genealogical mysteries.

First consider this: If Alexandra and Ptolemy Auletes were Mariamme's parents and also Cleopatra's parents, then Mariamme and Cleopatra are either sisters, or they are the same person. Cleopatra allegedly committed suicide c. 30 BCE; Herod allegedly executed Mariamme c. 29 BCE. These allegations will be examined in depth in Chapter Fourteen.

For the moment, as outrageous as it may seem, we will attempt to solve Josephus' "Alexandra-puzzle" by assuming that Mariamme and Cleopatra are threads to be spun together and tied to the same woman.

---

[66] Chris Bennett, *Tyndale House.*

[67] Chris Bennett, *Tyndale House:* Footnote #3: [Cleopatra's mother is not named in any of the classical sources.]

[68] Evidence to be explored in a later volume suggests that Pompey the Great was Julius Caesar's brother and Mariamme's father.

Josephus identifies Mariamme's husband, Herod the Great, as the son of a man he refers to as "Anti-pater,"[69] Greek for "not father." This could be an attempt to covertly reveal that Herod's father had another name.

The Ptolemy and Herodian women are infamous for marrying their uncles, frequently their mother's brother. Alexandra's brother is Antigonus II[70] and their father is Hyrcanus II. Therefore, the most likely solution to Anti-pater's real name is "Hyrcanus II." If so, Herod and Alexandra are siblings and Mariamme is Herod's niece. And the solution to the puzzle can be found by applying simple logic:

1. If Alexandra was Herod's sister and Alexandra's brother was Antigonus II, then Herod was also known as "Antigonus II."
2. Alexandra's daughter was Herod's wife Mariamme; Mariamme was also known as "Cleopatra"; Cleopatra was married to Marc Antony. Therefore, Antony was also known as "Antigonus II" and "Herod"; Antony was Mariamme-Cleopatra's uncle.

This means that Cleopatra produced children with her uncle Marcus Antonius as expected of Queens in the Hasmonean, Ptolemaic, and Herodian Dynasties.

Furthermore, Cleopatra's great-grandmother was another "Alexandra Salome" whose brother was Cleopatra's *great-granduncle*, Simeon ben Shatah, also known as "Hillel of the House of David." And the name of this "House" holds a clue to the uncle marriages common among Hasmoneans, Ptolemies, and Herodians: As we've already discovered, the name "David"[71] is, derived from *dod*,[72] translated as "beloved, lover, and, uncle."

Another word derived from *dod* is *dud*,[73] defined as "basket, pot, jar." This definition leads to yet another question: Did the

---

[69] Josephus, 1999, *Antiquities* 14.9.3 (167), 467.

[70] The name *Antigonus* also says he was not of the "seed" of Aristobulus: *anti* (against, opposite, instead of) or *ante* (before) + *gonus* ("seed, act of generation, race, family," related to *genos* "race, birth, descent").

[71] NAS (Strong's Hebrew 1732).

[72] NAS (Strong's Hebrew 1730).

[73] NAS (Strong's Hebrew 1731).

alabaster jar described in texts and depicted in ancient stone reliefs represent the *essence* or *seed* of the line of David? This question will be addressed in a later chapter. What can be derived from the etymology of *David* is that descendants of the House of David were *lovers* who were also *uncles*.

It's time to tie a few more threads together starting with the Pan-thread:

1. Abraham and Sarah's great-grandson Joseph, the Nazirite son of Rachel and Eloah, married an Egyptian woman and was given an Egyptian name: "Zaphenath-*Paneah*." Pan + YaH may be the inspiration for Ptolemy Soter's third century BCE, *Osiris + Apis* (Serapis), the second century BCE, *Hermes + Anubis* (Hermanubis), as well as the first century CE, *Yah + Zeus* (Iesous). God-synthesizing is clearly an established pattern among certain religious and government leaders of antiquity.

2. Joseph's step-father Jacob was renamed "Israel" (or *Ish zera El*); Joseph's mother was Rach-El, which means "The Way of El," "The Spirit of El," and "The Womb of El." The location of Rachel's tomb became the town called *Bat-el-ha-em*, translated "Daughter of El the Mother," the etymology behind *betulah-em*, which means "Virgin Mother."

3. Joseph married the *virgin* daughter of the Priest of the Temple of Shemesh; their firstborn was Manasseh, the progenitor of the Manassite Tribe. Gamaliel was the Nasi of the Manassites; Manassites are juxtaposed with Moses' Nazirites; Luke associates the Nazirites Samson and Samuel with Jesus and John.

4. Plato portrays "Pan" as the personification of the entire cosmos, embodying the lower animal nature (adam) as well as the higher spiritual nature (ish and ishshah) of humanity.[74]

5. Shabbat 104b associates Pandira (*PN DR*, "Pan of the Flocks") with Stada (*Shetada-Shatah*). Hillel-Shatah had at least one son, Simeon ben Hillel, father of Nasi Gamaliel. Simeon ben Hillel's

---

[74] Plato, *Cratylus.*

mother – Shatah-Hillel's wife – is not named, but she would be expected to come from the Hasmonean or Ptolemaic Dynasty.

6. Plutarch's account of the death of Pan (the flute-playing "Pan of the Flocks") identifies Emperor Tiberius Julius Caesar as "Pan." Therefore, Shatah-Hillel's son (Simeon ben Hillel) is also known as "Tiberius Julius Caesar."

7. Cleopatra also had a son; he was the same age as Simeon ben Hillel. Like her father, "Ptolemy XII the Flute-playing Bastard," Cleopatra's son was a Ptolemy (XV) nicknamed "Caesarion." Caesarion's father was Julius Caesar. (Ptolemy XIII was Cleopatra's step-brother; Ptolemy XIV was her half-brother).

8. Alexandra's daughter Mariamme was a Hasmonean Jew who is also known as "Cleopatra." Mariamme's great-granduncle is Simeon ben Shatah, also known as "Hillel," born c. 110-100 BCE. Therefore, Shatah is Cleopatra's great-granduncle.

9. "Helel ben Shatah" is Hebrew and is translated, "son of the bright morning star." Like Hillel, Julius Caesar was also born c. 110-100 BCE and claimed descent from Helel Shatah, also known as the planet and goddess Venus (Greek "Astar").

10. Hillel (also known as "Simeon son of Shatah") is Nasi Gamaliel ben Simeon's grandfather. Hillel was descended from the House of David, Julius Caesar was descended from Venus, and according to Rev 22:16 Jesus was descended from the House of David *and* Venus.

Of course these hypotheses present major problems. Plutarch's literal account of Julius Caesar's assassination is the first. So too is his claim that Octavian ordered the execution of Caesarion shortly after the Battle of Actium. These "facts" have never been questioned by historians because Plutarch's admonition regarding "stories about gods" has never been considered important to reading and understanding the history of Rome.

And so, even though multiple enigmas from several sources identify Julius Caesar as "Hillel," his son Caesarion as "Simeon ben Hillel" (also known as "Emperor Tiberius"), and his grandson as "Nasi Gamaliel ben Simeon" at whose feet Paul sat to be educated in "The Way of the Nasoraeans," two thousand years of scholarship says Julius was assassinated in 44 BCE and

Caesarion was executed fifteen years later. This presents a substantial hurdle.

Another problem is Plutarch's literal account of Antony's and Cleopatra's suicides after the Battle of Actium. The enigmas identify them as "Herod the Great" and "Mariamme," but historians – trained literalists – are required to resist embracing philological solutions as "historical accounts."

We can't deny that all these hypotheses seem unlikely. In fact, they seem outrageous and impossible. But... what was that admonition Plutarch addressed to Clea in "Isis and Osiris," his most popular myth? Clea, a shortened Cleapatra?

"Whenever you hear the traditional tales which the Egyptians tell *about the gods*, you must not think that *any of these tales* actually happened in the manner in which they are related."[75]

Julius Caesar's consort was Cleopatra, and according to Plutarch, she was also known as "The New Isis" – a goddess. Cleopatra had at least one other lover, Marc Antony, and according to Plutarch he was also known as "The New Dionysus." Therefore, the "New Isis" had lovers who were gods: Julius a descendant of Venus and Marcus the "New Dionysus" – all according to Plutarch.

Suetonius is our primary source for Julius Caesar's divinity:

> He died in the fifty-sixth year of his age, and was numbered among the gods, not only by a formal decree, but also in the conviction of the common people. For at the first of the games which *his heir Augustus* gave in honor of his apotheosis, a comet shone for seven successive days, rising about the eleventh hour, and was believed to be the soul of Caesar, who had been taken to heaven; and this is why *a star is set upon the crown of his head in his statue.*[76]

Is the "Star of Caesar" derived from the "Star of Kisar" and the genesis of the "Star of Betula Em" in the nativity of Jesus? "The Star" is the ancestral home of Ishtar and aNSaR, "Lord of Heaven." Their descendants, beginning with Kisar "Lady of Earth," are the Nasi-Sar, "Princes and Princesses."

---

[75] Plutarch, *Moralia*: "Isis and Osiris," 1st-2nd Century.
[76] Suetonius, *Life of Julius Caesar* (Loeb, 1914), (Thayer Online 88.1). Emphasis added.

Perhaps the similarities between the words "Kisar" and "Caesar" are not coincidental. Pliny the Elder attributes the cognomen "Caesar" to *caesum*, which means "cut out," because the first Caesar was cut from his mother's womb.[77] This may be tied to Gen 6:4, the story of the Nephilim, translated "giants," and described as "sons of "Elohim."

Ancient texts – Sumerian, Babylonian, and the Hebrew Bible – all agree that these "Beings" impregnated the daughters of the Adam-men and the offspring were *ha gibborim*, translated "mighty" and/or "strong."[78] The root, GB can also be rendered *GuB*, translated "plowman."[79] *Ha GuB BaR eM*, therefore, seems to identify the "plowman sons" born to the "sons of El the Mother" and the "daughters of the Adam Family."

Furthermore, these offspring were described as being quite large: "We saw the Nephilim there (*the descendants of Anak[80] come from the Nephilim*). We seemed like grasshoppers in our own eyes, and we looked the same to them" (Num 13:33).[81] "… a strong and tall people, the offspring of the Anakim… 'Who can stand up to the Anakim?'" (Deut 9:2).

The "descendants of Anak [*An* and *Ki*]," one tribe called "aN aph El Em" and another called "An ha Ki Em," were big and strong and probably delivered by Caesar-ian[82] section.

Julius' praenomen is equally intriguing. Gaius, Caius, and/or Kaius also associates this name with "Kisar" and leads to the Greek word *gaîa*, "earth" and *Gaia*, "Great Earth Mother." Pliny's enigmas suggest that "Gaius Caesar" and "Gaia Kisar" are to be tied to one another. They are, after all, exactly the same words.

But we still have an immense hurdle: the two-thousand-year-old historical accounts of the assassination of Julius Caesar and the suicides of Antony and Cleopatra.

---

[77] Healy (1991, 2004), *Natural History* 7.7.
[78] NAS (Strong's Hebrew 1368).
[79] NAS (Strong's Hebrew 1461).
[80] Equally valid is *An-Ki.*; the Sumerian texts refer to them as the *Annunaki*.
[81] Emphasis added.
[82] Equally valid is *Kisar ian*.

And so we return to an earlier question: Did Plutarch really suggest that his stories about Julius Caesar, Antony and Cleopatra did *not* actually happen in the manner in which he related them? That Julius was *not* assassinated on the Ides of March? That Antony and Cleopatra did *not* commit suicide after the Battle of Actium? That their assumed-dead children all survived into the first century and had children of their own? That Cleopatra may *not* have been a vicious killer of her brothers and sister Arsinoe? That Herod did *not* execute Mariamme's brother Aristobulus or his own sons Alexander and Aristobulus? That Octavian did *not* execute Caesarion and Antyllus?

How would one ever know?

Fortunately there is a way. In Chapter Fourteen we will re-examine Plutarch's accounts of Caesar's assassination, the Battle of Actium, and Antony and Cleopatra's suicides. We will test Philo's Philology for solving enigmas to answer these questions: Did Plutarch also use Philo's method, and if so, do his accounts support or dismantle our most controversial hypotheses:

Julius Caesar lived on after 44 BCE and emerged as "Hillel," and "Simeon ben Shetah," the most influential Jews since Moses;

Antony and Cleopatra lived on after their alleged suicides, first as "Herod and Mariamme" and later as other prominent historical figures;

Julius Caesar, as "Hillel the Elder," was the father of Simeon ben Hillel – born "Ptolemy," nicknamed, "Caesarion." Ptolemy Caesarion was also known as "Emperor Tiberius Julius Caesar," "Simeon ben Hillel," "Pandira," and the "Simeon" Jesus renamed "Peter," the enigmatic label that identifies one "Simon Peter" as "Jesus'" biological father, a Simeonite and a first-born Ptolemy. "Simon" and "Peter" also describe "Jesus'" elder brother and his elder brother's eldest son. They are identified in the Jesus Myth as "Judas the Galilean"; "James the Just"; "Ananias"; "Ananus"; "John the Baptist"; "Simon Peter II," and others.

Julius Caesar was the grandfather of Nasi Rabban Gamaliel ben Simeon (born c. 13-15 BCE) who was called "YaH-Zeus" in the "First Annual Passover-Passion Festival" in 37 when "Bar Jesus" was released and Jesus was crucified. And Julius Caesar was the great-grandfather of Nasi Rabban ben Gamaliel (b. 6 CE), "Bar YaH-Zeus" who was damned by Saul-Paul at Paphos.

Our quest for answers has raised several new questions. However, the chapter question, "Who was Paul's teacher Gamaliel," can now be answered: He was Nasi Gamaliel, son of Simeon and grandson of Hillel. Strong circumstantial evidence suggests he was also known as "Drusus Germanicus," Emperor Tiberius' biological son, Julius Caesar and Cleopatra's grandson.

However, before the search for answers to these new questions can commence, some additional threads must be gathered. We need to know more about the women in the life of Jesus. Who was "The Virgin Mary"? Who was "Mary The Magdalene"?

CHAPTER TWELVE

Following Philo to The Virgins

Part I

Mothers Mary

In the Roman Empire at the time of Jesus and Bar-Jesus, an ancient religion honored Virgins of Vesta, the goddess of a perpetual fire. Obscure verses in Leviticus seem to embrace the same doctrine, commanding: "The fire on the altar shall be kept burning; it shall not go out…" (Lev 6:12). "A perpetual fire shall be kept burning on the altar; it shall not go out" (Lev 6:13). This duplicated phrase says, "Hello enigma!"

The conclusion of Lev 6:12 is strategically placed between the duplicated phrases just quoted. It is traditionally interpreted and translated, "Every morning the priest shall add wood to it, lay out the burnt offering on it, and turn into smoke the fat pieces of the offerings of well-being."

However, looking at each Hebrew word, in the original order, and comparing Orthodox and Essene options, reveals what the "perpetual fire" meant to the Essenes:

Hebrew consonants, BR:

> Orthodox: *uBieR*, "and shall burn"
> Essene: *BaR*, "son of" and/or *aB oR* "Father Light."

Hebrew consonants, LH:

> Orthodox: *aLeHa*, "on"
> Essene: *eLoaH*, "El"

Hebrew consonants, *HKKHN*:

> Orthodox: *HaKKoHeN*, "the priest"
> Essene: *Ha Ka Ki Ha aN*, "The Ka[1] of Ki(sar) and An(sar)."

Hebrew consonants, SM:

> Orthodox: *eSiM*, "wood"
> Essene: *iSh eM*, "Ishene Mother."

Hebrew consonants, BBBQR:

> Orthodox: *BaBBoQeR*, "on it every"
> Essene: *aBBa BaQaR*,[2] "Abba seek"

Hebrew consonants, BBBQR:

> Orthodox: *BaBBoQeR*, "morning"
> Essene: *aBBa aB Ka oR*, "Abba, Father of Ka Light"

Hebrew consonants, WRKLH:

> Orthodox: *we aRaK aLeHa*, "and lay in order on"
> Essene: *we oRaKeL Hu*, "and Rachel herself"
> and/or *owR Ki eL Hu*, "Light of Ki of El Herself."

Hebrew consonants, HLH:

> Orthodox: *Ha oLaH*, "the burnt offering"
> Essene: *Ha eLoaH*, "The El Himself"

Hebrew consonants, WHQTR:

> Orthodox: We HiQTiR
> Essene: WeHa Ki Ti owR "and the Ki(sar) (Nin)Ti Light"

---

[1] In Egypt "Ka" was *conscience*, that which leads to acts of kindness, honor, and compassion; it was the giver of all good gifts, especially *eternal life*. "Ka: the Gods the Myths the Symbols the Land of Resources," 2014, n.p.

[2] NASB usage: care (1), concerned (1), inquire (1), make inquiry (1), meditate (1), seek (2).

Hebrew consonants, LH:

Orthodox: *aLeHa*, "thereon"
Essene: *eLoaH*, "El"

Hebrew consonants, HLB:

Orthodox: *HeLBe*, "fat"
Essene: *Ha El aB*, "The El Father"

Hebrew consonants, HSSLMM:

Orthodox: *Ha SSheLaMiM*, "of the peace offering"
Essene: *Ha Ishsha aLaM eM*, "the Ishshene secret Mother"

The Essene interpretation and translation says:

> "Son of El, Father Light, the Ka of Kisar and Ansar, Mother and Father of humankind. Seek *Abba Father* and Ki of Light, the Spirit of Rachel, the El Himself and the Ka, Life-force Light. El Himself, the El Father, the Ishshene secret Mother."

Mark 14:36 lends support to the Essene version: "He said, "Abba, Father, for you all things are possible…"

And, according to Josephus, the Essene "… will equally preserve the books belonging to their sect, and *the names of the Angels* [translator's added note "or messengers"].[3]

The Essenes' interpretation uses the perpetual fire to preserve the names of the messengers – the Beings that came from above: El, Abba Father, Ki and An, aBeL (or *BaaL*) and Rachel. The "fire" also represents "The Ka Light," something the Ishshenes had that man of Earth lacked. It is "An's Esh," the essence of Ansar. The Hebrew word is, *NPHS, nephesh*, defined as, "a soul, living being, life, self, person, desire, passion, appetite, emotion"[4] But the fire also represents the bloodline, and it was carried by the Virgins, the daughters of El the Mother.

Rachel's grandson was Manasseh; one option for the etymology is *nasa; nasah*, meaning, "to lift."[5] This choice renders Joseph's words at Gen 41:51, "Elohim has *lifted me above* all my hardships and all my father's house." And this option is supported by Jacob's blessing and prophecy for Joseph at Gen

---

[3] Josephus, 1999, *Wars*, 2.8.7 (142), 737-8.
[4] NAS (Strong's Hebrew 5315).
[5] NAS (Strong's Hebrew 5375).

49:22-26. Included in the blessing is a name and its etymology: "...by the SaDDaY who will bless you ... with ... blessings of the SaDaYim ["breasts"] and of the RaHaM ["womb"].[6]

"The SaDDaY" is translated, "the Almighty." However, attaching it to "the SaDaYim" reveals its actual meaning: "The One with Breasts." And the first appearance of The One with Breasts is Gen 17:1 when she speaks to Abram and renames him "Abraham." And it is important to note this overlooked but critical detail: YHWH's covenant was *not* with Abraham but with Abram:

> "On that day YHWH made a covenant with Abram, saying, 'To your descendants I give this land, from the river of Egypt to the great river, the river Euphrates ...'" (Gen 15:18).

However, Shadday's covenant isn't binding until *Ab ram* ("father exalted") becomes *Ab RaHaM* ("Father (of) Womb"):

> I am El Shadday;[7] walk before me, and be blameless. And I will make my covenant between me and you, and will make you exceedingly numerous. Then Abram fell on his face; LHM said to him [Hebrew, LMR[8]] 'As for me, this is my covenant with you: You shall be the ancestor of a multitude of nations. No longer shall your name be Abram, but your name shall be Abraham; for I have made you the ancestor of a multitude of nations. I will make you exceedingly fruitful; and I will make nations of you, and kings [malak] shall come from you. I will establish my covenant between me and you, and your offspring [ZeRa] after you throughout their generations, for an everlasting covenant, to be LHM [LK LLHM[9]] to you and to your offspring [zera] after you. And I will give to you, and to your offspring [zera] after you, the land where you are now an alien, all the land of Canaan for a perpetual holding; and I will be their God [LHM LLHM[10]]" (Gen 17:1-8).[11]

This Covenant is between El Shadday and Ab-raham; furthermore, El Shadday tells Ab-raham that SHE will also be

---

[6] Gen 49:25, excerpted for clarity.
[7] Traditionally translated, "I am God the Almighty."
[8] *LHM LMR*: equally valid is *eL Ha eM, eL eM oR*: "El the Mother, El Mother Light."
[9] Equally valid is *eL Ki eL Ha eM*: "Goddess Kisar, El the Mother."
[10] Equally valid is *eL Ha eM eL eLoHiM*, "God, the Mother El, Gods.
[11] Authors' translation; Hebrew insertions; emphasis added.

known to him and his offspring as LHM, "El the Mother," LLHM, "Praise be the Mother."

Eventually, the Lady of Breasts and Womb addresses the problem of Sarai's barrenness:

"LHM said to Abraham, 'As for Sarai your wife, you shall not call her Sarai but Sarah shall be her name. I will *bless*[12] her, and moreover, I will give you a son by her. I will *bless* her, and she shall give rise to nations; kings [*melek*] of peoples shall come from her" (Gen 17:15-16).[13]

Sarai blamed YHWH for her barrenness;[14] furthermore, she remained barren until El Shadday renamed her "Sarah" and Abram, "Abraham." Not only did El Shadday *bless* them with a son, She also gave them and their descendants the land of Canaan – *Ki aNNan*.

Ezra helps [Hebrew, ZR ZR] solve these enigmas with his naming methodology:

1. "Rachel," from racham and El, represents the Virgins of Shadday, Lady of Shaddayim ("breasts") and Racham ("womb").
2. El Shadday is also called *LHM* (eL Ha eM), "El the Mother" and *LMR* (eL eM oR), "El Mother Light."
3. Ab-RaHaM and Sarah's descendants via their son Isaac (*Isha Ki*) are sons and daughters of *Ki-SaR*, "Princess of Earth."

El Shadday Racham is the Israelite's version of *Anahita*, Mithra's Virgin of fertility and water. Anahita was responsible for "purifying the seed of men, purifying the wombs of women, and encouraging the flow of milk for newborns."[15] Anahita and her duties are explained in the fourth century BCE Zoroastrian Holy Book, *Avesta*, specifically, Yashts 5, also known as the *Aban Yasht*.)[16]

---

[12] The repeated word, *BRK*, can be rendered *BaRaK*, "blessed," and *BaR Ki*, "son of Kisar." Therefore, those who are "blessed" are "Sons and Daughters of Kisar."
[13] Emphasis added
[14] Gen 16:2.
[15] Joseph H. Peterson, digital edition (1995): Avesta: Khorda Avesta; translated by James Darmesteter (from *Sacred Books of the East*, American Edition, 1898). Aban Yasht 5.1: "Hymn to the Waters." Yashts 5.1.
[16] Peterson (1995), Avesta: Aban Yashts 5.2.

Abraham and Sarah's son Isaac passed El Shadday's blessing on to his son Jacob:

> Then Isaac called Jacob and *blessed* him, and charged him, "You shall not marry one of the Canaanite women. Go at once to Paddan-aram to the house of *Bethuel*,[17] your mother's father; and take as wife from there one of the daughters of *Laban*,[18] your mother's brother. May *El Shadday bless* you and make you *fruitful* and numerous, that you may become a company of peoples" (Gen 28:1-3).[19]

Additionally, it was El Shadday who renamed Jacob, "Israel," and who blessed him with the Covenant of Abraham and Isaac (Gen 35:11-15).

When Jacob arrived at Bethel's house, he did even better than Isaac hoped; he married *two* of Laban's daughters. The eldest was Leah, a wife he neither wanted nor loved, and Rachel, the wife he loved and desperately wanted (Gen 29:1-30).

The House of Jacob's first four sons were conceived when, "YHWH saw that Leah was unloved, he opened her womb ... Leah *conceived* and *bore a son* ... Reuben ... She *conceived* again and *bore a son* ... Simeon ... she *conceived* and *bore a son* ... Levi ... She *conceived* again and *bore a son* ... Judah" (excerpts from Gen 29:31-35).

None of the first four sons were "conceived with" or "bore *to* Jacob." They were "conceived" when YHWH opened Leah's womb. Nevertheless, they were "of the house of Jacob."

Jacob's first two *biological* sons were born when Rachel offered him the handmaid Laban had given to her: "Jacob *went into* her and "Bilhah *conceived* and *bore Jacob* a son" (Gen 30:4); "Rachel's maid Bilhah conceived again and *bore Jacob* a *second* son" (Gen 30:7). Bilhah's sons were Dan and Naphtali.

In addition, Zilpah, the handmaid Laban gave to Rachel's sister Leah, also "bore Jacob" two sons (Gen 30:10-12). Zilpah's sons were Gad and Asher.

---

[17] BeThueL: *BeTuLa*, "Virgin," and/or *BaT eL*, "daughter of El" and/or *BeiT eL*, "House of El."

[18] LaBaN: *eL aB aN*, "El Father An," and/or "El Cloud (of) An."

[19] Emphasis added.

At this point in the narrative, after four step-sons and four sons, the story gets weird:

> In the days of wheat harvest Reuben [Leah's eldest son] went and found *mandrakes* [Hebrew, *duday*] in the field, and brought them to his mother Leah. Then Rachel said to Leah, "Please give me some of your *son's mandrakes* [*duday*]." But she said to her, "Is it a small matter that you have taken away my husband? Would you take away my *son's mandrakes* [*duday*] also?" Rachel said, "Then he may lie with you tonight for your *son's mandrakes* [*duday*]." When Jacob came from the field in the evening, Leah went out to meet him, and said, "You must come in to me; for I have *hired* [Hebrew, *sakar*] *you with my son's mandrakes* [*duday*]." So he lay with her that night (Gen 30:14-16).

Five "mandrakes" in these two verses signal enigma: "mandrakes," Hebrew, *duday*, is "from the same as *dod*,"[20] defined as "beloved, love, *uncle*."[21] The name "David" is also "from the same as *dod*."[22] It seems that "mandrake" is used in these verses to "adorn" a "beloved uncle" who impregnates Leah. "Uncle" and "David" are derived from the same word and this story may be the genesis of the term, "House of David."

Reuben's "uncles" were his father's and mother's brothers; his mother's brothers are never named. Therefore, "uncle" must refer to his father's brother. YHWH opened Leah's womb when she conceived Rueben and his three younger brothers. But who is YHWH's brother?

In the Sumerian story of creation, Ea's brother is EnLiL; In Genesis, YHWH is often attached to LH (Eloah) as, "YHWH-LH," suggesting that *YaH* and *Eloah* may have been brothers or half-brothers. And indeed, Eloah appears in the scene just before Leah conceives thanks to "her son's *duday*":

> And God *heeded* [Hebrew, *LHM ShaMa*] Leah, and she *conceived* and *bore Jacob a fifth son* [Hebrew, *BeN Ha MiSi*[23]]. Leah said, 'God

---

[20] NAS (Strong's Hebrew 1736).
[21] NAS (Strong's Hebrew 1730).
[22] NAS (Strong's Hebrew 1732).
[23] NAS (Strong's Hebrew 2549).

[*LHM*] has given me my *hire* [Hebrew, *SaKaR*[24]] because I gave my maid to my husband'; so she named him Issachar (Gen 30:17-18).

The Hebrew word translated, "heeded," is *ShaMa*; the Essenes could render it *iSh eM*. The Hebrew word translated "fifth," is *chamishia*; the Essenes could render it, *Ki eM iSh*. Leah bore Jacob a "son of *Ki-Mother Ish*. The enigmatic *mandrake* who was "hired" to impregnate Leah was an Ishene-uncle; his son was an *Ish of the line of Kisar and Ansar*; therefore, they named him *Isha-Ki oR*, Issachar.

"Leah conceived again and bore a *sixth son* [Hebrew, *ben shi-shi*] to Jacob. Then Leah said, "God [*LHM*] has endowed me with a good gift; now my husband will *dwell* [Hebrew, *zabal*] with me, because I have borne him six [*shishi*] sons." So she named him Zebulun[25] (NAS; Gen 30:19-20).[26] Like Issachar, Zebulun's biological father was the "Mandrake" uncle.

Let's stop to review The House of Jacob as it stands just before Joseph is conceived: Jacob's wife Leah bore six sons; however, none was Jacob's biological son; four were YHWH's, two were with YHWH's brother, Eloah. The two handmaids bore Jacob biological sons, two each, so the total sons and step-sons in Jacob's house is ten with two more yet to come.

"Then *LHM* remembered Rachel and *LHM* listened unto her [Hebrew, *wayyisma eleha*], opened her womb, *she conceived and bore a son...*" (Gen 30:22-3; author's translation).

Joseph is The House of Jacob's eleventh, but Jacob isn't present during Joseph's conception; his conception is attended by (1) Rachel, (2) *eL Ha eM*, the Mother who "remembered Rachel," and (3) *LH* (*Eloah*), "the God" who "opened her womb." Joseph's biological father is Eloah.

The text explains that Joseph's name is derived from the Hebrew word *yasaph*, defined as "to add."[27] However, an equally valid option is to combine *Io + suph*. *Suph* (*tsuph*) is de-

---

[24] NAS (Strong's Hebrew 7939).
[25] Zebulun = Z (ish) aB eL aN.
[26] Emphasis added.
[27] NAS (Strong's Hebrew 3254).

fined as "(honey) comb."[28] Io was an ancient *Egyptian* goddess whose myth tells how and by whom she was turned into a cow.[29] Therefore, *Io-suph's* name ties him to both "Milk and Honey."

The identity of the father of Rachel's second son – whose birth brought about her death – is also shrouded in enigmas. Rachel named her son "Benoni," which means "son of my sorrow."[30] However, "...*his father* called him Benjamin" which means "son of the right hand"[31] (Gen 35:18).

The identity of "his father" is hidden in the Hebrew word for "right hand," *yamin*. "Your right hand, O YHWH glorious in power – your right hand, O YHWH shattered the enemy" (Ex 15:6). YHWH's *yamin* is a match; therefore, Rachel's second son – "son of sorrow" and the cause of her death and burial – was YHWH's *ben yamin*.

Neither of Laban's daughters bore any of Jacob's biological sons; two of Laban's "handmaids"[32] bore Jacob four sons. Laban's name identifies him as a descendant of the Ish and Ishshah of *eL aB aN*, "El Father An"; and so, they named him *LaBaN*.

The evidence suggests that Leah and Rachel were Elohim's "Temple Virgins" and required to bear children to YHWH and Eloah. They may have been married to Jacob and *slept* with him, but they did not have *sex* with him. Bilhah and Zilpah were given to Jacob for sex and to bear his biological children.

On his deathbed, Jacob gathered his twelve sons and stepsons; the reason given, "... that I may tell you what will happen to you in days to come." Jacob, it seems, was a prophet,

---

[28] NAS (Strong's Hebrew 6688)

[29] Encyclopedia.com. *Myths and Legends of the World*. "Io."

[30] NAS (Strong's Hebrew 1126).

[31] NAS (Strong's Hebrew 1144).

[32] Gerald Friedlander, trans., *Pirke De-Rabbi Eliezar*, Abraham Epstein Manuscript (New York: The Bloch Publishing Company, 1916), 271-2. This second century Midrash explains that "...according to the law of the land, the daughters of a man by his concubines are called handmaids." If so, then Bilhah and Zilpah were also Laban's daughters.

which isn't hard when prophesies are recorded centuries after
they occur and designed to solve enigmas.

To Judah, Jacob said, "... your *brothers* shall praise you ...
your father's sons shall bow down before you" (Gen 49:8).

Only YHWH's sons, Reuben, Levi, Simeon, and Benjamin –
Judah's biological *father's* biological sons – would bow down
before him. His step-brothers – Jacob's sons with the handmaids, Leah's sons with Eloah, and Rachel's son Joseph –
would *praise* him, but they would not "bow down before" him.

Jacob continues his "Judah Prophecy":

> Binding his *foal* [Hebrew, *ayir*; "male donkey"[33]] to the vine and
> his donkey's [Hebrew, *athonson* "female donkey"[34]] son to the
> choice vine, he washes his garments in wine and his robe *in the
> blood of grapes* [Hebrew, *u ve dam aNaB*]" (Gen 49:11).

Note that Judah *has* donkeys, but he is not identified as *being*
a donkey; this infers, therefore, that his wife or wives were descendants of Ansar and Kisar, cloaked as "donkeys," and became mothers of "donkeys."

The "choice vine" is Joseph, the NZR among Jacob's sons.
And, the only way Judah can bind his "female donkey's son" to
Joseph's choice vine is if Joseph's daughter is Judah's "female
donkey" and gives birth to an Ishene son. And as might be expected, the story of how this comes about is imbedded in
enigmas:

First, Judah marries a Canaanite woman whose name is
"Shuah"; their eldest son Er[35] marries Tamar (Gen 38:6), whose
name means "tree"[36] and whose parents are unknown. Tamar
is called a 'Temple Prostitute" (Gen 38:14-21), and the marriage
so angers YHWH that he kills Er. YHWH also kills Onan,
Shuah and Judah's second son, because he "spilled his seed on
the ground" to avoid giving his dead elder brother sons, a requirement under Jewish law (Gen 38:7-10).

---

[33] NAS (Strong's Hebrew 5895).

[34] NAS (Strong's Hebrew 860).

[35] *Er*: NAS (Strong's Hebrew 5782), defined as "to rouse oneself, awake." Equally valid
is owR, "light," (Strong's Hebrew 216).

[36] From *tomer*, another Hebrew word for "tree," NAS (Strong's Hebrew 8560).

Judah promised Tamar that his third son Shelah would become her husband once he reached the age to marry (Gen
38:11). However, Shuah died and Judah reneged on his promise, angering Tamar who devised a plan that would allow her
to bear children. She posed as a prostitute, and Judah unwit-
tingly impregnated her. Under Jewish law, Tamar's offspring
were considered to be Er's, not Judah's (Gen 38:6-10).

Jacob's "Judah Prophesy" could only be fulfilled if Tamar is
from the "choice vine," Joseph's daughter, Judah's niece. She
would be Judah's "female donkey," and her son – conceived
from Judah's seed but not his legal son – would be grafted onto
the "choice vine" of Joseph the NZR. Prophesy fulfilled!

Tamar, in fact, gave birth to *twin* sons, and while she was in
labor "one put out a hand; and the midwife took and bound on
his hand a crimson thread" (Gen 38:28). However, he "drew
back his hand and out came his brother..." The twin Perez delivered first, but his brother arrived wearing the crimson
thread. The thread, and his name, identify "Zerah" as Israel's
"choice vine." His robes would be crimson, dyed in the "blood
of grapes."

When Jacob speaks to Leah's fifth son whose father is Eloah,
he says,

> Issachar is a *strong donkey* [Hebrew, *GeRaM* ("a bone; strength"[37])
> *cHaMoR* ("male donkey"[38])], lying down between the sheepfolds;
> he saw that a resting place was good, and that the land was pleas-
> ant; so he bowed his shoulder to the burden, and became a slave
> at forced labor (Gen 49:14).

Notably, the word for "donkey" in this verse is not *pere*, but
chamor. *Pere* is used to describe just one son: "Joseph is the foal
[Hebrew, *ben*] of a *wild donkey*, [Hebrew, *PeRe*] the foal of a *wild
donkey at a spring* – one of the *wild donkeys on the ridge*" (Gen
49:22).[39]

---

[37] NAS (Strong's Hebrew 1634).
[38] NAS (Strong's Hebrew 2543).
[39] New Living Translation, Tyndale House Publishers.

This verse is the hypotext for Mk 11:2 as Jesus gives instructions to two of his disciples: "… and said to them, 'Go into the village ahead of you, and immediately as you enter it, you will find tied there a colt that has never been ridden; untie it and bring it.'"[40]

In Genesis, "Joseph" is "the colt of a wild donkey"; therefore, in Mark's hypertext, the "colt" also refers to "Joseph," Jesus' father. Apparently, Joseph had a role to play in the Crucifixion, and most likely it was as "Joseph of Arimathea," or Joseph of o*R eM Thea*, "Light Mother Goddess."

Judah's descendants, it seems, were to marry into both bloodlines. And it appears that Judah's step-father Jacob had done the same; here's how:

Laban was Leah and Rachel's father; however, his wife or wives are unknown. And apparently, Leah's bloodline is inferior to Rachel's, suggesting they had different mothers. Perhaps Le YaH's ancestors were *El the Mother* (eL) and YHWH (YaH), therefore they named her, *Le YaH*. And perhaps Rachel's ancestors were Kisar and EloaH, hence, o*R a Ki eL* ("Light of Kisar and Eloah"); o*RaK el* ("Spirit of El"); *DeRaK eL* ("The Way of El"); *RaKaM El* ("Womb of El").

This means, of course, that *only* Joseph carried the pure, undiluted blood that originated with Ansar and Ishtar, also called *Kisar*; that this bloodline was passed on through their son En-LiL and his wife NinLiL (*Elohim*) and eventually reached Rachel, her son Joseph, and his son Manasseh.

Jacob's name, "YaaKoB," identifies his parents: YKB can also be rendered *Ya Ki Ab*, which identifies Jacob as a descendant of YHWH and Kisar.

The evidence is enigmatic but strong: YHWH is the root of "The Vine" and *eLoaH* is the root of "The *Choice* Vine." The important "secret" is that Joseph the NZR is the only son of "The

---

[40] Gen 49:22 is also the hypotext for Zech 9:9: "Rejoice greatly, O daughter Zion! Shout aloud, O daughter Jerusalem! Lo, your king comes to you; triumphant and victorious is he, humble and riding on a donkey, on a colt, the foal of a donkey."

House of Jacob" who can claim Eloah and Ishtar, "The Choice Vine," as his ancestors via Abraham and Sarah.

"The Fire" (Hebrew, *Ha eSh*) that was to be kept burning was the "Choice Vine," the undiluted *Ishene and Ishshah bloodline of Kisar*. And this bloodline was passed on in the *BetuLaH Em*, Rachel, but not her sister LeeYaH.

And so clearly, "Temple Virgins" were nothing new at the time of Jesus. And the early Church recognized a Jewish tradition that honored virgins who resided in the temple where the Virgin Mary might have been when, "The messenger said, 'Greetings, favored one! Kurios is with you … for you have found favor with Theos'" (Lk 1:28).

When Luke's introduction of The Virgin Mary is examined carefully and objectively, it can be seen that the messenger brought someone along. "The Virgin" is introduced to "Kurios," and the reason given is that Theos favored her above all the other virgins.

Tacitus identified a Vestal Virgin by name when he reported that a gift of two million sesterces was decreed to the Vestal Cornelia.[41] And Josephus' enigmatic tale of the chaste and naïve Paulina raises questions: What was a Vestal Virgin? What were the *Sacred Duties of Vestal Virgins*? Was one of their sacred functions having sex in the temple with Theos and/or Kurios and bearing their children? And new questions relevant to this investigation that can now be asked:

Are the virgins called *Mary* temple virgins chosen specifically by the *Theos* to bear children to Rome's *Kurios*?

Are these men and the virgins descendants of *The Spirit of Rachel* and *The Father of Light*?

A careful examination of Lk 1:26-27 uncovers more clues: "In the sixth month the angel Gabriel was sent by *Theos* to a virgin [Greek, *parthenon*; Hebrew, *betulah*) betrothed to a man whose name was Joseph, of the House of David. The virgin's name was Mary."[42]

[41] Tacitus, *Annals; The Works* (1864-1877), (Sacred Texts Online 4.16).
[42] Hebrew *MR* ("Mary) can also be rendered *eM oR*, "Mother Light."

The Greek word *angelos*, translated "angel," can also be translated "messenger." *Kurios* is defined as "having power; a lord, master."[43] When viewed without preconceived notions, a messenger – sent by someone identified as "Theos" – introduces Mary to a man identified as "Lord and Master," Hebrew, *Nasi-Sar*.

Often noted but generally ignored is the important fact that "The Caesars, beginning with Augustus Caesar, were called 'Theos.'"[44] And whether this "Mary" is the "Virgin" who gave birth to Bar-Jesus and his twin brother in 6 CE, or the Virgin Mary who gave birth to Jesus the Elder when Herod was King, Augustus Caesar was known as "Theos."

In 6 CE, Augustus Caesar's step-son, future Emperor Tiberius Julius Caesar (born c. 46 BCE), was about fifty-two. Tiberius' son was about twenty-one; because of his royal blood, he was a "Lord and Master," and his "Royal Seed" was of immense value to the Roman Empire. But does anything suggest that a *Jewish* temple virgin[45] was the equivalent of a *Vestal* temple virgin?

Most of what is known of the Vestal Virgins comes from *Roman Antiquities* by Dionysius of Halicarnassus, a Greek historian who lived and worked during the time of Augustus Caesar. This historian's name – "Dionysius" – recalls his contemporary Marc Antony because it can be tied to one of Plutarch's revelations: "Now, Antony ... was called the New Dionysus."[46]

Dionysius the historian details the origin, functions, trials and tribulations of the Vestal Virgins. He writes:

> King Numa ordered that Romulus himself, as one who had shown a greatness beyond mortal nature, should be honored, under the name of Quirinus, by the erection of a temple and by sacrifices throughout the year ... a man named Julius (descended from Ascanius) who would never have told an untruth for his private

[43] Middle Liddell.
[44] Philip W. Comfort and Eugene E. Carpenter. *Holman Treasury of Key Bible Words: 200 Greek and 200 Hebrew Words Defined and Explained*; 290.
[45] References to Israelite Temple Virgins: Ex 38:8; 1 Sam 2:22; 2 Mac 3:19-20.
[46] Plutarch, *Life of Antony* (Loeb 1920) 54.6.

advantage arrived in the Forum and said that, as he was coming in from the country, he saw Romulus departing from the city and that he heard him say: "Julius, announce to the Romans from me, that the genius to whom I was allotted at my birth is conducting me to the gods, now that I have finished my mortal life, and that I am Quirinus." Numa, having reduced his whole system of religious laws to writing, divided them into eight parts, that being the number of the different classes of religious ceremonies.[47]

Romulus ascended to become the "Invincible God Quirinus," and he sent his messages to the people of Rome through a trustworthy man whom Vergil ties to Julius Caesar.

Dionysius describes the duties assigned to the Vestal Virgins in ancient times – or as Tacitus calls it, "rude antiquity" – and it is the "Fifth Part" that addresses the Virgins:

> The fifth part Numa assigned to the virgins who are the guardians of the *sacred fire* [Hebrew, *Qodesh esh*] and who are called Vestals by the Romans, after the goddess whom they serve, Numa himself having been the first to build a temple at Rome to Vesta and to appoint virgins to be her priestesses. But concerning them it is necessary to make a few statements that are most essential ... for there are problems that have been thought worthy of investigation by many Roman historians in connection with this topic and those authors who have not diligently examined into the causes of these matters have published rather worthless accounts.[48]

In other words, PAY ATTENTION! You are about to get *the account that matters.*

Regarding the building of the temple of Vesta, some ascribe it to Romulus, looking upon it as an inconceivable thing that, when a city was being founded by a man skilled in divination, a public hearth should not have been erected first of all, particularly since the founder had been brought up at Alba, where the temple of this goddess had been established from ancient times, and since *his mother had been her priestess.* And recognizing two classes of religious ceremonies – the one public and common to all the citizens,

---

[47] Dionysius of Halicarnassus, *Roman Antiquities* (Loeb, 1916), (Thayer Online 63.3-4). (Condensed and paraphrased.)
[48] Dionysius, *Roman Antiquities* (Loeb 1916) 64.5.

and *the other private and confined to particular families* – they declare
that on both these grounds Romulus was under every obligation
to worship this goddess.[49]

It is the ceremony that was "private and confined to particular families" that the enigmas are attempting to explain.

For they say that nothing is more necessary for men than a public hearth, and that nothing more nearly concerned Romulus, in
view of his descent, since his ancestors had brought the sacred
rites of this goddess from Ilium and *his mother had been her priestess.*[50] Those, then, who for these reasons ascribe the building of the
temple to Romulus rather than to Numa seem to be right, insofar
as the general principle is concerned, that when a city was being
founded, it was necessary for a hearth to be established first of all,
particularly by a man who was not unskilled in matters of religion; but of the details relating to the building of the present temple and to the virgins who are in the service of the goddess, they
seem to have been ignorant. For … it was not Romulus who consecrated to the goddess this place where the sacred fire is preserved (a strong proof of this is that it is outside of what they call
"Roma Quadrata," which he surrounded with a wall, whereas all
men place the shrine of the public hearth in the best part of a city
and nobody outside of the walls); and, in the second place, he did
not appoint the service of the goddess to be performed by virgins,
being mindful, I believe, of the experience that had befallen his
mother, *who while she was serving the goddess lost her virginity*; for he
doubtless felt that the remembrance of his domestic misfortunes
would make it impossible for him to punish according to the traditional laws any of the priestesses he should find to have been
violated.[51]

"Lost her virginity" suggests the virgin was impregnated by
a male who was not, like her, descended from the "First Parents." These "Parent" and/or "Creator Beings" are known by a
multitude of names including *Vesta, Hestia, Gaia, Kisar, Asherah,*
and *Ishtar.* The male "First Fathers" and/or "Creator Beings"

---

[49] Dionysius, *Roman Antiquities* (Loeb, 1916), (Thayer Online 64.5). Emphasis added.
[50] Philo's rule no. 1: doubling of a phrase.
[51] Dionysius of Halicarnassus, *Roman Antiquities* (Loeb, 1916), (Thayer Online 65.2-3).
Emphasis added.

include *Jupiter, Zeus, Ouranos, Ansar* and sons *Enlil* and *Enki-ea*; *eLoaH,* and *YHWH.*

This Roman tradition that required death for defiled Vestals supports our proposed alternative version of Lev 20:13 that required death for the defiled Asherah Virgins. Furthermore, these parallels associate the Romans' "Vesta" with the Israelites' "Asherah." The "eSH" in the names, Hebrew for "fire," also highlights the "perpetual fire" tradition prevalent in both religions.

YHWH demanded that the "defiled Israelite Virgin" be put to death; the manner of death is unspecified. Ancient Roman law required that a "defiled Vestal Virgin" be buried alive within the city, a breach of Roman law which forbade burial within the city. To get around this conundrum, the offending Virgin was entombed alive in an underground chamber near the Colline Gate with a few days' food, water, and a loaf of bread. The Vestal would not technically be buried alive in the city but simply descend into a habitable room where she would die willingly.[52]

> For this reason, therefore, he did not build a common temple of Vesta nor did he appoint virgins to be her priestesses; but having erected a hearth in each of the thirty curiae on which the members sacrificed, he appointed the chiefs of the curiae to be the priests of those hearths, therein imitating the customs of the Greeks that are still observed in the most ancient cities. At any rate, what are called *pyrtaneia* among them are temples of Hestia, and are served by the chief magistrates of the cities.[53]

Romulus did not appoint Virgins to serve the goddess because of what happened to his own mother; however, this ancient tradition is reinstated when:

> Numa, upon taking over the rule, did not disturb the individual hearths of the curiae, but erected one common to them all in the space between the Capitoline Hill and the Palatine (for these hills had already been united by a single wall into one city, and the Forum, in which the temple is built, lies between them), and he en-

[52] Plutarch, *Numa* 10.5.
[53] Dionysius of Halicarnassus, *Roman Antiquities* (Loeb, 1916), (Thayer Online 65.4).

acted, in accordance with the ancestral custom of the Latins, that the guarding of the holy things should be committed to virgins. There is some doubt, however, what it is that is kept in this temple and for what reason the care of it has been assigned to virgins, some affirming that nothing is preserved there but the fire, which is visible to everybody. And they very reasonably argue that the custody of the fire was committed to virgins, rather than to men, because fire is incorrupt and a virgin is undefiled, and the most chaste of mortal things must be agreeable to the purest of those that are divine. And they regard the fire as consecrated to Vesta because that goddess, being the earth [Sumerian, *Ki*] and occupying the central place in the universe, kindles the celestial fires from herself. But there are some who say that *besides the fire there are some holy things* in the temple of the goddess that may not be revealed to the public, of which *only the pontiffs and the virgins have knowledge*. As a strong confirmation of this story they cite what happened at the burning of the temple during the First Punic War [264-241 BCE] between the Romans and the Carthaginians over Sicily. For when the temple caught fire and the virgins fled from the flames, one of the pontiffs, Lucius Caecilius, called Metellus, a man of consular rank, the same who exhibited a hundred and thirty-eight elephants in the memorable triumph which he celebrated for his defeat of the Carthaginians in Sicily, neglecting his own safety for the sake of the public good, ventured to force his way into the burning structure, and, snatching up the holy things which the virgins had abandoned, saved them from the fire; for which he received the honors from the State, as the inscription upon his statue on the Capitol testifies.[54]

One of the descendants of Lucius Caecilius Metellus is Metellus Scipio (born Publius Cornelius Scipio Nasica but upon adoption became Quintus Caecilius Metellus Pius Scipio Nasica). Scipio married Aemilia Lepida, daughter of Mamercus Aemilius Lepidus Livianus. Their daughter Cornelia was Pompey the Great's fifth wife. Notably, Pompey's fourth wife was Julia, daughter of Julius Caesar.[55]

---

[54] Dionysius of Halicarnassus, *Roman Antiquities* (Loeb, 1916), 66.1-4. Emphasis added.
[55] Shelly P. Haley, "The Five Wives of Pompey the Great." *Greece & Rome*, 2nd Ser., Vol. 32, No. 1. (1985), 49-59. (Published by: Cambridge University Press on behalf of The Classical Association.)

The critical portion of Dionysius' account of the Vestal Virgins addresses the Sacred Fire. He writes:

> For my part, I find from very many evidences that there are indeed some holy things, unknown to the public, kept by the virgins, and not the fire alone; but what they are I do not think should be inquired into too curiously, either by me or by anyone else who wishes to observe the reverence due to the gods.[56]

What better way to arouse curiosity than to suggest that questions should not be asked.

> The virgins who serve the goddess were originally four and were chosen by the kings according to the principles established by Numa, but afterwards, from the multiplicity of the sacred rites they perform, their number was increased to six, and has so remained down to our time. They live in the temple of the goddess, into which none who wish are hindered from entering in the daytime, whereas it is not lawful for any *man* to remain there at night. They were required to remain undefiled by marriage for the space of thirty years, devoting themselves to offering sacrifices and performing the other rites ordained by law.[57]

Recall that Tacitus reported Tiberius held a meeting to discuss the duties of the Priest and the Vestal Virgins: "A law was passed that the priestess, in regard to her sacred functions, was to be under the husband's control..."[58] The topic was the Vestal Virgins and their sacred functions. Therefore *the priestess* refers to the Vestal Virgin who is married but not defiled by it. This could suggest the marriage was without sex, or it could suggest that sex with the husband in some cases did not result in defilement of the Virgin. Furthermore, the fact that neither Paulina nor Aemilia Lepida Paulus were killed lends support to our proposal that a Virgin's "death" simply meant she was no longer a divine and pure vessel for bearing children to gods, but a mortal woman bearing mortal children.

> During the first ten years their duty was to learn their functions, in the second ten to perform them, and during the remaining ten

---

[56] Dionysius of Halicarnassus, *Roman Antiquities* (Loeb, 1916), (Thayer Online 66.6).

[57] Emphasis added to note that no men, only gods, could remain at night.

[58] Tacitus, *Annals; The Works* (1864-1877), (Sacred Texts Online 4.16)

to teach others. After the expiration of the term of thirty years, nothing hindered those who so desired from marrying, upon laying aside their fillets and the other insignia of their priesthood.[59]

However, it is also well worth relating in what manner the goddess has manifested herself in favor of those virgins who have been falsely accused ... It is said, then, that once, when the fire had been extinguished through some negligence on the part of *Aemilia*, who had the care of it at the time and had entrusted it to another virgin ... they say, *Aemilia ... who was innocent...*[60]

Dionysius identifies a second Vestal Virgin by name, the falsely accused Aemilia. He does not identify Pompey's fifth wife Cornelia as a Vestal Virgin, but one of her descendants (gens Cornelia) would have been the Vestal Virgin who was the recipient of two million sesterces awarded by Emperor Tiberius.

At the time Herod the Great was King, the names "Aemilia" and "Cornelia" were associated with *one* prominent Roman woman of high standing. And she, like her daughter Aemilia Lepida Paulina, also claimed Pompey and Sulla as ancestors. Her name was "Cornelia Scipio," her husband was one of the men named "Lucius Aemilius Lepidus Paulus," and her mother was Scribonia.

Scribonia was Augustus Caesar's second wife and Julia the Elder's mother. Therefore, Scribonia's granddaughter was Julia the Younger, also known as "Julia Vipsania Paulus," mother of Paulus the Younger and his "brother-of-the-rib."

These threads may be curious, but does this history of the Vestal Virgins have any bearing on the question, *Is The Virgin Mary a Temple Virgin*? To answer this question we turn again to Luke's story of the Virgin Mary:

But she was much perplexed by his words and pondered what sort of greeting this might be. The angel said to her, "Do not be afraid, Mary, for you have found favor with [*Theos*]. And now, you will conceive in your womb and bear a son, and you will name him [*Iesous*]. He will be great, and will be called the *Son of the Most High*

[59] Dionysius of Halicarnassus, *Roman Antiquities*, (Loeb, 1916), (Thayer Online 67.1-2).
[60] Dionysius of Halicarnassus, *Roman Antiquities*, (Loeb, 1916), Thayer Online 68.1-5).

[Hebrew, *bar Shadday*], and the [*Kurios of Theos*] will give to him the throne of his ancestor David. He will reign over the house of Jacob forever, and of his kingdom there will be no end (Lk 1:29-33).[61]

"Mary asked the angel, 'How can this happen, since I have not had relations with a man?'" (Lk 1:34).[62]

Kurios Tiberius was the son of Theos Augustus - both were considered deities. Therefore, the Virgin did not know a *man* before she conceived; the Virgin knew a *deity*. And even after having sex with a deity, as Josephus' story of Saturnius and Paulina suggests, the Virgin remained chaste.

Dionysius seems determined to pique his readers' curiosity about the secret duty the Vestal Virgins performed that could never be made known to the public. Tacitus danced around the same issue when the new law was passed that gave authority over the priestesses to their husbands. The story of Paulina reveals the secret: A Vestal Virgin could be married and remain chaste if her husband was also descended from a deity ("Saturnius" a descendant of the god Saturn, and "Io-seph" a descendant of the goddess Io). Moreover, she was required to have sex in the temple with gods and sons of gods. And this "Law" may answer the question of what the primitive form of marriage entailed and why it became unpopular.

The virtuous Virgin, it seems, had to remain available to serve sexually when Theos requested her to do so. This sounds very much like the seed purification rituals performed by Mithra's priestesses in the temples of Anahita, the Zoroastrian goddess of fertility and water.

Eusebius writes that "temple prostitution" was still being practiced in some places in the Roman Empire in the fourth century. He names Sicily, the Kingdom of Pontus, Cyprus, Cappadocia (home of princess Glapyra), and Corinth at the Temple of Aphrodite.[63] The apocryphal Second Book of Maccabees also addresses this practice:

---

[61] NRSV with Greek insertions; emphasis added.
[62] ISV.
[63] Eusebius, *Life of Constantine*, 3.55 and 3.58.

Not long after this, the king sent an Athenian senator to compel the Jews to forsake the laws of their ancestors and no longer to live by the laws of God; also to pollute the temple in Jerusalem and to call it the *Temple of Olympian Zeus*, and to call the one in Gerizim the *Temple of Zeus-the-Friend-of-Strangers*, as did the people who lived in that place. Harsh and utterly grievous was the onslaught of evil. For the temple was filled with debauchery and reveling by the Gentiles, who dallied with prostitutes and had intercourse with women within the sacred precincts, and besides brought in things for sacrifice that were unfit (2 Macc 6:1-4).[64]

Often forgotten is the fact that the dispute was between conservative Jews and Hellenized Jews. Hellenistic Judaism emphasized monotheistic doctrine (*heis theos*), and represented "knowledge" (*gnosis*) and "wisdom" (*sophia*) as emanations from God – two aspects, but One God.

A little more than a century after the Maccabean Revolt was resolved the Jerusalem Temple was controlled by Hillel the Elder, a man who claimed descent from King David. This is where the enigmas lead to allegories written in ancient times but never truly comprehended by those who did not have access to the *Key*.

Many of the clues are found in ancient terms, some of which we've already examined: the word translated as "woman" in Genesis is *ishshah*; the word translated as, "bearing" [fruit], is *asah*; the word translated as "tree" is *es*; the word translated as "fire" is *esh*; the word translated as "alabaster" is *shayish*. Prominent in each word is the sound made by the letters *SH*, and the same root can be found in *"Ash-erah, Ish-tar, As-tarte, Sh-abbat, Isis, H-es-tia,* and *V-es-ta,* all representations of the "First Mother" of compassionate women and men.

Fire, too, plays a prominent role: "There the messenger of YHWH appeared to him in a flame of fire out of a bush; he looked, and the bush was burning yet it was not consumed" (Ex 3:2). And as previously quoted, "A perpetual fire shall be kept burning on the altar; it shall not go out" (Lev 6:13).

---

[64] NOAB.

If *Ish/Ash/Esh* represented the Feminine Energy of Creation to the Nazirites and Nasoraeans, then the words Epiphanius uses to debunk the Nasoraean Heresy now make sense:

> I mean the Nasoraeans, whom I am presenting here. They were Jewish, were attached to the Law, and had circumcision. But it was as though people had seen fire under a misapprehension. Not understanding why, or for [what] use, the ones who had kindled this fire were doing it – either to cook their rations with the fire, or burn some dead trees and brush, which are ordinarily destroyed by fire – they kindled fire too, in imitation, and set themselves ablaze.[65]

The secret sacred function of the Temple Virgin was to keep pure the Royal Blood represented by the Sacred Fire. Abraham's wife Sarah, Isaac's wife Rebekah, Jacob's wife Rachel, and Moses' wife Sephora were introduced as they *drew water* (Hebrew *SB, sha-ab*) from a well (Hebrew *BR, be-er*).

Notably, *SB* can also be rendered *iSh aB*, "Ish Father" or "Father of Ish," and *BR* can be rendered *aB oR*, "Father (is) Light," and BaR, "son of." And these options are supported by the Hebrew word for "fountain," MKR, rendered M*eQowR* and/or *eM Ki Or*, "Mother Ki Light." The "Virgin" descendants of Sarah, Rebekah, and Rachel, were called *MRM*, "Miriam," Greek "Maria," and "Mary," perhaps to denote they are *eM Owr*, "Mothers (of) Light," and *MaRoM*, "high places." Furthermore, *MaYiM*, is Hebrew for "water."

King Numa increased the number of Vestals from four to six with each devoting thirty years to service: The first ten years (approximate ages 6-15) they were in training, learning the ceremonies and preparing for the second ten years (ages 16-25) when a Prima, Secunda, and Tertia were chosen to perform the Sacred Function of bearing sons and daughters to gods. The remaining ten years (ages 26-35) were spent teaching novices and assisting the active Vestal Virgin Priestesses.[66]

---

[65] Epiphanius, *Panarion* 29:5.4-5.
[66] William Ramsay: "Vestales": *A Dictionary of Greek and Roman Antiquities*, William Smith ed. (London: John Murray, 1875), 1189-1191. LacusCurtius: Bill Thayer Website.

Tacitus explains: "... the old custom to nominate together three patricians, sons of parents wedded according to the primitive ceremony. One of these three men was chosen to be High Priest. Now however there was not the same choice as formerly, the primitive form of marriage having been given up or being observed only by a few persons."

Each of these "sons of parents wedded according to the primitive ceremony" was mated with the three chosen Virgins during their ten years of active service. The evidence indicates the three patricians were often the Virgins' uncles and granduncles. (A reminder: "David," "uncle," "mandrakes," and "jar" share the same root, *dod*.)

The threads that tie the Vestal Virgins to the Israelite Temple Virgins are the enigmatic fire and water and the secrecy of their Sacred Duties. The term "Virgin" had a special meaning when applied to the priestesses selected to serve in the Temples. Sex with a *man* during her thirty-years of service was forbidden; however, sex with deities was required. What Eusebius viewed as "temple prostitution" was the Sacred Function of Jewish priestesses, like the Virgin Mary, chosen to bear children to "gods and sons of gods."

The threads collected and examined provide a reasonable answer to the question: *Mothers Mary: Literal Virgins or Temple Virgins?* Philo's Philology points to a conclusion that has abundant support from ancient texts: The Virgins Mary were Israelite Temple Virgins. It was their duty as the "purifying water" and "Daughters of El the Mother" to preserve the Ishta and Ansar bloodline, the "fire" that was the "The Way of Rachel" and "The House of David."

Evidence suggests this bloodline is identified by and tied to the color crimson. The Hebrew word *SN*, *sani* (*ish ani*), is defined as "scarlet" but often translated "crimson." A "sani thread" is a recurring theme in Exodus 25 through 39. Moreover, *sani* shares its root, *SN*, with the Sumerian-Babylonian deity, *Sin*, as well as with "Sin" the desert wilderness, "Sin-ai" a mountain, and a city in Egypt later renamed "Pelusium."

The color crimson is also identified by another Hebrew word, *KML, kamil,* but equally valid rendered *Ki Em El.* Perhaps members of the "Ish of An" bloodline that began with *Ki Em El* and *Ansar* ("Ki Mother of El and An the Prince of heaven") are depicted in ancient art by women and men clad in crimson and/or scarlet. If so, our cover image carries more meaning than we recognized when we chose it.

Furthermore, the robe given to Jesus at the Crucifixion is described as "porphyra" in Mark's and Luke's gospels, but "kokken-in" in Matthew's. "Porphyra" is defined as "... purple, symbolic of 'royal status' ... three familiar shades of purple in the ancient world: deep violet, deep scarlet (or crimson), and deep blue ..."[67] "kokkenin is defined as "...crimson, scarlet, dyed with Kermes (coccum), the female coccus of the Kermes oak."[68] And both words were probably selected to link with the hypotext, Exodus 25 through 39, where *SN (sani),* repeated forty times, is tied to Moses and the Israelites. And notably, "Bezalel son of Uri" is introduced in the very midst of these "crimson threads" at Ex 35:30.

---

[67] NAS (Strong's Greek 4209),
[68] NAS (Strong's Greek 2847).

CHAPTER TWELVE

Following Philo to The Virgins

Part II

Who are the Israelite Temple Virgins?

The enigmas suggest that "Sacred Fire" represents the Royal Bloodline that can be traced to Ansar, the "Father from Heaven," also known as *Ab Or*, "Father Light," and Kisar, the "Mother of Earth." Some argue that the Sumerian texts indicate the first "virgins" may have been literal virgins, artificially inseminated and the baby delivered by Caesarian section.[1]

Hebrew and Christian scripture point to a "Father from Heaven" (Akkadian, *Ansar*) whose bloodline was preserved and passed on by Temple Virgins. These Virgins were forbidden to have sex with *mortal* men, descendants of YHWH's *adam*-men.

The search is now on for additional Jewish Virgins and the historical identities of the mothers of Jesus and Bar-Jesus. And the search takes us back to Luke: "In those days a decree went out from Emperor Augustus that all the world should be registered. This was the first registration and was taken while Quirinius was governor of Syria" (Lk 1:1-2).

Mother Mary isn't the only virgin thread tied to the Census of Quirinius; Josephus introduces another intriguing virgin in both *Wars* and *Antiquities*. We find her when we return to the

---

[1] "Ancient Aliens," cable channel *H2*, based in part on Zecharia Sitchin's *The Earth Chronicles*.

Census and are reminded that, "Quirinius had disposed of Archelaus' money ... when the census was concluded, which was made in the thirty-seventh year of Caesar's victory over Antony at Actium..."[2]

As previously shown, the reason Augustus Caesar dispatched Quirinius to conduct the census – and to dispose of Archelaus' money – was reported in *Antiquities*, Book Seventeen. It is the story of a virgin whose name may be a combination of "Glaucus" (Athena's Owl of Wisdom) and "pyra," Greek for "fire." Her name was "Gla-pyra," sometimes spelled, "Glaphyra."

The Virgin Glapyra was the daughter of Archelaus, King of Cappadocia, a hotbed of temple prostitution, according to Eusebius.[3] Her mother was not identified, but she would have been the same age as Cleopatra's elder sister, Bernice.

Josephus reports that Glapyra was married, "while she was a virgin,"[4] to Alexander, the son of Herod and the Hasmonean princess Mariamme. It should be noted that Antony and Cleopatra also had a son named "Alexander Helios" who was the same age.

The Jewish King Herod allegedly killed his son, Prince Alexander, c. 7 BCE. Later the widow Glapyra married Juba the king of Libya, whose first wife was Cleopatra Selene, Cleopatra's daughter. Josephus reports erroneously that Juba died c. 6 CE,[5] at which time Prince Alexander's half-brother Archelaus (Herod's son with a non-Jew) divorced his wife, another Mariamme. He then married Glapyra,

> ...who, during her marriage to him, saw the following dream: She thought she saw Alexander ... at which she rejoiced, and embraced him ... but he complained ... "O Glapyra! You have proved the saying to be true, that saying which assures us that

---

[2] Josephus, 1999, *Antiquities* 18.2.1 (26), 588.
[3] Eusebius, *Life of Constantine*, 3.55 and 3.58.
[4] Josephus, 1999, *Antiquities* 17.13.4 (349), 584.
[5] Josephus, 1999, *Antiquities* 17.13.4 (350), 584.

women are not to be trusted. Did you not pledge your faith to me? And were you not married to me when you were a virgin?"[6]

Immediately preceding the story of the Virgin Glapyra, Josephus tells the story of the "Spurious Alexander" who claimed to be her husband, Herod's Jewish son.[7] This Alexander swore that he and his brother Aristobulus had not been executed as Herod ordered.

However, Augustus Caesar personally judged him to be "spurious" because his hands were rough[8] from the work he did – i.e., carpentry. Through the telling of these two stories, Josephus identifies Glapyra as a "Virgin" and her husband as a "tekton." If they are also known as "The Virgin Mary" and the "carpenter Ioseph," then their son was Jesus I, born when Herod was King.

Pulling at this "Virgin Glapyra" thread reveals that the "Virgin Glapyra" was preceded by another "Glapyra," perhaps her unidentified mother. The first century historian Martial leaves the impression that she might have been a very willing Temple Virgin herself. In a particularly vulgar epigram, Martial claims to have read a complaint that Augustus Caesar lodged against Fulvia, one of Marc Antony's wives. In it he reveals the Elder Glapyra's relationship with Marc Antony. It's a little racy, but we're just the messengers:

> Spiteful censor of the Latin language, read six insolent verses of Caesar Augustus:
>
> Because Antony fucks Glapyra, Fulvia has arranged this punishment for me: that I fuck her too.
>
> That I fuck Fulvia? What if Manius begged me to bugger him? Would I? I don't think so, if I were sane.
>
> "Either fuck or let's fight," she says. Doesn't she know my prick is dearer to me than life itself?
>
> Let the trumpets blare!

[6] Josephus, 1999, *Antiquities* 17.13.4 (349-351), 584.
[7] Josephus, 1999, *Antiquities* 17.12.1-2 (324-338), 582-3.
[8] Josephus, 1999, *Antiquities* 17.12.2 (333), 583.

Augustus, you certainly grant my clever little books pardon, since
you are the expert at speaking with Roman frankness.[9]

Glapyra's lover Antony was "The New Dionysus"; therefore, to have sex with Antony – as with Theos and Kurios – was
to have sex with a deity. And the Virgin in these cases remained chaste even after a night of love making.

In another section of *Antiquities* Josephus reports that Caesar
made a present to each of Herod's two "virgin daughters" of
two hundred and fifty thousand [drachmae] of silver, and married them to Pheroras' sons.[10] Herod the Great and Pheroras
were brothers; their children were first cousins.

However, Josephus contradicts himself, writing that Herod
the Great had two daughters by Mariamme, the granddaughter
of the Jewish High Priest Hyrcanus. One is Salampsio and the
other is Cypros. The two sons of Pheroras are not named, a notable omission.

Equally strange, Herod's two Jewish virgin daughters – first
cousins of Pheroras' sons whom Josephus reported they married – did indeed marry their first cousins, but not the sons of
Pheroras. Salampsio married Phasaulus (son of Herod's brother Phasaulus), and Cypros married Antipater, son of Herod's
sister Salome[11] and one of her three husbands, Costobarus, notably, another "brother-of-the-rib." Furthermore, "Antipater"
or "Antepater" implies the biological father may not have been
Costobarus but preceded him.

The search for "Virgins" in the Works of Josephus continues:

Claudius took away from Antiochus that kingdom which he
possessed but gave him a certain part of Cilicia and Commagena:
he also set Alexander Lysimachus, the [Jewish] Alabarch [of Alex-
andria], at liberty, who had been his old friend, and steward to his
mother Antonia, but had been imprisoned by Gaius [Caligula] ...
Alexander's son Marcus married Bernice, the daughter of Agrip-

---

[9] Prudence Jones, *Cleopatra: A Sourcebook* (Norman: University of Oklahoma Press, 2006), 99; Martial (c. 96 CE), Epigram 11.20.

[10] Josephus, 1999, *Antiquities* 17.11.5 (322), 581.

[11] Josephus, 1999, *Antiquities* 18.5.4 (130), 596.

pa. But when Marcus was dead, who had married her *when she was a virgin*, Agrippa gave her in marriage to his brother Herod, and begged for him of Claudius the kingdom of Chalcis.[12]

And thus did Jewish king Agrippa depart this life [c. 44]. But he left behind him a son, Agrippa, a youth in the seventeenth year of his age, and three daughters; one of which, Bernice, was married to Herod, his father's brother, and was sixteen years old; the other two, Mariamme and Drusilla, were *still virgins*; the former was ten years old, and Drusilla six. Now these daughters were espoused by their father; Mariamme to Julius Archelaus Epiphanes, the son of Antiochus, the son of Chelcias; and Drusilla to the king of Commagena[13]

It seems strange that Josephus would specify that six and ten-year-old girls were "still virgins." Coincidentally six to ten was the age range during which a Vestal Virgin was chosen to begin training.

As previously noted, the early Church Fathers had no problem with Israelite Temple Virgins. In fact, they honored The Virgin Mary as the purest, most virtuous, and most blessed of them all. Church tradition, documented in the non-canonical "Infancy Gospel of James," holds that as a young girl the Virgin Mary was taken by her parents, Joachim and Anna, to the Temple in Jerusalem. The priest Zacharias, John the Baptist's father, took her into the Holy of Holies where only the High Priest was permitted to enter once a year on the Day of Atonement. There she was fed by a heavenly messenger[14] (perhaps the same messenger who introduced the Virgin Mary to Kurios). The Virgin lived and served in the Temple until her betrothal to Joseph of the House of David.[15]

"The Infancy Gospel of James" is dated to the mid-second century, about the time the New Testament was most likely finalized in its present form. It became quite popular among some segments of the early church, and certain traditions

[12] Josephus, 1999, *Antiquities* 19.5.1 (276-7), 633.
[13] Josephus, 1999, *Antiquities* 19.1.9 (354-5), 640. Emphasis added.
[14] Robert J. Miller, ed., *The Complete Gospels. Infancy Gospel of James*, 389, No. 13.
[15] Miller, *Infancy James*, 387, No. 9.

drawn from it remain popular today. Additionally, it may well hold some enigmatic clues; for instance, the parent's names, "Io-achim" and "Anna." Evidence that follows in Chapter Thirteen will show how Luke's character "Io Anna" is tied to this Virgin named "Mary."

Luke 1:28-33 – previously quoted – picks up the virgin thread at the time when Mary reaches the age to begin her ten years of active service. What follows Luke's introduction of the Messenger and Kurios to Mary is quite astounding when the key Greek words are examined for valid alternative meanings:

> The angel said, "The *Sacred Breath* will come upon you, and the *Most High Dynamis* will be a shadow over you; *Dio*, the child to be born to you, will be holy; he will be called 'Son of Theos'" (Lk 1:35; authors' interpretation with Greek insertions).

The angel signals enigma, and "sacred breath" in Hebrew is *Qodesh* (also *Kadesh*) *orach*. *Kadesh* is the location where Moses' sister Miriam died and was buried (Num 20:1); "orach" and "Rachel" share the same root.

"Dynamis" was a "Most High" Queen who left inscriptions referring to August Caesar as "Theos" and "son of Theos" (more about her in a moment). Luke's enigmas identify Dynamis as the "angel" who prophesies that "*Dio* ... will be holy; he will be called 'Son of Theos.'"

Homer (*Iliad* and *Odyssey*) identifies "Dia/Dio" as "Zeus" (Latin, *Jupiter*).[16] Given this interpretation of Dio, this verse can be tied to the name given three verses earlier: "...you will name him 'Ie-Sous'" (Lk 1:31). However, Dio at Lk 1:35 is usually translated as "therefore," sometimes as "so." No wonder Irenaeus railed against using Homer to interpret scripture! "Name him YaH-Zeus" followed by "Zeus, the child to be born to you..." was indeed a heresy. But this is exactly the name that was transmitted in these two verses.

"Dynamis" was "Most High Dynamis Philoromaios," Queen of the Bosporus Empire. Her grandfather was King

---

[16] Middle Liddell.

Mithridates the Great Eupator Dionysius of Pontus,[17] and her uncle was Mithridates Chrestus.[18] Ie-sous was not the first to be called "Chrestus."

Archaeologists have discovered three statues that Dynamis erected and dedicated to herself. Another was erected in honor of Augustus Caesar's wife, the first Roman Empress, Livia Drusilla. In Phanagoria (a peninsula in the area of the Black Sea and the Sea of Azov), Dynamis dedicated an inscription honoring Augustus as, "The emperor, Caesar, son of theos, the Theos Augustus, the overseer of every land and sea."[19]

In another inscription at the same location Dynamis refers to herself as "Empress and friend to Rome." In the temple of Aphrodite (home of the "Lady of Cypros"), Dynamis dedicated a statue of Livia, and the inscription refers to Livia as the "Empress and benefactress of Dynamis."

An early first century CE bust of Empress Livia was discovered at Arsinoe, Egypt, and Cleopatra's younger sister was named "Arsinoe." Dynamis seems to have gone to great lengths to identify Livia as Cleopatra's younger sister Arsinoe. And in doing so she also ties a thread from herself to Cleopatra.

Queen Dynamis' husband was Asander, a derivative of Alexander, surnamed "Philocaesar Philoromaios" ("lover of Caesar, lover of Rome"). Like Julius Caesar, Asander was born c. 110 BCE, but he outlived Julius by twenty-seven years. Asander died in 17 BCE, the year Augustus reinstated the Secular Games, the same year that money maker M. Sanquinius fashioned coins that depict a comet over the head of a wreathed man, assumed to be Julius Caesar. This conclusion is drawn from Suetonius, who reports that shortly after Julius was assassinated in 44 BCE, and just as the *Ludi Victoriae Cae-*

[17] Adrienne Mayor, *The Poison King: the life and legend of Mithridates, Rome's deadliest enemy* (Princeton: Princeton University Press, 2009), 364.
[18] Mayor, 2009, 45.
[19] S.T. Davis, D. Kendall, G. O'Collins. *The Trinity.* (Oxford: Oxford University Press, 2002), 30. (N.V.)

saris was getting underway, "a comet shone for seven successive days, rising about the eleventh hour, and was believed to be the soul of Caesar."[20]

Julius initiated the Ludi Victoriae Caesaris in 46 BCE to dedicate his Temple of Venus and to affirm that he was descended from Venus through Iulus, the son of Aeneas. Vergil wrote the *Aeneid* to emphasize this connection between the Julii bloodline and Venus – the planet and the goddess.

Asander and Dynamis had one known son, Tiberius Julius Aspurgus Philoromaios.[21] His wife, known only through numismatic evidence, was Gepae-pyris.[22]

Tiberius and Gepaepyris had two sons; the eldest was "Tiberius Julius Mithridates Philo-Germanicus Philopatris" ("son of Mithra, lover of Germanicus, lover of father").[23] Their second son was "Tiberius Julius Cotys I Philocaesar Philoromaios Eusebes" ("lover of Caesar, lover of Rome who is the Pious One").[24] Two sons: "Lover of father Germanicus" and "Lover of Caesar, Lover of Rome, The Pious One."

The name "Germanicus" associates this son of Tiberius Julius Aspurgus with Emperor Tiberius Julius Caesar's adopted son and heir, Germanicus. Do any of our philologists know of a Pious man of about the same age? Indeed: "There was a man in Jerusalem whose name was Simeon … he was righteous and pious…" (Lk 2:25).

Simeon is a "Pious One" and a "Righteous One"; therefore, we'll expand our search to look for Pious Ones and Righteous Ones. As might be expected, Luke offers some candidates, reporting:

---

[20] Suetonius, *Life of Julius Caesar* (Loeb, 1914), (Thayer Online 88.1).
[21] Ellis Hovell Minns, *Scythians and Greeks: A Survey of Ancient History and Archaeology on the North Coast of the Euxine from the Danube to the Caucasus.* (Cambridge: Cambridge University Press, 2011), 590-6. This book supports with archaeological and numismatic evidence the summarizing Wikipedia article, "Tiberius Julius Aspurgus."
[22] Minns, 1913, 594-596 , in support of Wikipedia, "Gepaepyris."
[23] Minns, 1913, 598, in support of Wikipedia, "Tiberius Julius Mithridates."
[24] Minns, 1913, 598, in support of Wikipedia, "Tiberius Julius Cotys."

In Caesarea there was a man named Cornelius, a centurion of the Italian Cohort ... He was a *pious* man ... One afternoon at about three o'clock he had a vision[25] ... he saw an angel of Theos[26] coming and saying, "Cornelius ... send men to Joppa for a certain *Simeon* who is called Peter; he is lodging with *Simeon* a tanner..." When the angel had left, he called two of his slaves and a *pious* soldier from the ranks of those who served him (excerpts from Acts 10:1-8 with Greek word insertions).

With the yellow-flag words "vision" and "angel of Theos," Luke signals "watch for enigmas." He then identifies two Simeons and a second man called "Pious." Two Simeons in one sentence says "dig deeper into the origin of Simeons."

Leah's second son with YHWH was Simeon; Simeon was "bound" by Joseph just long enough to father a son with a Canaanite[27] woman (Gen 42:24; 43:23); and this son's name was "Saul" (Gen 46:10).

According to "The Book of Numbers" in Hebrew Scripture, thousands of Simeonites disappeared between Moses' first and second censuses. The reason? Phineas, Moses' nephew (son of Aaron the Levite), killed a Simeonite, the son of Zimri the Nasi, and the Medianite woman he married. Phineas believed the double murder would appease YHWH and stave off a deadly plague.[28] Curiously his Uncle Moses also married a Medianite woman, daughter of Jethro-Reuel the Median High Priest.

Forty years after the Levite son of Aaron killed the Medianite woman and the son of the Simeonite Nasi, Moses' second census found that the number of Simeonites had dropped from 59,300[29] to 22,200,[30] a reduction of 37,100 men. What happened to them has remained a mystery.

However, "Simeons," "Simeonites" and "Medianites" reappear on a regular basis in Scripture – Hebrew, Christian, and

---

[25] Philo No. 20, striking statement.
[26] Philo No. 20, striking statement.
[27] Recall that *Ki aNNanite* women were descended from An and Ki.
[28] Num 25:7-9.
[29] Num 1:22.
[30] Num 26:14.

Apocryphal. Moses and the son of a Nasi of the Tribe of Simeon both married Medianite women. A Median High Priest re-
appears in *Acts* when Luke identifies Bar-Jesus as a "Magos," a
High Priest of the Median tribe, "one of the wise men in Persia
who interpreted dreams."[31] Theudas who came after Judas was
also a Magos, according to Josephus.[32]

What this tells us is that marriages between Simeonite Nasi
and Medianite women go at least as far back as Moses who
married the High Priest's daughter. And apparently, YHWH
did not approve of these marriages although LHM apparently
did.

At Acts 10:6, *Simeon*, a tanner, is lodging with a Simeon
called Peter; at Acts 18:3 Luke reveals that Paul is a tentmaker
and thus a tanner. These threads identify the two Simeons in
this scene as "Simeon called Peter" ("Simon of Petra") and
"Simeon the tentmaker."

What does all this mean: Two Simeons in *Acts*; Moses and a
Simeonite Nasi marry Medianite women; Medianites are associated with Mithra and Mithridates Chrestus; the appearance
and reappearance of Magoi, High Priests of the Medians?
Questions abound.

These Mithra-clues point to one of the competing religions
that concerned the Orthodox Church of the second through
fourth centuries: Roman Mithraism. It became a common practice to build Christian Churches over the ruins of the underground houses of worship called "Mithraea." Archaeologists

---

[31] Perseus: Middle Liddell.
[32] Josephus, 1999, *Antiquities* 20.5.1 (97), 648.

date most of the Mithraea to between 100 BCE and 300 CE, and most have been discovered in the Roman Empire.[33]

Is there something more to be learned from the family of Asander and Dynamis and their two sons, Mithridates, "Lover of father Germanicus" and "The Pious One"? Where shall we look?

According to *Acts*, Ananias was a pious man as well as Saul/Paul's brother:

> "Ananias a certain man ... *pious* ... stood beside me and said, "*Brother* Saul, receive your sight!" And at that very moment I was able to *see him*. Then he said: "Theos *our father* has chosen you to know his will and *to see the Righteous One* and to *hear words from his mouth* ... be his witness ... be baptized and wash your sins away, calling on his name" (excerpts from Acts 22:12-16).[34]

Who are these men identified as "The Pious One" and "The Righteous One"? Did the Pious One "restore Paul's vision" by making him *see* that war against his family and Rome was futile? And did words from the mouth of the "Righteous One" guide Paul when he was "sitting at the feet" of his teacher Gamaliel?

A few more threads are yet to be gathered before taking the final step of analyzing the meanings and answering these questions. And more threads will be identified in Chapter Thirteen.

---

[33] Tertullian notes that prior to the Mithraic initiation ceremony the initiate is given a ritual bath and at the end of the ceremony, receives a mark on the forehead. He describes these rites as a "diabolical counterfeit of the baptism and chrismation of Christians." Louis Bouyer, The Christian Mystery. (London: T.T. Clark International, 2004), 70; (footnote: *De praescriptione, Laer.*, 40 (Turchi, no. 341), 288 N.V.) Justin Martyr compares Mithraic initiation communion with the Eucharist: "Wherefore also the evil demons in mimicry have handed down that the same thing should be done in the Mysteries of Mithras. For that bread and a cup of water are in these mysteries set before the initiate with certain speeches you either know or can learn." Martyr, Justin Trans. Leslie William Barnard, ed. *The First and Second Apologies*. (New York: Paulist Press, 1997), 260.

[34] Emphasis added.

CHAPTER THIRTEEN

Following Philo to The Magdalene

Part I

Watchtower of the Flock

Orthodox Christianity has paid little attention to Hebrew Scripture that seems to prophesy a Jewish High Priestess and/or a Goddess: "And you, O Magdala of the flock, hill of daughter Zion, to you it shall come, the former dominion shall come, the sovereignty of daughter Jerusalem" (Mic 4:8; Hebrew word insertion).

As a result, the possibility that prophecy existed – and was fulfilled – has never been seriously explored. Philo's Philology applied to Mark's Gospel reveals her arrival at the time of Jesus: "When the Sabbath was over, Mary Magdalene, and Mary the mother of James and Salome, brought spices so that they might go and anoint him" (Mk 16:1).

A careful examination of each part of the key Greek words in Mk 16:1 allows equally valid translation options that carry a vastly different connotation. Mark's opening words in his final chapter are: "When the Sabbath was over..." [Greek, *Kai diagenomenou tou sabbatou...*]

"Dia," as previously noted, was used by Homer and others to identify Zeus. It is also defined as "heavenly (of or from

Zeus); through (to express conditions or states)";[1] *genomenou* is defined as "to come into a new state of being."[2]

Another source adds, "*ginomai* (Strong's No. 1096): ... to emerge, become, transitioning from one point (realm, condition) to another ... a change of condition, state or place (attributed to Vine, Unger, White, NT, 109),"[3] and concludes with this intriguing option, quoting M. Vincent: "to come into being/manifestation implying motion, movement, or growth (at 2 Pet 1:4). Thus it is used for God's actions as emerging from eternity and becoming (showing themselves) in time (physical space)."[4]

Therefore, even orthodox sources agree that "diagenomenou" can be translated as "a deity crossed over from the realm of spirit and became visible at a place in time and space."

The word "Shabbat," translated as "Sabbath" is Strong's No. 4520. The Hebrew word from which "Sabbath" is derived is the same word from which the name of an ancient, virtually unknown Hebrew goddess is derived. Her name was "Shabbat Hamalka":

> Among the goddesses representing either the female side of Yahweh or his consorts, such as Asherah, Shekinah, Anath, and Lilith, Shabbat Hamalka[5] has a unique personality and origin. Her myth strongly influenced Jewish thought, and contributed to the strength of home and family that had improved the odds for physical and spiritual Jewish survival.
>
> The name means Queen of the Sabbath, and the entity is the personification of the Jewish day of rest, Saturday. She still possesses a prominent position in Judaic mythology. For example, Israeli children, even in completely nonreligious surroundings, still sing songs to her every Friday afternoon (in Hebrew *Erev Shabatt* meaning the "Sabbath Eve") *before the Queen "descends" from Heaven to grace the world for twenty-four hours.*[6]

---

[1] Middle Liddell.
[2] Middle Liddell.
[3] Helps™ Word-studies (1987, 2011) Help Ministries, Inc.; Biblehub Online.
[4] Ibid.
[5] Also valid: *Ish aBBa et Ha eM eL Ki,* "Humankind Father the Mother El Ki."
[6] Ilil Arbel, 2002, "Shabbat Hamalka."

Hebrew words that are similar to Μαρία (Mary) include *Merom*, defined as "exalted, high"; *mayim*, translated as "water"; *sha-mayim*, translated as "heaven"; *meiromai*, defined as "a part, share, portion."[7] And as previously shown, the Hebrew word *MGDL* is translated as "watchtower." Furthermore, MRM can be rendered *eM oR eM*, "Mother Light, Mother."

With this added information, Mk 16:1 can be reexamined for an esoteric message. And it appears to be another merging of ancient deities, this time a Goddess. A translation – as correct as the traditional version – is: "Shabbat (YHWH's consort) crossed over from the realm of Spirit into the visible realm. Merom (Shadday's "Light Mother") Magdalene (the Watchtower), accompanied by the exalted mother of James and Salome, took spices to the tomb to anoint Jesus."

The Egyptian myth which runs parallel to portions of "The Jesus Story" reports that on the third day after Osiris/Serapis' death, his mother and his sister-wife – the goddess Isis – entered the tomb with healing spices. They were there to bring Osiris back to life. To the Egyptians the three days in the tomb represented the time it takes a small, lifeless seed of grain to break through the earth on its way to becoming the primary source of food. And as previously noted, the most popular version of the Osiris myth in the first century was written by Lucius Mestrius Plutarchus.

Myths are created to explain the visible and the invisible realms in stories everyone can understand, remember, and repeat. And they are written so that they can be performed to entertain the people. The purpose is twofold: (1) to create fear (to manipulate the thinking and actions of the fearful); (2) to provide answers that will calm those fears (to gain the trust and obedience of the dependent people).

With the introduction of a "Fourth sect of Judaism," a "Iesous Myth" was needed to do the same for the Israelites and Judeans of the Roman Empire. YHWH's temper and retribu-

---

[7] NAS (Strong's Greek 3313).

tions put quite a strain on his people, and without the moderating mediation of a goddess such as Shabbat or Asherah, YHWH's wrath knew no bounds. The Goddess, identified with "Wisdom," puts YHWH's power to work in ways that are less retaliatory and more constructive.

The evidence in Mark 16 suggests that the myths of Osiris/Serapis and Isis are woven into the story of the return of the Jewish King from the House of David. Accompanying him is YHWH's ancient bride, "Shabbat," but with a new name which fulfills Micah's Prophecy: "Magdala." "Maria" is added to signify that she represents the "Mother of the Children of Light." She is "Mary The Magdalene." And she may be more, a thread that will be picked up in the second part of this chapter.

CHAPTER THIRTEEN

Following Philo to The Magdalene

Part II

Anointing Sinner

For nearly two thousand years, Mary Magdalene, identified by the Church as Luke's anointing sinner, has been labeled a prostitute. And although Luke is quoted as the source, he is not to blame:

> And a woman in the city, who was a sinner,[1] having learned that he was eating in the Pharisee's house, brought an *alabaster jar of ointment*. She stood behind him at his feet, weeping, and began to bathe his feet with her tears and to dry them with her hair. Then she continued kissing his feet and anointing them with the ointment (Lk 7:37-38).[2]

Soon after Jesus is anointed by the "sinner" with an alabaster jar of ointment, Mary Magdalene begins traveling with him and the twelve:

> Soon afterwards he went on through cities and villages … The twelve were with him, as well as some women who had been cured of evil spirits and infirmities: 'Mary,' called 'Magdalene' … and 'Ioanna…[3] (excerpted from Lk 8:1-2).

It's easy to see why the Early Church Fathers identified Mary Magdalene as the anointing sinner. And their conclusion

---

[1] Strong's Greek 268, *hamartólos*.
[2] Emphasis added.
[3] Philo's rule no. 5: different meaning from different combination of words; Philo's rule no. 6: study synonyms.

that her sin was prostitution is to be expected – after all, she was a woman.

Additionally, around 591 Pope Gregory I issued a homily on Luke's gospel, and "settled doctrine" for nearly fourteen hundred years proclaimed that Mary Magdalene *was* the anointing woman, and her sin *was* prostitution.

However, the Vatican reversed its position via the 1969 Roman Missal. But alas, it was too late; her reputation was forever ruined. Most people today still believe The Magdalene was a repentant prostitute and certainly not a "Temple Virgin."

The questions to be answered: (1) Was Mary Magdalene Luke's "Anointing Sinner"? (2) Did Luke intend to cast her as a "prostitute," or was he leaving enigmas that lead to the woman in historians' accounts who was called "Mary Magdalene" in Scripture?

The key to solving Luke's 7:37 enigma is to unlock the secrets of the "alabaster jar." The Egyptian word *a-la-baste* refers to vessels of Bastet, an important but little-known Egyptian lioness-goddess dated to c. 3200 BCE.

Bastet is the daughter of Ra, wife of the lion-god known as both "Bes" and "Ptah," and mother of Mihos, also known as "Miysis," "Maihesa," and "Maahes." Perhaps the name "MoSeS" is derived from this "son of Bastet and Bes." And perhaps the Essenes rendered "MSS," "Moses" *and* "eM iShShah," "mother (was) Ishshah."

Bastet was the goddess of sunrise, music, dance, family, fertility, birth, and healing. She is depicted as a lioness in figures sitting atop alabaster vessels; the hieroglyph for her name is "ointment jar." She is associated with protective and healing ointments and is the goddess of protection against contagious diseases and evil spirits.[4]

The attributes associated with Bastet's husband Bes began during the Old Kingdom when he was associated with fertility,

---

[4] Herman te Velde; "Bastet." In Karel van der Toorn, Bob Becking and Pieter W. van der Horst. *Dictionary of Demons and Deities in the Bible* (2nd ed.). Leiden: Brill Academic (1999), 164–5.

circumcision, and harvest rituals. By the Middle Kingdom he had become a guardian of the home, infants, and new mothers and was a protector of pregnant women.

Other archaeological evidence – The Warka Vase,[5] an alabaster jar also dated to c. 3200-3000 BCE – was discovered by German Assyriologists between 1929 and 1934 in the temple complex of the goddess Inanna,[6] whose father was the Moon-God, Sin. It is among the earliest surviving works of narrative relief sculpture yet found.

Ten tiers of carvings seem to depict the story of creation. On the lowest tier are images of vegetation found in the Tigris and Euphrates delta – the location of the Garden of Eden.

The layer above depicts animals – oxen and sheep followed by nude males – "men of Earth" (Hebrew *Adam*), carrying containers of fruit and grain.

The earliest Sumerian rulers were Enlil, Ninlil, their son the Moon-god Sin, and his daughter Inanna.[7] And a procession of plants followed by animals followed by "Adam" eventually reaches the top tier where a male Adam offers a bowl of fruit and grain to Inanna. Standing nearby is a figure in ceremonial clothing – presumably a chieftain/priest – (Hebrew, *Nasi*).

Bastet and Bes represent reproduction, and the "El Ab Istar Jar" represents a specific lineage, "beloved uncles" descended from Ishtar-Venus.

The Wilderness and the Mountain made famous by Moses were surely named after this god called "Sin."

---

[5] See photograph, p. 350.

[6] Recorded as find number W14873 in the expedition's field book under an entry dated 2 January 1929, which read "Großes Gefäß aus Alabaster, ca. 96 cm hoch mit Flachrelief" ("large container of alabaster, circa 96 cm high with flat-reliefs"). Ralf B. Wartke, "Eine Vermißtenliste (2): Die 'Warka-Vase' aus Bagdad," Frankfurter Allgemeine Zeitung 26 April 2003, Nbr 97, page 39.

[7] Elizabeth Simpson, "Phrygian Furniture from Gordion," in Georgina Herrmann (ed.), *The Furniture of Ancient Western Asia*, Mainz: Philipp Von Zabern 1996), 198–201. In Phrygian art of the 8th century BCE, the attributes of the Phrygian mother-goddess include attendant lions. The Hurrian goddess *Hannahannah* was also earlier associated with lions, as was Sumerian *Inanna*, daughter of the Moon-god, *Sin*.

Furthermore, "Sinner" identifies those who were devoted to the god, Sin. And "Sin," Hebrew *SN*, can also be rendered *Ish An*, translated "Man of An." Not "Man of Earth, Adam," but rather "Mankind descended from Ansar and Ishtar." His identity in Egypt is "Bes," and "BS" can be rendered *Ab Ish*, "father of Ish-sons." This "god-lineage," "Bes," "An," "El," and "Sin" was the genesis of intelligent humankind, according to Sumerian, Babylonian, and Egyptian Scripture.

Furthermore, "Sin" is more than a deity, a wilderness, and a mountain. It is also the name of an ancient city in Egypt that has an intriguing history before and after its name was changed to "Pelusium":

333 BCE: Sin/Pelusium welcomed Alexander the Great who placed a garrison in the city under the command of one of the "Companions of the King."[8]

173 BCE: Antiochus Epiphanes defeated Ptolemy Philometor's troops under the walls of Sin/Pelusium which he retained after he left the rest of Egypt.[9] By the time Syria was conquered, Sin/Pelusium had been restored to the Ptolemies.

55 BCE: Ptolemy Auletes, Cleopatra's father, called on the Romans for assistance. Marc Antony came to the rescue but made himself *Master of the City* when he learned that Ptolemy planned to slaughter Sin/Pelusium's citizens.[10]

48 BCE: Pompey the Great was allegedly murdered in Sin/ Pelusium. He was already known as "Ptolemy Auletes," Cleopatra's father.

30 BCE: Shortly after his victory at the Battle of Actium, Augustus appeared before Sin/Pelusium and was admitted within its walls.

This reconstructed etymology for the word "sinner" works to perfection; people who rejected YHWH and turned to the moon-god Sin were "Sinners." Sin's family, including his daughter Inanna, were "Sinners" and their descendants were "Sinners"; therefore, Luke's anointing sinner was identified as

---

[8]Arrian, *Exp. Alex.* iii. 1, seq.; Quintus Curtius iv. 33.

[9] Polybius, *Legat.* § 82; Hieronym. *in Dan.* xi.

[10] Plutarch, *Life of Antony*; Valerius Maximus. 9.1.

a descendant of Sin and Inanna, and the city of Sin, Egypt, was her family's abode.

According to Webster, the English word "sinner" is derived from the Anglo Saxon, *synn*. It is noted as, "akin to"[11] the older Germanic, *sunde*. We propose that *sunde* may be akin to the even older Akkadian, *Su'en*, *Sîn*, the moon god. It seems likely that the name of a competing deity, "Sin," evolved into a word that means "an offense against religious or moral law."[12]

However, we have one little problem: the Christian Bible was composed in Greek; Luke's "sinner" (Lk 7:37) is *hamartolos*, derived from *ha-martanó*.[13] In Greek, *ha* means "not" and *martano* from *meros* is defined as: "from meiromai (to receive one's portion)."[14] Therefore, a "hamartolos" is one who will not receive a portion of an inheritance.

Perhaps Luke's enigmatic "sinner" is to be converted to Hebrew where *ha* means "the" and *meros* can be rendered *eM Or iSh*.

We should also look to the Babylonian precursor of Genesis where a similar word, *harimtu*, is found in the *Epic of Gilgamesh*. The Sumerian goddess, Shamkat, is described as "the Temple harimtu." Her purpose and power is revealed in the story of Gilgamesh's adversary, Enkidu, whose father is described as a "donkey." After six days and seven nights of lovemaking, the goddess Shamkat turned Enkidu from a wild man into Gilgamesh's cultured sidekick and best friend.[15] It appears that the Israelites' "Temple ha-martanó," like the Sumerians' "Temple harimtu," were "Sacred Vessels" descended from the "First Parents."

There is one other possibility: no one has ever seen Luke's original composition; therefore, no one can know if he attached

---

[11] *Webster's New Twentieth Century Dictionary, Second Edition* (New York: Simon & Schuster, 1979), 1693.

[12] Merriam-Webster Dictionary, Online.

[13] NAS (Strong's Greek 268).

[14] NAS (Strong's Greek 3313).

[15] *Myths from Mesopotamia*, Stephanie Dalley ed. and trans. (Oxford: Oxford 1989), Introduction xxvii-xxviii.

the proper noun "Sinner" to the anointing woman and a later translator changed it to the Greek, *hamartolos*. Perhaps it's irrelevant since all options tie the "anointing sinner" to Temple Virgins whose ancestors were the First Parents of Ishshah and Ishenes.

Luke offers two more critical clues about this particular Temple Virgin: Mary was called "Magdalene ... and Ioanna" [Greek Ἰωάννα] (Lk 8:2-3; 24:10). The thread picked up in The Infancy Gospel of James, the daughter of Io-chim and Anna, can now be tied to Luke's, "Mary Magdalene, Io-Anna."

As with Jesus the Elder and Bar-Jesus, more than one woman is called "Virgin Mary." And this answers the question of how Jesus' brother James, the purported author of The Infancy Gospel, could have written a first-hand account of the birth and early years of the Virgin Mary. James and Jesus were of the same generation; the *first* Virgin Mary was a generation older; therefore, James could not have written a first-hand account of her birth and childhood.

The answer is quite simple: James' story is about the Io-Anna who became the "Virgin Mary Magdalene II," the second generation "Virgin Mary" portrayed in the later versions of the annual festival.

This is not to say that James actually authored this work. However, it does say that attributing it to him was not a careless mistake. In fact, his name might have been chosen in order to report this second generation "Virgin Mary Magdalene." The closing paragraph tells us that James authored the account at the time of the death of Herod, which refers to the death of Herod *Agrippa* c. 44 CE, not the death of Herod *the Great* prior to 4 BCE.

Luke leaves a companion clue to the identity of Mary Magdalene Ioanna when he later adds:

> For just as Jonah [Greek Ἰωνᾶ] became a sign to the people of Nineveh,[16] so the Son of Man will be to this generation. The Queen

---

16 Philo's rule no. 1: doubling of a phrase.

of the South will rise at the judgment with the people of this generation and condemn them, because she came from the ends of the earth to listen to the Wisdom of Solomon, and see, something greater than Solomon is here! The people of Nineveh[17] will rise up at the judgment with this generation and condemn it, because they repented at the proclamation of Jonah, and see, something greater than Jonah [Greek, Ἰωνᾶ] is here! (Lk 11:30-2; NRSV with Greek insertion).

Enigmatically, "something greater than Ἰωνᾶ" is Ἰωάννα. "Ioanna" contains a greater number of letters than does "Iona." Also notable, the city of Nineveh plays a key role in the story of another first century religious leader, Apollonius of Tyana.

Roman Empress Julia Domna (170-217 CE) sponsored the reconstruction of the biography of Apollonius which was written in the late second or early third century by Philostratus. His work, "Life of Apollonius," is allegedly based on an earlier text curiously titled, "Scraps from the Manger." Philostratus attributed this source to Apollonius' loyal companion Damis.[18] According to Philostratus, Apollonius:

> reached the ancient city of Nineveh, where he found an idol set up of barbarous aspect, and it is, they say, *Io*, the daughter of Inachus, with little horns budding on her temples. While he was staying there and forming wiser conclusions about the image than could the priests and prophets, one Damis, a native of Nineveh, joined him as a pupil, the same, as I said at the beginning, who became the companion of his wanderings abroad and his fellow-traveler and *associate in all wisdom*, and who has preserved to us many particulars of the sage.[19]

"Life of Apollonius" describes him as the son of the god Apollo and a mortal woman; he was born about the same time as Bar-Jesus. The name of the city associated with Apollonius, Nineveh, may have been derived from *Nina*, one of the Babylonian names for the goddess Ishtar. "The ideogram means

---

[17] Philo's rule no. 1: doubling of a phrase.

[18] *Damis* in Hebrew means "blood of Ish."

[19] Philostratus, *Life of Apollonius* 1.19. Emphasis added.

'house or place of fish,'" and "the Aramaic word, nuna, denotes fish."[20]

How Apollonius is related to Bar-Jesus is a topic that will be addressed in Chapter Fifteen.

The answer to the chapter question is that Mary Magdalene *is* the "hamartolos" with the alabaster jar. She was a Temple Virgin, mated with Theos to produce Sons of Theos. But she was not a common whore as many still believe.

Another Hebrew Bible hypotext carries clues to finding the historical Mary Magdalene. It is a poem about another "anointing woman" who is also the "shepherd of a flock," a MGDL DR:

> If you do not know,
> O fairest among women,
> follow the tracks of the flock,
> and pasture your kids
> beside the shepherds' tents.

> I compare you, my love,
> to a mare among Pharaoh's
> chariots (Song 1:8-9).

> While the king was on his couch,
> My nard gave forth its fragrance (Song 1:12).

> I adjure you, O daughters of
> Jerusalem, (Song 2:7).

> Daughters of Jerusalem,
> Come out. (Song 3:10-11).

> You have ravished my heart, my
> Sister, my bride …(Song 4:9)

> How sweet is your love, my sister,
> My bride! (Song 4:10).

> A garden locked is my sister,
> My bride… (Song 4:12).

---

[20] Jewish Encyclopedia Online: "Nineveh."

I come to my garden, my sister,
My bride;
I gather my myrrh with my
Spice,
I eat my honeycomb with my
Honey,
I drink my wine with my milk (Song 5:1).

If Solomon's anointing "watchtower of the flock" is a "sister and a bride," it is probable that Jesus' anointing woman, Mary Magdalene, was also his sister – more likely his step-sister and bride. We have already encountered a "virgin" who became a "widow" and remarried. Her name was Glapyra, and she had two sons and two subsequent husbands, one of whom had a daughter of about the same age as her sons.

Chapter Eleven ended with a series of questions still awaiting answers: Did Plutarch really mean to say that his stories about Julius Caesar, Antony and Cleopatra did not actually happen in the manner in which he related them? That Julius was not assassinated on the Ides of March? That Antony and Cleopatra did not commit suicide after the Battle of Actium? That their assumed-dead children all survived into the first century and had children of their own? That Cleopatra may not have been a vicious killer of her brothers and sister Arsinoe? That Caesar Augustus did not execute Caesarion and Antyllus?

These lingering questions require a re-examination of Julius Caesar and Marc Antony and the blending of their bloodlines with the Ptolemaic Dynasty that culminated with Cleopatra. The Julii-Ptolemaic bloodline was passed on through the children born to Cleopatra and Julius Caesar (Plutarch alludes to a child born after the assassination in 44 BCE[21]).

---

[21] Plutarch, *Life of Antony*. (Loeb 1920 translation), 54.4, 262-3.

However, this doubly-royal bloodline appeared to come to an abrupt end following Cleopatra's defeat in the Battle of Actium. Plutarch reports that,

> Caesarion, who was said to be Cleopatra's son by Julius Caesar, was sent by his mother, with much treasure, into India, by way of Ethiopia. There Rhodon, another tutor like Theodorus, persuaded him to go back on the ground that Augustus Caesar invited him to take the kingdom.[22]

Notably, Plutarch fails to disclose the circumstances surrounding Caesarion's alleged death. And as he himself warned, what he wrote about gods and goddesses should not be interpreted literally. The enigmatic evidence reveals that "Tiberius Julius Caesar," Octavian's alleged step-son, was in fact Caesarion, son of Julius and Cleopatra. If true, Caesar's promise was fulfilled when Tiberius "took the Kingdom" as Emperor of Rome in 14 CE following Augustus Caesar's death.

---

[22] Plutarch, *Life of Antony*, (Loeb, 1920), (Thayer Online 81.1).

CHAPTER FOURTEEN

Following Philo to the Ides of March
and the Battle of Actium

Plutarch was quite unambiguous when he wrote the introduction to "Isis and Osiris" and addressed it to "My Dear Clea":

> Whenever you hear the traditional tales which the Egyptians tell about the gods, their wanderings, dismemberments, and many experiences ... you must not think that any of these tales actually happened in the manner in which they are related.[1]

Why then has History interpreted Plutarch's stories about the people literally identified as "gods" literally? Apparently, historians have considered Plutarch's admonition regarding "stories about gods" to be irrelevant to his "histories." And even though stories about Julius, Antony, and Cleopatra contain outrageously impossible sections, students and scholars of history use logic to pick and choose which portions of Plutarch's "Parallel Lives" are historical and which are fictional. If a portion of the story is simply too extraordinary to be credible it is judged "fictional"; portions that are believable are judged "historical."

Plutarch, however, left specific instructions about how to read his histories when a god or goddess is the subject. And it quickly becomes apparent that he inserted clues when his story is about to deliver a fictional account of events. In fact, Plutarch seems to employ Philo's method to signal enigmas when he writes a paragraph containing multiple yellow flags:

> But destiny, it would seem, is not so much unexpected as it is unavoidable, since they say that amazing signs and apparitions were seen. Now, as for lights in the heavens, crashing sounds

---

[1] Plutarch, Moralia: Isis and Osiris, 1st-2nd Century.

borne all about by night, and birds of *omen* coming down into the forum, it is perhaps not worthwhile to mention these *precursors* of so great an event; but Strabo the philosopher says that multitudes of men all on fire were seen rushing up, and a soldier's slave threw from his hand a copious flame and seemed to the spectators to be burning, but when the *flame ceased the man was uninjured*; he says, moreover, that when Caesar himself was sacrificing, the heart of the victim was not to be found, and the prodigy caused fear, since in the course of nature, certainly, an animal without a heart could not exist. The following story, too, is told by many. A certain *seer* warned Caesar to be on his guard against a great peril on the day of the month of March which the Romans call the Ides; and when the day had come and Caesar was on his way to the senate-house, he greeted the seer with a jest and said: "Well, the Ides of March are come," and the seer said to him softly: "Ay, they are come, but they are not gone."[2]

These otherworldly events are superstitions, and Plutarch also warns that "… superstition is no less an evil than atheism." Plutarch is signaling that the narrative which follows did not actually happen as he describes it.

Plutarch continues reciting more of these signs that signal "enigmas":

On the day before when Marcus Lepidus was entertaining him at supper, Caesar chanced to be signing letters, as his custom was, while reclining at table, and the discourse turned suddenly upon the question what sort of death was the best; before anyone could answer Caesar cried out: "That which is unexpected." After this, while he was sleeping as usual by the side of his wife, all the windows and doors of the chamber flew open at once, and Caesar, confounded by the noise and the light of the moon shining down upon him, noticed that Calpurnia was in a deep slumber, but was uttering indistinct words and inarticulate groans in her sleep; for she dreamed, as it proved, that she was holding her murdered husband in her arms and bewailing him.

Some, however, say that this was not the vision which the woman had; but that there was attached to Caesar's house to give it adornment and distinction, by vote of the senate, a gable-

---

[2] Plutarch, *Life of Julius Caesar* (Loeb, 1919), (Thayer Online 63.1-6). Emphasis added.

ornament, as Livy says, and it was this which Calpurnia in her dreams saw torn down, and therefore, as she thought, wailed and wept. Then day came, she begged Caesar, if it was possible, not to go out, but to postpone the meeting of the senate; if, however, he had no concern at all for her dreams, she besought him to inquire by other modes of divination and by sacrifices concerning the future.

And Caesar also, as it would appear, was in some suspicion and fear. For never before had he perceived in Calpurnia any womanish superstition, but now he saw that she was in great distress. And when the seers also, after many sacrifices, told him that the omens were unfavorable, he resolved to send Antony and dismiss the senate.[3]

So, even though he notes that "superstition is no less evil than atheism," Plutarch describes the omens and superstitions that convinced Julius his life was in danger. And these omens continue to pour forth as his fable slowly unfolds:

Decimus Brutus, surnamed Albinus, who was so trusted by Caesar that he was in his will as his second heir, had joined in the conspiracy of the other Brutus and Cassius. Fearing that Caesar might avoid the Senate that day, and their plot would be discovered, Albinus ridiculed the seers and chided Caesar for believing the senators could be so malicious as to plot his assassination. Albinus took Caesar by the hand and began to lead him along toward his pending death when a slave belonging to someone else, eager to get at Caesar, but unable to do so for the press of numbers about him, forced his way into the house, gave himself into the hands of Calpurnia, and bade her keep him secure until Caesar came back, since he had important matters to report to him.[4]

Artemidorus, a Cnidian by birth,[5] a teacher of Greek philosophy[6]... delivered a small roll to Caesar on which he had written the warning that his life was in danger; but seeing that Caesar took all such rolls and handed them to his attendants, he came

---

[3] Plutarch, *Life of Julius Caesar* (Loeb, 1919), (Thayer Online 63.7-12).
[4] Plutarch, *Life of Julius Caesar* (Loeb, 1919), (Thayer Online 64.1-6).
[5] Philo's rule no. 2: an apparently superfluous expression.
[6] Philo's rule no. 2: an apparently superfluous expression.

quite near, and said: "Read this, Caesar, by thyself, and speedily; for it contains matters of importance and of concern to thee."[7]

Plutarch probably assumed that everyone would know the most famous Cnidian of all time is the goddess Aphrodite whose other names are "Venus," "Artemis," "and Ishtar." In fact, Artemi-dorus who delivered the warning is named for the goddess Artemis. And the second half of the name, "Doris," is Greek for "gift," identifying this Greek philosopher as a "gift from Artemis."

Perhaps Plutarch chose the name "Artemi-dorus" to identify this participant in the drama as a descendant of the goddess and a goddess herself. And perhaps "Artemi-dorus" was to be tied to Doris, Herod the Great's *first* wife. Their son was Antipater, a name that can be separated into "anti" or "ante" ("not" or "before") and "pater" ("father").

Enigmatically then, Antipater's father came before Doris married Herod. Furthermore, when the Marc Antony thread is tied to the Herod the Great thread, as multiple clues suggest, then Julius Caesar is the one who came before. Therefore, Antipater would have been *his* son and "Doris" would have been Cleopatra.

Plutarch's enigmas continue as he reaches the "moral of the story":

Caesar took the roll and would have read it, but was prevented by the multitude of people who engaged his attention, although he set out to do so many times, and holding in his hand and retaining that roll alone, he passed on into the senate.[8]

These things may have happened of their own accord; the place, however, which was the scene of that struggle and murder, and in which the senate was then assembled, since it contained a statue of Pompey and had been dedicated by Pompey as an additional ornament to his theatre, made it wholly clear that *it was the work of some heavenly power which was calling and guiding the action.*[9]

---

[7] Plutarch, *Life of Julius Caesar* (Loeb, 1919), (Thayer Online 65.1-2).

[8] Plutarch, *Life of Julius Caesar* (Loeb, 1919), (Thayer Online 65.3).

[9] Plutarch, *Life of Julius Caesar* (Loeb, 1919), (Thayer Online 66.1).

Tucked within the last sentence is the moral of this story – the literal history. It was "the work of some *Ouranios Dynamis* that was guiding the action." And that "heavenly power" was wielded by the gods and goddess in this narrative, identified as "Ouranios" (Plato's "Venus-Urania") and "Dynamis"; "Dynamis," Asander's wife and mother of Tiberius Julius Aspurgus Philoromaios; "Dynamis," the "messenger" who introduced the Virgin Mary to Kurios. Add more threads to the "Dynamis-Cleopatra" strand.

What is Plutarch's message – the foremost *fact* in this fable? *Julius, Antony and Cleopatra were behind the faked assassination of the Divine Julius son of Venus on the Ides of March.* Why would they want to fake his death? One reason for faking someone's death is because a dead person can't be assassinated. Furthermore, the wars for control of Rome – whether factual or fictional – had been won; the duties of Rome's leader could be safely passed on to Julius' descendants. All that remained unresolved was the war that was still being waged between Orthodox and Hellenized Jews.[10]

Plutarch's account of The Battle of Actium recited in "Life of Antony" is equally stunning when examined carefully for the moral of the story. Plutarch writes:

> Cleopatra, indeed, both then and at other times when she appeared in public, assumed a robe sacred to Isis, and was addressed as the *New Isis*.[11]

> When Antony made his entry into Ephesus, women arrayed like *Bacchanals*, and men and boys like *Satyrs* and *Pans*, led the way before him, and the city was full of ivy and thyrsus-wands and harps and pipes and flutes, the people hailing him as *Dionysus* Carnivorous and Savage."[12]

---

[10] James Ponet, "The Maccabees and the Hellenists: Hanukkah as Jewish Civil War"; Slate Magazine Online, 2005.

[11] Plutarch, *Life of Antony* (Loeb, 1920), (Thayer Online 54.6).

[12] Plutarch, *Life of Antony* (Loeb, 1920), (Thayer Online 24.3). Emphasis added.

Antony associated himself with Heracles in lineage, and with Dionysus in the mode of life which he adopted, as I have said, and he was called the New Dionysus.[13]

Once again, Plutarch establishes for his readers that the stories about Antony and Cleopatra are about a god and goddess. And as with the story of Julius' assassination, he opens the fable with obvious signals that it is not to be interpreted literally:

The following signs are said to have been given before the war. Pisaurum, a city colonized by Antony situated near the Adriatic, was swallowed by chasms in the earth.

From one of the marble statues of Antony near Alba sweat oozed for many days, and though it was wiped away it did not cease. In Patrae, while Antony was staying there, the Heracleium was destroyed by lightning; and at Athens the Dionysus in the Battle of the Giants was dislodged by the winds and carried down into the theatre.

The same tempest fell upon the colossal figures of Eumenes and Attalus at Athens, on which the name of Antony had been inscribed, and prostrated them, and them alone out of many. Moreover the admiral's ship of Cleopatra was called Antonius, and a dire sign was given with regard to it. Some swallows, namely, made their nest under its stern; but other swallows attacked these, drove them out and destroyed their nestlings.

Plutarch inserts the clues necessary to alert philologists that the literal elements of the accounts that follow these otherworldly signs are to be disregarded. To find the true story – the *history* – the "moral" of the fable must be identified.

Now examine carefully the resources of the two combatants and what ultimately happens during the Battle of Actium. First,

Antony had no fewer than five hundred fighting ships, among which were many vessels of eight and ten banks of oars, arrayed in pompous and festal fashion; he also had one hundred thousand infantry soldiers and twelve thousand horsemen.[14]

Now pay close attention to what Plutarch reports regarding Octavian's resources?

---

[13] Plutarch, *Life of Antony* (Loeb, 1920), (Thayer Online 60.2).
[14] Plutarch, *Life of Antony* (Loeb, 1920), (Thayer Online 61.1).

> Caesar had two hundred and fifty ships of war, eighty thousand infantry and about as many horsemen as his enemies.[15]

Antony has twice as many ships, twenty thousand more infantry, and equal numbers of horsemen. Octavian is in trouble, right? Oh, but wait... a woman is involved in this tragic tale:

> Antony was an appendage of the woman ... that although he was far superior on land, he wished the decision to rest with his navy, to please Cleopatra, and that too when he saw that for lack of crews his trierarchs were haling together out of long-suffering Greek wayfarers, mule-drivers, harvesters, and ephebi, and that even then their ships were not fully manned, but most of them were deficient and sailed wretchedly.[16]

Any fool can see that Antony's land forces can easily crush Octavian's and that he will most certainly use that superior power to defeat the inexperienced younger man:

> Caesar's fleet, on the other hand, was perfectly equipped, and consisted of ships which had not been built for a display of height or mass, but were easily steered, swift, and fully manned.[17]

> But Antony, when the enemy sailed against him at daybreak, was afraid lest they should capture his ships while they had no fighting crews, and therefore armed the rowers and drew them up on the decks so as to make a show; then he grouped his ships at the mouth of the gulf near Actium, their ranks of oars on either side lifted and poised as for the stroke, and their prows towards the enemy, as if they were fully manned and prepared to fight. Caesar, thus outwitted and deceived, withdrew.[18]

Some questions should immediately come to mind: Could anyone really believe Octavian and Marc Antony wouldn't have known what the other's resources were – if there had been "the other's resources" in this fantasy?

Plutarch continues, placing the blame on the powerful woman who pulls Antony's strings:

> However, Cleopatra prevailed with her opinion that the war should be decided by the ships, although *she was already contem-*

---

[15] Plutarch, *Life of Antony* (Loeb, 1920), (Thayer Online 61.2).

[16] Plutarch, *Life of Antony* (Loeb, 1920), (Thayer Online) 62.1).

[17] Plutarch, *Life of Antony* (Loeb, 1920), (Thayer Online 62.2).

[18] Plutarch, *Life of Antony* (Loeb, 1920), (Thayer Online 63.1-2).

plating flight, and was disposing her own forces, *not where they would be helpful in winning the victory*, but where they *could most easily get away* if the cause was lost.[19]

So Cleopatra, rather than using Antony's advantage on land to win, chooses to go to war on water because it will be easier for her to escape? That's a woman for you! Except that Cleopatra is not known for being a stupid and cowardly woman. It is inconceivable that the intelligent and dynamic woman who produced children with the two most powerful men in the Empire insists on a naval battle when Antony's forces are superior on land and quite inferior on water. Unless, of course, all had agreed that Octavian would emerge as the "Victor."

Equally ridiculous is her reason for making this choice: to enable her to escape, abandoning her beloved Antony rather than engaging in the battle against Octavian to determine who will become the Ruler of Rome. When they could have easily won the war if it had been fought on land? Unbelievable! Which is the point.

But it gets even more incredible as Plutarch continues laying out clues:

> It was on this occasion, we are told, that an infantry centurion, a man who had fought many a battle for Antony and was covered with scars, burst into laments as Antony was passing by, and said; "Imperator, why dost thou distrust these wounds and this sword and put thy hopes in miserable logs of wood? Let Egyptians and Phoenicians do their fighting at sea, but give us land, on which we are accustomed to stand and either conquer our enemies or die."
>
> To this Antony made no reply, but merely encouraged the man by a gesture and a look to be of good heart and passed on. He had no good hopes himself, since, when the masters of his ships wished to leave their sails behind, he compelled them to put them on board and carry them, saying that not one fugitive of the enemy should be allowed to make his escape.[20]

---

[19] Plutarch, *Life of Antony* (Loeb, 1920), (Thayer Online 63.5). Emphasis added.
[20] Plutarch, *Life of Antony* (Loeb, 1920), (Thayer Online 64.1-2).

Plutarch says, "Readers take note! Antony assures us with a gesture and sly look that we need not worry." Plutarch continues, adding a bit of humor and more clues:

> Octavian, we are told, who had left his tent while it was still dark and was going round to visit his ships, was met by a man driving an ass. Octavian asked the man his name, and he, *recognizing Octavian*, replied: "My name is *Prosper*, and my ass's name is *Victor*."

> Therefore, when Caesar afterwards decorated the place with the beaks of ships, he set up bronze figures of an ass and a man. After surveying the rest of his line of battle, he was carried in a small boat to his right wing, and there was astonished to see the enemy lying motionless in the narrows; indeed, their ships had the appearance of riding at anchor.[21]

If someone wanted to immortalize the legend of Simeon ben Shetah and the donkey, bronze figures of a man and a donkey would be ideal. Moreover, the Greek word for "Prosper" is derived from *eu* and *hodos,* translated "good," and "The Way." The Greek word for "Victor" is *NiKe,* a Roman goddess but easily identified as a combination of *An* and *Ki.* By adding "Prosper" and "Victor" to this fable, Plutarch creates a cameo role for the man responsible for the farcical Battle of Actium – Julius Caesar. And the donkey ties him once again to Simeon ben Shetah.

Plutarch offers more reminders that this story is strictly for entertainment; the factual historical elements are yet to come:

> For a long time he was convinced that this was really the case, and kept his own ships at a distance of about eight furlongs from the enemy. But it was now the sixth hour, and since a wind was rising from the sea, the soldiers of Antony became impatient at the delay, and, relying on the height and size of their own ships as making them unassailable, they put their left wing in motion.

> When Caesar saw this he was delighted, and ordered his right wing to row backwards, wishing to draw the enemy still farther out from the gulf and the narrows, and then to surround them with his own agile vessels and come to close quarters with ships

---

[21] Plutarch, *Life of Antony* (Loeb, 1920), (Thayer Online 64.5.3-4).

which, owing to their great size and the smallness of their crews, were slow and ineffective.[22]

Though the struggle was beginning to be at close range, the ships did not ram or crush one another at all, since Antony's, owing to their weight, had no impetus, which chiefly gives effect to the blows of the beaks, while Caesar's not only avoided dashing front to front against rough and hard bronze armor, but did not even venture to ram the enemy's ships in the side. For their beaks would easily have been broken off by impact against vessels constructed of huge square timbers fastened together with iron. The struggle was therefore like a land battle; or, to speak more truly, like the storming of a walled town.[23]

It must have been a sight to see, this famous Battle of Actium, the sea battle fought to determine who will rule Rome; the battle Josephus invokes to date the census of Quirinius, therefore dating the birth of Jesus and tying Him to Antony and Cleopatra.

Antony's massive ships barely move at all, pushed not by oars but only by the gentle waves of the mighty but calm sea, their movement nothing more than the up and down of ships at anchor. Octavian's ships with their proud beaks for ramming also sit still.

After about four hours of this sea-dance, the final hours of the Battle for Rome approach. Plutarch slowly works toward the surprising victory for one and the humiliating defeat for the other:

> Although the sea-fight was still undecided and equally favorable to both sides, suddenly the sixty ships of Cleopatra were seen hoisting their sails for flight and making off through the midst of the combatants; for they had been posted in the rear of the large vessels, and threw them into confusion as they plunged through. The enemy looked on with amazement, seeing that they took advantage of the wind and made for Peloponnesus.[24]

---

[22] Plutarch, *Life of Antony* (Loeb, 1920), (Thayer Online 65.4-5).
[23] Plutarch, *Life of Antony* (Loeb, 1920), (Thayer Online 66.1-2).
[24] Plutarch, *Life of Antony* (Loeb, 1920), (Thayer Online 66.3-4).

If this production was actually played out for the benefit of Rome's military combatants, one can just imagine the confusion on the faces of Octavian's men as they watched in disbelief as Cleopatra sailed away with her sixty ships, leaving Antony to look like an abandoned fool.

> Antony made it clear to all the world that he was swayed neither by the sentiments of a commander nor of a brave man, nor even by his own, but, as someone in pleasantry said that the soul of the lover dwells in another's body, he was dragged along by the woman as if he had become incorporate with her and must go where she did. For no sooner did he see her ship sailing off than he forgot everything else, betrayed and ran away from those who were fighting and dying in his cause, got into a five-oared galley, where Alexas the Syrian and Scellius were his only companions, and hastened after the woman who had already ruined him and would make his ruin still more complete.[25]

This sounds less like Roman History and more like Greek Comedy, which is exactly what it was.

> Cleopatra recognized him and raised a signal on her ship; so Antony came up and was taken on board, but he neither saw nor was seen by her. Instead, he went forward alone to the prow and sat down by himself in silence, holding his head in both hands.[26]

He couldn't let his loyal but clueless men see him in tear-draining laughter over what he and Cleopatra had just pulled off. And it gets even better as the story moves to Cleopatra's palace in Alexandria. Plutarch's account of their suicides – overflowing with enigmas – continues to say, "You cannot read this literally because it never happened!"

> *It is said* that the asp was brought with those figs and leaves and lay hidden beneath them, for thus Cleopatra had given orders, that the reptile might fasten itself upon her body without her being aware of it. But when she took away some of the figs and saw it, she said: "There it is, you see," and baring her arm she held it out for the bite.
>
> *But others say* that the asp was kept carefully shut up in a water jar, and that while Cleopatra was stirring it up and irritating it

---

[25] Plutarch, *Life of Antony* (Loeb, 1920), (Thayer Online 66.4-5).
[26] Plutarch, *Life of Antony* (Loeb, 1920), (Thayer Online 66.1).

with a golden distaff it sprang and fastened itself upon her arm. But *the truth of the matter no one knows*; for *it was also said* that she carried about poison in a hollow comb and kept the comb hidden in her hair; and yet neither spot nor other sign of poison broke out upon her body.[27]

This should have raised questions. The asp story that has survived all these centuries was just one of several possibilities Plutarch put forth to explain how Cleopatra died. And he raises more questions himself, noting:

> Moreover, not even was the reptile seen within the chamber, though people said they saw some traces of it near the sea, where the chamber looked out upon it with its windows. *And some also say* that Cleopatra's arm was seen to have two slight and indistinct punctures; and this Caesar also seems to have believed. For in his triumph an image of Cleopatra herself with the asp clinging to her was carried in the procession. *These, then, are the various accounts of what happened.*[28]

Suetonius repeats the version that Cleopatra died from an asp bite.[29] Apparently he served as the second source that relates the "historical account" that Plutarch was unable to ascertain. However, Plutarch delivers the moral of this story: "… the truth of the matter no one knows." And it can still be said today, *No one knows the truth of the matter because Cleopatra did not commit suicide.*

Plutarch's account of Antony's suicide is the most entertaining of all. In a scene Shakespeare borrowed for Romeo and Juliet, Plutarch created a story that is, in a word, preposterous – humorous and entertaining, but preposterous. He writes:

> No sooner had Antony seen this than he was deserted by his cavalry, which went over to the enemy, and after being defeated with his infantry he retired into the city, crying out that he had been betrayed by Cleopatra to those with whom he waged war for her sake. But she, fearing his anger and his madness, fled for refuge into her tomb and let fall the drop-doors, which were made

[27] Plutarch, *Life of Antony* (Loeb, 1920), (Thayer Online 86.1-2). Emphasis added.
[28] Plutarch, *Life of Antony* (Loeb, 1920), (Thayer Online 86.3). Emphasis added.
[29] Suetonius, *Life of Augustus* (Loeb,1914), (Thayer Online 17.40).

strong with bolts and bars; then she sent messengers to tell Antony that she was dead.

Antony believed that message, and saying to himself, "Why doest thou longer delay, Antony? Fortune has taken away thy sole remaining excuse for clinging to life," he went into his chamber. Here, as he unfastened his breastplate and laid it aside, he said: "O Cleopatra, I am not grieved to be bereft of thee, for I shall straightway join thee; but I am grieved that such an imperator as I am has been found to be inferior to a woman in courage."

Now, Antony had a trusty slave named *Eros*. [Eros? The god of love? Really?] Antony had long before engaged Eros to kill him if circumstances ever warranted it. Antony now demanded the fulfillment of his promise.

So Eros drew his sword and held it up as though he would smite his master, but then turned his face away and slew himself. And as he fell at his master's feet Antony said: "Well done, Eros! Though you were not able to do it yourself you taught me what I must do" and running himself through the belly he dropped upon the couch.[30]

How convenient that Antony positioned himself next to the couch. Those marble floors were hard!

But the wound did not bring a speedy death. Therefore, as the blood ceased flowing after he had lain down, he came to himself and besought the bystanders to give him the finishing stroke.[31]

It seems that the wound is just a scratch because it stops bleeding immediately. Fortunately the bystanders wanted no part of finishing Antony off:

They fled from the chamber, and he lay writhing and crying out, until Diomedes [Greek, "advised by Zeus"] the secretary came from Cleopatra with orders to bring him to her in the tomb.[32]

Having learned, then, that Cleopatra was alive, Antony eagerly ordered his servants to raise him up, and he was carried in their arms to the doors of her tomb.[33]

His servants believed Antony had just fallen on his sword because of a woman who first abandoned him and then de-

---

[30] Plutarch, *Life of Antony* (Loeb, 1920), (Thayer Online 76.2-4).
[31] Plutarch, *Life of Antony* (Loeb, 1920), (Thayer Online 76.5).
[32] Plutarch, *Life of Antony* (Loeb, 1920), (Thayer Online 76.5).
[33] Plutarch, *Life of Antony* (Loeb, 1920), (Thayer Online 77.1).

ceived him into believing she was dead. Shouldn't they be furi-
ous with her? And shouldn't they expect him to be at least a
little miffed at what she had done? And yet Antony and his
servants continue to follow her orders and he is carried to the
doors of her tomb.

But it gets better:

> Cleopatra, however, would not open the doors, but showed her-
> self at a window, from which she let down ropes and cords.[34]

Yes, Cleopatra had conveniently stored ropes and cords in
her tomb. Otherwise, she might have been forced to resort to
using her hair!

> To these Antony was fastened, and she drew him up herself,
> with the aid of the two women whom alone she had admitted
> with her into the tomb.

> Never, as those who were present tell us, was there a more pite-
> ous sight. Smeared with blood and struggling with death he was
> drawn up, stretching out his hands to her even as he dangled in
> the air.[35]

Now how's that for drama? Or humor?

> For the task was not an easy one for the women, and scarcely
> could Cleopatra, with clinging hands and strained face, pull up
> the rope, while those below called out encouragement to her and
> shared her agony.[36]

Wouldn't you like to see a reenactment of this scene; three
women pulling a dangling Antony with outstretched arms –
smeared with blood but not bleeding – up a wall and into a
window, the crowd below cheering the women on? Hasn't anyone ever asked why they didn't just open the damn door so
Antony could be carried in?

> And when she had thus got him in and laid him down, she rent
> her garments over him, beat and tore her breasts with her hands,
> wiped off some of his blood upon her face … [the original drama
> queen!] … and called him master, husband, and imperator; in-
> deed, she almost forgot her own ills in her pity for his. But Antony

---

[34] Plutarch, *Life of Antony* (Loeb, 1920), (Thayer Online 77.1).
[35] Plutarch, *Life of Antony* (Loeb, 1920), (Thayer Online 77.1-2).
[36] Plutarch, *Life of Antony* (Loeb, 1920), (Thayer Online 77.2).

stopped her lamentations and asked for a drink of wine, either because he was thirsty, or in the hope of a speedier release.[37]

Actually it would have been time to celebrate getting up the wall and into the room – if it had happened, of course.

> When he had drunk, he advised her to be concerned about her own safety if she could do it without disgrace and not to feel pity for him because of his last defeat, but to consider him happy for the good things that had been his, since he had become most illustrious of men, had won greatest power, and now had been not ignobly conquered, a Roman by a Roman.[38]

Seems a little late to worry about disgracing herself – and him. Plutarch must have been concerned that these stories of the deaths of Antony and Cleopatra might be seen by subsequent "Victors" for what they were, especially since he carefully explained that he used the Pythagorean method of transmitting secrets to tell them. Even without his help, anyone familiar with Greek Tragedy, Romance, and Comedy should have seen through it immediately. Yet these fables have been passed along as "history" in spite of Plutarch's admonition and in spite of how laughable they are.

Just think about it for a moment. The most powerful woman in the world, considered above average in intelligence, chosen to bear children to Julius Caesar and Marc Antony, and she takes her own life before making any attempt to negotiate with the much younger and inexperienced Octavian? How could anyone really believe she would choose to make her royal sons and daughters orphans? Choose to leave them in the hands of her mortal enemy? The story is clearly pure fantasy just as Plutarch explained it would be. No wonder Shakespeare used it as a hypotext for Romeo and Juliet, surely an intentional play on the names, "Rome" and "Julius."

---

[37] Plutarch, *Life of Antony* (Loeb, 1920), (Thayer Online 77.3).
[38] Plutarch, *Life of Antony* (Loeb, 1920), (Thayer Online 77.4).

It's time to ask: Can Philo's Philology weave a new tapestry to demonstrate an ingenious plan for preserving history and the True Story of Jesus? The evidence is circumstantial, perhaps, but it is as strong – if not stronger – than commonly accepted conclusions.

The threads, rewoven, tell a new tale. And support for our hypothesis that Antony and Cleopatra metamorphosed into Herod and Mariamme after the Battle of Actium may be found tucked away on page 82, footnote 39, in Duane Roller's *The World of Juba II and Kleopatra Selene*:

> The [children's] tutors Euphronios and Rhodon disappear from the record at this time. Theodoros was executed for stealing Antyllus' possessions (Plutarch, *Antonius* 81). Conspicuously absent in these last days is Nikolaos of Damaskos, who may have been successful in suppressing his role, or more likely, had wisely *fled to Herod in Judea*, beginning forty years of service to that dynasty, and thus saving both his life and his career. *In fact, a number of scholars and intellectuals moved from the Alexandrian court to Judea at this time.*[39]

Lo and behold! The children's tutors along with the "scholars and intellectuals" moved from Cleopatra's palace in Alexandria to Herod's palace in Judea where the dramas continued to unfold and enigmas continued to pour forth.

The small threads are getting longer, and they continue to suggest that Antony and Cleopatra "died" so that Herod and Mariamme could emerge: "Whenever you read stories about the gods you must not think that any of these tales actually happened in the manner in which they are related."

Philo's Philology applied to Plutarch's accounts leaves little doubt: the Battle of Actium is a fable; there was no asp, no poisoned comb. Antony and Cleopatra did not kill themselves. Marc Antony metamorphosed into "Herod the Great." He later became "Marcus Agrippa," husband of Julia the Elder. Cleo-

[39] Duane W. Roller, *The World of Juba II and Kleopatra Selene*; (New York and London: Routledge Taylor & Frances Group, 2003), 55-7. Emphasis added.

patra became "Doris" then "Mariamme," and after her "death,"
"Dynamis."

And what of Julius Caesar? If his assassination was faked as
the evidence indicates, then the coincidences that tie him to
Hillel Simeon ben Shatah become plausible. Hillel is patterned
after Moses and chosen to lead the Israelites of Elohim – "the
Simeons" (Hebrew, *Ha smoneans*) – in a final victory over the
dark forces of the "evil" YHWH. It seems that Julius Caesar
"took to himself the name" prophesied at Isa 14:12: "Hillel ben
Shatah."

But he took other names as well, names created to serve the
method of keeping the "Secret History" intact and thereby preserving it for later generations. Julius chose the name
"Asander," from Alexander the Great, his ancestor. The name
"Alexander" was also assumed by Ha-smonean Jews: "Alexander Jannaeus"; Antony and Cleopatra's son "Alexander Helios"; Mariamme and Herod's son "Alexander III," and grandson "Alexander IV," and by their great-grandson, "Alexander
son of Simeon Quirinius" who carried the cross for Jesus (Mk
15:21).

Asander's wife is called "Dynamis," which means "Powerful One." A Temple Virgin herself, she is the "messenger" who
brings Kurios of Theos to the Temple Virgin who was chosen
to bear their grandson, Jesus. When key Greek words in Lk 1:35
are converted to the Hebrew equivalent, more important characters are uncovered:

"Kadesh Ruach tislah alah and Elyon Dynamis will be baselel
alakem; Dio (Homer's "Zeus") yalad Kadesh; he will be called
'Son of Theos.'"

As previously noted, Moses' sister Miriam was buried at
Kadesh, a word defined as "Holy woman." Kadesh was renamed "Emessa," *Em* plus *Ishshah* is translated, "Mother of *Ishtar's* women."

The King of the Emessenes was Sam-Caesar-amis. His
younger son Azizus (Isis + Zeus) was briefly married to the He-

rodian princess Drusilla.[40] Drusilla divorced Azizus to marry a freedman, Marcus Antonius Felix; Drusilla and Felix met with Paul (Acts 24:24).

Samcaesaramis' daughter Iotapa married the Herodian prince, Aristobulus; their daughter was deaf and mute.[41] A later volume will pursue these relationships in depth and how "mute" might have become "silent," then "tacit" and finally "Tacitus."

Julius Caesar's eldest son with Cleopatra, called "Caesarion," is also known as "Tiberius Julius Aspurgus Philoromaios," son of Dynamis and Asander. His names were chosen for the messages they carry. *Aspurgus* is an Iranian name derived from *aspa* ("horse") and *aspabara* ("horseman"). "Tiberius Julius Horseman Lover of Rome" and "Tiberius Julius Caesar Augustus" were born at the same time and died the same year. That should have called for questions and raised suspicion.

Suetonius also left clues to the horseman's parentage in *Lives of the Twelve Caesars*. It would be impossible to think of Julius Caesar without also remembering his horses, especially the horse with toes:

Julius Caesar was highly skilled in arms and horsemanship, and of incredible powers of endurance...[42] He rode a remarkable horse, too, with feet that were almost human; for its hoofs were cloven in such a way as to look like toes. This horse was foaled on his own place, and since the soothsayers had declared that it foretold the rule of the world for its master, he reared it with the greatest care, and was the first to mount it, for it would endure no other rider. Afterwards, too, he dedicated a statue of it before the temple of Venus Genetrix.[43]

Shortly before his death, as he was told, the herds of horses which he had dedicated to the river Rubicon when he crossed it, and had let loose without a keeper, stubbornly refused to graze and wept copiously. Again, when he was offering sacrifice, the

[40] Josephus, 1999, *Antiquities* 20.7.1 (139) 651.

[41] Josephus 1999, Antiquities 18.5.4 (135), 596.

[42] Suetonius, *Life of Julius Caesar* (Loeb 1914), (Thayer Online 57.1).

[43] Suetonius, *Life of Julius Caesar* (Loeb 1914), (Thayer Online 61.1).

soothsayer Spurinna warned him to beware of danger, which would come not later than the Ides of March.[44]

"Asander Lover of Caesar, Lover of Rome" died in 17 BCE, the year Augustus Caesar called for the reinstitution of the *Ludi Saeculares*. And it was the same year that construction began on the Pyramid of Romulus that was destroyed c. 1500. Its marble was used in St. Peter's Basilica.[45]

When Asander died, so the story goes, a man by the name of "Scribonius" pretended to be a relative of the widow Dynamis and forced her to marry him, making her a "Scribonia." And Augustus Caesar's second wife – mother of Julia the Elder – was also named "Scribonia." In fact, Scribonia was the grandmother of cousins, Paulus the Younger and Germanicus the Younger.

And Dynamis-Scribonia's story doesn't end with this fictional marriage. Scribonia's son-in-law, Marcus Vipsanius Agrippa, comes to her rescue and orders the usurping fictional con-man Scribonius killed. Marcus then asks a much younger Polemon I of Pontus to marry the widow Dynamis. When she dies in 14 BCE – just two years after their fictional marriage – Polemon married a younger woman, Pythodorida of Pontus, who, coincidentally, was Marc Antony's first grandchild – just one more coincidence to note.[46]

And what an amazing coincidence this is! Dynamis becomes a "Scribonia" and Emperor Augustus' second wife is "Scribonia." She is the mother of Julia the Elder, Emperor Tiberius' second wife. And notably, Julia and Tiberius had no children together. This childlessness would be explained if they were full siblings and Julius and Cleopatra were their parents.

Moreover, Scribonia is also Emperor Gaius Caligula's great grandmother, Empress Agrippina the Younger's great grandmother, Emperor Claudius' great grandmother-in-law, and Emperor Nero's great-great grandmother. Queen Cleopatra

---

[44] Suetonius, *Life of Julius Caesar* (Loeb 1914), (Thayer Online 81.2).
[45] Famous Wonders (2015), Pyramid of Cestius.
[46] Cassius Dio, *Roman History* (Loeb, 1917), (Thayer Online 54.24.4-6).

would have been quite envious of a woman with such elite posterity – had she not been that woman.

The women called "Dynamis," "Scribonia," "Mariamme," and "Cleopatra" have now been identified as *one* woman, a "Virgin of El." But another Virgin identity remains to be unmasked, and this one was believed to be a man: Publius Vergilius Maro.

Suetonius writes of Vergil Maro: "… at Naples he was commonly called *'Parthenias'* … whenever he appeared in public in Rome, where he very rarely went, he would take refuge in the nearest house, *to avoid those who followed and pointed him out.*"[47]

The curious exegete will ask if he "rarely went to Rome," how could anyone living there recognize him? An introvert who wanted to remain anonymous could do so quite easily in the first century BCE. In fact, only a few people would have been recognized by the common citizen, and one, especially, stands out: Cleopatra.

We know she would have been recognized because Julius Caesar placed a gilded statue of her in the newly constructed Forum Julium. It was placed next to a marble statue of Venus Genetrix, the Mother and Founder of the Julian clan.[48] Therefore, Cleopatra's face would have been well-known to all who visited the Forum Julium. And Plutarch gave Cleopatra a good reason to "take refuge" in a safehouse if someone pointed her out; she was supposed to be dead.

Furthermore, a name almost identical to "Parthenias Maro" can be found at Lk 1:27, "The name of parthenou Maria." These enigmatic clues suggest that "Vergil Maro" was a "Virgin of El," all of whom were called "Mariam," "Maria," "or Mary" (Hebrew *MR*, "Mother Light." And to be certain that "Vergil Maro" would be seen as an enigma to be solved, Suetonius reported that his birth was accompanied by miracles:

---

[47] Suetonius, *Life of Vergil*, (Loeb, 1913), (Thayer Online 2.11). Emphasis added.
[48] Cassius Dio, *Roman History* (Loeb, 1917), (Thayer Online 51.22.3).

He was born in the first consulship of Gnaeus Pompeius the Great[49] and Marcus Licinius Crassus, on the Ides of October, in a district called Andes, not far distant from Mantua. While he was in his mother's womb, she dreamt that she gave birth to a *laurel branch*, [Hebrew, NSR] which on touching the earth took root and grew at once to the size of a full-grown tree, covered with fruits and flowers of various kinds; and on the following day, when she was on the way to a neighboring part of the country with her husband, she turned aside and gave birth to her child in a ditch beside the road ... There was added another omen; for a *poplar branch*,[50] which, as was usual in that region on such occasions, was at once planted where the birth occurred, grew so fast in a short time that it equaled in size poplars planted long fore. It was called from him "Vergil's tree" and was besides worshipped with great veneration by pregnant and newly delivered women, who made and paid vows beneath it.[51] (Note that Suetonius chose "child," "infant," and "its" which are genderless).

New Year rites in ancient Rome were held on March 1 and led by Vestal Virgins. Purification rituals within the temple consisted of replacing the old *laurel* branches with new ones and relighting the sacred fire.[52]

Ovid's version of the myth of the laurel tree, composed a generation *after* Vergil, carries intriguing clues that pertain to Vergil. It is the story of Apollo's love for Daphne (Greek for *Laurel*) and his desire to possess her. In this story of unrequited love, fearful Daphne flees with Apollo in hot pursuit:

> I am the lord of Delphi; Tenedos and Patara and Claros[53] are my realms. I am the son of Jupiter [aka, "Zeus"]. By me things future, past and present are revealed; I shape the harmony of songs and strings. Sure are my arrows, but one surer still has struck me to the heart, my carefree heart. The art of medicine I gave the world and all men call me 'Healer'; I possess the power of every herb.

---

[49] "Pompey the Great" "metamorphosed" into "Ptolemy Auletes," Cleopatra's father.
[50] "Poplar Branch" in Hebrew is *LiBNeH NSR*; Strong's Hebrew No. 3839, Gen 30:37: "Then Jacob took fresh rods of *poplar*..." The Hebrew consonants, *LBNH NSR*, can also be used to create *eL aB aN Ha AnSaR*, translated, "El Father An the Nasarean"].
[51] Suetonius, *Life of Vergil* (Loeb, 1914), (Thayer Online 2-5). Emphasis added.
[52] Robin Lorsch Wildfang, *Rome's Vestal Virgins*; (New York: Routledge, 2006) 1-31.
[53] *Claros* and *Patera* are remarkably similar to *Cleopatra*.

Alas! That love no herb can cure, that skills which help afford to all mankind fail now to help their lord!

Daphne's father was Peneius, also called "Peneus," a Thessalian river god, and a son of Oceanus and Tethys.[54] Daphne prays to her father for help:

> Scarce had she made her prayer when through her limbs a dragging languor spread, her tender bosom was wrapped in thin smooth bark, her slender arms were changed to branches and her hair to leaves; her feet but now so swift were anchored fast in numb stiff roots, her face and had become the crown of a green tree; all that remained of Daphne was her shining loveliness. And still [Apollo] loved her; on the trunk he placed his hand and felt beneath the bark her heart still beating, held in his embrace her branches, pressed his kisses on the wood; yet from his kisses the wood recoiled. "My bride", he said, "since you can never be, at least, sweet laurel, you shall be my tree. My lure, my locks, my quiver you shall wreathe." ... Thus spoke the god; the laurel in assent inclined her new-made branches and bent down, or seemed to bend, her head, her leafy crown.[55]

Equally informative and revealing is Suetonius' poplar tree enigma; Greco-Roman mythology links the white poplar to Leuce, a nymph and Oceanus' daughter. Pluto fell in love with Leuce, abducted her, and forced her to live with him in the underworld. When Leuce died, Pluto created a white poplar, and Herakles crowned himself with a wreath made from its branches to celebrate his return from the underworld.[56]

The white poplar, therefore, is tied to resurrection. And it is possible that "Lucius Mestrius Plutarchus" chose that enigmatic name in order to be tied to this myth about a *daughter* of Oceanus." *Leuce Em Ishtar*, "Mother of Star," wife of Pluto, was converted to a male name, "Lucius Mestrius Plutarchus." It's beginning to look as if several ancient poets and philosophers, including Vergil and Plutarch, may have been women disguised as men.

---

[54] Homer, *Iliad.* ii. 757; Ovid *Metamorphoses* i. 568, &c.
[55] Ovid, *Metamorphoses 1. 452 ff (trans. Melville).*
[56] Aaron J. Atsma, *Theoi Project*, "Lueke" (2000-2011).

According to Suetonius, "Vergil" was born on the Ides of October, 70 or 69 BCE; Cleopatra was also born 70 or 69 BCE (some websites note October but cite no source).

Vergil's prophecy in the *Aeneid* that Ascanius-Julius (Julius Caesar's ancestor), "a son of god who will have gods as sons," is carried forward by Vergil's "Fourth Eclogue" which prophesies the birth of a holy child. This Eclogue is addressed to the poet's patron Gaius Asinius Pollio, which dates it and identifies it as a reference to Augustus Caesar, also known as Octavian.

However, Eusebius (c. 260-340) removed Pollio's name and appended the interpolated poem to "The Life of Constantine" as the "Oration of Constantine." From that time forward Vergil's "savior-child" was linked to Christ and the Isa 7:14 prophecy: "Look, the almah[57] is with child and shall bear a son, and shall name him Immanuel."[58] The association stuck, and Vergil—the "Virgin of El," also known as "Cleopatra"—became a "Christian prophet." Evidence presented in Gott's *Plutarch's Parable*[59] suggests that Lucius Mestrius Plutarchus authored *Luke-Acts*. Additionally, "Leuce 'Mother Istar' Pluto" was probably Cleopatra's great-great granddaughter. Can it get any more ironic?

---

[57] "LMH" can also be rendered *eL eM Ha*, "El; Mother; the," or "The Mother El."
[58] "MMNL" can also be rendered *eM eM aN eL*, "Mother; Mother; An; El."
[59] Gott (2005), *Plutarch's Parable*.

CHAPTER FIFTEEN

Following Philo to the Antichrist and the Second Coming

With some of the mysteries solved and a bundle of loose threads still in hand, we return to the unanswered questions from Chapter Six:

> What happened that turned Paul against Jesus and generated immense hatred that spewed forth in the encounter with Bar-Jesus at Paphos?

> Is the perceived "double-cross" the precipitating event that Josephus points to as the cause of the destruction of the Second Temple when he writes: "Jesus the son of Gamaliel succeeded Jesus the son of Damneus in the high priesthood"?

> These questions lead back to the family of Germanicus and the three young men born c. 6 CE who sat at his feet.

Suetonius reports that Germanicus and Agrippina had three sons and three daughters. Their sons were:

Nero Julius Caesar Germanicus

Drusus Julius Caesar

Gaius Julius Caesar

When Germanicus allegedly died in 19 CE, his eldest son Nero Germanicus moved to the front of the line to succeed Tiberius. However, Nero Germanicus (not to be confused with the Emperor Nero a generation later) was accused of treason and exiled to the island of Ponza where he committed suicide or starved to death.[1]

Notably, another prominent character of approximately the same age surfaces in Jerusalem at about this time. His enigmatic name is "Pontius Pilate." The *pileus* is an identifying cap

---

[1] Suetonius, *Life of Tiberius* (Loeb, 1914), (Thayer Online 54).

freedmen were given in a manumission ceremony; "Pontius" suggests he was from Pontus, whose King, Polemon I, married Dynamis in 16 BCE after Asander's death. Dynamis and Asander's son, Tiberius Julius Aspurgus became Polemon's stepson, and when Dynamis died in 14 BCE, Polemon became the sole ruler of the Bosporus Kingdom.

With Nero Germanicus out of the way, Germanicus' second son Drusus moved to the front of the line to succeed Tiberius. But one year after his elder brother's exile, Drusus was accused of plotting against Tiberius, also exiled and imprisoned. According to the philologist Tacitus, Drusus starved to death in prison c. 33, reduced to chewing the stuffing of his bed.[2]

However – as with his brother – a more likely outcome of Drusus' disappearance is a metamorphosis. And a lot was going on in the Judean countryside at about this time.

Next in line to become Emperor was Gaius, Germanicus' only remaining son. Unfortunately, the entire section of Tacitus' *Annals* that covers the life of Gaius Caligula – including the three-and-a-half years he ruled – has been lost.

Suetonius seems unsure exactly when and where Caligula was born, noting that he was, *born in the year of the consulship of his father*. Germanicus was consul in 12, but evidence implies that Germanicus may not have been Gaius Caligula's biological father. And it is Suetonius who creates the enigma that throws Caligula's parentage and year of birth into question.

Suetonius quotes from a letter, which he attributes to Augustus Caesar, written to Agrippina the Elder. It reads:

> Yesterday I arranged with Talarius and Asillius to bring your boy Gaius on the fifteenth day before the Kalends of June, if it be *the will of the gods* [note yellow flag]. I send with him besides one of my slaves who is a physician, and I have written Germanicus to *keep him* if he wishes. Farewell, my own Agrippina, and take care to come in good health to your Germanicus.[3]

---

[2] Tacitus, *Annals; The Works* (1864-1877), (Sacred Texts Online 6.23).
[3] Suetonius, *Life of Caligula* (Loeb, 1914), (Thayer Online 8.1-5).

Augustus informs granddaughter Agrippina that he had written to her husband Germanicus to tell him he could "keep him" if he wished. Were it not for the striking statement "will of the gods" that serves as a yellow flag, it might be assumed that "him" refers to "the slave who is a physician." However, because a signal for enigma *is* inserted, it is more likely that "him" refers to Gaius. This suggests that Germanicus and Agrippina are not Gaius' biological parents and that he came to them via Agrippina's grandfather Augustus. It also hints that Gaius may have been under the care of a physician.

Suetonius also provides two name clues: "Talarius" and "Asillius." Talaria are the winged boots worn by the Greek god Hermes. And a Hermes thread is conspicuous in *Acts*: "Barnabas they called Zeus, and Paul they called Hermes, because he was the chief speaker" (Acts 14:12).[4] Matching boot threads lead back to Gaius – coincidentally. The nickname "Caligula" is derived from the Latin word *caligae*, which also means "boots."

However, Talarius is not alone in arranging the adoption of Gaius. Suetonius identifies a second person, "Asillius," a name that is just one letter shy of the word *basillius*. Basillius (Basileus) and the feminine Basilissa, resurrected for Alexander the Great and the Ptolemies of Egypt including Cleopatra, came to designate the Roman Emperor in the everyday and literary speech of the Greek-speaking Eastern Mediterranean during the time of Tiberius.[5]

And so it seems that Suetonius composed Augustus Caesar's fictitious letter to identify the people who arranged the adoption of Gaius. "Asillius," the "almost B-assilius" is Tiberius who became Basileus in 14 CE. The first person named, "Talarius" is to be tied to Hermes, and Luke associates Hermes with Paul. Therefore, it appears that Talarius may be related in some way to Paul. But what is the relationship?

---

[4] Emphasis added.
[5] Alexander Kazhdan, ed. (1991), Oxford Dictionary of Byzantium, Oxford University Press, 264, ISBN 978-0-19-504652-6 (N.V.).

This question can be answered but to do so requires a quick review of threads previously collected:

Agrippina's sister was Julia Vipsania *Paulus* whose son Lucius Paulus was just two years old when his mother was exiled, leaving him a virtual orphan. He disappeared from history at that time with nothing more written about his fate.

The letter from Augustus to Agrippina seems to suggest that she and Germanicus agreed to take "Gaius" into their home. But where did Gaius come from? Who is he? Their orphaned nephew is Lucius (or Marcus) Aemilius *Paulus*, whereas the adopted child is *Gaius* Julius Caesar.

Did "Lucius Paulus" become "Gaius Caesar" when Germanicus and Agrippina adopted him? Was he passed off as being Germanicus and Agrippina's *third* son when he was, in fact, Julia the Younger's *eldest* son, Lucius Marcus Paulus? What better place for the semi-orphaned two year old Paulus than with his mother's sister Agrippina, wife of Germanicus. Raised by these close relatives, little Lucius Paulus would "sit at the feet of Germanicus," identified through multiple enigmas as Nasi Gamaliel.

The implication of this possibility is monumental because it suggests that the man who is known as the Emperor Caligula was also known as the Apostle Paul.

Additional support for this stunning hypothesis comes from the dating of Caligula's birth, "when his father was consul." Germanicus was consul in 12 CE; however, Lucius Aemilius Paulus, Julia the Younger's husband and father of her eldest son born in 6, was consul in 6. With the first two in line to become Emperor out of the way, it was Germanicus' third son Gaius who moved to the head of the line.

However, the evidence says that Gaius was not Germanicus' biological son but his wife's sister's son whom they adopted. Gaius was hardly next in line – unless his father Lucius also had a secret identity. And only one identity could have moved his son ahead of the sons of Germanicus: Emperor Tiberius must have been his biological father. And Lucius must have been "the eldest" – "*ha Peter*"[6] – and first in line, putting his eldest son first in line as well.

A careful examination of each of the prominent characters in historians' accounts yields just *one* man who could have been Emperor Tiberius' elder secret son. And like Julia's husband Paulus, his first name was "Lucius." He is Lucius Aelius Sejanus Strabo, prefect of the Roman imperial Praetorian Guard, better known as "Sejanus."

During his tenure as Commander, c. 14-31 CE, the Guard evolved into a powerful branch of government. When Tiberius withdrew to Capri in 26, Sejanus became de facto ruler of the Empire.[7] And as has frequently been the case, his name carries the clue: *Se Janus*. It seems that Emperor Tiberius had two sons: *Lucius Se-Janus* and *Quirinus*, also known as Drusus Germanicus the Elder." Two sons, *Janus* and *Quirinus* named after the two-headed deity. We find no evidence they were twins; however, one of them became the father of twins in 6 CE.

When Sejanus was removed from power c. 31, a man of the same age replaced him: Quintus Naevius Cordus Sutorius Macro. Macro's wife was Eunia, the granddaughter of Thrasyllus, the influential imperial astrologer introduced in Chapter Ten. According to Suetonius, Macro looked the other way as Caligula seduced Eunia and promised to marry her if he became Emperor. And Caligula used Macro to get to Tiberius, suggesting that – like Sejanus and Thrasyllus – Macro wielded immense power with the Emperor.

When Tiberius allegedly died in 37, the rumor spread that Caligula poisoned him and ordered that his ring be taken from him while he still breathed. "…and then suspecting that he was trying to hold fast to it, that a pillow be put over his face; or even strangled the old man with his own hand, immediately *ordering the crucifixion of a freedman* who cried out at the awful deed."[8]

---

[6] Brown-Driver-Briggs (Strong's Hebrew 6363).

[7] Suetonius, *Life of Tiberius* (Loeb, 1914), (Thayer Online 65).

[8] Suetonius, *Life of Caligula* (Loeb, 1914), (Thayer Online 12.2-3).

This scene is dated to March 16, 37 CE, the day Tiberius died. The next Jewish Passover would follow a month later – April 19, 37 CE. From Capri to Jerusalem took less than a month; therefore, this enigmatic "freedman who cried out" could have been transported to Jerusalem in time for the "First Annual Passover-Passion Festival" and a notable "Crucifixion."

But who is this "crucified freedman"? He must have been especially trusted to be allowed into the room while Caligula allegedly assassinated Tiberius. You will recall that we've already encountered a powerful freedman who helped Vespasian several decades after Tiberius' death: Vespasian was "sent in command of a legion to Germany, *through the influence* of [the freedman] Narcissus."[9]

Ancient historians agree that the second most powerful "freedman" in first century Rome was Claudius' secretary, Narcissus;[10] only Pallas wielded more power. However, if Narcissus was the freedman whom Caligula ordered to be crucified, it would mean he survived the Crucifixion and returned to Rome after Caligula's alleged assassination.

And who is Macro other than a man of the same age as Sejanus who arrives on the scene just as Sejanus exits? It is another woman who supplies the evidence to solve this puzzle: Macro's wife Eunia. Macro's marriage to the granddaughter of Thrasyllus would be an expected mating for gods and Temple Virgins in this family – but only if Macro and Thrasyllus are brothers and secret sons of Tiberius. Their power and influence over the Emperor, and Macro's marriage to Eunia, are explained if Macro is a metamorphosed Sejanus and Thrasyllus is a metamorphosed Germanicus.

Suetonius' report of Augustus Caesar's enigmatic letter to Agrippina identifies the two people who had to agree to allow Germanicus and Agrippina to adopt Caligula ("little boots"). First, his father Lucius Paulus-Sejanus, called "Talarius" (Her-

---

[9] Suetonius, *Life of Vespasian*; (Loeb,1914), (Thayer Online 4.1-5).
[10] Suetonius, *Life of Claudius* (Loeb, 1914), (Thayer Online 1.28).

mes' boots), and second, his grandfather Tiberius, identified as "Assillius" who became B-Assillius when Augustus Caesar died.

Also explained is Macro's willingness to look the other way as Caligula and Eunia plan to marry. After producing a child or two with her grandfather's brother, Macro-Sejanus, the Temple Virgin Eunia might then be required to produce one or more with Macro's son Caligula.

The evidence once again is circumstantial but compelling: It appears that Tiberius' two secret biological sons were Lucius Paulus (also known as "Sejanus" and "Macro") and his younger brother Germanicus (also known as "Gamaliel" and "Thrasyllus"). Lucius Paulus Sejanus' eldest son was Gaius Julius Caesar, also known as, "Caligula," but born, "Lucius Aemilius Paulus."[11]

And evidence continues to accumulate as Church Father Irenaeus returns with more clues. He delivers another thread that can be tied to both Caligula and the Apostle Paul, and he shares a revealing interpretation of the meaning of Daniel's apocalyptic vision:

> The fourth beast shall speak words against the *Most High*, shall wear out the holy ones of the Most High, and shall attempt to change the sacred seasons and the law: and they shall be given into his power for a time, two times, and a half a time (Dan 7:25).

According to Irenaeus, the duration of power is to be understood as three and one-half *literal* years.

Curiously Daniel was unable to interpret the vision himself, although it was this very ability that had been his primary claim to fame. But the Angel Gabriel arrives on the scene, bringing help and saying:

> At the end of their rule, when the transgressions have reached their full measure, a king of bold countenance shall arise, skilled

---

[11] Josephus, 1999, Antiquities 18.6.8 (206), 601: Josephus appears to confirm that Caligula was not Germanicus' biological son: "Now he [Tiberius] had no sons of his own alive, for Drusus, who was his only son, was dead; but Drusus's son Tiberius was still living, whose additional name was Gemellus. There was also living Caius [Caligula], the son of Germanicus, who was the son of his brother."

in intrigue. He shall grow strong in power, shall cause fearful destruction, and shall succeed in what he does. He shall destroy the powerful and the people of the holy ones. By his cunning *he shall make deceit prosper* under his hand, and *in his own mind* he shall be great. Without warning he shall destroy many and *shall even rise up against the Prince of Princes*. But he shall be broken, and not by human hands (Dan 8:23-6).[12]

Furthermore Irenaeus declares that the Antichrist's reign would be terminated by the Second Coming, the "resurrection of the righteous and the destruction of the wicked."[13] Is it possible that Irenaeus is referring to the resurrection of the "Righteous One"? The Righteous One who was surnamed "Germanicus"? Does Irenaeus identify the man who is the Antichrist as well as the man who is called "Jesus"? And does he leave clues to the date of his Second Coming?

So it seems. Caligula, whose biography the historians filled with an extensive listing of horrendous acts any Antichrist would envy,[14] ruled from March 37 until January 41 – just over three-and-a-half years. Contemporary historians Philo and Seneca the Younger also describe a madman and a reign of terror.[15]

Suetonius a generation later accuses Caligula of incest with his sisters and prostituting them to other men, turning the palace into a brothel.[16] Furthermore,

> He was sound neither of body nor mind. As a boy he was troubled with the falling sickness, and while in his youth he had some endurance, yet at times because of sudden faintness he was hardly able to walk, to stand up, to collect his thoughts, or to hold up his head. He himself realized his mental infirmity, and thought at times of going into retirement and clearing his brain. It is thought that his wife Caesonia gave him a drug intended for a love potion, which however had the effect of driving him mad. He was espe-

---

[12] Emphasis added.

[13] Irenaeus, "Against Heresies" 5.30.4.

[14] Suetonius, *Life of Caligula* (Loeb,1914), (Thayer Online 27.1-49.3).

[15] Seneca the Younger, *On Anger* xviii.1; *On the Shortness of Life* xviii.5; Philo of Alexandria, "On the Embassy to Gaius" 24.

[16] Suetonius, *Life of Caligula* (Loeb, 1914), (Thayer Online 41.1).

cially tormented with sleeplessness; for he never rested more than three hours at night, and even for that length of time he did not sleep quietly, but was terrified by *strange apparitions,* once for example dreaming that *the spirit of the Ocean talked with him.*[17]

We can now understand why a physician accompanied Caligula when he was sent to live with Germanicus and Agrippina. He was a very sick child and remained so his entire life. According to Plutarch, Caligula appeared in public dressed as various gods and demigods, including Mercury, the Roman version of the Greek god Hermes.[18]

Cassius Dio reports that Caligula frequently referred to himself as a god when meeting with politicians and that he was addressed as Jupiter in some public documents.[19] Jupiter, of course, is the Roman version of the Greek god Zeus.

However, it is Suetonius' report that Caligula saw "strange apparitions" and dreamed that "the spirit of the Ocean talked with him" that is most significant to solving the puzzle of Caligula's relationship to the Apostle Paul. The "Spirit of the Ocean" is the water deity Oceanus whose parents were Uranus (Heaven) and Gaia (Earth).[20] In other words, Oceanus had a "Heavenly Father" and an "Earthly Mother," *An* and *Ki* in the Sumerian language.

According to Homer, Oceanus and his sister-wife Tethys are the father and mother of all the gods: "I go now to the ends of the generous earth on a visit to Oceanos, whence the gods have risen, and Tethys our mother."[21]

Ovid returns once again to tie Oceanus and Tethys to a well-known Christian chant and to the rite of baptism as the sea-god Glaukos says: "Tethys and Oceanus ... [took] away my mortal essences. *They purified me with a nine-fold chant that purges my sins;* then bade me plunge my body beneath a hundred rivers.

---

[17] Suetonius, *Life of Caligula* (Loeb, 1914), (Thayer Online 50.2). Emphasis added.
[18] Philo of Alexandria, *On the Embassy to Gaius, 11-15.*
[19] Cassius Dio, *Roman History* 59.26; 59.28.
[20] The Theoi Classical Texts Library: "Okeanos."
[21] Homer, *Iliad,* 14.200.

Instantly torrents cascaded down from near and far and poured whole seas of waters on my head."[22]

An echo of this nine-fold chant to Oceanus that "purges sin" can be found in the nine-fold chant for mercy, directed to Jesus, found in the *Kyrie Eleison Litany*:

1. Lord, King and Father unbegotten, True Essence of the God-head, have mercy on us.
2. Lord, Fount of light and Creator of all things, have mercy on us.
3. Lord, Thou who hast signed us with the seal of Thine image, have mercy on us.
4. Christ, True God and True Man, have mercy on us.
5. Christ, Rising Sun, through whom are all things, have mercy on us.
6. Christ, Perfection of Wisdom, have mercy on us.
7. Lord, vivifying Spirit and power of life, have mercy on us.
8. Lord, Breath of the Father and the Son, in Whom are all things, have mercy on us.
9. Lord, Purger of sin and Almoner of grace, we beseech Thee abandon us not because of our Sins, O Consoler of the sorrowing soul, have mercy on us[23]

Luke's three conflicting accounts of Paul's vision of Jesus[24] – the "purger of sins" – can now be tied to Suetonius' story of Caligula's vision of Oceanus – an earlier "purger of sins."

Additionally, John – who wrote the Book of Revelation while on the island of Patmos – ties the "Spirit of the Ocean and his bride Tethys" to "Jesus and his Bride": "The Spirit and The Bride say, 'Come' ... And let everyone who is thirsty, Come. Let anyone who wishes take the water of life as a gift'" (Rev 22:17). The Hebrew word for "water" is *Mayim*, identifying "The Bride" enigmatically as *Mayim, The MGDLene*.

According to an ancient Greek myth, the island of Patmos once sat on the bottom of the sea. It was originally called "Letois," named after the goddess Artemis, daughter of Leto. The Legend of Patmos goes something like this:

---

[22] Ovid, *Metamorphoses*, 13.949. Emphasis added.
[23] Kevin Knight, *New Advent* 2014).
[24] Acts 9:3-19; Acts 22:6-16; Acts 26:12-18.

The goddess Artemis was a frequent visitor to her shrine on Mount Latmos at Caria, the mainland across the shore from Patmos. She was often joined there by the moon goddess Selene, whose light revealed the beauty of the sunken island. Artemis fell in love with Patmos and wanted it for herself. She turned to her brother Apollo for help, and he in turn went to their father Zeus. Zeus petitioned his brother Poseidon to allow Patmos to arise from the sea, which he agreed to do. "Potamoi" are the river deities in Greek mythology, sons of Oceanus and Tethys.[25]

Unique characteristics – Patmos and a nine-fold chant for mercy and baptism – tie Oceanus (Spirit of the Ocean) and Tethys (His sister-wife; "embodiment of the waters of the world"[26]) to Jesus ("The Spirit") and The Bride (His sister-wife, "Mayim"; "the waters of life"). Therefore, Paul's vision of Jesus and Caligula's vision of Oceanus can be added to the many threads that identify Paul as the "metamorphosed" Caligula after his downfall, "death," and exile from Rome.

Notably, Caligula's downfall did not come about as a result of insane acts of violence and depravity. Nor did it come about because he claimed to be Mercury/Hermes, Jupiter/Zeus, or any of the other Roman and Greek gods. Caligula's downfall came about, according to Josephus, because he ordered that his statue be erected in the Jerusalem Temple. He was determined that the Jews be forced to worship him as *their* God. He ordered Petronius to take troops to Jerusalem, and he issued clear instructions: If the Jews agreed to erect his statue in the Temple, Petronius was to do so. But if they refused, he was to kill them and then erect it over their dead bodies.[27]

The Nasi in Jerusalem at the time was Gamaliel ben Simeon. Evidence examined in previous chapters indicates he was the "metamorphosed" Germanicus, the man who helped raise his elder brother's eldest son Gaius Caligula.

---

[25] The Theoi Classical Texts Library: "Okeanos."
[26] The Theoi Classical Texts Library: "Potamoi."
[27] Josephus, 1999, *Antiquities* 18.8.2 (261), 605.

Josephus' account of the imprisonment and release of Alexander the Alabarch of Alexandria is his contribution to the meaning of Paul's damning of Jesus and Bar-Jesus at Paphos. "Alabarch Alexander" was yet another name for Nasi Gamaliel; it was he who traveled to Rome and met with Caligula to explain that his prophesied three and a half years had expired.

Caligula threw Alexander (aka, Gamaliel) into prison, and then attempted to claim another title: "God of the Jews." His uncle Gamaliel (also known as, Alexander) could not allow that happen. The many decades of work that had gone into the effort to peacefully merge Judaism and The Way of Ansar and Kisar would have been for naught.

Josephus' enigmatic recitation of what transpired is tediously detailed in *Antiquities* 18.8.3-9. He describes the Jews' dramatic refusal to honor Caligula as God, their willingness to die for their faith, the efforts of Aristobulus, Temple Treasurer Helcias, and the other principal men of the family of King Herod. He describes Petronius' growing sympathy for the Jews, King Agrippa's intervention, and Caligula's eventual retreat from his unreasonable demands.

And then in January of 41, Caligula's reign of terror ended. The Antichrist was killed – or more correctly, the Antichrist was "metamorphosed." Suetonius is careful to note that the people did not believe Caligula was dead; rather, they suspected he concocted and circulated the story to find out how they felt about him.[28]

As a result of his removal as Emperor after only three-and-a-half years, the enigmatic narratives tell us that Caligula believed his uncle had double-crossed him. After all, he agreed to drop his demand to be honored as God of the Jews, and he was still forcibly dethroned.

Apparently, the explanation that his reign was to be the fulfillment of Daniel's Prophecy did not satisfy him. This perceived betrayal planted the seed of intense hatred for his pow-

---

[28] Suetonius, *Life of Caligula* (Loeb, 1914), (Thayer Online 60).

erful uncle and foster father Germanicus, later called Gamaliel but best known as "Jesus the Nazarean." His hatred was exposed when "Saul" is first identified as "Paul" during his encounter with Bar-Jesus at Paphos.

The accumulated evidence suggests that after he was dethroned in 41, "Lucius Aemilius Paulus" became "Lucius Sergius Paulus." He was sent from Rome to become proconsul of Cyprus. However, the stories suggest that his hatred simmered beneath the surface until c. 46 when he was betrayed a second time. It was after this second betrayal that Saul-Paul began his missionary work as Jesus' chief opponent under the guise of his chief apostle. It became his life's work to turn "The Jesus Myth" into a "Jesus History" and "The Nazarean Way" into a heresy.

Complicating the events, Caligula promised to pass the sceptrum Augusti to his cousin and foster-brother Marcus, Germanicus and Agrippina's younger son. But when Germanicus' half-brother Claudius was named Emperor instead, Marcus joined Caligula in a crusade against the man they blamed for the double-cross. And though given high positions in Cyprus and Gischala, they wanted more. They wanted revenge.

Over time – because they *were* grandsons of Marc Antony and Emperor Tiberius – Saulus and John of Gischala were able to draw together a substantial number of rebels and robbers. Josephus refers to Saulus as "Eleazar" the chief Sicarii and his half-brother as "Simeon Gioras." "John of Gischala," whose other name was "Marcus," was Germanicus' son, the younger twin.

In their mid-thirties when forcefully escorted from Rome – the prime of their lives – Paulus and John Mark set about to conquer or destroy the people who ruled the Empire – the very people who had raised them. After the encounter at Paphos, John Mark returned to Jerusalem with Bar-Jesus (his twin brother), but "Joseph called Barnabas" remained with Paul (Acts 13:13).

The identity of "Joseph called Barnabas" may be hidden in his surname: *Bar-abba* means "son of father." Therefore, it is likely that this "Joseph Barnabas" was the son of the man with whom he traveled – Paul.

Paul and Barnabas traveled alone to Perga, Antioch, Iconium, and Lystra, eventually returning to Jerusalem. It was then that Paul convinced James to waive the circumcision requirement for converts. They introduced Paulus' half-brother Silas Vespasian and his son Judas called *Barsabbas*, whose other name was "Titus."

These four then traveled to Antioch where they convinced more people to join in their cause. Eventually Silas and Barsabbas were sent back to Jerusalem while Paul and Barnabas remained in Antioch (Acts 15:22-35).

However, as they are preparing for another long journey, Barnabas tells Paul that he wants to take John Mark with them. Whatever took Mark to Jerusalem had apparently been resolved but not to his satisfaction. He was back and ready to rejoin the opposition party.

But Paul refuses. "The disagreement became so sharp that they parted company; Barnabas took Mark with him and sailed away to Cyprus. But Paul chose Silas..." (Acts 15:30-41).

Paul and Silas "went on to Derbe and to Lystra, where there was a disciple named Timothy, the son of a Jewish woman who was a believer; but his father was a Greek."

Derbe is also tied to a "Gaius" (Acts 24:4); a "Gaius" is called a *zenos*, translated thirteen times of fourteen uses as "stranger."[29] The one exception is when Tertius, the scribe of Romans, writes, "Gaius, who is *zenos*[30] to me and to the whole church, greets you." This exception can be defined as "the artificial interpretation of a single expression."[31] In other words,

---

[29] NASB, Strong's Greek 3581: "strange (2), strange thing (1), stranger (4), strangers (6)."
[30] Ibid, "host."
[31] Philo's Rule 16.

Tertius reports that Gaius, whom we suspect of being Paul, was, or had become, "a stranger."

In this same letter Paul greets certain Romans by name: *tous ek ton Narkissou tous ontas en Kyrio*; the word for word translation is, "he from the Narcissus who being among Lord."[32]

Furthermore, it sounds as if Paul is attempting to apologize for something: "I do not understand my own actions. For I do not do what I want, but I do the very thing I hate." And, "So then, with my mind I am a slave to the law of God, but with my flesh I am a slave to the law of sin" (Rom 7:15; 25).

And although it was no longer required, Paul forces Timothy to be circumcised (Acts 16:3). From this point forward, Saulus and Silas are together, accompanied for the most part by Timothy and Barsabbas.

It is Paul himself – or more likely our final editor – who reveals his relationship to Timothy: "For this reason I am sent you Timothy, who is *my beloved and faithful child* in the Lord, to remind you of my ways in Christ Jesus, as I teach them everywhere in every church" (1 Cor 4:17).[33] Not "The Way," but "my ways," a notable difference.

Timothy's grandmother and mother are identified in the Second Epistle to Timothy: "I am reminded of your sincere faith, which first lived in your grandmother Lois and in your mother Eunice and, I am persuaded, now lives in you also" (2 Timothy 1:5).

As previously noted, the name "Bar-n-abbas" identifies "Joseph called Barnabas" as Paul's son. This woman called "Eunice," Timothy's mother, was probably Julia Eunia, whose mother was Julia Iotapa, John Mark's elder sister. Therefore, "Joseph called Barnabas" and "Timothy" were brothers, and Paul was their father; Josephus' father "Matthias" was one of four men born in 6 CE.

---

[32] Words chosen are the most frequently used according to NASB count.
[33] Emphasis added.

After Barnabas and John Mark abandoned Paul and returned to Cyprus,[34] Paul enlisted his younger son Timothy
and continued the rampage. However, after twelve years as
Costobarus Silas, Vespasian's mind was also changed. Perhaps he received an offer from Rome that convinced him it
was time to reject Paul and his war. The defector – Paul's
half-brother – was joined by his son Titus and the historian
Josephus, Luke's "Joseph Barnabas."[35] Paul and Timothy are
later captured and shipped to Rome where they received another reassignment.

Curiously, each time Timothy joins Paul in the Acts' narrative, a "we passage" follows within a few verses, pointing
to Timothy as the author of Luke-Acts. And "Tim" is found
in the family of one of our prominent philologists whose
name was Luke: Lucius Mestrius Plutarchus. Plutarch's writings identify one of his brothers as "Timon," and Plutarch's
wife was "Timoxena."[36] Their daughter – who died at the age
of two – was also named "Timoxena."[37]

The question, "Was Plutarch also known as the gospel
writer Luke?" is a current topic of interest and debate among
biblical bloggers, Christians versus Skeptics. Many cite *Plutarch's Parable*, by Gott,[38] which identifies more than three
dozen unique characteristics that apply to both Lukes: Luc
Plutarch and the author of Luke-Acts. The synopsis and one-
page comparison of the similarities between the two men is
compelling. It can be found on several websites.[39]

[34] Col 4:10 discloses that Barnabas and Mark were cousins.
[35] Acts 4:36.
[36] Plutarch, *Consolation to His Wife*; Loeb Edition, 608 (C). Bill Thayer's Website.
[37] Plutarch, *Consolation to His Wife*; Loeb Edition, 611 (D). Bill Thayer's Website.
[38] Gott, *Plutarch's Parable: Lux Gospel and the Axe of the Apostle* (2005), 13-20.
[39] Nazannia. The Nazarene Way Website.

Only a few loose threads remain before this Volume I can be concluded:

Emperor Tiberius had twin grandsons, born to his son's wife, Livilla, at the very time her brother Germanicus died – or was "metamorphosed":

> While men's sorrow was yet fresh, Germanicus' sister Livilla, who was *married to* Drusus, gave birth to twin sons. This, as a rare event, causing joy even in humble homes, so delighted the emperor that he did not refrain from boasting before the senators that no Roman of the same rank had twin offspring ever before been born. In fact, he would turn to his own glory every incident, however casual. But at such a time, even this brought grief to the people, who thought that the increase of Drusus' family still further depressed the house of Germanicus.[40]

Three men named *Drusus* were closely related to Emperor Tiberius:

1. His younger brother, Nero Claudius Drusus the Elder, born c. 38 BCE.
2. His brother's son, Nero Claudius Drusus Germanicus, born c. 13–15 BCE.
3. His only known son, Drusus Julius Caesar, born c. 13–15 BCE.

Let's attempt to unravel these similar and potentially confusing threads:

1. In Luke's account of Jesus' birth, Tiberius was called "Kurios"; as "Kurios," his biological son "Jesus" was conceived and born to The Temple Virgin "Mary" while she was married (or betrothed) to "Joseph."
2. Luke's "Joseph" (Jesus' stepfather) was Tiberius' *brother* Drusus #1. Josephus called him "Spurious Alexander III"; to Plutarch he was "Alexander Helios."
3. The "Virgin Mary #1" was married to Drusus #1 (Jesus' stepfather) when she gave birth to his brother's son, Drusus #2 Germanicus (Jesus the Elder); therefore, Germanicus was Drusus #1's stepson and his brother's step-nephew.

---

[40] Tacitus, *Annals; The Works* (1864-1877), (Sacred Texts Online 2.84). Emphasis added.

4.   Drusus #1's brother was Tiberius, the Kurios who impregnated
     Drusus #1's wife, the "Virgin Mary." Therefore, Tiberius was
     Drusus #2's biological father as well as his step-uncle.

Therefore, Drusus #2 (Tiberius' brother's stepson) and Drusus #3 (Tiberius' biological son and step-nephew) was the same
man. He played the role of Jesus in Mark and Luke's Crucifixion of 37.

Tacitus' claim that Tiberius' son Drusus and wife Livilla had
a daughter in 5 CE and twin sons fifteen years later is possible
but unlikely. Temple Virgin mothers of gods were permitted to
serve in the child-producing capacity for only ten years.

It is more likely that these twin boys were sons of Drusus
Julius Caesar Germanicus, who was in fact Tiberius' biological
son, also known as Drusus Julius Caesar.

The Twins' mother was the Temple Virgin Mary Magdalene,
also known as "Agrippina the Elder" and "Livilla." Livilla-
Agrippina was Germanicus' step-sister; therefore, their marriage did not constitute incest. Furthermore, as "Jesus," his
"Sister-wife," a required relationship for gods and goddesses,
was Mary Magdalene.

Twin sons born to Germanicus and Agrippina in 6 CE were
hidden by the philologists for good reason. It would have been
far too easy for antagonistic censors to associate "Jesus and his
Twin" with twin boys born at the time of the Census. Their
birth had to be reported by way of small threads scattered
among multiple accounts, threads that could be pulled out and
reassembled.

Therefore, the solution to "The Twin Mystery" is that John
Mark of Gischala is the younger twin born in 6. Germanicus the
younger is the firstborn twin, the one Luke refers to as "Bar-
Jesus."

Luke's account of Gamaliel's contradiction with Josephus,
previously examined in Chapter Eight, identifies members of
the most important historical family to participate in "The Jesus Story": "Then came Tiberius Alexander ... the son of Alexander the Alabarch of Alexandria ... a great famine happened

in Judea, in which Queen Helena bought grain in Egypt and contributed it to those in need."[41]

The Drusus-Germanicus-Gamaliel threads can now be tied to the Alabarch Alexander thread. Alexander's unknown mother was the Virgin Glapyra whose second husband was Juba II; Alexander's sons were Julius Tiberius Alexander and Marcus Tiberius Alexander. They were Emperor Tiberius' grandsons, "The Twins" born to Drusus (Germanicus) and Livilla (Agrippina), not in 19 CE but in 6, concurrent with the Census.

In some cases, as with Julius Caesar and Hillel, one character "dies" just as the next arrives on the scene with little known of the earlier years of his/her life or genealogy. At other times, as with Jerusalem's Nasi Gamaliel and Alexandria's El-Ah-bararch Alexander, the identities are contemporaneous.

The "heavenly forces" behind "The Jesus Story" also created archaeological evidence to support the multiple identities. Examples include Dynamis' inscriptions and the bust of Livia found in Arsinoe, Egypt. All the evidence was created with a sole purpose: to carry abundant threads so that no matter how many might be destroyed, enough would survive that the whole story – and, therefore, the history – could be reconstructed.

This evidence added to Josephus' Alexandra-puzzle leads to stunning revelations supported by strong circumstantial evidence from multiple sources:

1. Hillel of the House of David and Julius Caesar descended from Venus, also known as "Shatah," are not two men, but one. He was Cleopatra's great-grandmother's brother. As "Hillel," he and Cleopatra had a son, Simeon ben Hillel. As "Julius Caesar," he and Cleopatra had a son – the same son – and called him "Ptolemy (XV) Caesarion." As "Asander and Dynamis" this son was "Tiberius Julius Aspurgus Philoromaios."

2. Caesarion was raised by Empress Livia, also known as "Arsinoe," Cleopatra's younger half-sister. Volume Two of our series

---

[41] Josephus, 1999, *Antiquities* 20.5.2 (100-1), 648.

will offer evidence that Arsinoe was also known as "Octavia" (whose brother was Emperor Octavian Augustus Caesar) and "Junia Tertia," Ovid's mother,[42] and "Tertulla," Vespasian's paternal grandmother.

3.   Cleopatra's mother, Alexandra, and Alexandra's grandmother's brother, Julius Caesar, are Octavian and Arsinoe's parents; Octavian was also known as Ptolemy XIV, Cleopatra's half-brother. Ptolemy XIII was Juba II, Cleopatra's step-brother. Like the Virgin Glapyra, his mother married Cleopatra's father. Juba was also known as Marcus Antonius, Lepidus, and Agrippa. Cleopatra Selene was his step-daughter; her father was Julius Caesar, and she was also known as Julia the Elder.

4.   As Livia's son and Octavian's step-son, Caesarion would be known as "Emperor Tiberius Julius Caesar." Furthermore, Tiberius' son Drusus Julius Caesar was also known as Simeon ben Hillel's son, Nasi Gamaliel, who, according to Josephus, had a son named "Jesus" – the historical and still popular "Jesus Christ Superstar."

John Mark the Twin, also known as "John of Gischala," was also known as the freedman-turned-governor, "Marcus Antonius Felix." He was accused of taking bribes[43] from Paul, and he was shipped to Rome with Paul, Timothy, and others. The Twins' elder cousin – six months older according to Luke – was John the Baptist. His parents were Lucius and Julia Paulus. He was also known as "Matthew," "Apostle Paul," and "Emperor Gaius Caligula."

Several more threads are now ready to be reassembled and Irenaeus returns yet again to participate in the task, asking rhetorical questions about Jesus:

For how could He have had disciples, if He did not teach? And how could He have taught, unless He had reached the age of a Master? For when He came to be baptized, He had not yet completed His thirtieth year, but was beginning to be about thirty years of age (for thus Luke, who has mentioned His years, has ex-

---

[42] Enigmatic evidence suggests that Ovid and Julia the Younger's biological father was Marc Antony. Their unapproved and incestuous relationship resulted in the conception and birth of future Emperor Vespasian.

[43] Acts 24:26.

pressed it: *Now Jesus was ... beginning to be thirty years old, when He came to receive baptism*); and, *He preached only one year reckoning from His baptism*. On completing His thirtieth year He suffered, being in fact still a young man, and who had by no means attained to advanced age. Now, that the first stage of early life embraces thirty years, and that this extends onwards to the fortieth year, everyone will admit; but from the *fortieth and fiftieth* year a man begins to decline towards *old age, which our Lord possessed* while *He* still fulfilled the office of a Teacher, even as the Gospel and all the elders testify; those who were conversant in Asia with John, the disciple of the Lord, reported that *John conveyed to them that information. And he remained among them up to the times of Trajan.* Some of them, moreover, saw not only John, but the *other apostles* also, and *heard the very same account from them, and bear testimony as to the statement.* Whom then should we rather believe? Whether such men as these, or Ptolemaeus, who never saw the apostles, and who never even in his dreams attained to the slightest trace of an apostle?"[44]

Demonstrating his knowledge of Philo's Philology, Irenaeus left it unclear whether the "he" who "remained among them up to the times of Trajan" referred to Jesus or to John. However, the subject under discussion was what age *Jesus* reached. And Irenaeus states unequivocally that "our Lord possessed old age." Moreover, the subsequent sentence reports that "the other apostles" confirmed John's account that "Jesus possessed old age" and that *He* fulfilled the office of a Teacher. And since the subject is how long Jesus lived, and the previous "He" clearly refers to "Jesus," it seems more likely that the "he" who "remained among them up to the time of Trajan" was Jesus, rather than John. Or it could have been both.

Trajan was born c. 53 and ruled from c. 98 until c. 115 CE. Irenaeus is certain that John and other apostles bore witness to the fact that Jesus was still alive up to the time of Trajan. He is adamant that their account – and, therefore, his – should be trusted above any other. It seems that Irenaeus believed that Jesus survived the Crucifixion and became a Teacher.

---

[44] Irenaeus, "Against Heresies," 2.22.5. Emphasis added.

In another work Irenaeus writes: "'For Herod the king of the Jews and Pontius Pilate, *the governor of Claudius Caesar*, came together and condemned Him to be crucified.'"[45]

Claudius did not become Emperor until 41; Pontius Pilate was relieved of his position as prefect of Judea in 36; he arrived in Rome to face charges of the mass murder of Samaritans in 37. Therefore, this stunning revelation requires careful investigation. These claims about Jesus that Irenaeus introduced in the second century should have raised questions about the Crucifixions – the *annual* Crucifixions that are conflated into the biblical accounts misinterpreted as being just one.

We can now identify three different Crucifixions spanning ten years and two generations of sons and daughters called "Jesus and Mary Magdalene."

The collected enigmatic evidence dates the first Crucifixion to April 19, 37, the first Passover after the reported death of Emperor Tiberius. Pontius Pilate succeeded Valerius Gratus c. 26 CE, not as "governor of Claudius" but as Prefect of Judaea.[46] And ten years later he was ordered back to Rome, arriving there *after* the death of Tiberius in 37.[47]

However, Irenaeus reports that Pontius Pilate was also "governor under Claudius," which could be any time after 41 and before 54. But Herod the King died in 44; therefore, Irenaeus' Crucifixion under Claudius and Herod – pinpointed to between 41 and 44 – is a different Crucifixion than the Crucifixion of 37.

Josephus reports yet another Crucifixion – number three – which takes us back to the promised examination of "Gamaliel's contradiction" in Chapter Eight, Part Two:

...the sons of Judas of Galilee were now *killed*; [48] I mean of that Judas who caused the people to revolt, when Quirinius came to take an account of the estates of the Jews, as we have showed in a

---

[45] Irenaeus, "Demonstration" 74. Emphasis added.

[46] Josephus, 1999, *Antiquities* 18.2.2 (35), 588.

[47] Josephus, 1999, *Antiquities* 18.4.2 (89-90), 592-3.

[48] The Greek words are more accurately translated, "were now taken away."

foregoing book. The names of those sons were James and Simon, whom Alexander commanded to be crucified.[49]

Julius Tiberius Alexander arrived in Judea Province to replace Fadus c. 46 and served in that capacity until c. 48. Josephus states that one of his first acts was to command that two of the sons of Judas the Galilean, James and Simon, be crucified.

Luke, Matthew, and Mark also write of a Crucifixion in which Simon plays a key role: "They compelled a passer-by, who was coming in from the country to carry his cross; it was Simon Cyrenius (Quirinius),[50] the father of Alexander and Rufus" (Mk 15:21). James, of course was Jesus' brother's name, and "Jesus" was related to "Ha Simoneans," rendered "Hasmonean."

Ten years may have marked the time for another generational change, and 47 may have been the year it was enacted and performed. Emperor Tiberius' sons Se-Janus and Quirinius arrived in Jerusalem for their final Passover-Passion performance.

SeJanus, also known as "James," and his brother Simeon Quirinius, also known as "Jesus," had taken on other duties. Sejanus, as Jesus' elder brother James, stayed in Jerusalem as High Priest. But Sejanus' younger brother Germanicus and step-brother Claudius had work to do in Rome. And so "The Twins," Alexander and Rufus, arrived with their father to assume their roles in the Annual Passover-Passion Festival of 47.

Simeon "carried the cross ... to the place called Golgotha," a word derived from the Hebrew *galal* which is defined as "roll; roll away."[51] It seems that someone slips out of sight and "rolls away" in order that another can be strapped to the cross.

Simeon ben Gamaliel takes the cross from his father, Gamaliel ben Simeon, who portrayed Jesus in previous performances; the role of "Jesus" is passed to the next generation. The

---

[49] Josephus, 1999, *Antiquities* 20.5.2 (100-102) 648.
[50] Translation of name is directly from the Greek.
[51] NAS (Strong's Greek 1556).

crowd's enthusiastic support for the release of Jesus Bar-abbas signals that The Sons' time has come.

The circumcised twin (Rufus-Thomas-Marcus) was the Jew who was stripped of his robe and tied to the cross. The uncircumcised twin Judas Didymos, also known as the son of Apollo, left Jerusalem for a life of teaching Pythagorean philosophy as "Apollonius of Tyana."

The philologists left no detail unanswered for anyone willing to search for clues. Gamaliel's contradiction in *Acts* points to *Antiquities* and Queen Helena of Adiabene.[52] Josephus' account of Queen Helena, her husband Mono-ba-zeus, and sons Monobazeus II and Is-ates explains how the circumcision of the younger son came about:

> ...a certain other Jew that came out of Galilee, whose name was Eleazar ... asked, "How long will you continue uncircumcised? If you have not yet read the law about circumcision, and do not know how great the impiety you are guilty of by neglecting it read it now." [Izates] delayed no longer but retired to another room and sent for a surgeon and did what he was commanded to do.[53]

Just as Paul did with his own son Timothy, he demanded circumcision for his cousin, as well, before they set out to oppose their perceived betrayer.

The Festival of the Crucifixion and Resurrection was to be an annual event. Irenaeus dates one festival between 41 and 44, the only years Claudius was Emperor and Herod Agrippa was alive. Luke and Josephus conspire to date two others: April 19, 37, and the third just after Tiberius Alexander became procurator c. 46.

Irenaeus seems to make a careless mistake when he reports that Pilate was governor under Claudius. However, this mistake now appears to be an intentional and valuable clue for solving the mystery of the contradictory accounts of the Crucifixion. It provides the final pieces of a portion of a much larger tapestry to be picked up again in Volume Two. And this thread

---

[52] Josephus, 1999, *Antiquities*, 20.5.2 (101), 648.
[53] Josephus, 1999, *Antiquities* 20.2.4 (43-44) 644.

– plus others found in *The Works of Irenaeus* – may identify him as being, like Polycarp his fellow citizen of Smyrna, *one of them* – a Nasoraean.

More clues to Irenaeus' important participation are found in Matthew's and John's Gospels: "At that time they had an *episemon* prisoner called Jesus Barabbas...Pilate said, 'Whom do you want me to release for you, Jesus Barabbas or Jesus who is called the Messiah?'... And they said, 'Barabbas'" (Mt 27:16-17; 21).

"Episemon" is a rarely-used word, but it represents a most significant number: 6. And, were it not for Irenaeus quoting from the teachings of the Gnostic Marcion, we could not know the heretics' understanding of the number 6 and their use of the term:

> For that perfect being Nous, knowing that the number *six* had the power both of *formation and regeneration*, declared to the *children of light*, that regeneration which has been wrought out by *Him who appeared as the Episemon* in regard to that number. For that perfect being Nous, knowing that the number six had the power both of formation and regeneration, declared to the children of light, that regeneration which has been wrought out by Him who appeared as the *Episemon* in regard to that number. Whence also he declares it is that the double letters contain the Episemon number; for this Episemon, when joined to the twenty-four elements, completed the name of thirty letters. Consider this present Episemon ... Him who was formed after the [original] Episemon, as being, as it were, *divided or cut into two parts*, and remaining outside; who, by His own power and wisdom, through means of that which had been produced by Himself, gave life to this world, consisting of *seven* powers. after the likeness of the power of the Hebdomad, and so formed it, that it is *the soul of everything visible*.[54]

Thanks to Irenaeus, we can see that "Episemon Iesous Barabbas" meant something to the Children of Light that others did not understand. To these Gnostics – whom the Church Fathers labeled "heretics" – "Episemon Iesous Barabbas" identifies the prisoner who was released as one of the Sons of the Fa-

---

[54] Irenaeus, "Against Heresies" 1.14.6-7. Emphasis added.

ther Jesus. "This present Episemon ... half of the two parts" refers to one of the twins born to the elder Episemon.

"Episemon" is made up of two words: *epi* ("on, to, against") and *sémainó* ("signify, indicate"). The editor of John's Gospel, whose voice can be easily identified, uses this term three times as the climax of the festival draws near. Coincidentally Jesus thrice asks, "Simon son of John, do you love me?" (Jn 21:15-17).

The lament that YH-Zeus utters as he prepares to die are words that Serapis surely spoke to the gathered masses in Egypt: "The hour has come for the *Son of Man* to be glorified ... unless a grain of wheat falls into the earth and dies, it remains just a single grain; but if it dies, it bears much fruit" (Jn 12:23-24).

It is easy to imagine Jesus bending down to plant seeds in a facsimile of the Osiris Bed as a visible example of the repeating cycle of life, death, and rebirth. "Jesus said: 'Now is the judgment of this world; now the ruler of this world will be driven out'" (Jn 12:31).

Josephus reports what happened to "the ruler of this world" during the first festival: "... on the fourth day letters came which informed him that Emperor Tiberius had died." And according to Plutarch, a "Twin" (Thamus), informed Tiberius of the *permanent* death of the pipe-playing, goat-footed Pan at this very same time.

The flute is used to identify Cleopatra's father, the "flute-playing bastard," as Tiberius' maternal grandfather, adding compelling evidence that supports our hypothesis that Tiberius Julius Caesar was born "Ptolemy" and called "Caesarion" by his father Julius Caesar.

Jesus also said, "And I, when *I am lifted up from the earth*,[55] will draw all things to myself. He said this to indicate [Greek *sémainó*] the kind of death he was to die" (Jn 12:32).

The "kind of death" is the same as the death of Serapis – a symbolic death to demonstrate the cycles of life that assure ev-

---

[55] Hebrew, *Anoki NaSa Ki* and/or *aNoKi aN iSh Ki.*

erlasting life – seed to plant to seed; parents to children to parents.

Finally, Jesus said, "The light is with you for a little longer. Walk while you have the light, so that the darkness may not overtake you. If you walk in the darkness, you do not know where you are going. While you have the light, believe in the light, so that you may become Children of Light" (Jn 12:35-36).

"Pilate said … 'Take him yourselves and judge him according to your law.' The Jews replied, 'We are not permitted to put anyone to death.' (This was to fulfill what Jesus had said when he indicated [sémainó] the kind of death he was to die)" (Jn 18:31-32).

A reminder once again that the death is symbolic and that no one actually died during these annual festivals.

"When Jesus had received the wine, he said, 'It is finished'" (Jn 19:30). A spear pierced his side and he bled, echoing Attis' Day of Blood ritual and fulfilling Zechariah's Prophecy (12:10).

When the tomb was found empty on the third day, this festival had encompassed the "kinds of death" suffered by all the gods of all time in all the Empire – except, according to Plutarch, the death of the god Pan. Pan's death was final, but it was immediately followed by the birth of Pandira's son, Ie-Zeus.

Jesus returns for some final words directed to Simon Peter: "But when you grow old, you will stretch out your hands, and someone else will fasten a belt around you and take you where you do not wish to go. (He said this to indicate [sémainó] the kind of death by which he would glorify Theos)" (Jn 21:18-19).

These words deliver two notable messages: (1) No nails were driven through the hands, wrists, or feet. Belts were used to fasten the Messiah-Savior to the cross before it was lifted up from the earth with him tied to it; (2) Simeon of Petra was to be a future "Jesus." But how far in the future might have been the problem. Perhaps Jesus envisioned twenty years and Phasaulus of Petra envisioned no more than ten.

And perhaps this was the second betrayal and the beginning of the Great Revolt. Paulus was the eldest son (Hebrew, *peter*) of the eldest son, SeJanus. He should have been the man chosen to portray – and, therefore, become – the next generation Messiah Savior. However, it appears that he was passed over, possibly because of the power of the Sacred Twins in the psyche of Rome. He was made High Priest of the Jerusalem Temple and given the name An-an-nous ("knowledge of An"). But apparently that did not appease him, for Josephus notes:

> ... this younger Ananus who took the high priesthood had a bold and insolent temper; he was also of the sect of the Sadducees. Festus was now dead and Albinus had not yet arrived from Alexandria; so Ananus assembled the Sanhedrim of judges and brought before them the brother of Jesus, who was called Christ, whose name was James, and some others ... and when he had accused them of breaking the law he delivered them to be stoned. Some of the people went to meet Albinus and informed him that it was not lawful for Ananus to assemble a Sanhedrim without his consent. Albinus agreed and wrote in anger to Ananus threatening punishment. King Agrippa took the high priesthood from Ananus after he had ruled only three months, and made Jesus, the son of Damneus, high priest.[56]

The second betrayal is Paul's removal from the High Priesthood after only three months. Adding insult to injury, he is replaced by Jesus the son of Damneus, Luke's "Bar-Jesus the magos" whom Paul cursed at Paphos. It must have been the final straw.

James-Sejanus wasn't actually killed – and Josephus doesn't indicate he was. He was *delivered* to be stoned, but there is no indication he *was* stoned. After all, James' brother was the Nasi Gamaliel, and the man who ordered that he be stoned was James' own son, Paulus.

It's more likely that Josephus created this fictional account of James' death to reveal the second betrayal and the motive for

---

[56] Josephus, 1999, *Antiquities*, 20.9.1 (199-203), 656.

Paul's revolt as "Eleazar the Zealot," a descendant of Judas the Galilean, also known as "Sejanus" and "James."

One of Claudius' first acts when he became Emperor in 41 was to release Philo's brother Alabarch Alexander from prison.[57] And Alexander's release and the high-profile position he assumed in Rome is the Second Coming of Iesous Chrestus, ending the reign of the Antichrist, Lucius Paulus Caligula.

Alexander was released just over three-and-a-half years after the Crucifixion of 37, the First Easter. The Prophecy in Revelation that has terrified the literalist-Christian world for two thousand years was fulfilled decades before it was written.

Still alive and waiting for him was the disciple whom Jesus loved, Ioanna, a woman of many names, including "Mary Magdalene." Inscriptions excavated in Athens – near the location of the statue of Athena – help identify two of her other identities. One inscription reads, "daughter of King Juba,"[58] and another is dedicated to the memory of a daughter of a Libyan King.[59] The ancient Greek geographer Pausanias identifies King Juba II as "Juba the Libyan," and Josephus also refers to him as "Juba, the king of Libya."[60]

To earn two inscriptions near the colossal statue of Athena, this daughter of Juba must have done something remarkable. Yet the daughter of Cleopatra Selene and Juba is a mystery no one has been able to satisfactorily solve. Historians and genealogists agree that she would almost certainly have been named "Cleopatra Thea Philo Pater" after her Grandmother, the Basilissa of Egypt.[61] However, no trace of Juba's daughter or her fate has been found – until now.

The last "Saying" in The Gospel of Thomas has sparked debate among scholars since it was discovered at Nag Hammadi in 1945 and published in a modern language in 1959. Most

---

[57] Josephus, 1999, *Antiquities* 19.5.1 (276), 633.
[58] Athenian inscription, IG II 3439.
[59] Athenian inscription *IG* III¹ 1309.
[60] Josephus, 1999, *Antiquities* 17.13.4 (349), 584.
[61] Chris Bennett: Genealogy of Cleopatra Selene (2001).

have attempted to explain it allegorically. However, in this particular case, the saying is to be taken literally:

> Simon Peter said to them, "Let's put Mary out of our group, for women are not worthy of life."
>
> Jesus replied, "Look, I myself will lead her to make her male, so that even she may become a live spirit, like you males; for every female making herself male will come under the *Imperial Rule of Heaven*"[62] (Gospel of Thomas, Saying 114).[63]

The solution to this enigmatic saying takes us back to the Virgin Glapyra, widow of Herod's eldest son Alexander III. After her husband's death, the widow Glapyra first married Juba II then Alexander's half-brother Archelaus. It was this marriage to her first husband's half-brother that Josephus blames for the Census of Quirinius.

When Glapyra married Juba, their children became step-siblings. And Glapyra's son Alexander IV and Juba and Cleopatra Selene's eldest daughter – almost certainly a "Cleopatra" – were about the same age, both with royal blood, both descendants of Ansar and Kisar, also known as the "Ka of Ptah."

When these step-siblings married one another, sister Clea became Alexander's "Sister and Bride," and it is this sibling who led the Embassy to Gaius in order to be in Rome for her brother's release – The Second Coming of Jesus.

This Sister-Bride's mother and grandmother's full name was the same: "Clea-patra Thea Philo Pater." And, as the first-born daughter, she was given the same name. She is Alabarch Alexander's unknown and unnamed wife – mother of Julius and Marcus.

Furthermore, since she was also Alexander's step-sister, the two boys were not only her sons but also her nephews. Alabarch Alexander (IV), also known as "Jesus," "helped make Mary male" – more than once. The first time he did so, he helped make her their sons' "Uncle Philo."

---

[62] Possible Essene version from Greek and Hebrew: *Basileus of Or an an, "Basilides of Light of An of Heaven."*

[63] Hedrick, Charles, *Unlocking the Secrets of the Gospel According to Thomas.* (Eugene: Cascade Books, 2010), 186. Emphasis added.

Judas the twin explained it: Jesus renamed Mary, calling her Philo and making her appear to be male. Her memory as "Philo Judeaus of Alexandria" has lived on these two thousand years just as Jesus promised it would – but only because she became a male philosopher. She was also "the disciple Jesus loved"; "Ioanna" was also known as the gospel writer "John."

However, the inscription at Athens honoring "Juba's daughter" has nothing to do with her work as Philo the Jew or the disciple called "John." It is in recognition of all she did for Rome as Claudius' freedman "Pallas" – as in Homer's "Pallas-Athena," the "goddess of wisdom, weaving, and every kind of craft."

Pallas-Athena frequently disguised herself as a man. And it was almost certainly Pallas who directed the plan to weave the history among a multitude of sources – all of whom carried Julius and Cleopatra's blood: sons and daughters, grandsons and granddaughters, great-grandsons and great-granddaughters.

An extant letter, an enigma written tongue-in-cheek by a "disgusted" Pliny the Younger to his friend Montanus, details Pallas the freedman's accomplishments and honors. It answers our final question: was the most powerful *man* in first century Rome a *woman*?

> Gaius Plinius to his friend Montanus: Greetings. As you know from my last letter,[64] I recently saw the monument of Pallas with this inscription: The senate decreed the praetorian ornaments and 15,000,000 HS for this man on account of his extraordinary loyalty and pietas towards his patrons. He was content with the honor.
>
> I then decided that it might be worth the effort to look up the actual decree of the senate. I found it so effusive and verbose that the arrogant inscription seemed moderate and humble by comparison. If all the Africani, Achaici, Numantini – and I will not speak only of the ancient, but even more recent characters such as the Marri, Sullae, and Pompeys (I will not go on any longer) – should they put themselves all together they would still fall short of the praise of Pallas.

---

[64] The referenced letter (Loeb, VII. 29) also quotes the inscription on "the monument" and places this monument to a freedman on the east side of Rome.

Should I think that the people who voted on this were witty or wretched? I would say witty, if wit was appropriate for the senate; I would say wretched, but I have no idea how wretched one would have to be that he could be compelled to say this sort of thing. Maybe it was ambition and a desire to get ahead. But who could be so insane that he would want to get ahead through his own and the state's disgrace in a state in which the reward for the highest office is to be the first person in the senate to be able to praise Pallas?

I pass over the fact that praetorian ornaments were offered to the slave Pallas (since they were offered by slaves); I pass over the fact that they voted that he should not just be encouraged, but actually compelled to wear a golden ring, for it would lower the dignity of the senate if an ex-praetor wore the iron ring of a slave.

These trivialities may be ignored; what must stand on record is that the senate, on behalf of Pallas – (the senate house has not subsequently been purified) – that the senate gave thanks to Caesar on behalf of Pallas because he spoke about him with the highest honor and gave the senate the chance to testify to their appreciation of him.

What could be more pleasant for the senate than that it should seem to be sufficiently grateful to Pallas? It was added, "That Pallas, to whom all say that they are obliged with the best of their ability, has received the most justly deserved reward for his singular faith and industry." You would think that he had extended the borders of the Empire, or that he had brought the armies of the state home again!

And there follows that, "Since there will be no more gratifying occasion for the Roman senate and people to display their generosity than if it should be able to add to the resources of the most abstemious and faithful manager of the Emperor's wealth." This then was the prayer of the senate; this was the particular joy of the people; this was the most pleasant material for demonstrating liberality: that the fortune of Pallas should be increased by wasting public money.

What next? The senate wished that he be given 15,000,000 HS from the treasury, and since his soul was so far removed for all desires of this sort, the senate should ask all the more fervently that the Father of the state should compel him to accede to the wishes of the senate!

The only thing that was missing was for Pallas to be approached on public authority, for Pallas to be begged to accede to the wishes of the senate, that Caesar himself, the patron of that arrogant abstinence, should make the request in person that he should not spurn 15,000,000 HS!

Pallas did reject it! The only thing he could have done that was more arrogant than to accept so much money from the public treasury was to reject it. The senate took this with further praises, though this time couched with a complaint, in these words: "When the best Emperor and Father of the State was asked by Pallas that the part of the decree of the senate that pertained to giving him 15,000,000 HS from the public treasury be rescinded, the senate states that it bestowed this amount freely and with good reason amongst the other honors that it voted because of Pallas' faith and diligence; and since it felt that it was not right to oppose the will of the Emperor in any manner, he ought to obey him in this manner as well."

Can you imagine Pallas, vetoing, as it were, a decree of the senate, moderating his own honors, refusing 15,000,000 HS as too much, and taking praetorian insignia as being of less importance! Imagine the Emperor obedient to the prayers, or rather, the orders, of his freedman before the senate (for the freedman ordered his patron that he should make this request in the senate)!

Imagine the senate going so far as to assert that it offered this sum, amongst other honors, freely and deservedly to Pallas, and that it would persevere if it did not have to bow to the will of the Emperor, whom it was not right to oppose in any way. So, in order that Pallas not take 15,000,000 HS out of the public treasury, it took his modesty, and the obedience of the senate, which would not have happened in this case, if it had not been thought right to disobey on any point!

You think that this is all? Hold on and hear some more. "Since it will be a good thing that the generous promptness of the Emperor to praise and reward deserving people be known everywhere, and especially in those places where those who are entrusted with the management of affairs might be incited to imitation, and where outstanding loyalty and innocence, as exemplified by Pallas should be able to encourage zeal for honest emulation, that those things that the Emperor had said before a full meeting of the senate on January 23, and the decrees of the senate that had been passed in subsequent meeting, should be inscribed on bronze and that the bronze tablet[65] should be erected next to the armored statue of the Divine Julius."

It was not enough for the senate house to be witness to these disgraceful events, but a very public place was chosen in which these events would be published so that they could be read by contemporaries and members of future generations! It was decreed that all the honors of this dutiful slave should be inscribed on bronze, along with those that he had refused, and those that he took up insofar as those voting them had the power to do it. The praetorian ornaments of Pallas were cut and inscribed on a public monument[66] for all time just like ancient treaties, just as if they were sacred laws.[67] So far did the Emperor, so far did the senate, so far did the – I don't know what to call it – of Pallas go that they wished to display the insolence of Pallas, the subservience of Caesar and the humiliation of the senate for all to see! Nor were they ashamed to find a reason for their wretched conduct, a wonderful and beautiful reason, that others would be encouraged by the example of Pallas with enthusiasm for rewards and emulation!

Honors, even those that Pallas did not refuse, were to be cheap. Nevertheless, people of good family could be found who competed for and desired those very honors that they saw given to freedmen and promised to slaves.

How glad I am that I did not live in those days, I would be ashamed if I had. I don't doubt that you feel the same way since I know what a lively and freeborn mind you have; it has been easier for me, even though I have allowed my indignation in places to go beyond the accepted limits of a letter, you will know that I have grieved less rather than too much. Farewell.[68]

How in the world could a woman disguise herself as a man? Her voice would surely give her away. We turn to Tacitus who explains *how* she got away with it:

---

[65] In addition to a "monument," a "bronze tablet" with inscriptions. Recall that the Hebrew word for "bronze" is *naschash*, the enigma identified in Genesis and Exodus that can also be translated "shining" and "serpent."

[66] Again, Pliny refers to a "monument for all time" with inscriptions.

[67] Possibly a reference to the inscriptions in Athens honoring Juba's daughter.

[68] Pliny the Younger, *The Letters of Pliny the Consul with Occasional Remarks*, William Melmoth, Esq, ed. (Edinburgh: 1807) 2.8.6 (85). Emphasis added.

...the proved innocence of Pallas did not please men so much as his arrogance offended them. When his freedmen, his alleged accomplices, were called, they reported that at home Pallas signified his wishes only by a nod or a gesture, or, if further explanation was required, he used writing, so as not to degrade his voice in such company.[69]

As Claudius' powerful freedmen Narcissus[70] and Pallas, this Divine Duo continued to build on the foundation established by their ancestors. Their ambitious goal was to create Plato's Ideal City, The Golden Age of Rome, and The New Jerusalem.

History has treated Julius Caesar kindly. As "Hillel the Elder,"
Julius is listed as one of the most important figures in Jewish history. His descendants continued his policies built on the "Law of Cause and Effect," rather than the "Law written in stone."

Marc Antony metamorphosed into Marcus Agrippa, the prolific husband of Julia the Elder and an honored statesman, general, and architect. Agrippa is credited with designing and constructing some of the most stunning buildings in the history of Rome. He was also involved in massive projects to renovate aqueducts, giving all Romans access to the best of public accommodations. His government-funded projects also provided jobs and created a vibrant and productive middle class.

Cleopatra, however, became one of the most reviled women in history, a manipulator of powerful men and a merciless killer of her siblings. Of course, she participated in creating the

---

[69] Tacitus, *Annals; The Works* (1864-1877), (Sacred Texts Online 13.23).
[70] The Gnostics' "Secret Book of John" alludes to *Narcissus* just before "the image of the Perfect and Invisible Virgin Spirit," appears. She is called "Barbelo," *BaR aB eL* and/or *aB oR aB eL.* Her name identifies her ancestors as "Sons of Father/Cloud (of) El" and "Father Light Father/Cloud (of) El." See Meyer, 2008, 110. "The Secret Book of John," *The Nag Hammadi Scriptures,* footnote 13: "The Father gazes into the water and falls in love with his own image in a manner that calls to mind Narcissus in Greek mythology (see Ovid *Metamorphoses* 3.402-510)."

stories that would make her the unacknowledged power be-hind the glory of Rome. She probably had no idea how long it would take before her work would be recognized and her rep-utation repaired.

Cleopatra helped make her younger sister Arsinoe "Em-press of Rome" while she hovered in the background as Scribonia (Julia the Elder's mother) and the insignificant, "Queen Dynamis." As "Vergil," of course, she has remained significant to classicists; she may also have been published un-der other pseudonyms, the most likely being Lucius of *Patrae*[71] (derived from Cleo-*patra*), and *Chariton*[72] (*chera* is the Greek word for "widow" + "An").

But Luke managed to also get her into the Christian Bible as the "Angel of the Lord" in the conception scene and as the "widow Anna," the prophetess who participated in Jesus' con-secration ceremony. Thanks to her great-great-granddaughter Leuce, Cleopatra remains an unrecognized but important fig-ure in Orthodox Christianity:

> There was also a prophet, *Anna* the daughter of *Phanuel*, of the tribe of *Asher*. She was of a great age, having lived with her *hus-band seven* years after her marriage [Greek, *parthenias*], then as a widow to the age of *eighty-four*. *She never left the temple* but wor-shiped there with fasting and prayer night and day. At that mo-ment she came, and began to *praise God* [Hebrew, *Hillel*] and to speak about the child to all who were looking for the redemption of Jerusalem (Lk 2:36-8).[73]

To the Essenes, the word "prophet" (Hebrew, *NaBi*) was *aN aB*, "An Father" and "An's cloud," reinforced by the name "Anna." Her father *Phanuel*, from *Phanes*, represents light[74] but is also tied to "Pan of the flocks, the flute player." Luke's enig-mas say that Anna is a daughter of the Light of El of the tribe of Asherah, also known as "Ishtar."

Believed to be the author of the original version of *The Ass*.
[72] Author of *Chaereas and Callirhoe*.
[73] Emphasis added.
[74] Liddell-Scott.

The Greek word translated "husband" is *Andros*, from *aner*, defined as "man," but suggestive of the Sumerian deity, *An Or*, "An of Light," and King Asander (*Ish An Or*), Queen Dynamis' husband.

In Hebrew "seven" is *Shabbat*, the name of an ancient Hebrew goddess; *Shabbat* can also be rendered, *iSh ha ab bat* and translated, "Ish the cloud daughter." *Parthenias*, translated here as "marriage," is translated elsewhere in Luke's Gospel as "virgin." Therefore, Anna is identified enigmatically as a Temple Virgin.

But it was Anna's age that jumped off the page as I read the story of the birth of Jesus back in 2002. Who could possibly care that Anna lived to be 84? Only an Essene or a "Wise Man with knowledge" would have cared to pass on this superfluous number. It seems they wanted to leave a clue to the extent of the "Gnosis" they possessed, and Anna's age is the key:

The Pythagorean Mystery Schools, which Josephus associates with the Essenes, used several values for *pi* to calculate the circumference of a circle.[75] The most convenient, 22/7, applied to Anna's age, 84, equals 264:

264 times 20 is 5,280, the number of feet in a mile;
264 times 30 is 7,920, the diameter of the Earth;
264 times 900 is 237,600, the distance to the Moon;
264 times the biblical number 12 is 3168, a *Sacred Number.*[76]

But the number 264 is much, much more, especially as it pertains to the *birth* of Jesus:

264 divided by the Gnostic's "episemon number 6"[77] is 44. Each human cell normally contains *twenty-two pairs* of chromosomes, called *autosomes*, which look the same in both males and females.

---

[75] John Michell, *The Dimensions of Paradise: The Proportions and Symbolic Numbers of Ancient Cosmology* (Kempton: Adventures Unlimited Press, 2001), 66.

[76] Michell, 2001, 55: "… *Lord Jesus Christ*… has the value of gematria of 3168, the Key number in the New Jerusalem dimensions."

[77] "For that perfect being Nous, knowing that the number *six had the power both of formation and regeneration,* declared to the *children of light,* that regeneration which has been wrought out by Him who appeared as the Episemon in regard to that number." Irenaeus, "Against Heresies" 1.14.6-7.

The 23rd pair determines gender: females (*Ishish or Isis*) have two X chromosomes, males (*Ish or Ishenes*) have one X and one Y.[78]

Finally, 264 times 100 is 26,400. And this number is hidden in the work of Buckminster Fuller which relies on the Watson-Crick model of DNA. Fuller composed a complicated gem of scientific jargon that attempts to explain the origin of human-kind. It isn't necessary to grasp the technical aspects of Fuller's words; we quote him only to demonstrate the complexity of the subject matter and what the word, "Gnosis," may have meant to those who identified themselves as "Gnostics":

> Five tetrahedra triple bonded to one another around a common edge axis leave an angular sinus of 7 degrees 20 minutes as the birth unzipping angle of the DNA-RNA behaviors.[79]

> This gap could be shared 10 ways, i.e., by two faces each of the five circle-closing tetrahedra, and only 44 minutes of circular arc per each tetra face, each of whose two faces might be only alter-natingly edge-bonded, or hinged, to the next, which almost-closed, face-toward-face, hinge condition would mechanically ac-commodate the spanned coherence of this humanly-invisible, 44-minutes-of-circular-arc, distance of interadherence.[80]

> Making such a tetrahelix column could be exactly accomplished by only hinging one edge of each tetrahedron to the next, always making the next hinge with one of the two-out-of-three edges not employed in the previous hinge. Whatever the method of inter-linkage, this birth dichotomy is apparently both *accommodated by* and *caused by* [Fuller's emphases] this invisible, molecular biolo-gist's 1 degree 28 minutes per tetra and 7 degrees 20 minutes per helical-cycle hinge opening.[81]

---

[78] National Institutes of Health, "How Many Chromosomes do People Have?"

[79] Converting 7 degrees 20 *minutes* of arc to *seconds* of arc: $(7 \times 60 \times 60) + (20 \times 60) = 26{,}400$ seconds of arc.

[80] 44 *minutes* of circular arc times $60 = 2{,}640$ *seconds* of arc.

[81] $(1 \times 60 \times 60) + (28 \times 60) = 5280$ *seconds* of arc per tetra.)

R. Buckminster Fuller (in collaboration with E.J. Applewhite), *Synergetics: Explorations in the Geometry of Thinking. Unzipping Angle* (934.02). (New York: Macmillan, Vol. 1, 1975 (with a preface and contribution by Arthur L. Loeb;); (Vol. 2, 1979), as two hard-bound volumes, re-editions in paperback. Online edition hosted by R. W. Gray with permission; Copyright © 1997 Estate of R. Buckminster Fuller.

Fuller's choice of words, "Invisible molecular biologist" suggests he, like Crick, may have considered the possibility that human DNA was "Intelligently Designed."

The evidence suggests that our ancient ancestors who compiled the Torah believed that humankind was "designed," *not* by a "Supreme Being," but by Beings from Venus whose knowledge was *superior* to ours. They believed "Adam's Ishshah helper" was "from Venus" and that her children with Adam were half Venusian, half Earthling. The sons and daughters of Ansar and Kisar were pure-blooded Venusians; they became the "Caesars of Kisar" and the "Ptolemies of Ptah."

Modern reconstructions of DNA look remarkably similar to two coiled snakes and the Caduceus, a winged staff with two snakes. A more ancient symbol, the "Rod of Asclepius," is associated with healing and resembles Moses' serpent on the Asherah pole used to save the lives of his followers.

Today, scientists and clinicians involved with the Human Genome Project and other genomic research are finding that DNA may hold the secrets to medical cures and extending lives.[82]

Is this nothing more than coincidence? The odds of the *"birth* unzipping angle" being coincidentally imbedded in the story of the *birth of Jesus* must be astronomical. Then add the odds that DNA is similar in appearance to coiled snakes. These odds, whatever they might be, imply that the Pythagorean-

---

[82] *A Brief Guide to Genomics: DNA, Genes and Genomes*; National Human Genome Research Institute; National Institutes of Health.

Essene author of Luke's Gospel knew of this characteristic of DNA/RNA behavior.

Furthermore, 264 is hidden in such a way that only a Pythagorean-trained person with knowledge of his 22/7 value for *pi* could find it. And it would be recognized as important only when technology discovered, or rediscovered, its significance to the origins of intelligent humankind.

Nevertheless, "coincidence" remains a possibility that we reluctantly acknowledge as long as our work is added to the growing body of evidence – archaeological, textual, and circumstantial – that points to the existence of similar knowledge in ancient cultures. At some point the scales may tip.

LATE ADDITION

Rome's Bethlehem Monument
June 2015

By Gott

When my Yoga teacher announced a June 2015 Yoga Retreat to Porto Santo Stefano in Tuscany, I immediately signed up. The airport that serves this area of Tuscany also serves Rome, so I decided to leave a week early to visit the Pyramid of Cestius as well as the better known and more popular Roman antiquities. So, on May 25, 2015, we sent the manuscript to our publisher, and I began preparing for this exciting trip.

I coaxed my friend Pam Miller into going along to photograph me in front of the Pyramid. And just before we left, I found some Internet-suggested "off the beaten track" places of interest that I thought we might want to visit. I printed out the information to take along – just in case.

One of the suggestions was a little-known monument called "The Baker's Tomb." The Baker was believed to have been a freedman, based in part on his name: he had a Roman praenomen and nomen followed by a Greek cognomen, typical for former slaves. Also, the inscription lacks the filiation that identifies a freeborn Roman.

The fact that he was a first century Roman freedman piqued my interest; that he was also wealthy, as were the "freedmen" Narcissus and Pallas, added to my curiosity. And Pam is always an easy sell when it comes to exploring new things. So, we hopped on the Red Bus near our hotel and hopped off several blocks from the Tomb and the Porta Maggiore.

Our decision to visit this "monument to bread baking" proved to be monumental – although I didn't fully grasp this until I returned home and began researching the Tomb in light of what I suspected about it.

The Porta Maggiore that towers over this curious box-shaped structure, was, like the Pyramid of Cestius, incorporated into the Aurelian Wall between 271 and 275 CE. However, a hundred years after the wall was built, Emperor Honorius (384-423) buried the Gate and the Tomb and constructed a tower over and around them. They remained underground and unseen for fourteen hundred years – until 1838 when Pope Gregory XVI had the Honorius Tower removed and the area excavated.[1]

Most sources date the tomb's construction to c. 50-20 BCE. However, after examining the evidence through Philo's lens, I became convinced that the dating is off by more than one hundred years. Another week of research led to *The Archaeology of Rome*, by John Henry Parker (1806–1884). Parker was an English archaeologist who specialized in ancient architecture, and in 1877 he, too, challenged the BCE dating:

> The tomb was much mutilated, and the second inscription had to be collected from fragments, and amongst them was a sculpture in bas-relief of the baker Eurysacis and his wife Atistia.[2] These fragments and the figures are built into the wall on the opposite side of the road, together with part of the buildings of the time of Honorius, in which, together with the Porta Maggiore itself, it was concealed, having formed the interior of one of the round towers of Honorius; the Porta Maggiore having been also built over, and fortified with two flanking towers, like his other gateways; so that it is at least as early as the third century, and *it is believed to be of the first*.[3]

---

[1] Samuel Ball Platner; Thomas Ashby (1929). A Topographical Dictionary of Ancient Rome. Oxford University Press (1929), 479, "Sepulcrum Eurysacis."

[2] Pompey the Great's first wife was *Antistia*. Haley, 1985.

[3] Emphasis added.

The Baker's Tomb (South Side)
East side of Rome

Porta Maggiore; Baker's Tomb; Aurelian Wall[4]

---

[4] Photographs by Pam Miller, June 12, 2015.

Before Honorius became Rome's Emperor, his father Theodosius issued decrees that made orthodox Nicene Christianity the official state church of the Roman Empire.[5] All other versions of *The Story of Jesus and Mary Magdalene* became heresies; the Ophites, Nasoraeans, Platonists, and Neo-Pythagoreans became – officially – heretics.

Theodosius was Emperor when the Temple of Zeus in Apamea, the Temple of Serapis in Alexandria, and the Temple of Apollo in Delphi were destroyed. Theodosius also presided over the extinguishing of the sacred fire in of the Temple of the Vestal Virgins and the destruction of the Temple of Cybele on Palatine Hill, home to Cybele and Attis.[6]

Apparently, and curiously, Theodosius' son Honorius must have seen something in the Porta Maggiore and the Baker's Tomb that threatened his father's Orthodox Nicene agenda. But, what could he have seen in Claudius' "East Gate" and a former slave's monument to his trade that led him to bury these structures during the same era other major heretical Temples were destroyed? And how might a Gate and a Tomb be connected to Temples built to honor Greek and Roman Gods, Goddesses, and Temple Virgins?

Parker's observations help answer these questions:

An excellent account of this tomb was published by Canina at the time it was excavated, with engravings of the plan, elevations, and sculptures. A very early date was at first assigned to it, and Canina is disposed to think it of the time of the Republic, but it must be near the end of it; *the construction is evidently of later character than some of the aqueducts. The material is travertine and tufa, the sculpture also is too good for the early part of the Republic.* The very singular plan, wider at one end than the other, is accounted for by the situation between two roads converging at the double gate,

---

[5] "Edict of Thessolonica": Codex Theodosianus XVI.1.2.

[6] Gilbert Grindle, *The Destruction of Paganism in the Roman Empire From Constantine to Justinian, the Chancellors Essay 1892*, (Ann Arbor: University of Michigan Library, 1892), 29–30. Ramsay MacMullen, *Christianizing the Roman Empire AD 100–400*, (New Haven: Yale University Press, 1984), 90.

and these roads are not likely to have been brought so near together before the gate was made. The chief argument in favour of
its being earlier than the aqueduct is, that no buildings were allowed to be erected so near the aqueducts; but that order was of
subsequent date to the time of this tomb, and a low ornamental
building of this kind might very well have been made an exception. [7]

Parker presented evidence that suggested to him (and to
me) that the Tomb was built *after* the aqueducts and the Porta
Maggiore. Nevertheless, Canina's original BCE dating remains
unchallenged and presented as factual; unfortunately, Parker's
disagreement and thoughtful argument are not mentioned in
easily-accessed sources.

Parker describes other important artifacts uncovered in 1838
that were later lost:

> The outer end of the tomb has been destroyed, probably because
> it was in the way of the builders of the round tower of Honorius;
> the fragments were found among the foundations of the tower,
> and have been preserved as mentioned; in the centre of this outer
> end were the figures of the baker and his wife, now built up in the
> wall on the opposite side of the road .[8]

As Parker notes, a marble relief portrait of a man wearing a
toga and tunic and a woman wearing a palla and tunic, were
also found at this site in 1838.

The female head was stolen in 1934 after the grainy photo
(p. 298) was taken, and the relief was later lost, an unexpected
tragedy for a city known for religiously preserving its ancient
artifacts, whether Christian or Pagan.

The epitaph (photo p. 296) found with the relief portrait is
written in Latin:

---

[7] Emphasis added.
[8] John Henry Parker, *The Archaeology of Rome, Part IX*, "Tombs in and Near Rome" (Oxford: James Parker and Co; London: John Murray, Albemarle Street, 1877), 34-5. Public
Domain.

FVIT ATISTIA VXOR MIHEI
FVIT ATISTIA
Atistia was my wife
FEMINA OPITVMA VEIXSIT
A most excellent lady in life
QVOIVS CORPORIS RELIQVIAE
the surviving remains of her body
QUOD SVPERANT SVNT IN
which are in
HOC PANARIO
this breadbasket[9]

Recall that "most excellent" (Greek, *kratistos*) was Philo's favorite adjective; *she* used it more than three hundred times in extant writings. Luke's Gospel and The Acts of the Apostles are also addressed to "kratiste Theophilus," the clue we followed to the Theologian Philo and her "Rules" for interpreting scripture.

Parker's observations coincide with and add to mine, and enigmatic evidence – not recognized by Parker – dates the Tomb's construction to c. 74-75 CE: First, Claudius was Emperor from 41 to 54 CE when the Aqua Claudia and Anio Novus aqueducts were completed.[10] His top advisors were the freedmen Narcissus and Pallas.[11] We know now, of course, that Pallas was not a man but a woman, and neither was ever a slave. They were, in fact, Julius Caesar and Cleopatra's grandchildren, Germanicus and Agrippina the Elder, also known as Drusus and Livilla. In Mark's version of the Crucifixion pageant of 37, they were "Jesus and Mary Magdalene."

---

[9] Robert Burn, Old Rome: (London: George Bell and Sons; Cambridge: Deighton, Bell & Co., 1880), 81. Current location: Baths of Diocletian. Corpus inscriptorum latinarum, 1.2, 1206. Photograph by Jastrow, 2006.
[10] The aqueducts were begun by Caligula in 38 CE and completed by Claudius (41-54 CE). Suetonius, *Life of Caligula*, (Loeb, 1914), (Thayer Online 21).
[11] Suetonius, *Life of Claudius*, (Loeb, 1914), (Thayer Online 59).

After completing the aqueducts, Claudius constructed the massive and costly Porta Maggiore c. 52 CE to celebrate the entrance of these waterways into Rome. And a question as large as the Porta Maggiore looms: why would Claudius, Narcissus, and Pallas place this colossal gate and waterway *behind* a freedman's Tomb that partially blocks its view when entering Rome from the East? If the Baker's Tomb was already in place, why not construct the gate several yards to the north or the south so it could be viewed in all its glory with no impediments?

As Parker's observations suggest, it seems more likely that the Tomb was constructed *after* the Porta Maggiore. And I propose that it stands at the entrance to attract attention and raise questions: What is the meaning of the Tomb? Who are the people buried in it? What did they do to deserve such a prominent location at Rome's East Gate?

Enigmatic clues to answers can be identified in a detailed relief that runs along the top.[12]

The south side depicts the delivery and grinding of grain and sifting of flour. Note two donkeys near the center are turning the grinding stones.

The west side depicts loaves of bread in baskets being carried to scales, weighed, then carried away.

---

[12] The three images are from *The Online Database of Ancient Art*: © Photo, text: M.E. Sergeenko. Prostie lyudi drevnei Italii — Izdatel'stvo "Nauka". Moskva — Leningrad, 1964, s. 66—67. From: M. Rostovzeff. *The social and economic history of the Roman Empire*, tabl. II.

The north side depicts the mixing and kneading of dough, forming loaves, and baking in ovens. Note the horse on the right, and recall that Julius Caesar placed a statue of his beloved "horse with toes" in front of the Venus Genetrix.[13] A portion of the left side of this relief was not recovered, but the leg of what appears to be a second baker, probably with another oven, can be seen.

The East side of the tomb, including inscriptions on the relief if one existed, was not recovered.

More clues can be pulled from the surviving inscriptions written in Latin and repeated on the three recovered sides:

EST HOC MONIMENTVM MARCEI VERGILEI EVRYSAC
MARCEI VERGILEI EVRYSACIS
PISTORIS REDEMPTORIS APPARET

The words are most often translated:

"This is the monument of Marcus Vergilius Eurysacis, baker, contractor, public servant."

However, this common translation is problematic and deficient for several reasons:

First, "APPARET" is not a noun ("public servant") but a verb, and it means "to come in sight, to appear, become visible, make one's appearance (class. in prose and poetry)." Also, "to be seen, to show one's self, be in public, appear."[14]

---

[13] Suetonius, *Life of Julius Caesar* (Loeb, 1914), (Thayer Online 61.1).
[14] Perseus Digital Library, Gregory R. Crain, Editor in Chief, Tufts University. Latin Word Study Tool, online.

Top:
EST HOC MONIMENTVM MARCEI VERGILEI EVRYSAC
(The remaining letters on this side are missing.)

Middle:
MARCEI VERGILEI EVRYSACIS
(This is a closer look at the names.)

Bottom:
PISTORIS REDEMPTORIS APPARET[15]

---

[15] Photographs by Pam Miller, June 12, 2015 (enlarged and enhanced).

Second, included in the definition of "PISTORIS" is one revealed by Ovid: "A surname of Jupiter, because, when the Romans were besieged in the Capitol, he gave them the idea of hurling bread, as though they had an abundance of it, at the besieging Gauls."[16]

"Jupiter," of course, was the Roman name for the deity the Greeks called "Zeus" – as in *YaH-Zeus*. Therefore, if Jupiter's surname was *Pistoris*, then Zeus' surname was *Pistoris* as well.

The key hypotext, however, is Genesis: a "baker" of bread is with Rachel's son Joseph and a "cupbearer" who serves wine.[17] The three are imprisoned in Egypt: "Some time after this, the cupbearer of *the king of Egypt* and his baker offended their lord *the king of Egypt*" (Gen 40:1; NIV).[18]

The key words between the repeated phrase are, "baker," and "Lord." Therefore, Philo's method for solving puzzles using a hypotext reveals that "the baker" is "the Lord," and perhaps "the king" of Egypt.

Equally informative is the fate of this baker: "… the chief baker he hanged, just as Joseph had interpreted to them"[19] (Gen 40:22).

Philo's brother, Alexander the Alabarch of Alexandria, was the equivalent of a King during the first century CE. "Allah ab arch" means "Allah (or El) Father highest." The enigmatic message on the tomb is: PISTORIS, "the baker" is "Lord of Lords," and "King of Kings," and "descended from El the Mother."

The second word, REDEMPTORIS, can be tied to the MGDL DR, "the watchtower of the flock," introduced immediately before the Bethlehem Prophecy (Mic 5:2-3) at Mic 4:8:

---

[16] Perseus Digital Library: Latin Word Study Tool. Ovid, *Fasti* 6.350; 394.

[17] Wine: from "a vine" or a "choice vine."

[18] Emphasis added to note the repetition of a phrase.

[19] Hebrew consonants in Gen 40:22: WT SR HFYM T LH KShR PTR LHM YSF. Essene interpretation: "The chief baker is eLoaH-Kisar's first-born (son of) El the Mother, Joseph."

"As for you, watchtower of the flock, stronghold of Daughter Zion, the former dominion will be restored to you; the Kingdom will come to Daughter Jerusalem."

Can this be interpreted as anything other than a prophecy that Daughter Zion, Daughter Jerusalem – the Watchtower of the Flock – would be resurrected from the ashes of Asherah that YHWH demanded be destroyed?

Break down their altars, smash their sacred stones and burn their Asherah poles in the fire; cut down the idols of their gods and wipe out their names from those places (Deut 12:3).

Micah's prophecy continues:

Why do you now cry aloud -- have you no king? Has your ruler perished, that pain seizes you like that of a woman in labor?

Writhe in agony, Daughter Zion, like a woman in labor, for now you must leave the city to camp in the open field. You will go to Babylon; there you will be delivered, *Redemptoris* from the hand of YHWH, your adversary (Micah 4:9-10).[20]

Micah's Prophecy promises the Ishraelites that Isherah, the Goddess YHWH despised and whose temples were repeatedly destroyed,[21] would be restored to her Kingdom *in Babylon* – "redeemed" – in the very place the Hebrew Bible was compiled and edited before Ezra delivered it to Jerusalem. This ignored Prophecy is followed by the better known,

But you, *Bethlehem Ephrathah*,[22] though you are small among the clans of Judah, out of you will come for me one who will be ruler over Israel, whose origins are from of old, from ancient times. Therefore Israel will be abandoned until the time when *she who is in labor* bears a son, and the rest of his brothers return to join the *Israelites* (Mic 5:2-3).[23]

The "Redemptoris" on the Tomb refers to the Virgin of El, Daughter Jerusalem, the Watchtower of the Flock, the Virgin

---

[20] Author's interpretation using Essene methodology; Latin *Redemptoris* replacing Hebrew *gaal*; emphasis added.
[21] Ex 34:13; Deut 12:3; Judg 6:25, 26, 28, 30; 2 Kings 18:4; 2 Kings 23:14, 15; 2 Chron 31:1; 2 Chron 34:4, 7; and others.
[22] These two words can be translated, "Betulah Em of the Ashes" (NAS, Strong's Hebrew 665, *epher*, "ashes").
[23] Emphasis added.

Mary Magdalene. And in 1987, Pope John Paul II wrote a controversial encyclical titled, *Redemptoris Mater*. He concluded by quoting a hymn attributed to Hermannus Contractus (1013-1054), who composed it based on writings of Early Church Fathers, including our friend, Irenaeus. The hymn's opening words restore the Kingdom to the Virgins and the Feminine deity she represents:

> Alma Redemptoris Mater, Gate of Heaven, Star of the Sea, assist your people who have fallen yet strive to rise again.[24]

To these words – long overdue – I would like to add, "Awomen and Amen!"

According to linguists, the suffix *ei* in the names, "Marcei Vergilei Eurysacis" denotes the generative (possessive) form of a name. This would render "Marcei" and "Vergilei," "of Marc and Vergil," the common translation. However, two thousand years ago in the now extinct Oscan language of southern Italy, *ei* denoted the dative form "to," not the possessive, "of."[25] The difference is significant because it creates a puzzle that must be solved: Is this the monument "*of* Marcei Vergilei Eurysacis" or is this the monument "*to* Marcei Vergilei Eurysacis"?

Just a little research into the Oscan language leads to the answer and adds support to previous conclusions:

First, Oscan was spoken by the Samnite tribe;[26] "Samnite" and "Simeonite" in biblical Hebrew are both written SMNT. Additionally, a common Samnite name was "Pontius" – as in "Pontius Pilate."[27] In Chapter Fifteen we presented evidence that "Pontius Pilate" was Germanicus and Agrippina's firstborn twin son and that the name "Pilate" can be associated with the freedman's *pileus* (also *pilos* and *pilleus* or Latin, *pille-*

[24] The Monks of Saint Meinrad Monastery, *The Tradition of Catholic Prayer*, Christian Raab and Harry Hagen, eds. (Collegeville: Liturgical Press, 2007), 234.
[25] Philip Baldi, *The Foundations of Latin* (Berlin: Walter de Gruyter GmB H & Co. 2002), 324.
[26] Ibid.
[27] William Smith, *A Dictionary of the Bible* (London: John Murray, Albermarle Street 1863), 872.

um). So, clearly, the Oscan language might have been used by a first century Samnite inscriber of a tomb, perhaps the Samnite known as "Pontius Pilate."

The pileus was a particular type of hat placed on the head of freedmen during manumission ceremonies. It closely resembles the Phyrgian cap worn by Cybele's priests and by Attis himself, and it became the emblem of liberty and freedom in Rome.[28]

In fact, Rome's annual celebration of Cybele and Attis (examined in Chapter Eight) began on the Ides of March with the *Canna intrat* ("The Reed Enters") celebrating Attis' birth among reeds. Of course, Moses birth narrative features reeds, as well.

Relevant to our search for the people in the Tomb, the pileus is also associated with Julius Caesar: Brutus issued a denarius to commemorate his assassination on the Ides of March, and the reverse side shows a pileus between two swords.

Evidence presented throughout this book explains the probable meaning of these symbols: Julius Caesar's descendants are disguised as freedmen and freedwomen. His grandson Germanicus, also known as the freedman "Narcissus," would be, like Attis, tied to a tree in the form of a cross in his role as "Jesus the Nazarean." Julius' granddaughter, the freedman Pallas as a "Virgin Mother," would be associated with a perpetual fire kept burning by "Temple Virgins."

The pileus was surely designed to be associated with the Phyrgian cap worn by Attis which was also tied to Roman Mithraism. Not only would it have represented "freedom and liberty," it would have represented allegiance to Cybele and Attis whose annual celebrations began on the Ides of March.

---

[28] Diodorus Siculus (Exc. Leg. 22), 625, ed. Wess.; Plaut. Amphit. I.1.306; Persius, V.82).

Top left: Attis as a child in Phrygian cap, 2nd century ACE.[29]

Top right: Denarius featuring a pileus, issued by Brutus c. 44 BCE. The handle of one sword appears to be a cross, the other seems to suggest a flame.[30]

Bottom left: Dioscure in pileus, 4th Century CE. Rome, Italy, Piazza del Campidoglio.[31]

Bottom right: Dioscure in pileus, c. 460-450 BCE. Paris, France, Louvre Museum.[32]

---

[29]Currently at Cabinet des Medailles. Photograph by Jastrow, 2006

[30] Image from Wikimedia Commons; no source cited.

[31] Photograph: Carlomorino public domain. Wikimedia Commons.

[32] Photograph by Jastrow, 2008.

These associations with Samnites, Pontius Pilate, the twins, and the Oscan language leave but one choice for accurately interpreting the *ei* suffix added to the names on the Tomb. The Samnite's ancient Oscan dative *ei* turns "Marcei" into "*to* Marc" and "Vergilei" into "*to* Vergil." Therefore, the Tomb is dedicated *to* Marc and *to* Vergil Eurysacis.

Additional evidence comes from the name "Marc," from Mars, the god of war. And, notably, Ovid's version of the genealogy and founding myths of Rome identifies Mars as the father of twins, Romulus and Remus; their mother was the Vestal Virgin Rhea Silvia. Mars and Venus would later become lovers, reconciling the two competing traditions of Rome's founding. Venus was the divine mother of Aeneas, Julius Caesar's ancestor – according to Vergil's *Aeneid*.

A search for prominent first century Roman freedmen who were bakers came up empty except for "a baker and a cook" who accompanied Emperor, Aulus Vitellius, out of Rome in 69 CE. This forced removal was in preparation for the arrival of Emperor-to-be Vespasian, Saulus-Paulus' half-brother. Vespasian was on his way back to Rome from Alexandria where he miraculously cured two men, one blind the other lame.[33]

However, before we examine Aulus Vitellius and his unnamed "baker and cook," we need to look at an intriguing first century "freed*woman*" who ran with this same crowd. Her name was "Antonia Caenis" (Greek, *Kaenis*); she is described as "secretary of Antonia Minor," daughter of Marcus Antonius and Octavia Minor. Caenis was, according to Suetonius, Emperor Vespasian's mistress whom "he treated … almost as a lawful wife."[34]

Cassius Dio adds:

It was at this time [c. 74 CE] that Caenis, the concubine of Vespasian, died. I mention her because she was exceedingly faithful and was gifted with a *most excellent* memory. Here is an illustration. Her mistress Antonia, the mother of Claudius, had once employed

---

[33] Tacitus, *Histories*; *The Works* (1864-1877), (Sacred Texts Online 4.80.1).
[34] Suetonius, *Life of Vespasian*, (Loeb, 1914) (Thayer Online 3.1).

her as secretary in writing a secret letter *to Tiberius about Sejanus* and had immediately ordered the message to be erased, in order that no trace of it might be left.[35]

According to Josephus, this letter warning Tiberius about Sejanus's malice against him (dictated by Antonia and written by Caenis) was delivered to Tiberius by the freedman Pallas.[36] This raises a question: if the letter was erased as Antonia ordered, how could it be delivered to Tiberius? Dio answers this question:

> Thereupon she replied: "It is useless, mistress, for you to give this command; for not only this but as whatever else you dictate to me I always carry in my mind and it can never be erased."

The only way an erased letter could be delivered to Tiberius is by recitation from memory. And the woman with the photographic memory of the contents of the letter was Caenis, not Pallas. However according to Dio, Caenis and Pallas share common characteristics, and these characteristics tie them together and tie both to The Baker's Tomb:

> And not only for this reason does she seem to me to have been a remarkable woman, but also because Vespasian took such excessive delight in her. This gave her the *greatest influence* and *she amassed untold wealth*, so that it was even thought that he made money through Caenis herself as his intermediary. For she received vast sums from many sources, sometimes selling governorships, sometimes procuratorships, generalships and priest-hoods, *and in some instance even imperial decisions.* For although Vespasian killed no one on account of his money, he did spare the lives of many who gave it; and while it was Caenis who received the money, people suspected that Vespasian willingly allowed her to do as she did.[37]

A monument dedicated to Caenis was found near the Porta Nomentana in Rome on her estate on the Via Nomentana (image p. 310). Perhaps the etymology for the naming of this gate and street is "Name (eT) Anna," identifying Caenis as a woman

[35] Cassius Dio, *Roman History: Epitome of Book 65*, (Thayer Online 14.1-4).

[36] Josephus, 1999, *Antiquities* 18.6.6 (182), 599.

[37] Cassius Dio, *Roman History*, "Epitome of Book 65" (Loeb, 1925), (Thayer Online 14.1-4). Emphasis added.

also known as "Anna." And as noted earlier, Luke refers to Mary Magdalene as "Mary Magdalene IoAnna" (Lk 24:10). It can also be interpreted as, "Name Ti An," associating Caenis with the Sumerians' Ti, "Life giver" and Ansar, "First Father" of compassionate humanity.

On one side of the monument is a relief of two figures riding on swans holding inverted and intertwined laurel branches. The other side is a relief of two winged cherubs holding a large floral garland with vittae tied on either end. Vittae were head-dresses worn by Vestal Virgins.[38]

A multitude of ancient myths associate swans with Castor and Pollux, the twins born to Zeus and Leda, whose daughter was Helen of Troy.[39]

Ovid's story of Apollo's love for the virgin sea nymph Daphne,[40] quoted in an earlier chapter, explains the laurel branches and the wreath:

And still [Apollo] loved her; on the trunk he placed his hand and felt beneath the bark her heart still beating, held in his embrace her branches, pressed his kisses on the wood; yet from his kisses the wood recoiled. "My bride", he said, "since you can never be, at least, sweet laurel, you shall be my tree. My lure, my locks, my quiver you shall wreathe." … Thus spoke the god; the laurel in assent inclined her new-made branches and bent down, or seemed to bend, her head, her leafy crown.[41]

The monument was dedicated to Caenis by a man who identified himself as "Aglaus" and his three children. The epitaph reads:

---

[38] Photographs (front and two sides): Ann R. Raia; Judith Lynn Sebeste. *Online Companion to The Worlds of Roman Women*.

[39] Atsma, Greek Mythology (2000-2011): "Dioskouroi."

[40] Greek for "laurel."

[41] Ovid, *Metamorphoses* 1. 452 ff (trans. Melville).

DIS MANIB: "To the memory of"

ANTONIAE AVG: "Antonia the Great's"[42]

L CAENIDIS: "freedwoman Caenis"

OPTVMAE:[43] "Most Excellent"

PATRON: "Protector of the People"

AGLAVS LCVM: *Aglaus* is derived from the Greek word *aglaos*, which means, *shining, bright*. The Homeric Hymn to Hermes[44] places this word next to *Dio*, translated as "Zeus").[45] Furthermore, Ie-sous said, "I am ... the *bright*[46] morning star" (Rev 22:16).

AGLAO: Aglaus' son, another "shining one," was also known as "Bar-Jesus." He was Tiberius's grandson, the twin called "Germanicus Gemellus,"[47] born in 6 CE (not 19), to Livilla and Drusus.[48][49]

ET GLENE: means "and Mirror" (Bar-Jesus' "mirror image," the twin John Mark). Josephus calls him "Tiberius Gemellus."[50]

ET AUGLAIDE: means "and Auglaide," Aglaus' daughter, also known as Drusus and Livilla's daughter "Julia," born c. 5 CE.

FILIIS: "Children."

On the back of the altar is a relief of two trees (The photographer Ann Raia did not provide a photograph and I've been unable to find one). Both Jesus and Attis are associated with a tree which represents cycles of life and immortality.

---

[42] Antonia Minor, Marc Antony's daughter.

[43] The same word, *OPTVMA*, is in Atistia's epitaph.

[44] *Homeric Hymns*, "To Hermes." Editions and translations: Greek (ed. Hugh G. Evelyn-White); English (ed. Hugh G. Evelyn-White); Perseus Lookup Tools: 4.430.

[45] Liddell-Scott.

[46] NAS Greek 2986, *lampros*, also means "bright."

[47] *Gemellus* is the Greek word for "twin."

[48] Tacitus, *Histories*; *The Works*, (1864-1877), (Sacred Texts Online 2.84).

[49] Josephus, 1999, Antiquities 18.6.8 (206), 601.

[50] Josephus, 1999, Antiquities 18.6.8 (206), 601.

Monument to Caenis, Antonia's Freedwoman.[51]

---

[51] Photographs (front and two sides): Ann R. Raia; Judith Lynn Sebeste. *Online Companion to The Worlds of Roman Women.*

The etymology of "Attis" might be the Hebrew word for tree, *Ets*. Furthermore, Daphne, Apollo's beloved, was turned into a laurel tree which plays a prominent role in the birth-myth of the poet "Vergil," a "Virgin of El."

Aglaus and his children, "Aglao," "Glene," and "Aglaide," are assumed to have been Caenis' freedmen and freedwoman. However, the inscription and their names suggest a far different relationship:

In Ovid's *Metamorphoses,* Caenis was a Greek goddess who was transformed into a man – a "transgender" of sorts. This myth brings to mind Jesus' mysterious words in the Gospel of Thomas: "Look, I myself will lead [Mary] to make her male..."[52]

Evidence previously presented solved this Gospel of Thomas Saying: "Mary Magdalene" can be found in historians' accounts hiding behind a man's name. We identified *two* men, Philo of Alexandria and the freedman Pallas, as women who are remembered as prominent first century males. They were the woman Jesus referred to as "Mary" – Mary Magdalene.

Caenis, Pallas, and the builder of the Baker's monument were all described as powerful, influential, and extremely wealthy former slaves. "They" were, however, one woman, Agrippina the Elder, also known as "Livilla." She was co-ruler with Emperors Claudius (Livilla's half-brother), Nero (Agrippina's grandson), and Vespasian (Agrippina's nephew who was also her father's grandson).

Furthermore, she was a Vestal Virgin who would have participated in their rituals, and baking was an important part of more than one.

The Vestals' most important festival was the annual *Vestalia* that ran from June 9 until June 15. The Virgins prepared sacred *Mola Salsa Wafers* made from parched spelt, a kind of wheat grown only in mountainous regions. The water used to make the

---

[52] Hedrick, Charles, *Unlocking the Secrets of the Gospel According to Thomas*. (Eugene: Cascade Books, 2010), 186.

sacred cakes came from a holy spring and was transported in consecrated jugs. The containers were never permitted to touch the
earth between the spring and the baking of the cakes in order to
preserve its sacred nature. The Wafers were cut into slices and
offered to Vesta as a bloodless sacrifice. The last day of the festival
the shrine was cleaned and the ashes from the altar discarded.[53]

The Virgins also used ovens to bake muries, which consisted of
impure salt ground with a mortar and pestle. It was then mixed
with holy water and also used in bloodless sacrificial rituals.[54]

And as noted in Chapter Fourteen, the Vestals led the annual New Year rites on March 1 when new laurel branches replaced the old branches as they relit the sacred fire to symbol-
ize a fresh start of the New Year.[55]

Bread in the form of the sacred Mola Salsa Wafers, sacred
spring water, and the sacred laurel branch were the three items
most often associated with the Vestal Virgins. The Baker's
Tomb and the Porta Maggiore represent the first two and the
monument to Caenis' adds the third. The Baker's Tomb is a
monument to Rome's Vestal Virgins and to the Israelites' Betula Em, Bat El ha Em, and Honorius must have known this.

Eurysacis' wife's name, Atistia, also offers important clues.
In Biblical Hebrew, "Atistia" is written *TST;* the Essene-
Nazarene's rendering could be *eT iShTa. Et,* defined as "un-
translatable mark of the accusative case, is found two times in
Genesis 1:1, *Ishta* and "bread" one time each:

BaR **iShTa** aB oR **LeHeM eT** Ha iSSaMaYiM We **eT** HaaRes.

The Essene-Nazareans' interpretation would be, "Son of
Star, Father Light, El the Mother (and/or "Bread") *eT* Heavens
and *eT* Earth."

Of course the Hebrew word, *eT* can also be rendered *Ti,* the
Sumerian goddess whose name, like *Chavvah* ("Eve"), means

[53] T. Cato Worsfold, *History of the Vestal Virgins,* (London: Rider & Co. Paternoster
House E.C., 1934), 148.
[54] Wildfang, 2006, 16.
[55] Wildfang, 2006, 1-31.

"Life Giver." It is surely no coincidence that Pompey the Great's first wife was Antistia[56] who may have been Cleopatra's unknown mother, also known as "Salome Alexandra."

The Greek name "Eurysacis" also helps explain Honorius' decision to bury the Tomb and the Gate:

"Eurysacis" can be broken into two Greek words: the prefix *Eury* means "wide; broad";[57] the suffix *sakis* means "little" or "small."[58] Once we tie in some biblical verses, Honorius' concern of a competing heresy comes into focus.

Jesus said:

> Enter through the narrow gate; for the gate is wide (Greek, *eury*) and the way is broad that leads to destruction, and there are many who enter through it. For the gate is small (Greek, *sakis*) and *the way*[59] is narrow that leads to *life,*[60] and there are few who find it (Mt 7:13-14).[61]

Now look closer at the Porta Maggiore relative to the placement of the Tomb. It would be impossible to enter or exit Rome through the "narrow gate" without walking into or around the monument that honors LHM, "bread," and/or "El the Mother."

Moreover, Jerusalem also had an "East Gate," and Nehemiah identifies the "keeper of the East Gate":

> After them Zadok[62] son of Immer [also, *Em Or*] made repairs opposite his own house. After him Shemaiah son of Shecaniah, the keeper of the East Gate, made repairs (Nehemiah 3:29).[63]

---

[56] Haley, 1985.

[57] Dictionary.com: *Eury*: "1. a combining form meaning 'broad,' 'wide,' used in the formation of compound words... "

[58] Greek Names: *Sakis*.

[59] Hebrew *derek*, root of Rachel "The Way of El."

[60] Hebrew, *chavvah*, translated "Eve."

[61] NAS; emphasis added.

[62] Josephus associates "Judah the Galilean and Zadok" with the fourth sect of Judaism, Josephus, 1999, *Antiquities*, 20.5.1 (97-99), 648.

[63] It is unclear whether "the keeper of the East Gate" was Shemaiah the son or his parent Shecaniah.

Porta Maggiore and Baker's Tomb[64]

---

[64] Photographs by Pam Miller June 12, 2015

Ezra steps in to identify Shecaniah as "son of Jehiel, of the descendants of Elam..." (Ezra 10:2). "Jehiel" can be translated, *Yah, El,* "Praise El." And according to Acts, Elymas (from *Elam*) was "the meaning of the name" ... "bar YH Zeus."

Now compare Rome's East Gate (from the inside looking out) with Jerusalem's East Gate (photographs p. 316).

Featured on Jerusalem's East Gate are two arches that come together to create one large entrance were it not filled in. Rome's East Gate has one narrow gate between two wide gates, and the narrow gate is aligned with the Baker's Tomb, nearly invisible from inside the Gate.

Nehemiah gives two names, "Shemaiah" and "Shecaniah," when identifying the keeper of Jerusalem's East Gate. Philo's rules say to look at similar words when trying to solve enigmas: "Shemaiah," "Shemesh," "Simeon," "Samuel" and "Samnites" share the same Hebrew root. In Chapters Eight and Eleven we examined the various translations for *shemesh,* most often "sun" which rises in the East; in fact, NASB translates *shemesh* as "east side" twice.[65]

"Shecaniah" can also be written "Shekhinah." Mythology and folklore scholar, Ilil Arbel, has written extensively on Judaic myths, including the Talmud's "Shekhina":

---

[65] Strong's Hebrew 8121.

Top: Porta Maggiore from the inside looking out.[66]
Bottom: Jerusalem Second East Gate, c. 520 CE[67]

[66] Photograph by Roberto Piperno.
[67] Photograph by Gary Combs.

The literature also calls her the "Holy Spirit" which, in Hebrew, is also a feminine form. The feminine nature of the Shekhina is so easy to establish in Hebrew, because the gender of the subject plays an important role in the sentence structure. In English, you can say "The Glorious Shekhina returned to bless us" without mentioning gender. In Hebrew, both verbs and adjectives have a male or female form, and many names suggest gender to anyone who understands the language. The simple sentence above indicates three times that the Shekhina is female, and the fact sinks easily into the consciousness of the reader.[68]

The Talmud also ties Shekhina to Nasi Gamaliel:

The Emperor said to Raban Gamaliel: "You say that wherever ten men are assembled, the Shekhina dwells among them. How many Shekhinas are there?"

Thereupon Raban Gamaliel beckoned a servant and began to beat him, saying: "Why did you let the sun enter the Emperor's house?"

"Have you gone mad?" said the Emperor, surprised at the violence of the usually gentle Raban Gamaliel, "the sun shines all over the world!"

"If the sun," answered Gamaliel "which is only one of a thousand myriad servants of God, shines all over the world, how much more so the Shekhina of God!"[69]

The "Keeper of the East Gate" in Hebrew Scripture was *Shecaniah*. But, alas, YHWH closed the East Gate!

Then he brought me back to the outer gate of the sanctuary, which faces east; and it was shut. YHWH said to me: "This gate shall remain shut; it shall not be opened, and no one shall enter by it; for YHWH, the LHM of Israel, has entered by it; therefore it shall remain shut. Only the prince [*nasi*], because he is a prince [*nasi*], may sit in it to *eat food* [Hebrew, *LKL LHM*] before YHWH; he shall enter by way [Hebrew, *DeReK*] of the vestibule [Hebrew, *uLaM*] of the gate [Hebrew, *Ha Shaar*], and shall go out by the same way [Hebrew, *DeReK*]" (Ezekiel 44: 1-3).

---

[68] Ilil Arbel, *Shekhina*. Encyclopedia Mythica. Retrieved July 08, 2015, from encyclopedia Mythica Online.

[69] Abulafia, 1170-1244. *Babylonian Talmud*, Sanhedrin Folio 39a.

Today, Jerusalem's East Gate built c. 520, like the Gate YHWH showed Ezekiel, remains closed; YHWH's "Judean prince" is yet to return. However, Rome's East Gate is wide open, and it stands next to the Monument to *LeHeM*. Silently it proclaims, "Let it be known that El Ha Em's Nasi of the Israelites returned with Daughter Jerusalem, the Watchtower of the Flock."

The East Gate was constructed and opened in Rome during the years that Narcissus and Pallas served with Claudius, the same years that Nasi Gamaliel and his son Jesus and grandson Jesus were high priests in Jerusalem.

Jerusalem's East Gate and Rome's East Gate are similar in appearance except for the "narrow gate" in Rome's, aligned with the Tomb. Honorious' attempt to destroy both during the purge of heretical structures throughout the Roman Empire shines a light of suspicion on the Gate and the Tomb. And his actions suggest he was aware of the connection between these structures and the Temples of Zeus; Apollo; Serapis; Cybele and Attis; the Vestal Virgins; and the Nazareans, Jesus and Mary Magdalene.

The woman known as "Mary Magdalene" died c. 74 CE as "Antonia Caenis." The year Caenis' husband died is a bit more difficult to pin down. Threads set aside for Volume II tie the man called "Jesus," born c. 13-15 BCE, to several other men not examined in this Volume. One of these, Basilides, was briefly introduced in Chapter One.[70]

Suetonius describes an event in which Vespasian sees a vision of his freedman Basilides in the Temple of Serapis in Alexandria immediately before Philo's step-nephew and son, Tiberius Julius Alexander, declares him Emperor on July 1, 69 CE.[71]

Tacitus reports a meeting between Vespasian and Basilides at Mount Carmel at about the same time. However, Tacitus describes Basilides as a priest.[72] Both Philologists agree that he

---

[70] Suetonius, *Life of Vespasian* (Loeb, 1914), (Thayer Online 8.7).

[71] Suetonius, *Life of Vespasian* (Loeb, 1914), (Thayer Online 6.37).

[72] Tacitus, *Histories*; The Works (1864-1877), (Sacred Texts Online 2.78).

was elderly and in poor health and that he encouraged Vespasian to accept the position of Emperor. This would most likely anger Aulus Vitellius who believed himself to be Rome's Emperor for eight months during 69, although not all Romans agreed.[73]

Suetonius confirms this expectation and offers some insight into the mind of Aulus Vitellius:

> Then he set fire to the temple of Jupiter Optimus Maximus and destroyed them, viewing the battle and the fire from the house of Tiberius, where he was feasting. Not long afterwards he repented of his action and throwing the blame upon others, called an assembly and took oath, compelling the rest to do the same, that there was nothing for which he would strive more earnestly than for the public peace. Then he took a dagger from his side and offered it first to the consul, and when he refused it, to the magistrates, and then to the senators, one by one. When no one would take it, he went off as if he would place it in the temple of Concord; but when some cried out that he himself was Concord, he returned and declared that he would not only retain the steel but would also adopt the surname Concordia.[74]

Concordia, also known as Harmonia, was the Goddess of Harmony and Concord. As a daughter of Mars she represented harmonious action in war. It might be argued that "harmonious action" means peace, not war, which was the guiding philosophy of Hillel, Gamaliel, and their descendants.

Notably, and probably not coincidentally, the Temple of Concordia in Rome housed a statue of Hygeia, a Greek deity the Romans named: "Salus."[75] This may explain why Suetonius keeps pointing to the Temple of Concordia in his detailed account of the last days of *Aulus* Vitellius.

Suetonius goes on to explain that Aulus Vitellius was escorted out of Rome with only two companions:

> He also persuaded the senate to send envoys *with the Vestal virgins*, to sue for peace or at least to gain time for conference. The

---

[73] Suetonius, *Life of Vitellius* (Loeb 1914), (Thayer Online 15.1).
[74] Suetonius, *Life of Vitellius* (Loeb 1914), (Thayer Online 15.1).
[75] Pliny the Elder, *Pliny's Natural Histories* (1949-54), (Thayer Online 34.19).

following day, as he was waiting for a reply, word was brought by a scout that the enemy were drawing near. Then he was at once hurried into a sedan *with only two companions, a baker and a cook*, and secretly went to his father's house on the Aventine, intending to flee from there to Campania.[76]

The Goddess of Cooks and Cooking was Vesta, and inserting the Vestal Virgins into this scene helps solve its puzzle: "The enemy were" the baker and the cook; they not only drew near, they arrived to negotiate a peaceful agreement and to escort Aulus Vitellius out of Rome – again. Another ... what's that word ... "double-cross."

In the years leading up to these changes in Rome, equally notable changes were taking place in Jerusalem. Between 62 and 64, King Agrippa II named a quick succession of high priests. In fact, the year 63 might be termed "The Year of the Four High Priests":

Joseph Cabi ben Simon (c. 62-63)

Ananus ben Ananus (c. 63)

Jesus son of Damneus (c. 63)

Jesus son of Gamaliel (c. 63-64)

Then, according to Josephus, Agrippa "deprived Jesus, the son of Gamaliel, of the high priesthood, and gave it to Matthias, the son of Theophilus, under whom the Jews' war with the Romans took its beginnings."[77]

Matthias was Jerusalem's high priest in 65 and 66 when the Zealot movement became an all-out war against Rome. And it can be reasonably assumed that it was during this tenure as High Priest that "Matthias" composed his own Gospel by copying and interpolating the older text now known as "The Gospel of Mark."

"Matthew's Gospel" was probably written to *replace* that earlier text, which was possibly the "lost" gospel Jerome describes as "written in the Hebrew alphabet."[78] Jerome also

---

[76] Suetonius, *Life of Vitellius*, (Loeb, 1914), (Thayer Online 16.1). Emphasis added.

[77] Josephus, 1999. *Antiquities* 20.9 (223), 658.

[78] Jerome, Epistle 120. *The Complete Gospels: Annotated Scholars Version* (New York: Harper Collins/Polebridge Press, 1994), 446.

writes that "the gospel written in Hebrew" was "used by the Nazoreans."[79] It was written after the Crucifixion of 37, and it would probably have been called *Sefer Ha Nazoraios*, "Book of the Nazareans." Is it the heretical gospel Paul attacks with these angry words addressed to the Galatians?

> I am astonished that you are so quickly deserting the one who called you in the grace of Christ and are turning to a different gospel – not that there is another gospel, but there are some who are confusing you and want to pervert the gospel of Christ. But even if we or an *angel from heaven* [watch for the enigma] should proclaim to you *a gospel contrary* to what we proclaimed to you, *let that one be accursed*! As we have said before, so now I repeat, if anyone proclaims to you *a gospel contrary* to what you received, *let that one be accursed*! (Gal 1:8).[80]

The *striking statement*, "angel from heaven," is followed by the repetition of two phrases; this signifies that the "contrary gospel" and "let that one be accursed" are enigmas. Galatians is dated c. 55 CE;[81] therefore, it was written before Matthias replaced Gamaliel's son Jesus as Jerusalem's High Priest. But compelling evidence suggests the final editing of the New Testament wasn't completed until the mid-second century.[82]

The "contrary gospel" was almost certainly the Nazareans' *Sefer Nazoraios*. And, if it was not written by Nasi Gamaliel himself, it was surely written by someone in his family. It would have been used in the Nazarean communities, and it may have even been added to the Tanakh. As Jerusalem's High Priest, Matthias would have been expected to also teach from it. He chose, instead, to replace it with his own gospel and go to war with the Roman authorities, especially his closest relatives. The New Testament's "final editor" added the enigmatic phrases to Galatians in order to tie this "contrary gospel" to the men Paul "accursed" at Paphos: Jesus and Bar-Jesus the Nazoraios.

---

[79] Jerome, "On Famous Men 3"; Miller, 1994, 443.
[80] Emphasis added.
[81] Metzger, 1994, New Annotated Bible, 263 NT.
[82] Trobisch, "Who Published the New Testament?", 2007/2008.

"Aulus" is just one letter shy of "Saulus" and "Paulus." And in this metamorphosis, "Aulus-Saulus-Paulus returned to Jerusalem c. 65 as "Matthias." He wrote his own gospel, plagiarizing portions of the "contrary gospel" Paul attacks in his letter to the Galatians. His interpolations and Greek translation of the *Sefer Nazoraios*, renamed "The Gospel of Marcus," supports the lie in "The Gospel of Matthew" that Jesus was called "The Nazarene" because "he came from Nazareth."

Moreover, Paul claimed that the bone of contention between him and the accursed's contrary gospel was circumcision.[83] However, the evidence points to another "bone" of contention – the rib – the "First Mother," "LHM" – not "Elohim," but "El ha Em" – one-third of the Essenes' "Holy Trinity" (Gen 1:1).

The daughters of El the Mother and The Virgins - including The Magdalene – would have a very different role in Matthew's Gospel and in Paul's Church. The Watchtower of the Flock, The Kingdom of Daughter Jerusalem, the Redemptoris Mater, would not be recognized as the first of *two* returnees identified in Micah's Prophecy. And other than donating time, energy, and resources, women would play no role in Paul's churches. In fact, women were forbidden to speak in Paul's churches (1 Cor 14:34), a prohibition that is still enforced in some denominations today.

An all-male Trinity and vicarious atonement, the foundation of Paul's Christianity, were preferred over The Goddess and the Golden Rule, Jesus' Nazarean philosophy. Paul's Church rejected "Bat El ha Em" and "Eloah's Son" in favor of YHWH. Equally abhorrent, it turned "The Watchtower of the Flock" into a repentant prostitute. In spite of Jesus' concerted effort to elevate the Feminine, women continued to be seen and treated as subservient and inferior for the next two thousand years – and still counting.

The rejection of Jesus' "Most Excellent Wife" and mother of his children leaves the first half of Micah's Prophecy unful-

---

[83] Gal 2:7-13; 5:2-6; 5:11-12; 6:12-15.

filled. And it will remain unfulfilled until Paul's Patriarchal doctrines are replaced by the teachings of Jesus, and Catholic Priestesses are given flocks.

Matthias would have had his Gospel copied and widely distributed before the fall of the Temple. And he would have collected and destroyed all known copies of *The Sefer Ha Nazoraios*. Indeed, the censored portions not copied for his own gospel are only found in brief quotations in the writings Early Church Fathers.

After the fall of the Temple, probably before the end of the 70s, "Leuce" would have taken sections from Mark and sections from Matthew and restored the interpolations and clues to the enigmas. The story of the return of the Israelites' Goddess could then be told.

By the time Luke's Gospel was published, however, Matthew's Gospel and Paul's letters had been widely circulated among the Churches, including those of the Nazareans. And there can be little doubt that the congregations were confused about which text was authentic and which teacher and teachings to follow.

And so, as David Trobisch proposes, Polycarp brought the texts and letters together to create a single volume that would satisfy the congregations of all the Churches. The textual evidence suggests that Polycarp may have added "The Acts of the Apostles" and "The Book of Revelation" to the corpus, for only then could the tapestry be woven together using threads from Scripture, Josephus, Tacitus, Suetonius, et. al. The history of Rome's rejection of Paul's "Christianity" and its promotion of "The Nazarean Way of Jesus" would eventually be revealed – as long as Philo's Philology was available and correctly employed.

"The baker and the cook" were Aulus Vitellius' adoptive parents, Germanicus and Agrippina, "Basilides and Caenis," "Jesus and Mary Magdalene." When Nero allegedly committed suicide in 68, "Aulus-Paulus-Saulus" thought he saw his chance to return to the position he held from 37 to 41 as "Caligula." In April 69, the Year of the Four Emperors, two legions of Roman soldiers proclaimed Vitellius Emperor, which he gladly embraced. Eight months later he was again escorted out of Rome, and by the end of 70, Jerusalem's East Gate and Temple had been destroyed – but not the sacred scrolls and writings housed in the Temple.

An event that occurred just prior to the destruction completes yet another circle. It also saved the Nasi Nazareans and their sacred texts. This circle began in 6 CE when Judas the Galilean and Zadok arrived at the time of the Census. In 69, a man identified in the Babylonian Talmud as "Rabban Johanan ben Zakkai" traveled to Rome, met with Vespasian, and informed him that he was to be Rome's next Basileus. When confirming news arrived that this prophecy had been fulfilled,

> Vespasian said; I am now going, and will send someone to take my place. You can, however, make a request of me and I will grant it. [Zakkai] said to him: Give me Jabneh and its Wise Men, and the family chain of Rabban Gamaliel, and physicians to heal R. Zadok."[84]

And, indeed, Jabneh (also called "Yavne") was the new headquarters of the Sanhedrin, and the Nasi leaders for several centuries would be the sons, grandsons, great grandsons, etc., of Gamaliel, son of Simeon son of Hillel. Furthermore, Rabban Zadok, as Zakkai requested, was given medical treatment and his health improved; four years later he would bury his "most excellent wife" in a "House of Bread."

Johanan ben Zakkai's biography is remarkably similar to that of Moses and Hillel: it was divided into three, forty-year segments, and he lived to be 120 years old.[85]

His name, "Johanan ben Zakkai" (from *zakah*),[86] identifies him as "John, son of the Pure Ones." The *zakah*, "Pure," were the Nazarean and the Virgin, Jesus and Mary Magdalene. Additionally, at Lam 4:7, the word *zakku* (from *zakah*) is placed

---

[84] Babylonian Talmud, Tractate Gittin 56 a and b.
[85] Babylonian Talmud, Tractate Sanhedrin 41 a.
[86] NAS, Strong's Hebrew 2135, *zakah*, defined as "to be clear, clean or pure."

next to and describes the word *Nazarites*. "Johanan ben Zak-kai," therefore, was the Zealot Josephus called, "John of Gis-chala," referred to as "John whose other name was Mark," at Acts 12:24. Josephus refers to him "Marcus Tiberius Alexander."

Josephus also identifies the commanders of the Roman troops that surrounded the Temple, and among those listed are Vespasian's son Titus and Philo's nephew (and son) Julius Tiberius Alexander, Marcus' twin brother. Josephus was the negotiator who failed to mediate a harmonious settlement between his father, Eleazar-Matthias-Vitellius, and the Roman authorities, Vespasian and Vitellius' "Baker and Cook."[87]

The epitaph on Atistia's tomb and the monument to Caenis reveal that Basilides outlived his "most excellent wife." As "Germanicus, he was born c. 13-15 BCE and would have been almost 90 years old when she died in 74 CE.

In Chapter One, we noted that Basilides was the author of two dozen books collectively titled, *Exegetica*, the lost hermeneutical system that Philo used to construct her method of exegesis. Surely the couple worked together on *Exegetica*, considering that "Caenis" was also known as "Philo."

And perhaps The Nazarean and The Magdalene worked together to design The House of Bread. Vespasian placed it in a *most excellent* location – Rome's East Gate – where it would be seen by anyone entering or exiting the city through the Porta Maggiore. They dedicated it to Mars and the Vestal Virgins of El, the parents of Remus and Romulus. They added *Eury sacis*, "wide/narrow," to represent the war-god "Mars" and the life-giving peacemakers, The Virgins of El. Then they added word and letter clues that would lead to their identities.

The evidence suggests that Honorius knew the Tomb and the Porto Maggiore were constructed to celebrate "The Betulah Em" and the "Bat El Ha Em" in Genesis, "The Waters of Life" in the Book of Revelation, and the re-opening of Ezekiel's East

---

[87] Josephus, 1999, *Wars*, 6.4.2 (232-235); 6.4.3 (.236) (895).

Gate in Rome. Matthew's "wide gate/narrow gate" parable would have been relatively easy to solve: it ties the Tomb to the Virgin and the Gate to the Nasi, "Jesus the Nazarean."

Rome's soldiers – all men – would march to war through the two wide gates; however, only a wise peace-maker, a "Pax Sophia," could pass through the narrow gate. The message from Jesus, paraphrased: "War is easy, but it leads to destruction and death. Peace is much harder, but it leads to life."

Evidence summarized in Chapter Fifteen identified "Mary Magdalene," "Philo," and "Pallas" as Agrippina the Elder, also known as Antonia's daughter "Livilla." As Livilla, her *stepbrother* was Germanicus; as Agrippina the Elder her *husband* was Germanicus, also known as, "Nasi Gamaliel," also known as, "Jesus." She can now be tied to Antonia Caenis, the freed-woman who died in 74 CE at the age of eighty-four.

One last look at the inscription on the Baker's Tomb brings a most important clue into focus.

The letter "T" (image above) in "EST" and "MONI-MENTVM" are the same size as the other letters.

However, the "T" (image below) is noticably larger than the other letters in the words:

PISTORIS REDEMPTORIS APPARET

The traditional depictions of the three crosses in the Crucifixion scene resemble the small letter "t." However, evidence from the first century suggests the cross used at the time resembled a capital "T,"[88] as seen in the inscription.

Three prominent crosses in these three words were clearly intentional. And Honorius must have worried that people familiar with Philo's Philology would eventually see the associations. He could have claimed The Baker was merely leaving clues that he was a secret Christian; but apparently, that did not occur to him.

---

[88] Barbet, 44-5, 57-60; Hengel, 8-9; E. M. Blaiklock, *The Archaeology of the New Testament* (Nashville, Tenn.: Thomas Nelson Publishers, 1984), 62-63.

And so he buried The Gate and The Tomb and built his tower over them.

Honorius surely believed that no one would ever find the tomb of the couple known as "Jesus the Nazarean and Mary the Magdalene." When the tower came down in 1838, the Tomb – possibly still holding their bodies – was uncovered, and the clues to the explosive secret were once again exposed for all to see.

Recall that in his rant to Montanus about the monument to honor Pallas, Pliny the Younger referred to a previous letter he had written about the same subject. In that first letter, Pliny placed the monument to Pallas "on the road to Tiber" (modern Tivoli), which is east of Rome.[89] If this monument to Mars and the Virgins of El is the monument to Pallas which Pliny describes, the quoted inscription was on the east side and too damaged to be repaired.

To Homer, the "ides" in "Basilides" identifies him as a "son of the Basileus" (Basil + ides); the Basileus was Emperor Tiberius, also known as "Theos," translated in the Christian Bible as "God." Basilides' mother was a "BeTuLaH eM," his wife was a "BaT eL Ha eM," and his final resting place is a "BeT LeHeM."

It appears that His life on earth is to be viewed as a completed cycle – perhaps the visible part of the cycle of life. Jesus, Attis, and other ancient deities were associated with a tree which loses its leaves annually and appears to die. But new leaves appear each spring and the "life" of the tree becomes apparent again. Were they trying to tell us that the cycles of life and death are perpetual? Does this suggest, perhaps, a belief in multiple cycles of life for descendants of the Ishshah and the Ishenes which by now we all are?

"Have you discovered the beginning, then, so that you are seeking the end? For where the beginning is the end will be."[90]

---

[89] Letters of Pliny the Younger, Loeb VII. 29.
[90] Meyer, 2008, 142. *Gospel of Thomas,* Saying 18 (2).

Jesus and Mary Magdalene's ignored and unkempt monument stands in front of the Porta Maggiore, leaving us to wonder and ask: How many other important tombs, structures, and artifacts are yet to be discovered? And of those already uncovered, what new insights can be gained by applying Philo's Philology to their inscriptions and epitaphs?

Are the bodies still in the tomb? Where is the marble relief portrait depicting Eurysacis and Atistia? Did their attire suggest a royal bloodline, perhaps crimson palla and tunic? Were their faces similar to busts of Germanicus and Agrippina?

The search for answers will continue.

The spring that flowed from distant mountain lakes and rivers, along the aqueduct above the Gate and the Tomb and into Rome, still produces drinking water for Romans and visitors to the area around the Coliseum and the Forum. Its cold refreshing gift can be savored by anyone walking through these ruins.

Philo rarely wrote of herself; however, the introduction to "The Special Laws, III" carries a clue to her identity and reveals her ardent hope which you, the reader, just fulfilled:

> "There was once a time when, devoting my leisure to philosophy and to the contemplation of the world and the things in it, I reaped the fruit of excellent, and desirable, and blessed intellectual feelings, being always living among the divine oracles and doctrines, on which I fed incessantly and insatiably, to my great delight, never entertaining any low or groveling thoughts, nor ever wallowing in the pursuit of glory or wealth, or the delights of the body, but I appeared to be raised on high and borne aloft by a certain inspiration of the soul, and to dwell in the regions of the sun and moon, and to associate with the whole heaven, and the whole universal world.

> "At that time, therefore, looking down from above, from the air, and straining the eye of my mind *as from a watchtower*, I surveyed the unspeakable contemplation of all the things on the earth, and looked upon myself as happy as having forcibly escaped from all the evil fates that can attack human life. Nevertheless, the most grievous of all evils was lying in wait for me, namely, envy, that hates every thing that is good, and which, suddenly attacking me, did not cease from dragging me after it by force till it had taken me and thrown me into the vast sea of the cares of public politics, in which I was and still am tossed about without being able to keep myself swimming at the top."[91]

> "Behold, therefore, I venture not only to study the sacred commands of Moses, but also with an ardent love of knowledge to investigate each separate one of them, and to endeavor to reveal and to explain to those who wish to understand them, things concerning them which are not known to the multitude."[92]

---

[91] C.D. Yonge, trans. The Works of Philo: Complete and Unabridged, (Peabody: Hendrickson Publishers, 2013), "Special Laws III," I.1-3 (594). Emphasis added.
[92] Ibid, I.6 (594).

Volume II will examine more mysteries including a curious monument housed in Rome's Church of Santa Maria Maggiore. An eye-catching, orange-colored pyramid stands in the background; allegorical figures of *Fortitude* (with a lion, the symbol of Cybele) and *Religion* (with a cross, the symbol of Attis) stand on either side of a putto (or Baby Jesus) who holds a book opened to a page which reads:

POST AVERNI
NON ABIIT
NEC SPER AVIT
IN PICVNIA
ET THESAVRIS

Monument to Cardinal Augostino Favoriti, 1685,
by Filippo Carcani from a design by Ludovico Gimignani[93]

---

[93] Photographs by Pam Miller, June 14, 2015

When the Great Pan died, his son was born as "IeZeus the Nazarean." His message is simple:

> In everything do to others as you would have them do to you; for this is the Law and the Prophets (Mt 7:12).

Iesous learned it from his grandfather Hillel:

> What is hateful to you, do not do to your fellow: this is the whole Torah; the rest is the explanation; go and learn (Shabbat 31a).

Ovid reveals the secret identity of the freedman Narcissus:

> When, looking for his corpse they only found,
> A rising stalk with yellow blossoms crowned.

The story of the god *Narcissus*,
Mythological origin of the Easter Lily.
From the fifteen-book narrative poem,
Metamorphoses, by Ovid

And Homer reveals the identity of "Narcissus'" partner:

> ... two of a kind we are, contrivers both.
> Of all men now alive,
> you are the best in plots and story-telling.
> My own fame is for wisdom among the gods –
> deceptions, too.

Pallas-Athena,
Goddess of wisdom, weaving,
and every kind of craft.
Homer, *Odyssey*[94]

---

[94] Homer, *The Odyssey* , Robert Fitzgerald translation, 1963 (13.296-99), 239.

The Second Coming came and went two thousand years ago, decades before "Jesus the Nazarean" was entombed in Nazareth and "The Way of Ansar and Kisar" declared a heresy.

Jesus' final Revelation – the climax of His Story – was to re-introduce the long-lost Goddess, the "Daughter of El ha Em." Together – as equals – The "Prince of Princes" and The "Watch-tower of the Flock" extend an invitation to *all* people – especially the poor but also the rich – whether black, brown, white; female, male, LGBT, straight; of all religions/philosophies and non-believers:

> The Spirit and his Bride say, "Come."
> And let *everyone* who hears say, "Come."
> And let *everyone* who is thirsty come.
> Let *anyone* who wishes take the Water of Life as a gift.

(Rev 22:17)

MAY WE COME TOGETHER
AS THEY ENVISIONED WE COULD,
IN PEACE,
WITH LOVE
AND RESPECT
FOR ALL LIVING THINGS.

PAX AMO LUX

EPILOGUE

Does Philo's Philology Pass the Tests?

The biblical texts examined and the historical sources utilized bear signs that their authors were aware of and used a method of writing secret messages into their stories. And Philo's Method applied to the texts leads to reasonable and repeatable solutions supported by multiple sources. The solutions we have offered are based on our interpretation of the enigmas. We have debated, whittled, cut, and weeded in an effort to keep each chapter as uncluttered as possible. We have discarded as much as we've retained, and what remains barely scratches the surface of what Philo's Philology can do. The identified examples number into the thousands; we've chosen only those easiest to demonstrate and comprehend. After all, it is a new "science," and we are continuing to learn how best to unlock all of its secrets.

We look forward to hearing from anyone curious enough to test it for themselves on these and other biblical questions, and we are open for debate. We expect to receive angry criticism from "the faithful," but we are hopeful that critics and detractors will test the method before attacking it and us. Ultimately, it will be up to seekers, students, and scholars to determine if Philo's Philology can be a useful tool in their search for reasonable answers to lingering questions in Hebrew and Christian Theology.

P.J. Gott
Logan Licht

Ptolemy and Hasmonean Genealogy

Generation I

Julius Caesar: Julius claimed descent from Venus, the "Bright Morning Star." Historians call him "Asander." In the Talmud he is "Simeon ben Shetah" and "Hillel," the influential Jew from Babylon and a descendant of King David.

Cleopatra, Queen of Egypt (the "New Isis"): As "Mariamme the Hasmonean princess," her great grandmother was Salome Alexandra, Simeon ben Shetah's sister. Historians also call her: "Scribonia" (mother of Julia the Elder and Aemilia Lepida); "Dynamis" (mother of Julius Aspurgus).

Julius and Cleopatra had a son and a daughter:

Ptolemy XV nicknamed "Caesarion": Historians and Josephus call him "Emperor Tiberius Julius Caesar" and "Julius Tiberius Aspurgus." In the Talmud he is "Simeon ben Hillel." In Luke's gospel, he is "Kurios."

Julia the Elder: Historians and Josephus also call her "Cleopatra Selene"; "Salampsio"; "Cornelia Scipio."

Marc Antony (the "New Dionysus"): Historians and Josephus call him "Herod the Great"; "Antigonus II" (a Hasmonean); "Juba II, King of Libya"; "Marcus Vipsanius Agrippa."

Arsinoe of Egypt, Cleopatra's half-sister: Historians call her "Octavia Minor"; "Junia Tertia"; "Empress Livia Drusilla," Caesar Augustus' third wife. Julius Caesar was her father.

Antony and Arsinoe (as "Octavia Minor") had a daughter:

Antonia Minor: Historians call her "Vipsania Agrippina"; "Gepaepyris" (wife of Aspurgus); "Aemilia Lepida" (wife of Publius Quirinius). Josephus calls her the "Virgin Glapyra." In Luke's gospel she is the "Virgin Mary."

Antony and Arsinoe (as Junia Tertia) had a son:

Decimus Junius Silanus, better known as Ovid.

Generation II

Ptolemy XV "Caesarion" (Julius and Cleopatra's son): As "Kurios," he was mated with "The Virgin Mary" (Antony and Arsinoe's daughter). As "Aspurgus" and "Gepaepyris," "Kurios" (the "Lord") and "The Virgin Mary" had two sons, both born "when Herod was King":

Tiberius Julius Mithridates Philo-Germanicus Philopatris: Born c. 19 BCE, historians call him "Lucius Aemilius Paulus" and "Lucius Aelius Sejanus." In *Antiquities* and *Luke-Acts* he is "James the brother of Jesus."

Tiberius Julius Cotys Philocaesar Eusebes: Born c. 13–15 BCE, historians and Josephus call him: "Drusus Julius Caesar"; "Nero Claudius Drusus Germanicus"; "Alexander son of Glapyra"; "Alexander the Alabarch"; "Narcissus a freedman." In the Talmud he is "Gamaliel ben Simeon" and "Gamaliel the Elder." In Luke's gospel he is "Jesus the Nazarean I."

Julia the Elder (Julius and Cleopatra's daughter): Julia was mated with Marcus Vipsanius Agrippa, also known as "Marc Antony." Julia and Antony (as Agrippa) had five children, two daughters:

Julia the Younger: In Luke's gospel she is called "Elizabeth," wife of Zechariah, mother of John the Baptist.

Agrippina the Elder: Historians and Josephus also call her: "Claudia Livia Julia" (nicknamed "Livilla"); "Juba's daughter"; "Pallas the Freedman"; "Philo of Alexandria." She married Germanicus (Drusus Julius Caesar, also called "Jesus the Nazarene I"), her step-brother and first cousin. Emperor Claudius was her half-brother. In Luke's gospel, she is called "**Mary Magdalene.**"

Generation III

Lucius Aemilius Paulus and Julia the Younger had a son:

Lucius (or Marcus) Aemilius Paulus, Jr.: Born in 6 CE, historians also call him "Gaius Julius Caesar" nicknamed "Caligula." Josephus calls him "Saulus, brother of Costobarus" and "Eleazar the Zealot." In Luke's gospel he is "John the Baptist" and in *Acts* he is the Apostle Paul.

D. Junius Silanus (Ovid) and Julia the Younger had a son:

Titus Flavius Caesar Vespasianus Augustus: Born in 9 CE, he is historians' Emperor Vespasian, Paul's "Silvanus" and Luke's "Silas." According to Suetonius, "… he was commonly known as 'the Muleteer.'"[1]

Drusus Germanicus (Tiberius' biological son) and Agrippina the Elder (as "Livilla") had a daughter and twin sons:

Julia Drusi Caesaris Filia: Born c. 5 CE, she was nicknamed "Junilla." Historians call her "Julia Urania"; Josephus calls her "Iotapa," daughter of Sampsiceramis and Iotapa, King and Queen of the Emessenes.

Tiberius Germanicus II: Born in 6 CE, he is called "Bar-Jesus" in *Acts*, "Iesous Barabbas" in Luke's gospel. As the eldest twin son of Gamaliel ben Simeon ("Jesus the Nazarean" I) and Agrippina the Elder ("Mary Magdalene"), he is "Jesus the Nazarean II." Historians and Josephus also call him "Julius Tiberius Alexander." In the Talmud he is "Simeon ben Gamaliel" and/or "Gamaliel the Younger."

Tiberius Gemellus: Born in 6 CE, historians and Josephus call him "Marcus Antonius Felix," a freedman. In *Acts* he is "John Mark" and "Governor Felix"; in the Gospels he is "Pontius Pilate." He is also known as "Judas the Betrayer" and "Judas Didymos Thomas."

---

[1] Suetonius, The Lives of the Caesars: The Life of Vespasian, 1st-2nd Century, 289. Mules are hybrids, half donkey half horse.

IMAGES

P.J. Gott and the Pyramid of Cestius
Rome, Italy[1]

The *Ludi Saeculares* were reinstituted and a pyramid-tomb constructed in Rome concurrent with Asander's death c. 17 BCE. Called the
"Pyramid of Romulus" and located between the Vatican and the
Mausoleum of Hadrian, it is known only through historians' descrip-
tions and artists' paintings. A slightly smaller pyramid, *The Pyramid of
Cestius* (above), was constructed in precisely 330 days (7,920 hours) c.
12 BCE. It still stands in Rome. *Caius Cestius Epulonius*, for whom the
pyramid was built and named, belonged to a group of priests responsible for sacred banquets. He died c. 13–12 BCE, as did Marcus Vipsanius Agrippa; Marcus Aemilius Lepidus; Lucius Aemilius Lepidus
Paullus, also known as Paullus Aemilius Lepidus (consul in 34 BCE),
et al. These names, coincidental deaths, and more, will be examined
in a later volume.

---

[1] Photograph by Pam Miller, June 12, 2015.

343

Germanicus Julius Caesar, born c. 15 BCE,
also known as
"Jesus, 'The Nazarean'"[2]

---

[2] Bust dated to c. 14 - 23 CE. Wikimedia Commons.
Photographer: Pierre Selim (2012).

Agrippina the Elder, also known as
"Maria, 'The Magdalene'"
Bust dated ca 1-50 CE[3]

Left: A young Emperor Caligula, born in 6 CE, reigned from 37 to 41 CE;[4]
Right: An elderly Emperor Vitellius reigned eight months in 69 CE[5]; he was
about 63 years old when the original bust was commissioned in 69.

Accumulated evidence presented throughout this book reveals that "Caligula" and "Aulus Vitellius" were not two men,
but one. He was also known as the Apostle Paulus. His mother
was Julia the Younger; his father was Lucius Paulus, also
known as Sejanus.

---

[4] The bust of Caligula is dated c. 39-40 CE. Photograph by ChrisO. Wikimedia Commons, Louvre Museum.
[5] The bust of Aulus Vitellius is a reproduction of another dated 69 CE. Photograph by
Jastrow (2008). Wikimedia Commons, Louvre Museum, Department of Sculptures
from the French royal collections. This reproduction is grey veined marble, Italian artwork of the first half of the 16th century, modern copy of an antique head of the Hadri-
anic era in the Grimani Collection in Venice, once thought to represent the Emperor
Vitellius.

Marcus Antonius[6]

Livia Drusilla (left),[7] also known as "Octavia Minor"(right).[8]

---

[6] Source: "A Smaller history of Rome." Author: Commons member Amadscientist created the file from the book by William Smith, Abel Hendy Jones Greenidge, Andrew Di. Wikimedia Commons.

[7] Left: "Livia Drusilla." Bust discovered in Arsinoe, Egypt. Currently on display in Rome at the Ara Pacis museum: From the collection of casts of busts showing the members of the Julio-Claudian dynasty. The original artwork is exhibited in the Ny Carlsberg Glyptotek (Copenhagen). Picture by Giovanni Dall'Orto, March 28, 2008.

[8] Right: "Octavia." Parian marble bust from Smyrna; Roman woman believed to be Octavia Minor. National Archaeological Museum in Athens. Picture by Giovanni Dall'Orto, November 11, 2009.

The notation describing the coin says,
"Coin minted by Augustus (c. 19–18 BC);[9]
Obverse: CAESAR AVGVSTVS,
laureate head right/Reverse: DIVVS IVLIV[S],
with comet (star) of eight rays, tail upward."[10]

---

[9] Evidence suggests the coin was minted by Augustus, also known as Octavian (Latin for "eight"), c. 17 BCE, concurrent with the death of *Asander*, also known as *Julius Caesar*, *Simeon ben Shatar*, and *Hillel the Elder*. The eight-pointed star is the ancient symbol for Venus, Ishtar, and Inanna. The flames may represent the bloodline of the Ishene and Ishshah who came to Earth from Venus, the "Perpetual Fire" preserved by the Israelite Temple Virgins.

[10] Classical Numismatic Group, Inc. CC BY-SA 3.0. File: S0484.4.jpg. Uploaded by Carlomorino, January 25, 2006.

Moregine Silver Treasury, Roman, late Republic, c. 40 BCE[11]

Two "little silver cups" are part of a 20-piece set of dining utensils found in 2000 in modern Moregine near Pompeii. The museum interprets the enlarged image (above middle) as "a priestess of Isis proffering a bunch of grapes toward a cock on an altar." Enlarged image (above right) is a tripod table on goats' legs (the deity Pan had goat's legs). Three silver vessels (Prima, Secunda, Tertia?) sit on the table, a long cylinder and a round pouch with fringed textile hangs above them (alabaster jar?).

These images are on the reverse of both cups.
Above left: Marc Antony (Octavia's husband).
Above right: Augustus Caesar (Octavia's brother)[12]

---

[11] Lent by the Republic of Italy to The New York, Metropolitan Museum of Art (2010-2015). Photographs by Ann Raia 2013.
[12] Photographs by Ann Raia.

Titus Flavius Caesar Vespasianus Augustus.[13]

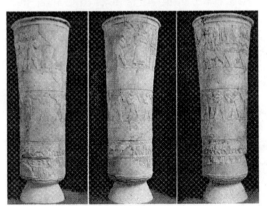

Warka Vase
Dated c. 3200-3000 BCE[14]

---

[13] Originally uploaded by user: shako. Plaster cast, Pushkin museum after original in Louvre Museum.
[14] Cyarthistory wiki site (2015).

Bibliography

Abulafia, M. (1170-1244). *Babylonian Talmud: Tractates on Sanhedrin.* (American-Israeli Cooperative Enterprise) Retrieved July 10, 2013, from Jewish Virtual Library:
http://www.jewishvirtuallibrary.org/jsource/Talmud/sanhedri n_toc.html

Arbel, I. (2002, September 28). *Shabbat hamalka.* Retrieved August 10, 2009, from Encyclopedia Mythica:
http://www.pantheon.org/articles/s/shabbat_hamalka.html

Arbel, I. (Revised 2000, April 27). *Shekhina.* Retrieved from Encyclopedia Mythica:
http://www.pantheon.org/articles/s/shekhina.html

Atsma, A. (2000-2011). *Theoi Project: Ovid's Metamorphoses.* Retrieved from Theoi Project:
http://www.theoi.com/Text/OvidMetamorphoses13.html

Atsma, A. J. (2000-2011). *Greek Mythology: Dioskouroi.* Retrieved July 2, 2015, from The Theoi Project:
http://www.theoi.com/Ouranios/Dioskouroi.html

Atsma, A. J. (Ed.). (2000-2011). *Greek Mythology: Leuke.* Retrieved April 30, 2014, from The Theoi Project:
http://www.theoi.com/Nymphe/NympheLeuke.html

Atsma, A. J. (Ed.). (2000-2011). *Greek Mythology: Okeanos.* Retrieved June 3, 2012, from The Theoi Project:
http://www.theor.com/Titan/TitanOkeanos.html

Atsma, A. J. (Ed.). (2000-2011). *Greek Mythology: Pan.* Retrieved April 6, 2012, from The Theoi Project:
www.theoi.com/Georgikos/Pan.html.

Atsma, A. J. (Ed.). (2000-2011). *Greek Mythology: Phaunos.* Retrieved May 9, 2013, from The Theoi Project:
http://www.theor.com/Georgikos/Phaunos.html

Audin, A. (1956). Dianus bifrons ou les deux stations solaires, piliers jumeaux et portiques solsticiaux. *Revue de geographie de Lyon,* 191-8.

Baldi, P. (2002). *The Foundations of Latin.* Berlin: Walter de Gruyter GmB H & Co.

Barbet, Hengel, & Blaiklock. (1984). *The Archaeology of the New Testament.* Nashville: Thomas Nelson Publishers.

Barnard, L. W. (1997). *The First and Second Apologies (Tertullian).* New York: Paulist Press.

Benaissa, A. (2010). *The Onomastic Evidence for the God Hermanubis.* Retrieved May 2, 2012, from Library University of Michigan: http://quod.lib.umich.edu/cgi/p/pod/dod-idx/onomastic-evidence-for-the-god-hermanubis.pdf?c=icp;idno=7523866.0025.116

Bennett, C. (2001, May). *Cleopatra Selene.* Retrieved May 5, 2006, from Egyptian Royal Genealogy: http://www.tyndalehouse.com/egypt/ptolemies/selene_ii_fr.htm

Bouyer, L. (2004). *The Christian Mystery (Illtyd Trethowan Translation).* London: T.T. Clark International.

Brisch, N. (2012). *Ansar and Kisar '(god and goddess)'.* Retrieved March 2, 2012, from Ancient Mesopotamian Gods and Goddesses: http://oracc.museum.upenn.edu/amgg/listofdeities/ansarandkisar/

Brisch, N. (2013). *Ninlil (Mulliltu, Mullissu, Mylitta) (goddess).* Retrieved March 20, 2014, from Ancient Mesopotamian Gods and Goddesses: http://oracc.museum.upenn.edu/amgg/listofdeities/ninlin

Brown, Frank and Fentress, Lisa, Archaeologists. (Intermittent 1948-present). *Cosa.* Retrieved March 12, 2015, from Ansedonia-Citta di Cosa; Museo Archeologico Nazionale di Cosa: http://www.stad.com/wiki.php?search=Cosa

Burn, R. (1880). *A Handbook to the Ruins of the City and the Campagna.* London; Cambridge: George Bell and Sons; Deighton, Bell & Co.

Burton. (n.d.). *The Howard Carter Archives.* Retrieved October 4, 2010, from The Griffith Institute: http://www.griffith.ox.ac.uk/gri/carter/288a-p2024.html

Carter, H. (n.d.). *The Howard Carter Archives.* Retrieved July 14, 2012, from The Griffith Institute: http://www.griffith.ox.ac.uk/gri/carter/288a-p2024.html

Cassius Dio. (3rd Century CE). *Roman History by Cassius Dio.* (Loeb, Trans.) Retrieved from Bill Thayer's Website (Loeb Classical Library 1916):

http://penelope.uchicago.edu/Thayer/E/Roman/Texts/Cassi
us_Dio/43*.html

ChrisO, Photographer. (n.d.). *Gaius Julius Caesar Bust: Louvre
Museum*. Retrieved from Wikimedia Commons:
https://commons.wikimedia.org/wiki/File:Caligula_bust.jpg

Classical Numismatic Group, Inc. (n.d.). Retrieved from
http://commons.wikimedia.org/wiki/FilePS0484.4.jpg

Clement of Alexandria. (ca. 182-201 CE). *Stromata: Early Christian
Writings: Clement of Alexandria*. (P. Kirby, Producer) Retrieved
April 10, 2010, from Early Christian Writings (2001-2015):
http://www.earlychristianwritings.com/text/clement-
stromata-book1.html

Combs, G. (n.d.). *The Gates of Zion*. Retrieved from
garycombs.org.: http://www.garycombs.org/blog/tag/eastern-
gate

Comfort, P. W. (2000). *Holman Treasury of Key Bible Words: 200
Greek and 200 Hebrew Words Defined and Explained*. Nashville:
Broadman and Holman.

Crane, G. R. (Ed.). (2006). *Latin Word Study Tool; servare*. Retrieved
from Perseus Digital Library:
http://www.perseus.tufts.edu/hopper/morph?la=la&l=servar
e

Dalley, S. (Ed.). (1989-2000). *Myths from Mesopotamia*. (S. Dalley,
Trans.) Oxford: Oxford University Press.

Dall'Orto, Giovanni. (2008, March 28). *Livia Drusilla Bust: Ara
Pacis Museum*. Retrieved from Wikimedia Commons:
https://commons.wikimedia.org/wiki/File:8093_-_Roma_-
_Ara_Pacis_-_Livia_-_Foto_Giovanni_Dall%27Orto_-_30-
Mar-2008.jpg

Dall'Orto, Giovanni. (2009, November 11). *Octavia Minor Bust:
National Archaeological Museum, Athens*. Retrieved from
Wikimedia Commons:
https://commons.wikimedia.org/wiki/File:8106_-_Roma_-
_Ara_Pacis_-_Ottavia_Minore_-
_Foto_Giovanni_Dall%27Orto_-_30-Mar-2008.jpg

Dictionary.com: Eury. (n.d.). Retrieved from Dictionary.com:
http://www.dictionary.reference.com/browse/eury

Dionysius of Halicarnassus. (1st Century BCE). *The Roman
Antiquities of Dionysius of Halicarnassus*. (University of Chicago)
Retrieved from Bill Thayer's Website:

http://penelope.uchicago.edu/Thayer/E/Roman/Texts/Dion ysius_of_Halicarnassus/home.html

Dunn, J. D. (2003). *Jesus Remembered.* Grand Rapids: Eerdmans.

Encyclopaedia Britannica Online: Sumerian Moon God Sin. (n.d.). Retrieved July 1, 2010, from Encyclopaedia Britannica Online: www.britannica.com/EBchecked/topic/545523/Sin

Epiphanius. (Late 3rd, early 4th Century CE). *The Panarion of Epiphanius of Salamis: A treatise Against Eighty Sects in Three Books.* Retrieved from Masseiana.org: http://www.masseiana.org/panarion_bk1.htm

Epstein, R. D. (Ed.). (1952). Soncino Babylonian Talmud. (H. Freedman, Trans.) Retrieved from http://www.come-and-hear.com/shabbath/shabbath_104.html#PARTb

Epstein, R. D. (Ed.). (2012). Soncino Babylonian Talmud: Tractate Sanhedrin Folio 67. (J. Shachter, Trans.) Teaneck. Retrieved from Halakhah.com: http://halakhah.com/sanhedrin/sanhedrin_67.html

Epstein, R. D. (Ed.). (n.d.). *Soncino Babylonian Talmud: Tractate Berakoth; Folio 55a.* Retrieved from Berakoth: Translated into English with Notes, Glossary and Indices: http://halakhah.com/berakoth/berakoth_55.html

Epstein, R. D. (Ed.). (n.d.). *Tractate Gittin: Folio 58a.* Retrieved January 15, 2015, from Soncino Babylonian Talmud: http://www.come-and-hear.com/gittin/gittin_58.html

Farrar, F. W. (1886). *History of Interpretation: Eight Lectures.* London: MacMillan and Co.

Fitzgerald, R. T. (1963). *The Odyssey Homer.* Garden City, NY: Anchor Books; Doubleday & Company, Inc.

Flickr (Photography). (n.d.). *Drusus Julius Caesar Bust: Museo Nacional del Prado, Madrid.* Retrieved from Museo Del Prado: http://museodelprado.es/en

Forbes, C. A. (1970). *The Error of the Pagan Religions.* New York: Paulist Press.

Fraser, P. (1972, 1986). *Ptolemaic Alexandria.* Oxford: Oxford University Press.

Frazer, S. J. (1922). *The Golden Bough: Attis Mythology.* Retrieved January 18, 2013, from Sacred Texts: www.sacred-texts.com/pag/frazer/gb03400. htm

Fuller, R. B. (1975; 1979). *Synergetics: Explorations in the Geometry of Thinking.* New York: Macmillan. Retrieved January 3, 2015,

from
http://www.rwgrayprojects.com/synergetics/synergetics.html
Garcia, L. (. (n.d.). *Agrippina the Elder Bust: National Archaeological Museum of Spain*. Retrieved from http://www.man.mcu.es/
Genette, G. (1997). *Palimpsests: Literature in the Second Degree*. Lincoln: University of Nebreska Press.
Goodacre, M. (2002). *The Case Against Q: Studies in Markan Priority and the Synoptic Problem*. Retrieved from The Case Against Q Web Site: http://NTGateway.com/Q
Gosling, L. A. (1996). *"Yeshu" "Yeshua" or "Jesus" - Which?* Retrieved May 5, 2014, from Biblical Research Institute: www.biblicalresearchinstitute.com/lectures/lec1
Gott. (2005). *Plutarch's Parable: Lux Gospel and the Axe of the Apostle*. Charleston: Booksurge.
Greek Names: Anatasios. (n.d.). Retrieved from Greek Names: http://www.greek-names.info/anastasios/
Greek Names: Dionissis. (n.d.). Retrieved from Greek Names: http://www.greek-names.info/dionissis/
Greek Names: Sakis. (n.d.). Retrieved from Greek Names: http://www.greek-names.info/sakis/
Greek Names: Sotirios. (n.d.). Retrieved from Greek Names: http://www.greek-names.info/sotirios/
Greek Names: Theodosis. (n.d.). Retrieved from Greek Names: http://www.greek-names.info/theodosis
Grindle, G. (1892). *The Destruction of Paganism in the Roman Empire From Constantine to Justinian*. Ann Arbor: University of Michigan Library.
Guthrie, K. S. (1920s). *The Complete Pythagoras*. Retrieved May 5, 2012, from Holy Books.com: http://www.holybooks.com/wp-content/uploads/The-Complete-Pythagoras
Haley, S. P. (1985). The Five Wives of Pompey the Great. *Greece & Rome, 32*(1), 49-59.
Hare, J. B. (2010). *Ancient Works in Public Domain*. Retrieved from Sacred Texts Archives: www.sacred-texts.com
Headley, S. (2015). *Coins: EID MAR: An Ancient roman Coin Commemorates the Assassination of Caesar*. Retrieved from About.com: http://coins.about.com/od/famousarecoinprofiles/p/eidmarprofile.html#

Healy, J. F. (1991, 2004). *Natural History by Pliny the Elder.* London: Penguin Books.

Hedrick, C. (2010). *Unlocking the Secrets of the Gospel According to Thomas.* Eugene: Cascade Books.

Heichelheim, F. (1938). Roman Syria. In F. Heichelheim, & T. Frank (Ed.), *Economic Survey of Ancient Rome* (p. 161). Baltimore: John Hopkins University Press.

Heiser, M. S. (n.d.). *The Nachash and His Seed: Some Explanatory Notes on Why the "Serpent" in Genesis 3 Wasn't a Sserpent.* Retrieved from MichaelSHeiser.com: http://www.michaelsheiser.com/nachashnotes.pdf

Homer. (1914). *Homeric Hymns: To Hermes.* (H. G. Evelyn-White, Ed.) Cambridge MA; London UK : Harvard University Press; William Heinemann Ltd. Retrieved from http://perseus.mpiwg-berlin.mpg.de/cgi-bin/ptext?doc=Perseus:text:1999.01.0138&query=hymn%3D4%3Acard%3D408

Hornblower, S., & Spawforth, A. (1970). *Oxford Classical Library, Second Edition.* Oxford: Oxford University Press.

Humphreys, C. J. (1991). The Star of Bethlehem—a Comet in 5 BC—and the Date of the Birth of Christ. *Quarterly Journal of the Royal Astronomical Society (32),* 389-406.

Iamblichus. (Late 3rd, early 4th Century CE.). *On the Pythagorean Way of Life.* (P. Rousell, Editor) Retrieved from The Complete Pythagoras: http://www.holybooks.com/wp-content/uploads/The-Complete-Pythagoras.pdf

Io. (2001). Retrieved from Encyclopedia.com: Myths and Legends of the World: http://www.encyclopedia.com/topic/Io_(mythology).aspx

Irenaeus. (2001-2015). *Basilides.* (P. Kirby, Producer) Retrieved December 2, 2012, from Early Christian Writings: http://www.earlychristianwritings.com/basilides.html

Irenaeus. (2nd Century CE). *Against Heresies.* (A. Roberts, Editor) Retrieved Februrary 15, 2012, from The Gnostic Society Library Online (1995): http://www.gnosis.org/library/advh1.htm.

Jastrow, Photographer. (2008). *Emperor Vitellius Bust: Louvre Museum.* Retrieved from https://commons.wikimedia.org/wiki/File:Pseudo-Vitellius_Louvre_MR684.jpg

Jerome. (4th-5th Century). *Jerome to Pammachius.* (K. Knight, Editor) Retrieved from New Advent: http://www.newadvent.org/fathers/3001057.htm

Jewish Encyclopedia: Hillel. (1906). Retrieved November 2, 2013, from Jewish Encyclopedia Online: http://www.jewishencyclopedia.com/articles/7698-hillel.

Jewish Encyclopedia: Nineveh. (1906). (Jewish Encyclopedia) Retrieved October 6, 2009, from Jewish Encyclopedia Online: http://www.jewishencyclopedia.com/articles/11549-nineveh

Jewish Encyclopedia: Philo Judaeus. (1906). Retrieved June 2, 2005, from Jewish Encyclopedia Online: http://www.jewishencyclopedia.com/articles/12116-philo-judaeus

Jones, P. (2006). *Cleopatra: A Sourcebook.* Norman: University of Oklahoma Press.

Josephus. (1999). *The New Complete Works of Josephus.* (W. Whiston, Trans.) Grand Rapids: Kregel Publications.

Ka: the Gods the Myths the Symbols the Land of Resources. (2014, August 17). Retrieved from Ancient Egypt: the Mythology: http://www.egyptianmyths.net/ka.htm

Killebrew. (2005). *Biblical Peoples And Ethnicity: An Archaeological Study of Egyptians, Canaanites, Philistines, And Early Israel 1300-1100 B.C.E.* Atlanta: Society of Biblical Literature.

Kilmon, J. (1997, October 8). *History and the New Testament.* Retrieved July 17, 2012, from The Scriptorium: http://www.historian.net/NTHX.html

Kirby, P. (2001-2015). *Basilides.* Retrieved from Early Christian Writings: http://www.earlychristianwritings.com/basilides.html

Lockman Foundation. (2015). *Hebrew-Aramaic and Greek Dictionaries.* Retrieved from Biblehub.com: http://biblehub.com

MacMullen, R. (1984). *Christianizing the Roman Empire AD 100-400.* New Haven: Yale University Press.

Mayor, A. (2009). *The Poison King: the life and legend of Mithradates, Rome's deadliest enemy.* Princeton: Princeton University Press.

Melmoth, W. (1807). *The Letters of Pliny the Consul with Occasional Remarks.* Edinburgh: James Ballantine.

Merriam-Webster Dictionary. (n.d.). Retrieved March 3, 2010, from Merriam-Webster Online: http://www.webster-dictionary.org/definition/enigma

Merriam-Webster Dictionary. (n.d.). Retrieved March 3, 2010, from Merriam-Webster Dictionary Online: http://www.webster-dictionary.org/definition/allegory

Merriam-Webster Dictionary. (n.d.). Retrieved from Merriam-Webster Online: http://www.merriam-webster.com/dictionary/sin

Metzger, B. M. (Ed.). (1994). *The New Oxford Annotated Bible with the Apocrypha New revised Standard Version.* New York: Oxford University Press.

Meyer, M. (Ed.). (2008). *The Nag Hammadi Scriptures: The Revised and Updated Translation of Sacred Gnostic Texts.* New York: HarperOne.

Michell, J. (2001). *The Dimensions of Paradise: The Proportions and Symbolic Numbers of Ancient Cosmology.* Kempton: Adventures Unlimited Press.

Miller, R. J. (Ed.). (1994). *The Complete Gospels: Annotated Scholars Version.* New York: Harper Collins by arrangement with Polebridge Press.

Minns, E. H. (1913; 2011). *Scythians and Greeks: A Survey of Ancient History and Archaeology on the North Coast of the Euxine from the Danube to the Caucasus.* Cambridge: Cambridge University Press.

Moran, W. L. (1992). *The Armana Letters.* Baltimore: Johns Hopkins University Press.

NAS Exhaustive Concordance of the Bible. (1998). *Biblehub.com.* (The Lockman Foundation) Retrieved from http://biblehub.com

National Center for Biomedical Communications. (2015, August 242). *How Many Chromosomes do People Have?* Retrieved from Lister Hill National Center for Biomedical Communications: http://ghr.nlm.nih.gov/handbook/basics/howmanychromosomes

National Institutes of Health. (n.d.). *A Brief Guide to Genomics: DNA, Genes and Genomes.* Retrieved from National Human Genome Research Institute; National Institutes of Health: http://www.genome.gov/18016863

Nazannia. (n.d.). *Plutarch and Luke.* Retrieved from The Nazarene Way:

http://www.thenazareneway.com/Plutarch%20and%20Luke.htm

Nebet, M. (2007, August 1). *The Egyptian World: The Passion Plays of Osiris*. Retrieved April 13, 2013, from Ancient Worlds: http://www.ancientworlds.net/aw/Article/743017

Norman, J. (2014, December 20). *Philology Probably Begins at the Royal Library of Alexandria (c. 280 BCE)*. Retrieved February 27, 2015, from Jeremy Norman's HistoryofInformation.com: http://www.historyofinformation.com/expanded.php?id=174

Ovid. (1st Century BCE to 1st Century CE). *Fasti Book I*. Retrieved May 5, 2012, from Poetry in Translation: http://www.poetryintranslation.com/PITBR/Latin/OvidFasti BkOne.htm

Ovid. (1st Century BCE to 1st Century CE). *Fasti Book III*. Retrieved November 1, 2012, from The Theoi Classical E-Texts Library: http://www.theoi.com/Text/OvidFasti3.html

Ovid. (1st Century BCE to 1st Century CE). *Fasti, Book III: Introduction*. Retrieved May 5, 2012, from Poetry in Translation: http://www.poetryintranslation.com/PITBR/Latin/OvidFasti BkThree.htm#_Toc69367772

Parker, J. H. (1877). *The Archaeology of Rome, Part IX: Tombs in and Near Rome*. Oxford; London: James Parker and Co; John Murray, Albemarle Street.

Peterson, J. H. (Ed.). (1898). Khorda Avesta: Aban Yashts. *Sacred Books of the East, American Edition, Five, Digital Edition*. (J. Darmesteter, Trans.) doi:1995

Philo of Alexandria. (1st Century). *The Complete Works of Philo: Complete and Unabridged*. (C. Yonge, Trans.) Peabody: Hendrickson Publishers.

Piperno, R. (n.d.). Retrieved from A Rome Art Lover's Web Page: http://www.romeartlover.it/Vasi07.html#Today

Pliny the Elder. (1949-54). *Pliny's Natural History*. (W. Jones, Trans.) Cambridge; London: Harvard University Press; William Heineman.

Pliny's Natural History. (1st Century). (Harvard University Press & William Heinemann (1949-54)) Retrieved 01 10, 2015, from Masseiana: http://www.masseiana.org/pliny.htm#BOOK VII

Plutarch. (1st-2nd Century). *Moralia: Isis and Osiris*. (Loeb Classical Library) Retrieved May 22, 2009, from Bill Thayer's Website: Loeb Classical Library (1914):

http://www.penelope.uchicago.edu/Thayer/E/Roman/Texts
/Plutarch/Moralia/Isis_and_Osiris*/A.html

Plutarch. (1st-2nd Century). *Parallel Lives: Life of Antony*. Retrieved
October 10, 2008, from Bill Thayer's Website: Loeb Classical
Library (1914):
http://penelope.uchicago.edu/Thayer/E/Roman/Texts/Pluta
rch/Lives/Antony*.html

Plutarch. (1st-2nd Century). *Parallel Lives: Life of Numa*. Retrieved
March 3, 2010, from Bill Thayer's Website: Loeb Classical
Library (1914):
www.penelope.uchicago.edu/Thayer/E/Roman/Texts/Plutarc
h/Lives/Numa*.html.

Ponet, J. (2005, December). *The Maccabees and the Hellenists:
Hanukkah as Jewish Civil War*. Retrieved November 2, 2011,
from Slate Magazine Online:
http://www.slate.com/articles/life/faithbased/2005/12/the_
maccabees_and_the_hellenists.html

Rabbi Eliezar. (1916). Pirke De-Rabbi Eliezar. *Abraham Epstein
Manuscript*. (G. Friedlander, Trans.) New York: Bloch
Publishing Company. Retrieved March 15, 2015, from
http://archive.org/stream/pirkderabbieli00frieuoft/pirkderabb
ieli00frieuoft_djvu.txt

Raia, A. R. (2015). Retrieved from Online Companion to The
Worlds of Roman Women:
http://www2.cnr.edu/home/araia/religion.html

Ramsay, W. (1875). *Vestales: A Dictionary of Greek and Roman
Antiquities*. Retrieved April 30, 2009, from LacusCurtius: Bill
Thayer:
http://penelope.uchicago.edu/Thayer/E/Roman/Texts/seco
ndary/SMIGRA*/Vestales.html

Reliefs of the Monument of Eurysaces. (n.d.). Retrieved from Online
Database of Ancient Art:
http://ancientrome.ru/art/artworken/img.htm?id=765

Roberts, A. (Ed.). (1995). *The Gnostic Library Online*. Retrieved
from http://www.gnosis.org/library/advh1.htm

Roberts, A., & Donaldson, J. (Eds.). (1867-1873). *Ante-Nicene
Fathers: The Writings of the Fathers Down to A.D. 325*. Edinburgh:
T. & T. Clark.

Rodkinson, M. L. (1903). *The History of the Talmud*. New York:
New Talmud Publishing Company. Retrieved from

http://www.come-and-
hear.com/talmud/rodkinson_1.html#p7

Roller, D. W. (2003). *The World of Juba II and Kleopatra Selene*. New
York and London: Routledge Taylor & Francis Group.

Rostovzeff, M. (n.d.). *The Online Database of Ancient Art*. (M.
Rostovzeff, Editor, & M. Sergeenki, Producer) Retrieved from
Ancient Rome:
http://ancientrome.ru/art/artworken/img.htm?id=765

Sami, N., & Dunn, J. (n.d.). *Egypt: The Origin of the Word, "Egypt"*.
Retrieved from Tour Egypt:
http://www.touregypt.net/featurestories/kmt.htm

Sbardella, L. (2007). Philitas of Cos. In H. Cancik, H. Schneider, &
C. Salazar (Eds.), *Brill's New Pauly-Antiquity*. Leiden: Brill.

Schafer, P. (2007). *Jesus in the Talmud*. Princeton: Princeton
University Press.

Selim, P. (. (2012, October 26). *Germanicus Bust: Musee Saint-
Raymond, Toulouse, France*. Retrieved from Wikimedia
Commons: https://commons.wikimedia.org/wiki/File:MSR_-
_Germanicus_Inv._30010.jpg

Shako, Photographer. (n.d.). *Vespasian Bust: Plaster Cast in Pushkin
Museum; Original in Louvre*. Retrieved from Wikimedia
Commons:
https://commons.wikimedia.org/wiki/File:Vespasianus01_pus
hkin_edit.png

Simpson, E. (1996). Phrygian furniture from Gordion. In G.
Herrmann (Ed.), *The Furniture of Ancient Western Asia* (pp. 198-
201). Mainz am Rhein: Philipp Von Zabern.

Sitchin, Z. (1976-2007). The Earth Chronicles. *Seven Volume Series*.
New York: Avon; Harper-Collins, et. al.

Smith, W. (1863). *A Dictionary of the Bible Comprising its Antiquities,
Biography, Geography, and Natural History*. London: John Murray
Albemarle Street.

Stone, A. (2012). *"Ansar and Kisar (god and goddess)"*. Retrieved from
Ancient Mesopotamian Gods and goddesses, Oracc and the
UK Higher Education Academy:
http://oracc.museum.upenn.edu/amgg/listofdeities/anarandki
sar/

Stone, A. (2013). *Enlil/Ellil (god)*. Retrieved from Ancient
Mesopotamian Gods and Goddesses:
http://oracc.museum.upenn.edu/amgg/listofdeities/enlil/

Suetonius. (1st-2nd Century). *The Lives of the Caesars: The Life of Vitellius*. Retrieved from Bill Thayer's Website: Loeb Classical Library (1914):
http://penelope.uchicago.edu/Thayer/E/Roman/Texts/Suetonius/12Caesars/Vitellius*.html

Suetonius. (1st-2nd Century). *The Life of Vergil*. (Loeb Classical Library) Retrieved April 5, 2014, from Bill Thayer's Website: Loeb Classical Library (1914):
http://penelope.uchicago.edu/Thayer/E/Roman/Texts/Suetonius/de_Poetis/Vergil*.html

Suetonius. (1st-2nd Century). *The Lives of the Caesars: The Life of Augustus*. (Loeb Classical Library) Retrieved from Bill Thayer's Website: Loeb Classical Library (1914):
http://penelope.uchicago.edu/Thayer/E/Roman/Texts/Suetonius/12Caesars/Augustus*.html

Suetonius. (1st-2nd Century). *The Lives of the Caesars: The Life of Caligula*. (Loeb Classical Library) Retrieved from Bill Thayer's Website: Loeb Classical Library (1914):
http://penelope.uchicago.edu/Thayer/E/Roman/Texts/Suetonius/12Caesars/Caligula*.html

Suetonius. (1st-2nd Century). *The Lives of the Caesars: The Life of Claudius*. (Loeb Classical Library) Retrieved March 28, 2015, from Bill Thayer's Website: Loeb Classical Library (1914):
http://penelope.uchicago.edu/Thayer/E/Roman/Texts/Suetonius/12Caesars/Claudius*.html

Suetonius. (1st-2nd Century). *The Lives of the Caesars: The Life of Julius Caesar*. Retrieved March 18, 2011, from Bill Thayer's Website: Loeb Classical Library (1914):
http://penelope.uchicago.edu/Thayer/E/Roman/Texts/Suetonius/12Caesars/Julius*.html

Suetonius. (1st-2nd Century). *The Lives of the Caesars: The Life of Tiberius*. (Loeb Classical Library) Retrieved from Bill Thayer's Website: Loeb Classical Library (1914):
http://penelope.uchicago.edu/Thayer/E/Roman/Texts/Suetonius/12Caesars/Tiberius*.html

Suetonius. (1st-2nd Century). *The Lives of the Caesars: The Life of Vespasian*. Retrieved July 1, 2010, from Bill Thayer's Website: Loeb Classical Library (1914):
http://penelope.uchicago.edu/Thayer/E/Roman/Texts/Suetonius/12Caesars/Vespasian*.html

Tacitus. (1942; 1964). *Complete Works of Tacitus.* (M. Hadas, Ed., A. J. Church, & W. Brodribb, Trans.) New York, New York: McGraw-Hill.

Tangient LLC. (2015). *Warka Vase.* Retrieved from Cyarthistory: https://cyarthistory.wikispaces.com/warka+vase

Taylor, T. (1818). *Iamblichus: Life of Pythagoras or Pythagoric Life.* London: J.M. Watkins.

Thayer's Greek Lexicon. (2002). Retrieved from Biblehub: http://www.biblehub.com

The Epic of Gilgamesh. (2000). (M. G. Kovacs, Trans.) Stanford, California: Stanford University Press.

The Gospel of Philip. (c. 150 - 300 CE). (W. t. Isenburg, Producer) Retrieved May 15, 2014, from The Gnostic Society Library: http://www.gnosis.org/naghamm/gop.html

The Gospel of Thomas. (c 40 - 150 CE). Retrieved July 3, 2010, from The Gnostic Society Library Online (1995): http://www.gnosis.org/naghamm/gth_pat_rob.htm

The Monks of Saint Meinrad Monastery. (2007). *The Tradition of Catholic Prayer.* (C. Raab, & H. Hagan, Eds.) Collegeville, Minnesota: Liturgical Press.

Trobisch, D. (1994). *Paul's Letter Collection: Tracing the Origins.* Minneapolis, MN: Fortress Press.

Trobisch, D. (2000). *The First Edition of the New Testament.* Oxford: Oxford University Press.

Trobisch, D. (2007/2008, December-January). Who Published the New Testament? *Free Inquiry,* pp. 30-33.

Trobisch, D. (2013). *Talitha and the Eyes of Saint Paul.* Bolivar: Leonard Press.

Velde, H. (1999). Bastet. In B. B. Karel van der Toorn, *Dictionary of Demons and Deities in the Bible* (pp. 164-5). Leiden: Brill Academic.

Vergil. (1st Century BCE). *The Aeneid.* (R. Fagles, Trans.) New York, New York: Penguin Books (2006).

Vermes, G. (2006). *The Nativity.* New York: Penguin.

Webster's New Twentieth Century Dictionary, Second Edition. (1979). New York: Simon & Schuster.

Wellhausen, J. (2003, December 1). *Prolegomena to the History of Israel.* Retrieved February 5, 2014, from Project Gutenberg: http://www.gutenberg.org/cache/epub/4732/pg4732.htm

Wells, G. (1996). *The Jesus Legend.* Chicago: Open Court.

West, M. (1971). *Early Greek Philosophy and the Orient*. Oxford, NY: Clarendon Press.

Wildfang, R. L. (2006). *Rome's Vestal Virgins*. New York: Routledge.

Witherington, B. I. (1998). *The Acts of the Apostles: A Socio-Rhetorical Commentary*. Grand Rapids, MI: Wm. B. Erdmans Publishing Co.

Worsfold, T. C. (1934). *History of the Vestal Virgins*. London: Rider & Co Paternoster House E.C.

Index

DISCARD

CPSIA information can be obtained at www.ICGtesting.com
Printed in the USA
LVOW12s2111190216

475870LV00004B/333/P